DISARMAMENT

Its Politics and Economics

Edited by
Seymour Melman

THE AMERICAN ACADEMY OF ARTS AND SCIENCES
BOSTON, MASSACHUSETTS

Disarmament: Its Politics and Economics

Edited by Seymour Melman

Contents

DOCUMENTS

Acknowledgment

THIS VOLUME originated in a set of papers prepared for a research conference on disarmament which met in December 1961 at Columbia University. Professor Seymour Melman of the Department of Industrial and Management Engineering served as chairman of the conference. Twenty communications on various disarmament topics were discussed by a hundred specialists drawn from universities, research institutes, private and governmental bodies.

Certain of the papers were subsequently revised and are printed in their new form in the present volume. Several not presented at the conference have been added to treat additional aspects of the problem which were only partly dealt with in the original papers.

BERNARD T. FELD

The Geneva Negotiations on General and Complete Disarmament

Two SIGNIFICANT documents have been presented to the eighteen-nation Conference on Disarmament assembled in Geneva on 13 March 1962. One is a proposed "Draft Treaty on General and Complete Disarmament under Strict International Control," accompanied by a Memorandum summarizing its main features, submitted by the Soviet Union on 15 March. The second is an "Outline of Basic Provisions of a Treaty on General and Complete Disarmament in a Peaceful World," presented to the Conference by the United States on 18 April. (A later version of the Soviet memorandum and the United States document are reprinted on pages 279 to 331.)

It is the purpose of this paper to compare the two proposals (or, more accurately, the main features of the two approaches) with a view toward ascertaining whether the positions of the United States and the USSR differ in any important respect from those previously taken in earlier negotiations, and in particular whether there appear to be any significantly new aspects of these proposals which would indicate a drawing together of the two approaches.

Both proposals envisage three stages, the last that of general and complete disarmament, in which the only arms remaining will be national-security forces. The Soviet proposal is that the whole process of disarmament should be effected within a period of four years. The American proposal envisages the completion of each of the first two stages within three years after their initiation; Stage III, however, "would be completed within an agreed period of time as promptly as possible."

Thus, there is at least a factor-of-two difference in the time scale

This paper was presented at the Ninth Pugwash Conference on Science and World Affairs, Cambridge, England, 25-30 August 1962.

for general and complete disarmament envisaged by the two plans, with the American plan vague as to the length of the last stage. This vagueness is a reflection of the greater uncertainty in the American plan concerning the mechanisms available for ensuring the orderly attainment of the final state of disarmament.

The Basic Problem of Inspection

It is not always easy to tell from these documents where there has been any basic alteration of the previous positions of the United States and the Soviet Union on inspection. (Roughly speaking, these positions were: widespread inspection before appreciable disarmament versus complete disarmament before significant inspection.) The main difficulty is that, while both the Russian and the American documents contain statements which could be taken to indicate a change in the previous positions, the documents also contain provisions of a hedging nature, which could be read to imply that the previous positions remain fundamentally unchanged.

For example, the United States document certainly introduces a new concept of inspection through the "zonal inspection" plan. This plan—in which inspection would be instituted step by step, with the progressive inspection of an increasing number of zones on each side, the number of zones inspected to be increased as the degree of disarmament grew—seems to represent a major step toward accommodating the Soviets' objection to the pervasive inspection requirements introduced into the early stages in previous American proposals. To quote from the United States document:

> Measures providing for reduction of armaments would be verified . . . at agreed depots. . . . Measures halting or limiting production, testing, and other specified activities would be verified [by] access to relevant facilities and activities. . . . Assurance that agreed levels . . . were not exceeded and that activities limited or prohibited . . . were not being conducted clandestinely would be provided . . . through agreed arrangements which would have the effect of providing that the extent of inspection during any step or stage would be related to the amount of disarmament and to the degree of risk to the parties . . . of possible violations. . . . For example . . . parties to the treaty would divide their territory into a number of appropriate zones . . . and would submit . . . a declaration stating the total level of armaments . . . subject to verification within each zone. . . . An agreed number of such zones would be progressively inspected . . . according to an agreed time schedule. . . . The zones . . . would be selected . . . by parties to the Treaty other than the party whose territory was to be inspected. Upon selection . . . the party

. . . whose territory was to be inspected would declare the exact location of armaments, forces and other agreed activities within the selected zone. . . . Arrangements would be made to provide assurance against undeclared movements of the objects of verification. . . . Aerial and mobile ground inspection would be employed. . . . Access within the zone would be free and unimpeded. . . . Once a zone had been inspected it would remain open for further inspection. . . . By the end of Stage III, inspection would have been extended to all parts of the territory of the Parties to the Treaty.

The principle and practice seem here to be clearly stated, and to adhere to the general concept that "verification arrangements would be instituted progressively *as necessary*" (italics mine). On the other hand, when it comes to specifics, it is not clear that the application of the above principle is consistently followed. Thus, there are at least three statements, in describing Stage I of the American plan (which calls for the limited reduction, by thirty percent, of delivery systems and correspondingly conservative limitations on other forms of armaments) that "the International Disarmament Organization would . . . provide assurance that retained armaments did not exceed agreed levels." The obvious question arises as to whether such statements represent an effective hedge on the principle of "inspection in proportion to disarmament." What kind of inspection measures, in nature and degree, are necessary to provide the required assurance? Can this be done short of completely free access to the territories of the Soviet Union and allied states? Or would access to only a fraction of the designated zones be acceptable in the first stage?

The Soviet proposals, on the other hand, are correspondingly ambiguous. Although "the Soviet Government bases itself on the fact that the institution of strict and reliable international control is an essential guarantee of, and an indispensable condition for, the successful implementation of general and complete disarmament," the application of this principle is far from clear. There is no ambiguity as to the end state: "After the accomplishment of general and complete disarmament control will become unrestricted and comprehensive." But there is much ambiguity relating to the controls which would be acceptable during the progress of disarmament. On the one hand, the Soviet proposals provide, in addition to "international control . . . over those enterprises which were previously engaged, wholly or in part, in the production of means of delivering nuclear weapons," for "access to objectives essential for purposes of effective verification"; on the other hand, the Soviet explanation goes out of its way to state that "it will be the implementation of disarmament measures, and not the armaments retained by States . . . that will be the subject of control."

Actually, the Soviet documents accept in principle the concept of the *verification* of remaining arms, by means commensurate with the degree of disarmament, as contrasted to the *control* over remaining arms: "Each disarmament measure shall be accompanied by such control measures as are necessary for verification of that measure." But there is a crucial and disturbing sentence in their Memorandum, namely: "In the course of disarmament both sides will reduce their armed forces in agreed proportions . . . though the quantities of armed forces and armaments retained by States will not be verified."

Possibly some of the evident ambiguities in the Soviet documents result from inaccurate translation. More likely, the obvious contradictions in their documents arise, as is undoubtedly the case for the United States statement, as a result of an attempt to compromise the positions of strongly antagonistic internal-pressure groups. If we remember that the documents are intended both as propaganda statements and as statements of initial negotiating positions, one should probably not make too much of some of the ambiguities, and it might be reasonable to assume that the significant features of both documents lie in the apparent attempts to accommodate previous positions to the reasonable objections of the other side. It is in this vein that I shall summarize the details of the proposals of the United States and the Soviet Union.

The Elimination of Delivery Vehicles

The plan of the USSR proposes in the first stage (eighteen months) "the complete elimination of the means of delivering nuclear weapons . . . including military rockets of any range, military aircraft, surface warships, submarine and artillery installations."*

* Note the remarks of Soviet Foreign Minister Gromyko, 21 September 1962, at the U. N. (*New York Times*, 22 September, 1962): "Taking account of the stand of the Western powers, the Soviet Government agrees that in the process of destroying nuclear weapons delivery vehicles, at the first stage exception be made for a strictly limited and agreed number of global (intercontinental) missiles, anti-missile missiles, and anti-aircraft missiles of the ground-to-air type which would remain at the disposal of the U.S.S.R. and the United States alone. Thus for a definite period the means of defense would remain in

This is an elaboration of a proposal first made by the French some years ago in an attempt to circumvent the enormous difficulties of inspection required for the elimination of nuclear weapons and stockpiles of fissionable materials; the purpose is to "preclude a nuclear attack by one group of states against another, even though nuclear weapons would still remain at the disposal of States," beginning at the earliest stages of the agreement. However, in the Russian proposal, this measure is coupled "with the dismantling of all military bases in foreign territory and with the withdrawal of foreign troops from such bases." Whether this old theme is really a rock-bottom Soviet desideratum or a negotiable issue is one of the important questions requiring clarification.

The United States proposes the reduction by thirty percent in the first stage of "armed combat aircraft, missiles, and anti-missile systems," together with "combat ships with standard displacement of 400 tons or greater," including "aircraft carriers, battleships, cruisers, destroyer types and submarines." In addition, the "production of all [such] armaments would be limited to agreed allowances during Stage I, and, by the beginning of Stage II, would be halted except for production within agreed limits of parts for maintenance of the agreed retained armaments. Any armament produced . . . would be compensated for by . . . the destruction of sufficient armaments within that category to the end that the [thirty percent] *reduction in destructive capability as well as numbers* in each of these categories . . . would be achieved" (italics mine). Note the introduction here of a new criterion. Is this intended as a hedge against anticipated Russian improvements in weapons and in the weight-carrying capability of their rockets? Is it, in fact, a criterion which can be applied without full knowledge of the details of the Soviet deterrent force? (The vexing problem of control over disarmament versus control over remaining armaments.)

The second stage (also lasting three years) of the American plan calls for a "further reduction of each type of [such] armaments by fifty percent of the inventory existing at the end of Stage I." Thus, by the end of Stage II, this plan would have reduced delivery sys-

---

case someone, as certain Western representatives fear, ventures to violate the treaty, and conceal missiles or combat aircraft. The Soviet Government is introducing the appropriate amendments to its draft Treaty on General and Complete Disarmament under Strict International Control which we are submitting for consideration by this session of the General Assembly of the United Nations."

tems by sixty-five percent. Finally, upon "determination that . . . all undertakings [agreed on in the first two stages] had been carried out, all preparations required for Stage III had been made, and all states possessing armed forces and armaments had become Parties to the Treaty . . . transition . . . to Stage III would take place." In this stage, of unspecified length, "the Parties of the Treaty would eliminate all remaining armaments . . . subject to agreed requirements for non-nuclear armaments . . . for national forces."

In the American plan, the question of foreign military bases is left until the second stage, when "the Parties to the Treaty would dismantle or convert to peaceful uses agreed military bases and facilities, wherever they might be located." On the other hand, even in the first stage, "the Parties . . . would undertake . . . to refrain . . . from the threat of use of force of any type . . . from indirect aggression and subversion." Clearly, the riding of hobby-horses is not confined to either side.

Nuclear Weapons and Stockpiles

In the Soviet proposal, it is in the second stage that provision is made "for the complete prohibition of nuclear, chemical, biological, and other weapons of mass destruction, together with the termination of their production and the destruction of all stockpiles of such weapons." (Note that this second stage would start fifteen months after the conclusion of the treaty; the whole disarmament process is to be concluded in four years.)

In the American plan, the parties "would halt the production of fissionable materials for use in nuclear weapons" in the first stage, and would "verify [these] measures at declared facilities and . . . provide assurance that [such] activities were not conducted at undeclared facilities." In the second stage, the parties "would reduce the amounts and types of fissionable materials declared for use in nuclear weapons to minimum levels *on the basis of agreed percentages*." (Italics mine. Does this mean reduction by an equal fraction of previously declared, verified stockpiles, or equal final stockpiles?) In the third stage, the parties "would eliminate all nuclear weapons remaining at their disposal [and] all facilities for production of such weapons."

As to chemical and biological weapons, these would in the American plan be reduced in Stage II "to levels fifty percent below those existing at the beginning of Stage II." In addition, there would be "the cessation of all production and field testing and . . . dismantling or conversion to peaceful uses of all facilities engaged in production and field testing." Probably through an oversight, no mention is made of a further reduction of these weapons in Stage III; but we may assume that these come under the provision to "eliminate all armaments remaining at their disposal at the end of Stage II."

Armed Forces and Conventional Armaments

The stages of dismantling the armed forces in the Soviet proposals are: in the first stage the armed forces of the USSR and the United States will be reduced to 1.7 million men each, and those of other states to levels to be agreed on. In the second stage, the maximum number for both the USSR and the United States will be 1 million men each. In the third stage, the "elimination of all remaining forces and conventional armaments and . . . the complete cessation of military production and appropriations for military purposes. In this stage war ministries, general staffs, and military institutions will be abolished, all laws on military conscription and other legislation concerning the recruitment of the armed forces will be abrogated, and all military courses and other forms of military training for citizens will be prohibited. . . . To maintain order, the states will have at their disposal only strictly limited agreed contingents of police or militia, equipped with light firearms."

In the American plan, the force levels of the United States and the USSR would be reduced in the first stage to 2.1 million each, and the forces of some other parties would be reduced to agreed levels not exceeding 2.1 million each. All other parties would reduce their force levels to 100,000, or to one percent of their population, whichever was higher. Armaments relating to conventional forces (tanks, artillery, etc.) would be reduced by thirty percent in the first stage. In the second stage, the force levels of the United States and the USSR would be reduced by a further fifty percent (to 1.05 million), and those of the other parties to agreed levels. In the third stage, the armed forces would be reduced to levels necessary "to maintain internal order" and "capable of providing agreed manpower for the United Nations Peace Force." Paramilitary forces would be eliminated. Although there are differences in detail and in numbers in the two proposals (mainly in the first stage), such differences would appear to be reconcilable through negotiation.

The International Disarmament Organization

Both proposals envisage the establishment of an International Control Council, at the outset of the agreement, to supervise the application of the disarmament treaty. However, generally speaking, the Soviet view is that the IDO will have only a verifying function; the American proposal is to invest the IDO with functions of both verification and enforcement. In both proposals, the IDO is to function within the framework of the United Nations Organization.

Specifically, the Soviet draft Treaty provides for "a control Council composed of representatives of the socialist countries, the countries participating in the Western Military Alliance, and of non-aligned countries [to] serve as the permanent organ of the IDO. . . . There is no need to introduce into it the unanimity principle or veto since . . . decisions would be taken by an appropriate majority. . . . [However] it goes without saying that the IDO will not and cannot be entrusted with any functions involving the execution of preventive or enforcement measures in regard to States. The business of the IDO is to establish facts. If . . . need should arise of taking action to safeguard peace and security, this would, as heretofore, be exclusively within the competence of the Security Council." Furthermore, "after the accomplishment of . . . general and complete disarmament the IDO will continue to supervise compliance . . . and will be able to send inspection teams to any point within the territory of the States." But, "if in the course of implementation of general and complete disarmament, any state or group of States were to take aggressive action, the powers of the Security Council under the Charter of the United Nations would be quite adequate to put an end to such action. . . . In the first stage of disarmament . . . states should negotiate agreements with the Security Council . . . that armed forces [be] made available . . . to the Security Council on its call. . . . [These forces] will form part of the national armed forces of the States concerned and will be stationed within their territories. . . . The same method . . . should also be retained in the second stage of disarmament. . . . In the third stage, international forces under the Security Council will be formed, whenever necessary, from the contingents of police (militia) retained by States. . . . The command of the international armed forces of the Security Council should be formed on the basis of equitable representation of the three groups of States . . . [and] decisions should be taken by agreement among them."

These proposals go much further than any previously set forth by the Soviet Union, and they indicate a much greater concern for implementing general and complete disarmament in the final stages; however, they still contain elements which have previously met with strong opposition from the West (the "troika" principle, the maintenance of the "veto" through control by the Security Council).

The American proposals, on the other hand, are much more strongly oriented toward the establishment of an IDO with effective capabilities for enforcement (in addition to the function of verifying compliance with the agreement), tending in the final stage toward an organ with functions strongly suggestive of a world government. Actually, in the first stage, the IDO functions are essentially confined to verifying compliance. However, during Stage I arrangements would be developed for establishing a United Nations Peace Force and a Peace Observation Corps in Stage II. By the end of Stage II, the United Nations Peace Force would have "sufficient armed forces and armaments so that no state could challenge it" (including nuclear weapons?).

The organization of the IDO would also, under the United States proposal, have a much more strongly centralized character. Thus, in addition to the Control Council "consisting of representatives of all the major signatory powers as permanent members and certain other Parties to the Treaty on a rotating basis," there would be "an Administrator . . . under the direction of the Control Council . . . who would have the authority, staff, and finances adequate to ensure effective and impartial implementation of the functions of the IDO."

Another important provision of the United States proposal concerns the use of the International Court of Justice. In the first stage, the Court could be requested "to give advisory opinions on legal questions concerning the interpretation or application of the Treaty." But in Stage II, "the Parties . . . would undertake to accept without reservation . . . the compulsory jurisdiction of that Court to decide international legal disputes."

The plans of both sides include many other measures. Thus, in the area of nuclear-weapon testing, the USSR as well as the United States would prohibit tests in the first stage (or before), although the Soviet Union would postpone the institution of a system for the inspection of possible underground tests, pending further technical developments (while asserting that such tests can already be detected by existing national systems). Both sides propose an agreement in the first stage to refrain from transferring control over nuclear weapons or transmitting information on their production to nonnuclear powers. Both sides would have the nonnuclear powers agree to refrain from acquiring or producing nuclear weapons; the Soviet Union would go even further, and have the nonnuclear powers agree to "refuse to permit such weapons to be stationed in their territories."

Both sides propose to prohibit from the outset the placing in orbit of weapons of mass destruction. Both sides propose the international supervision of the launching of all space vehicles, from the outset. The American proposals for the first stage contain a number of other measures designed to provide assurance against the possibility of a surprise attack. Such measures include: "advance notification of major military movements and manoeuvres, . . . observation posts . . . at agreed locations, including major ports, railway centers, motor highways, river crossings, and air bases . . . exchange of military missions . . . to improve communication and understanding . . . and establishment of rapid and reliable communications among their heads of government and with the Secretary General of the United Nations." The Soviet proposal regards its first-stage elimination of delivery systems as accomplishing the required assurance against surprise attack, since "the execution of these measures would in fact preclude a nuclear attack . . . even though nuclear weapons would still remain at the disposal of states."

Granted that much of the content of both the Russian and American proposals can be interpreted as repetitions of old formulae, originally designed to accomplish either a propaganda advantage or to ensure some kind of a military advantage for one side or the other, and recognizing serious internal contradictions and ambiguities in both, it appears that these proposals contain much that is new and serious which can serve as the basis for fruitful negotiations, should both sides desire to carry these forward. Clearly, both sides have given considerable thought to the deficiencies of their previous positions, and the documents analyzed above indicate some real attempts to move toward an accommodation of conflicting views.

A number of basic differences remain: the difference in the time scales proposed for the accomplishment of GCD; the widely divergent emphases on the importance of the verification of remaining arguments during the first two stages; and the disagreement as to the concept of the role of the IDO in the enforcement, as distinguished from the verification, of the agreements. In general, the opposing views on the role of the United Nations in a disarmed world, in my opinion, reflect as much the absence of serious study in depth of this problem as they do any basic divergence in the points of view of the United States and the Soviet Union.

Nevertheless, there are important new features in these documents: the recognition (albeit reluctant and inconsistently applied) by the Soviet Union of the necessity for the verification of agreed disarmament measures *when they are applied;* the adoption by the United States of Louis B. Sohn's scheme for the *graduated* introduction of inspection, through the technique of zonal inspection. With respect to this aspect of the American proposal, there remains some confusion between the use of the zonal-inspection scheme as a device for the "random sampling" of Soviet territories as a check on compliance in the early stages of the agreement, and the use of the scheme as a means of progressively opening up increasingly greater territories of the Soviet Union to free access by the International Inspectorate.

Some very difficult and vexing problems are only peripherally touched on in both documents. Foremost among these is the problem of the inclusion in a disarmament agreement of those powers now entering into, or about to enter into, the "nuclear club"—France, for one, *but most especially* the People's Republic of China. Sooner or later, both sides must yield to the inescapable necessity of negotiating in earnest to remove the frightful threat of mutual annihilation before circumstances, abetted by the stubborn adoption of irreconcilable positions, force us to the table in the shadow of—or as an aftermath to—an inexcusable tragedy of nuclear destruction. On the basis of the documents submitted to the eighteen-nation Geneva Disarmament Conference, I am inclined to conclude that neither the desire nor the basis is lacking for the initiation of serious negotiations aimed at averting the tragedy of a nuclear war. What seems to be lacking is the national will, and the strength of conviction that disarmament is an attainable goal. Still, we are closer than ever before to such serious negotiations. Perhaps what is now required is the united and unremitting pressure on our respective governments by enlightened and devoted advocates of disarmament.

BERTRAND RUSSELL

The Early History of the Pugwash Movement

The Pugwash Movement, as it is called, consists of periodical conferences of scientists from Eastern and Western and neutral countries intended to discuss in a scientific, nonpolemical spirit various problems arising out of modern methods of mass destruction. It came from a projected collaboration between Einstein and myself on the dangers connected with nuclear warfare. Unfortunately, Einstein was suffering from his last, fatal illness and, while still willing to collaborate, was unable to join in the work of drafting the appeal that we had in mind. He therefore left it to me to draw up a manifesto to which I sought signatures of a limited number of very eminent men of science. This manifesto was as follows:

> In the tragic situation which confronts humanity, we feel that scientists should assemble in conference to appraise the perils that have arisen as a result of the development of weapons of mass destruction, and to discuss a resolution in the spirit of the appended draft.
>
> We are speaking on this occasion, not as members of this or that nation, continent, or creed, but as human beings, members of the species Man, whose continued existence is in doubt. The world is full of conflicts; and, over-shadowing all minor conflicts, the titanic struggle between Communism and anti-Communism.
>
> Almost everybody who is politically conscious has strong feelings about one or more of these issues; but we want you, if you can, to set aside such feelings and consider yourselves only as members of a biological species which has had a remarkable history, and whose disappearance none of us can desire.
>
> We shall try to say no single word which should appeal to one group rather than to another. All, equally, are in peril, and, if the peril is understood, there is hope that they may collectively avert it.
>
> We have to learn to think in a new way. We have to learn to ask ourselves, not what steps can be taken to give military victory to whatever group we prefer, for there no longer are such steps; the question we have to ask ourselves is: what steps can be taken to prevent a military contest of which the issue must be disastrous to all parties?

The general public, and even many men in positions of authority, have not realized what would be involved in a war with nuclear bombs. The general public still thinks in terms of the obliteration of cities. It is understood that the new bombs are more powerful than the old, and that, while one A-bomb could obliterate Hiroshima, one H-bomb could obliterate the largest cities, such as London, New York, and Moscow.

No doubt in an H-bomb war great cities would be obliterated. But this is one of the minor disasters that would have to be faced. If everybody in London, New York, and Moscow were exterminated the world might, in the course of a few centuries, recover from the blow. But we now know, especially since the Bikini test, that nuclear bombs can gradually spread destruction over a very much wider area than had been supposed.

It is stated on very good authority that a bomb can now be manufactured which will be 2,500 times as powerful as that which destroyed Hiroshima. Such a bomb, if exploded near the ground or under water, sends radio-active particles into the upper air. They sink gradually and reach the surface of the earth in the form of a deadly dust or rain. It was this dust which infected the Japanese fishermen and their catch of fish.

No one knows how widely such lethal radio-active particles might be diffused, but the best authorities are unanimous in saying that a war with H-bombs might quite possibly put an end to the human race. It is feared that if many H-bombs are used there will be universal death—sudden only for a minority, but for the majority a slow torture of disease and disintegration.

Many warnings have been uttered by eminent men of science and by authorities in military strategy. None of them will say that the worst results are certain. What they do say is that these results are possible, and no one can be sure that they will not be realized. We have not yet found that the views of experts on this question depend in any degree upon their politics or prejudices. They depend only, so far as our researchers have revealed, upon the extent of the particular expert's knowledge. We have found that the men who know most are the most gloomy.

Here, then, is the problem which we present to you, stark and dreadful and inescapable: Shall we put an end to the human race; or shall mankind renounce war?* People will not face this alternative because it is so difficult to abolish war.

The abolition of war will demand distasteful limitations of national sovereignty.** But what perhaps impedes understanding of the situation more than anything else is that the term "mankind" feels vague and abstract. People scarcely realize in imagination that the danger is to themselves and their children and their grandchildren, and not only to a dimly apprehended humanity. They can scarcely bring themselves to grasp that they, individually, and those whom they love are in imminent danger of

* "Professor Joliot-Curie wishes to add the words: '. . . as a means of settling differences between States.' "

** "Professor Joliot-Curie wishes to add that these limitations are to be agreed by all and in the interests of all."

perishing agonizingly. And so they hope that perhaps war may be allowed to continue provided modern weapons are prohibited.

This hope is illusory. Whatever agreements not to use H-bombs had been reached in time of peace, they would no longer be considered binding in time of war, and both sides would set to work to manufacture H-bombs as soon as war broke out, for, if one side manufactured the bombs and the other did not, the side that manufactured them would inevitably be victorious.

Although an agreement to renounce nuclear weapons as part of a general reduction of armaments*** would not afford an ultimate solution, it would serve certain important purposes. First: any agreement between East and West is to the good in so far as it tends to diminish tension. Second: the abolition of thermo-nuclear weapons, if each side believed that the other side had carried it out sincerely, would lessen the fear of a sudden attack in the style of Pearl Harbour, which at present keeps both sides in a state of nervous apprehension. We should, therefore, welcome such an agreement, though only as a first step.

Most of us are not neutral in feeling, but, as human beings, we have to remember that, if the issues between East and West are to be decided in any manner that can give any possible satisfaction to anybody, whether Communist or anti-Communist, whether Asian or European or American, whether White or Black, then these issues must not be decided by war. We should wish this to be understood, both in the East and in the West.

There lies before us, if we choose, continual progress in happiness, knowledge, and wisdom. Shall we, instead, choose death, because we cannot forget our quarrels? We appeal, as human beings, to human beings: Remember your humanity, and forget the rest. If you can do so, the way lies open to a new Paradise; if you cannot, there lies before you the risk of universal death.

Resolution

We invite this Congress, and through it the scientists of the world and the general public to subscribe to the following resolution:

In view of the fact that in any future world war nuclear weapons will certainly be employed, and that such weapons threaten the continued existence of mankind, we urge the Governments of the world to realize, and to acknowledge publicly, that their purposes cannot be furthered by a world war, and we urge them, consequently, to find peaceful means for the settlement of all matters of dispute between them.

Einstein's signature to this manifesto was the last public act of his life. The other signatories were:

Professor Max Born (Professor of Theoretical Physics at Berlin, Frankfort, and Göttingen, and of Natural Philosophy, Edinburgh; Nobel Prize in physics).

*** "Professor Muller makes the reservation that this be taken to mean 'a concomitant balanced reduction of all armaments.'"

Professor P. W. Bridgman (Professor of Physics, Harvard University; Nobel Prize in physics).
Professor L. Infeld (Professor of Theoretical Physics, University of Warsaw).
Professor J. F. Joliot-Curie (Professor of Physics at the Collège de France; Nobel Prize in chemistry).
Professor H. J. Muller (Professor of Zoology at University of Indiana; Nobel Prize in physiology and medicine).
Professor Linus Pauling (Professor of Chemistry, California Institute of Technology; Nobel Prize in chemistry).
Professor C. F. Powell (Professor of Physics, Bristol University; Nobel Prize in physics).
Professor J. Rotblat (Professor of Physics, University of London; Medical College of St. Bartholomew's Hospital).
Bertrand Russell.
Professor Hideki Yukawa (Professor of Theoretical Physics, Kyoto University; Nobel Prize in physics).

This manifesto was published to the world at a press conference in London on 9 July 1955. Its purpose was to bring together men of science of the most divergent political opinions—Communist, anti-Communist and neutral—in a friendly atmosphere in which it was hoped that a scientific spirit would enable them to find a greater measure of agreement than the politicians had found possible. The press conference was attended by an enormous number of journalists and TV and wireless men from every part of the world. Professor Rotblat was brave enough to take the chair in spite of the fact that the bringing together of East and West was thought rash by many people. I read the manifesto and spent more than two hours answering questions. In the main the reception of the manifesto by the assembled journalists was surprisingly friendly. There were, of course, difficulties in obtaining general support for the manifesto. There were those among the public of the West who regarded any effort to avoid nuclear war and any friendly contact with Communists as Communist-inspired and, therefore, undesirable. There were also those who regarded all scientists as wicked, since it was their discoveries and inventions that caused the trouble. It was not, however, among men of science that such opinions prevailed, and from them the manifesto met with a very wide, favorable reception.

The organization of the first conference in response to the manifesto was by no means easy. The greatest difficulty was finance. Wherever the congress might be held, most of the participants would have to make long journeys which few of them could afford. This difficulty was solved by the generosity of Mr. Cyrus Eaton, who offered to pay all expenses of the conference (provided that it took place) at his estate in Pugwash, Nova Scotia.

This first conference (7-10 July 1957), as compared to the later ones, was not very large. There were twenty-two participants: fifteen physicists; two chemists; four biologists; and a lawyer. Of these participants, seven were from the United States, three from the U.S.S.R., three from Japan; two from Great Britain; two from Canada; and one each from Australia, Austria, China, France, and Poland. The organizing work, which was very considerable, was undertaken by Professors Rotblat, Burhop, and Powell. The conference, as well as all subsequent conferences of the Pugwash Movement, differed from more formal conferences in the fact that the participants, while the conference lasted, all lived together and saw each other socially and informally in addition to the more formal meetings. This made a friendly atmosphere much easier to preserve, and the participants came to regard each other as friendly human beings who could be understood, even liked, not as antagonists from a foreign and possibly inimical nation. In consequence, it was found that a surprisingly large measure of agreement was possible. The work of the conference was divided among three committees: the first, on radiation hazards; the second, on the control of nuclear weapons; and the third, on the social responsibility of scientists. Each committee drew up a report, and the conference as a whole issued a report saying, *inter alia:*

> Men of science are now well aware that the fruits of their labours are of paramount importance for the future of mankind, and they are thus compelled to consider the political implications of their work. Their opinions on politics are as diverse as those of other men. These facts make it difficult for a conference such as the present to issue an agreed statement on matters which are controversial. The discussion of such issues, however, allowed the points of difference and the areas of agreement to be defined, and led to a measure of mutual understanding of the opinions of one another. . . .
>
> The estimates of the hazards which have arisen from test explosions permitted a closer examination to be made of the probable consequences of an unrestricted nuclear war. This examination led to the unquestioned conclusion that a general war with nuclear weapons would indeed represent a disaster of unprecedented magnitude. The radiological hazards would be thousands of times greater than those due to the fall-out effects of test explosions. In the combatant countries, hundreds of millions of people would be killed outright by the blast and heat, and by the ionizing radiation produced at the instant of explosion whether bombs of the so-called "clean" or "dirty" kind were employed. If "dirty" bombs were used,

large areas would be made uninhabitable for extended periods of time, and additional hundreds of millions of people would die from delayed effects of radiation from local fall-out, some in the exposed population from direct radiation injury, and some in succeeding generations as a result of genetic effects. But even countries not directly hit by bombs would suffer through global fall-out, which, under certain conditions, might be of such intensity as to cause large-scale genetic and other injury. . . .

Finally, we should like to give expression to the high degree of unanimity we have found among all the members of the Conference on *fundamental aims*. We are all convinced that mankind must abolish war or suffer catastrophe; that the dilemma of opposing power groups and the arms race must be broken; and that the establishment of lasting peace will mark the opening of a new and triumphant epoch for the whole of mankind. We earnestly hope that our conference may make a modest contribution to these great aims.

This report was signed by all the participants except John Foster of Canada and Leo Szilard of the United States.

The first conference appointed a Continuing Committee to organize future conferences and undertake whatever additional work might be necessary. The members of this Continuing Committee were Professors Rotblat, Powell, Rabinowitch, Academician Skobeltzyn, and myself. The chief importance of the conference, from the point of view of the general public, consisted in the demonstration that men of science of the most diverse political opinions could agree on a large number of the most important questions connected with current political controversies. The impact in the West, however, was less than might have been hoped, since organs of publicity find agreement less newsworthy than disagreement. But gradually what one might call the Pugwash point of view has come to be increasingly favored among those who know enough to have a competent opinion. Subsequent conferences have been much more widely attended and somewhat better publicized—though never as fully as they should have been. The friendly co-operation between men of different nationalities and different political opinions has continued to be maintained.

The Second Pugwash Conference took place at Lac Beauport in Canada in March and April, 1958. Mr. Eaton again provided accommodation and paid expenses, but, owing to the northern prolongation of winter, the conference could not be held in Nova Scotia. The discussions of the conference were announced as being concerned with "the dangers of the present situation, and ways and means of diminishing them." At its conclusion, a statement was issued.

A third and larger conference was planned to take place in Austria. It was held in September, 1958, partly at Kitzbühel in the Tyrol, and partly in Vienna where it obtained the support of the Austrian Government. It issued a document which was called "The Vienna Declaration," which states more fully and adequately than any previous pronouncement the aims as to which the Pugwash conferences are agreed. This Declaration was accepted *nem. con.*, Leo Szilard being the only one to abstain. A hundred and one persons were present, of whom, however, only seventy were participating scientists, the others being observers or guests. The Vienna Declaration, in view of the fact that it was supported by scientists of East and West and of neutral countries, is a very important document. I think one may say, without exaggeration, that it proves that, if scientists had the power to decide world problems, the nuclear peril would soon be under control. The Declaration is as follows:

1. *Necessity to End Wars*

We meet in Kitzbühel and in Vienna at a time when it has become evident that the development of nuclear weapons makes it possible for man to destroy civilization and, indeed, himself; the means of destruction are being made ever more efficient. The scientists attending our meetings have long been concerned with this development, and they are unanimous in the opinion that a full-scale nuclear war would be a world-wide catastrophe of unprecedented magnitude.

In our opinion defence against nuclear attack is very difficult. Unfounded faith in defensive measures may even contribute to an outbreak of war.

Although the nations may agree to eliminate nuclear weapons and other weapons of mass destruction from the arsenals of the world, the knowledge of how to produce such weapons can never be destroyed. They remain for all time a potential threat for mankind. In any future major war, each belligerent state will feel not only free but compelled to undertake immediate production of nuclear weapons; for no state, when at war, can be sure that such steps are not being taken by the enemy. We believe that, in such a situation, a major industrial power would require less than one year to begin accumulating atomic weapons. From then on, the only restraint against their employment in war would be agreements not to use them, which were concluded in times of peace. The decisive power of nuclear weapons, however, would make the temptation to use them almost irresistible, particularly to leaders who are facing defeat. It appears, therefore, that atomic weapons are likely to be employed in any future major war with all their terrible consequences.

It is sometimes suggested that localized wars, with limited objectives, might still be fought without catastrophic consequences. History shows, however, that the risk of local conflicts growing into major wars is too great to be acceptable in the age of weapons of mass destruction. Mankind must, therefore, set itself the task of eliminating all wars, including local wars.

2. *Requirements for Ending the Arms Race*

The armaments race is the result of distrust between states; it also contributes to this distrust. Any step that mitigates the arms race, and leads to even small reductions in armaments and armed forces, on an equitable basis and subject to necessary control, is therefore desirable. We welcome all steps in this direction and, in particular, the recent agreement in Geneva between representatives of East and West about the feasibility of detecting test-explosions. As scientists, we take particular pleasure in the fact that this unanimous agreement, the first after a long series of unsuccessful international disarmament negotiations, was made possible by mutual understanding and a common objective approach by scientists from different countries. We note with satisfaction that the governments of the U.S.A., U.S.S.R., and U.K. have approved the statements and the conclusion contained in the report of the technical experts. This is a significant success; we most earnestly hope that this approval will soon be followed by an international agreement leading to the cessation of all nuclear weapon tests and an effective system of control. This would be a first step toward the relaxation of international tension and the end of the arms race.

It is generally agreed that any agreement on disarmament, and in particular nuclear disarmament, requires measures of control to protect every party from possible evasion. Through their technical competence, scientists are well aware that effective control will in some cases be relatively easy, while it is very difficult in others. For example, the conference of experts in Geneva has agreed that the cessation of bomb tests could be monitored by a suitable network of detecting stations. On the other hand, it will be a technical problem of great difficulty to account fully for existing stocks of nuclear weapons and other means of mass destruction. An agreement to cease production of nuclear weapons presents a problem of intermediate technical difficulty between these two extreme examples.

We recognize that the accumulation of large stocks of nuclear weapons has made a completely reliable system of controls for far-reaching nuclear disarmament extremely difficult, perhaps impossible. For this disarmament to become possible, nations may have to depend, in addition to a practical degree of technical verification, on a combination of political agreements, of successful international security arrangements, and of experience of successful co-operation in various areas. Together, these can create the climate of mutual trust, which does not now exist, and an assurance that nations recognize the mutual political advantages of avoiding suspicion.

Recognizing the difficulties of the technological situation, scientists feel an obligation to impress on their peoples and on their governments the need for policies which will encourage international trust and reduce mutual apprehension. Mutual apprehensions cannot be reduced by assertions of good will; their reduction will require political adjustment and the establishment of active co-operation.

3. *What War Would Mean*

Our conclusions about the possible consequences of war have been supported by reports and papers submitted to our Conference. These documents indicate that if, in a future war, a substantial proportion of the nuclear weapons already manufactured were delivered against urban targets, most centres of civilization in the belligerent countries would be totally destroyed, and most of their populations killed. This would be true whether the bombs used derived most of their power from fusion reactions (so-called "clean" bombs) or principally from fission reactions (so-called "dirty" bombs). In addition to destroying major centres of population and industry, such bombs would also wreck the economy of the country attacked, through the destruction of vital means of distribution and communication.

Major states have already accumulated large stocks of "dirty" nuclear weapons; it appears that they are continuing to do so. From a strictly military point of view, dirty bombs have advantages in some situations; this makes likely their use in a major war.

The local fall-out resulting from extensive use of "dirty" bombs would cause the death of a large part of the population in the country attacked. Following their explosion in large numbers (each explosion equivalent to that of millions of tons of ordinary chemical explosive), radio-active fall-out would be distributed, not only over the territory to which they were delivered but, in varying intensity, over the rest of the earth's surface. Many millions of deaths would thus be produced, not only in belligerent but also in non-belligerent countries, by the acute effects of radiation.

There would be, further, substantial long-term radiation damage, to human and other organisms everywhere, from somatic effects such as leukemia, bone cancer, and shortening of the life span; and from genetic damage affecting the hereditary traits transmitted to the progeny.

Knowledge of human genetics is not yet sufficient to allow precise predictions of consequences likely to arise from the considerable increase in the rate of mutation which would ensue from unrestricted nuclear war. However, geneticists believe that they may well be serious for the future of a surviving world population.

It is sometimes suggested that in a future war, the use of nuclear weapons might be restricted to objectives such as military bases, troop concentrations, airfields, and other communication centres; and that attacks on large centres of population could thus be avoided.

Even tactical weapons now have a large radius of action; cities and towns are commonly closely associated with centres of supply and transportation. We, therefore, believe that even a "restricted" war would lead, despite attempted limitation of targets, to widespread devastation of the territory in which it took place, and to the destruction of much of its population. Further, an agreement not to use cities for military purposes, entered into in order to justify their immunity from attack, is unlikely to be maintained to the end of a war, particularly by the losing side. The latter would also be strongly tempted to use nuclear bombs against the population centres of the enemy, in the hope of breaking his will to continue the war.

4. *Hazards of Bomb Tests*

At our first conference it had been agreed that while the biological hazards of bomb tests may be small compared with similar hazards to which mankind is exposed from other sources, hazards from tests exist and should receive close and continual study. Since then, an extensive investigation by the United Nations Scientific Committee on the Effects of Atomic Radiation has been carried out and its authoritative conclusions published. In this case, too, scientists from many different countries have been able to arrive at a unanimous agreement. Their conclusions confirm that the bomb tests produce a definite hazard and that they will claim a significant number of victims in present and following generations. Though the magnitude of the genetic damage appears to be relatively small compared with that produced by natural causes, the incidence of leukemia and bone cancer due to the radio-activity from test explosions may, in the estimate of the UN committee, add significantly to the natural incidence of these diseases. This conclusion depends on the assumption (not shared by all authorities in the field) that these effects can be produced even by the smallest amount of radiation. This uncertainty calls for extensive study and, in the meantime, for a prudent acceptance of the most pessimistic assumption. It lends emphasis to the generally agreed conclusion that all unnecessary exposure of mankind to radiation is undesirable and should be avoided.

It goes without saying that the biological damage from a war, in which many nuclear bombs would be used, would be incomparably larger than that from tests; the main immediate problem before mankind is thus the establishment of conditions that would eliminate war.

5. *Science and International Co-operation*

We believe that, as scientists, we have an important contribution to make toward establishing trust and co-operation among nations. Science is, by long tradition, an international undertaking. Scientists with different national allegiances easily find a common basis of understanding: they use the same concepts and the same methods; they work toward common intellectual goals, despite differences in philosophical, economic, or political views. The rapidly growing importance of science in the affairs of mankind increases the importance of the community of understanding.

The ability of scientists all over the world to understand one another, and to work together, is an excellent instrument for bridging the gap between nations and for uniting them around common aims. We believe that working together in every field where international co-operation proves possible makes an important contribution toward establishing an appreciation of the community of nations. It can contribute to the development of the climate of mutual trust, which is necessary for the resolution of political conflicts between nations, and which is an essential background to effective disarmament. We hope scientists everywhere will recognize their responsibility, to mankind and to their own nations, to contribute thought, time, and energy to the furthering of international co-operation.

Several international scientific undertakings have already had considerable success. We mention only the century-old, world-wide co-operation in weather science, the two International Polar Years which preceded (by seventy-five and twenty-five years respectively) the present International Geophysical Year, and the Atoms-for-Peace Conferences. We earnestly hope that efforts will be made to initiate similar collaboration in other fields of study. Certainly they will have the enthusiastic support of scientists all over the world.

We call for an increase in the unrestricted flow of scientific information among nations, and for a wide exchange of scientists. We believe that nations which build their national security on secrecy of scientific developments sacrifice the interests of peace, and of the progress of science, for temporary advantages. It is our belief that science can best serve mankind if it is free from interference by any dogma imposed from outside, and if it exercises its right to question all postulates, including its own.

6. *Technology in the Service of Peace*

In our time, pure and applied science have become increasingly interdependent. The achievements of fundamental, experimental, and theoretical science are more and more rapidly transformed into new technological developments. This accelerated trend is manifest alike in the creation of weapons of increased destructiveness and in the development of means for the increased wealth and well-being of mankind. We believe that the tradition of mutual understanding and of international co-operation, which have long existed in fundamental science, can and should be extended to many fields of technology. The International Atomic Energy Agency, for example, aims not merely at co-operation for establishing facts about atomic energy, but also at helping the nations of the world to develop a new source of energy as a basis for the improvement of their material welfare. We believe that international co-operation in this and other fields, such as economic development and the promotion of health, should be greatly strengthened.

The extremely low level of living in the industrially underdeveloped countries of the world is and will remain a source of international tension. We see an urgent need to forward studies and programmes for the effective industrialization of these countries. This would not only improve the level of living of the majority of the population of the world; it would also help reduce the sources of conflict between the highly industrialized powers. Such studies would offer fruitful scope for co-operative efforts between scientists of all nations.

The great increase in the ease and speed of communications, and our increasing understanding of how the forces of nature influence the living conditions of nations in different parts of the world, show us, in a way not previously possible, that the prosperity of individual nations is connected with, and dependent upon, that of mankind as a whole; and how rapidly it could be increased by common international effort. We believe that through such common effort, the coexistence between nations of different social and economic structure can become not merely peaceful and competitive, but to an increasing degree co-operative, and therefore more stable.

As scientists, we are deeply aware of the great change in the condition of mankind which has been brought about by the modern development and application of science. Given peace, mankind stands at the beginning of a great scientific age. Science can provide mankind with an ever-increasing understanding of the forces of nature and the means of harnessing them. This will bring about a great increase in the well-being, health, and prosperity of all men.

7. *The Responsibility of Scientists*

We believe it to be a responsibility of scientists in all countries to contribute to the education of the peoples by spreading among them a wide understanding of the dangers and potentialities offered by the unprecedented growth of science. We appeal to our colleagues everywhere to contribute to this effort, both through enlightenment of adult populations, and through education of the coming generations. In particular, education should stress improvement of all forms of human relations and should eliminate any glorification of war and violence.

Scientists are, because of their special knowledge, well equipped for early awareness of the danger and the promise arising from scientific discoveries. Hence, they have a special competence and a special responsibility in relation to the most pressing problems of our times.

In the present conditions of distrust between nations, and of the race for military supremacy which arises from it, all branches of science—physics, chemistry, biology, psychology—have become increasingly involved in military developments. In the eyes of the people of many countries, science has become associated with the development of weapons. Scientists are either admired for their contribution to national security, or damned for having brought mankind into jeopardy by their invention of weapons of mass destruction. The increasing material support which science now enjoys in many countries is mainly due to its importance, direct or indirect, to the military strength of the nation and to its degree of success in the arms race. This diverts science from its true purpose, which is to increase human knowledge, and to promote man's mastery over the forces of nature for the benefit of all.

We deplore the conditions which lead to this situation, and appeal to all peoples and their governments to establish conditions of lasting and stable peace.

I should like to emphasize one very important point in the Vienna Declaration, and that is that agreements for the abolition of nuclear weapons, however desirable, would not suffice to make the world safe from disaster and that safety can only be secured when means are found of entirely preventing war. Seven subsequent conferences have continued the work begun by the first three, and the scope of the conferences has been widened to embrace economic and other problems not belonging to the physical sciences. When such problems are discussed, authorities on the matters concerned are invited to participate in the conferences.

Although the measure of support obtained by the movement has increased, the impact upon public opinion has not been so great as might have been hoped. The general public tends to have an attitude of suspicion towards scientists, regarding them somewhat as magicians were regarded in former times. They are thought, partly, to be people with strange powers which they have acquired by something like a pact with the Devil, and, partly, as woolly-headed idealists totally divorced from reality. There is a resistance against their pronouncements which is due to the incomprehensibility of their work and a fear that they may establish a technical aristocracy. In the Armed Forces there is a different kind of resistance. The gallant General who rides a horse brandishing a sabre and shouting "Charge!" is a traditional figure easily understood and inheriting centuries of admiration. To a great extent, this traditional figure has been replaced by a new one—the gallant and ruthless Airman or Commando. But this new figure will be equally out of date in a nuclear war if it occurs. The scientist, ill-dressed, unmilitary, unaccustomed to horses and physical exercise, and perhaps even with long hair, is the sort of person whom eminent military officers have despised ever since they were schoolboys. They have to admit that those odd beings have strange but indispensable powers, but they admit it with reluctance and resent their incursion into military problems. When the A-bomb was new, all the scientists agreed that the Russians would very soon have it. When this proved true, the non-scientific world assumed that traitors must be responsible. There were traitors, but all competent scientists were agreed that they contributed little to Soviet acquisition of A- and H-bombs.

The Pugwash Conferences have proved that men of science, in the main, are better guides to policy than men who do not understand the problems concerned, even if such men are eminent statesmen or generals. I do not think that all scientists are noble men or that they are always wise. Like other men, they are fallible and, alas, sometimes cowardly. But they have information denied to others, and that information and such wisdom as they have should be made known to the public and built upon by the authorities, the men in power—as it is very definitely not at present. It is unfortunate that the organs of publicity—the press, radio and television—have not seen fit to give any but the most meager publicity to the pronouncements of scientists in conference, and that the best wisdom available has therefore remained unknown to all but a few. One must continue to hope that the wisdom of experts will gradually percolate to the general public and even to governments. Recent statements by Mr. McNamara and Mr. Rusk show that some members of the administration have become aware of some of the facts that Pugwash Conferences have tried to bring to the notice of the authorities and the public. These statements make it possible to hope that knowledge as to the possible effects of nuclear warfare and the risk of unintended war will come to be more generally known. If this happens, the Pugwash Movement, along with other similar movements, will have achieved its purpose.

DAVID F. CAVERS

Disarmament as a Cumulative Process for Peace

DISARMAMENT IS a political process that poses a political problem—the most important and the most difficult one confronting the world today. The purpose of "general and complete disarmament," accepted as a goal by West and East, is to change one basic characteristic of the political entities into which human society has been divided throughout history: we propose to take from every nation such power as it has for subjugating and defending itself against every other nation, and to repose that power in a suprastate body whose specifications today are far from clear.

The solution to the problem of disarmament is not going to be reached in four years. Conceivably, it may require generations before the nations become convinced that they can live in peace with one another, and so proceed to get rid of the fantastic weapons that will have been developed. However, were history to take such a course, disarmament would be merely a result, not a process that in itself exerted an influence for world peace and freedom. We are not resigned today to running the obvious hazards of a continuing arms race. Our aim is to set in motion a process which, possibly within a decade, would turn this deeply divided world into one world in which peace would coexist with freedom.

The thesis of the present paper is that this goal is not wholly utopian and that the disarmament process itself can generate cumulative forces making for its ultimate success. The subject I was asked to develop does not oblige me to confront the entire gamut of questions that must be met in moving from where we are today to where we hope to be—say, in ten years. My main concern relates to the second of two basic questions:

First, can the disarmament process actually be set in motion?

Second, can that process, once set in motion, be successfully carried through a series of stages to completion?

Unfortunately, it is very much harder to give an affirmative answer to the first question than to the second. To answer the first question affirmatively requires confidence that an uphill fight can be successfully waged (1) to overcome the suspicions that impede negotiations and cooperation between the rival blocs, (2) to resolve the important substantive differences that must be anticipated in formulating specific provisions of any disarmament plan, (3) to resolve or reduce the critical state of those serious political differences now outstanding that (if left as they are) would gravely jeopardize the disarmament program, and (4) to persuade enough people having the power of decision in both blocs to support whatever plan may ultimately be devised, in order that conventions or treaties embodying the plan may be signed and ratified.

An affirmative answer to the second question is easier to give. Once the plan is established, the world is over the hump and the going is mostly downhill. However, the successful implementation of a general and complete disarmament program requires that the participating nations agree on the moves called for by the earlier stages of the plan and carry them out to the final stage; that they administer the plan as a going concern with enough harmony to permit reasonable efficiency in conducting the complex operations involved; and that they resolve the inevitable disputes, including disputes on issues intrinsic to the plan, that might wreck it for all time if unchecked.

The Tactic of Deferring Difficult Problems

This division of the political problems posed by disarmament into two sets of questions is, of course, oversimplified. The break between agreement and operation is not as sharp as my two questions suggest. I have ignored a wise principle that has been especially prominent in United States disarmament proposals, "Don't try to settle all the problems at the start of the program." Some of the matters on which agreement is most difficult may be left until the basic plan has been accepted and operations are well under way. Moreover, the statement of principles for disarmament negotiations adopted by the United States and the Soviet Union in September 1961 encourages this approach. It permits any partial measure that may win acceptance during negotiations to be agreed on and implemented "without prejudicing progress on agreement on the total program and in such a way that these measures would facilitate and form part of that platform."

Whether by this kind of serendipity or by the deliberate phasing of the disarmament program, some matters that would logically fall under the first basic question will probably fall under the second. This has one major advantage: the gravitational pull of popular enthusiasm for arms reduction and the growth of governmental and public confidence in the good faith of the other parties would build pressures for agreement on the difficult points set aside for later negotiation. Like many good ideas, however, this one can be pushed too far. A disarmament treaty, when signed, must be both sufficiently far-reaching and specific to attest the reality of each signatory's commitment and must demonstrate that no nation is trying to entrap its adversaries in a protracted period of desultory negotiations designed to get nowhere. Many persons in this country suspect this was the Soviet intent in the test-ban negotiations, and the Soviet leaders seem to have thought that this was the intent of some of the disarmament proposals of the United States.

Pressures to Solve Political Problems

Whatever the basis for these suspicions, I believe that, to achieve agreement on disarmament with the U.S.S.R., the United States is going to find that we must go further toward disarmament in the early stages of the process than we should like. I am concerned less by the risks we may run in thus going further than I am by the greatly increased political problems of initial persuasion this poses for us. The bigger the commitment made abroad, the harder it will be to sell the plan at home. The reverse would seem to be true in the U.S.S.R.—if their emphasis on far-reaching agreements is genuine. Whatever the political factors, they doubtless are reinforced by the pressure in the Soviet Union to cut back Western offensive capability quickly, once the Soviet's own defensive posture is exposed. The Soviet military may be equally sensitive to exposure of its offensive potential, particularly if the potential is as low as we have recently assumed.

If my impressions are correct, important political commitments would have to be made and hard questions resolved if and when agreement to a disarmament plan was reached, or soon thereafter. Fortunately, however, the very achievement of agreement and settlements on this scale would add to the momentum of the disarmament plan and make the process a more effective influence for peace. To assess the political difficulties that must be overcome and to gauge the potency of the process set in motion, it may be useful to look briefly at the main political problems that must be faced in setting up a disarmament plan. As I see them, they include both political problems extrinsic to the plan that, if left unresolved, would jeopardize its successful operation, and political problems intrinsic to the plan, particularly to the design of the control machinery. Without attempting a detailed analysis, I shall make a few observations.

Related Political and Military Problems

The more rapid the cutback in armaments, the sooner will we have to deal with those political problems that are dangerous because they arise from, or bear directly upon, military situations. By way of example, I cite the two Chinas, the two Germanies (plus the two Berlins), the two Koreas, and the two Vietnams. I also note the nearly ubiquitous problem of how a disarming world is to respond to the overthrow of an established government by subversion or by violence, especially when the result is to shift allegiance from East to West or from West to East. Another problem, political as well as military, is that of foreign bases.

I do not know how many of these problems it would be possible to postpone until some later stage in the disarmament process, but it seems clear that the problem of the two Chinas could not be. Still more important than working out a schedule may be the recognition of the proposition that the settlement or deflation of such political problems is part and parcel of disarmament planning. In these situations, the *status quo* rests on bayonets—to use a quaint old-fashioned figure. Withdraw the bayonets, and you change the *status quo*. We cannot plan disarmament without thinking about these problems. We cannot settle these problems without thinking about disarmament.

Disarmament as an Aid in Problem Solving

Happily, these political problems are rendered easier to handle by reason of the fact that they are part of disarmament planning. This is a proposition I advanced in 1955; unlike some views I held then, I still believe it to be true. In *Foreign Affairs* I observed that:[1]

> . . . it may be easier to settle a dispute as a means to achieving some larger and independent purpose than it would be to resolve it wholly on

its own merits. Thus the United States could more easily recognize Red China's claim to a Security Council seat as a step in setting up an arms control plan under the U.N. than on grounds bearing exclusively on the merits of that claim. For its part, China would find it easier to give up the effort to capture Formosa by force if this were part of the procedure of joining a control plan.

Some further considerations might be noted. In so far as United States reluctance to admit Red China to the United Nations has been based on the warlike policies of Red China, the controlled reduction in armaments should progressively remove the dragon's teeth and so remove that reason for our opposition. The same operation would remove the military justification for the continued occupation of Quemoy and Matsu; moreover, it would so reduce the armed forces on Formosa as to destroy any illusion of their "liberating" the mainland by force. In these circumstances, the problem of finding a political solution for Formosa—possibly provisional—would not seem intractable.

The settlement of certain problems might be easier after disarmament rather than before. Presumably a United Nations Peace Force would then exist, constituting a more effective instrumentality than the improvised emergency forces resorted to in the past by the United Nations. However, a United Nations Peace Force cannot prop up shaky governments against shifts in popular allegiance in either direction, especially if there is no interference by a neighboring country. As military supports are withdrawn, both sides become exposed to such changes: the West, among the underdeveloped countries; the Soviet Union, among its European satellites. The tension created in a disarming world by such turnovers would, however, be distinctly less than that created today, when their effect would have to be assayed in terms of the existing military balance.

Political Control over Disarmament

Important among the political problems intrinsic to the disarmament plan and not readily deferrable is the question of the terms on which the signatory powers would accept the impairment of sovereignty by a suprastate control system. I do not refer to such consequential legal matters as the status and powers of inspectors or the duty of citizens to inform on wrong-doing conationals in official positions. Relatively speaking, these are details. The big disputes are more likely to arise with respect to the authority of the central administrative body (International Disarmament Organization—or IDO, as our latest proposal terms it); to the command of the suprastate military forces charged with keeping the peace; and especially to the authority of whatever body has the power to determine basic policies for IDO and the peace-keeping forces and to issue implementing directives.

In a world divided into two contending camps, with many unaligned nations, the task of devising control plans that are politically tolerable to enough of the members of all three groups to win acceptance is one of extreme difficulty, as shown by the Hammarskjöld succession. Furthermore, the task is roughly proportionate in difficulty to the importance of activities subject to control.

In contrast to the great responsibilities of the bodies charged with making disarmament work (including keeping a disarmed world peaceful), the duties of the Secretary General of the United Nations have been limited. This has rendered easier, though not easy, the task of providing effective means to make the Secretary General answerable to politically responsible bodies in the United Nations. The shape that disputes concerning political control will take has been foreshadowed in the "troika" proposals of the U.S.S.R. and in our out-of-hand rejection of them. Neither major power bloc is likely to accept a design for disarmament machinery that will expose it to the hegemony of its rival bloc; yet clearly, as the United Nations Secretariat compromise evidences, this is an area of controversy in which it is not wise to be intransigent. Arrangements are feasible to keep the gap between policy-making and administration from growing too wide.

On the other hand, I must concede that, whenever a political problem in shaping the disarmament plan is solved by compromising a position we have long held and widely publicized, the task of persuading opposition groups in the United States to accept the treaty becomes more difficult, to say nothing of that still more difficult task of enlisting the concurring votes of two-thirds of the Senators present. If this objective is to be attained, the plan must be defensible on the score of national security. Military danger to the nation will be the common rallying ground of all the opponents of any disarmament plan, whatever their underlying motivation. Though the plan's protagonists cannot guarantee absolute safety, they must be able to show that a reduction in armaments is so geared to progress in control that at no time would the United States be exposed to the grave danger of a surprise attack or a one-sided war. So far as practicable, the more difficult decisions bearing on security should be deferred to the later stages of the disarmament program, so that, in the assessment of the security hazard, due weight can be given to the cumulative effects of the disarmament process.

So far I have discussed problems posed by my first question: can the disarmament process actually be set in motion? For the purposes of the rest of this paper, I shall postulate that the United States has entered a disarmament convention signed by all other nations—including Red China; that IDO has been set up in the United Nations; that little IDO's have been created within most signatory powers. Once IDO begins its functions of organizing its verification and inspection activities, of disarming nations, of building up a United Nations Peace Force, many difficult, even dangerous problems lie ahead. What is there to prevent these from blowing up into war or simply into collapse?

Military Instability in Disarmament

One may too readily conclude that what would prevent either dénouement would be the progressive reduction in the military strength of the major powers. Ultimately, of course, this process, if not brought to an untimely halt, would reduce and finally eliminate nuclear weapons and the principal means for their delivery. In the interim, however, nuclear weaponry would exist in sufficient abundance to wipe out both democratic and totalitarian societies. Assessed in terms of military considerations alone, the changes wrought in the interim stages by the disarmament process would not be such as to remove all risk of armed conflict.

In a paper entitled "The Stability of Total Disarmament," distributed by the Institute of Defense Analyses, Professor Thomas C. Schelling of Harvard University analyzes the military situation that would be created by disarmament with his customary acumen and thoroughgoingness.[2] He examines the stability of partial as well as of total disarmament. He views the stability achieved in either of these conditions as a quite unstable stability. Indeed, he sees the instability in the stability of total disarmament as greater than the instability in the stability of partial disarmament.

As usual, I find it difficult to disagree with Professor Schelling's reasoning, once I have accepted his purpose and assumptions. He assumes that the disarmament he writes about is in the near term, and so, hopefully, do I. He assumes that disarmament does not follow but "precedes the settlement of international differences" and "is not limited to the pace at which trust and confidence might be developed." He refuses to "take for granted that the interests and anxieties of government would be automatically reduced by the substantial elimination of visible military threats." Indeed, one of the threats to which he devotes considerable attention is the threat of rearmament. His analysis extends to "preventive rearmament," to "pre-emptive rearmament," to rearmament catalyzed by mischief-makers, and even to accidental rearmament.

What seems to be missing in Professor Schelling's approach is the idea embodied in the title Seymour Melman suggested for the present paper, "Disarmament as a Cumulative Process for Peace and Freedom." Professor Schelling states: "To be realistic, we have to look at the military environment in relation to political and other relations that provide a basis for conflict." I would add that realism equally requires us to consider the emergent political and other relations that might remove the basis for conflict. This Professor Schelling has not attempted to do, and I shall try to fill the void.

In this undertaking I shall reject in part one of his assumptions, namely, that disarmament precedes the settlement of international differences. As I have indicated, I believe that the operation of the disarmament process would *compel* the readjustment of a number of important international differences, some at the start, others as the program progresses. The disarmament process itself would exert an independent and important tranquilizing influence. Therefore, on the day the agreement became effective, the world would not be bristling with as many menacing political issues as it does today.

Political Forces Making for Stability

To come to my main thesis, I believe entry into a disarmament treaty would set in motion political forces that would counter the consequences of such military instabilities as might persist and that it would sharply curtail the readiness of the participating powers to resort to armed force as an "instrument of policy" (to employ an ill-starred phrase). During the disarmament process, the existence of a *sure* military deterrent to the use of military force, or to rearmament, might be hard to demonstrate, but disincentives either to the use of such force or to rearmament would be building up apace. Without attempting to catalog all the tranquilizing forces that I believe would be potent in a disarming world, I shall present three.

Political Commitments in Securing the Adoption of the Plan. The very act of embarking on a disarmament program, with the break from ancient institutions and attitudes this entails, would constitute an open commitment to peaceful solutions in international disputes and to abstention from coercive threats and actions. This factor of commitment would be most evident in a democracy whose government had had to fight hard to enlist the support of a majority; inevitably, that government would be pitted against a sincere, anxious, and articulate opposition, reinforced by the vested interests that disarmament would destroy or depreciate. In its campaigning to convince the majority of the wisdom of its course, no such government could approach the disarmament program and the questions it posed in a tentative or experimental state of mind. In the early stages at least, its security forces would doubtless remain wary, but the policy makers would be compelled to do their utmost to execute the plan.

Undoubtedly, the business of carrying the agreements into execution would lead to many differences within IDO, and at times it would create tense and potentially disastrous situations; but the governments' commitment would work for patience. In no democracy would the campaign for IDO stop when the ink had dried on the treaty. The majority that had supported IDO would have to be kept a majority, and an ever growing one. As Fred C. Iklé of the RAND Corporation warned,[3] this tendency to persevere in efforts to make the system work might render democratic government overly indulgent to violators. In the absence of violations plainly making the continuance of disarmament perilous, such governments would doubtless be slow to react to controversy-breeding charges and suspicions in ways that might cause the program to collapse. What makes this prospect tolerable—indeed, a good thing—is the fact that comparable, if less conspicuous, pressures to abide by the agreement would have arisen in the Communist states as well, especially in their bellwether, the Soviet Union.

In totalitarian states, the process I have been describing would take place within the much narrower circle of those whose voices can be heard in the formulation of policy. In securing the adoption of the plan, an opposition would have had to be persuaded or overridden. Vested interests would have had to be curtailed or destroyed. Not even a dictator would embark on such a course without solid support. To be sure, one could conjure up a plot in which the dictator and an inner inner circle had devised a scheme to wage war as soon as the trusting democracies had disarmed themselves to a vulnerable level; but, given the ponderous character of the instrumentalities that they would be obliged to manipulate secretly over a period of years to accomplish their objective, this diabolic hypothesis does not carry conviction. In a world in which some chances have to be taken, the risk of such a scheme seems one of the lesser chances.

Popular Enthusiasm for the Benefits of Disarmament. The second factor building up pressure for perseverance in the disarmament program springs from the response of people everywhere to the activities the program would generate. Probably this would manifest itself most plainly when the plan began to have a noticeable impact on the military, somewhere in the first stage. Three actions would signal it: cutbacks in calls for military service; reductions in military budgets; and the deposit for ultimate destruction in internationally supervised depots of military matériel in excess of the ceilings set. The third development would be the most dramatic; and doubtless each great power would strive to publicize its good faith in carrying out the plan by propaganda photographs of the vast parks of matériel it was building up. Yet more important, if less conspicuous, would be the concurrent measures reflecting the reduction in military budgets. These might take various forms, all welcome to the citizenry: investment in needed public works, educational and health programs, increases in the pay of government employees and teachers, and, in the United States at least, some reduction in taxes. As military cutbacks continued, sums released by these processes might begin to swell to tremendous dimensions. They would soon build up powerful vested interests for their continuation.

The enthusiasm with which the peoples of both the democracies and the totalitarian states would respond to this beating of costly swords into wanted plowshares would be vast. Any government that tried to reverse this policy, save under the strongest provocation, would find itself in the same sort of political danger as our wartime administrations would have faced, had they tried to slow the headlong pace of our postwar demobilizations. To be sure, there would be some persons in every nation for whom progressive demilitarization would represent the loss of career, of prestige, and of economic benefits, but doubtless they would have made their fight in advance of the decision: *ex hypothesi,* they would have been defeated. Their efforts to turn back the tide would become increasingly futile as the peace economy steadily supplanted the defense economy.

Public rejoicing would not be inspired solely by economic gains. Two years or so ago all of us experienced a lift from the temporary success of the technical conference on the nuclear test ban. Imagine how much greater would be the world-wide exhilaration produced by the successful negotiation and the putting into effect of a scheme looking to "general and complete disarmament," even though major portions of the plan were still in skeletal form. Naturally, the public, always inclined to wishful thinking, would tend to exaggerate the assurance of peace that the initiation of disarmament would bring, but it would be a hardy government indeed that attempted to deny its people the sense of emancipation from fear that its action had achieved. Moreover, the pressure for peaceful policies would not be evanescent. The longer the new peace was maintained, the further the disarming went, the harder it would be to reverse the process.

The Soviet leaders' familiar practice of talking tough when things do not go their way would be at once less convincing and more antagonizing. We would soon find ourselves getting much less of it. And though, of course, there would still be bellicose American editors and columnists ever ready to view with alarm, their influence would dwindle, becoming comparable in dimension to the influence exerted by the convinced pacifists today.

A New Pattern for Handling International Problems. A third factor in accumulating support for the disarmament program would be the creation of a new pattern for handling problems between nations, problems that heretofore have not been subject to effective international control. At the start, there would arise a multitude of questions as to the interpretation, application, and elaboration of the control plan. As a model for its functioning, the pessimists customarily choose the Korean armistice and assume that the Communist states would adhere to that model in a global disarmament program. This, however, not only disregards the two points just considered but also ignores the fact that the Korean armistice brought a halt to a war that might at any time have been resumed. In the hostile climate in which the armistice violations took place, military advantages might understandably have been put ahead of establishing a reputation for fidelity in keeping agreements. One is not warranted in assuming that the attitudes manifest at Panmunjom, or more recently in the cockpit of Laos, would recur in case a convention for general and complete disarmament were negotiated and actually put into effect. They might recur—but the odds seem against it.

Once established, the pattern for resolving issues in accordance with rules and standards that were administered pursuant to rational procedures would begin to exert a force of its own. It would be recognized as the way disarmament disputes and problems were to be handled, and it would take a deliberated decision at a high level for any nation to decide to ignore or undermine the system. Moreover, the system's tranquilizing influence on the major powers operating it would extend well beyond the operations of the system itself. If the major powers were respecting the rules for restraining their own conduct in an effort to keep the system operative, one could be sure that they would not readily permit smaller countries to disregard the system or put its operation into jeopardy. From this concern would come new pressures for the peaceful settlement of disputes upon countries that did not possess much military power yet had enough to produce military problems. The business of seeing to it that other countries kept the peace would become a much livelier concern of the great powers, once they came to realize that a breach would imperil the disarmament plan and might even lead to the use of the United Nations Peace Force, at some expense to all concerned.

The Need for Balance in Assessing Risks

If I seem to present an arrogantly optimistic view of the cumulative growth of the disarmament process, once under way, as a force for world peace with freedom, I plead the need of restoring, through emphasizing the constructive side, a balance I feel has all too often been lacking. How often have the participants in discussions of the disarmament process been confronted by seemingly insuperable difficulties and horrendous dangers, and how often have these proved on analysis to have sprung from the usually inarticulate premise that the political stress-patterns of the disarming or disarmed world would be essentially the same as those in the trigger-tense world of today! At the least, we should recognize the interaction of the relevant factors in our analyses.

I am not striving to emulate Dr. Pangloss and close my eyes to the obvious possibility that dangerous mischief or serious disagreements in the disarming or inspection processes would lead to a breakdown of the system—or worse. My contention is that such hazards must be gauged in the light of an imposing array of political factors tending either to prevent them from occurring or to minimize their consequences. If there is a place for pessimism, I think it lies not in this calculation of the viability of a disarmament program but in reckoning the chance for the necessary consensus to make the adoption of any disarmament plan possible.

Overcoming Opposition Here to Disarmament

I am by no means sure that the opposition of the combined forces of crusading anti-Communism, of vested interests in armaments, and of natural, honest conservatism can be overcome, unless and until many more years pass without a nuclear war, during which increasingly amicable relations are maintained with the nations in the Communist bloc. If, as I hope, we strive to reach an earlier agreement, United States leadership must keep three points constantly in mind.

1. *The Importance of Reducing East-West Tensions.* The United States government cannot conduct a cold war with the Soviet bloc until the day a disarmament treaty is signed, and then turn it off. This trick seems to be possible for the men in the Kremlin, but if we could see inside its walls we might find that those men were confronted by the same problem. Hence we might discover—both here and in Moscow—that it was at once possible and mutually profitable to make disarmament negotiations coincide with a soft-pedaling, even a postponement, of political issues likely to exacerbate present differences. Once substantial progress had been made in formulating a plan, it might be feasible (as I have already suggested) to tie the resolution of such issues to agreement on the plan.

How *not* to pave the way for political agreement on disarmament was graphically demonstrated by the collapse of the test-ban negotiations last year, by the resumption of the tests, and by the blowing up of the Laos, Berlin, and South Vietnam crises. All these preceded by short intervals the acceptance by the United States and the U.S.S.R. in September 1961 of the "statement of principles" for the conduct of disarmament negotiations—the most forward-looking document to emerge out of such negotiations in years. The result: the statement has not been taken seriously, its good faith is suspect, and it has been virtually ignored. Coming at a more propitious time, it would have given fresh hope and renewed heart to the champions of disarmament on both sides.

With much justification we can claim that the eclipse of the statement of principles by this series of political setbacks and crises is the fault of the Soviet Union and its allies. But we are too easily satisfied with the fact that we can fasten the blame for such a failure on the other side. More important is the fact that the failure was a setback for our own policies. Our government may not have been able to accomplish more, in view of Soviet intractability, but surely it might have done more to keep the American people from writing off disarmament and concentrating on shelters. The American people will have just as much to say about whether there is to be disarmament in this generation as the men in the Kremlin.

2. *The Use of Disarmament in Handling Political Problems.* The main questions we have to answer are: Could we have minimized the effects of the failure even though we could not prevent it? Could we conceivably have turned the statement of principles to good account in handling the then current crises? A comparison of two presidential addresses will give my point specificity.

In December 1953 President Eisenhower addressed the United Nations Assembly on the horrors of nuclear war, with special emphasis on our own ability to wage it. He concluded his grim recital with a few paragraphs about the possibility of turning atomic energy to peaceful uses through international agreement and machinery. The response was tremendous. This address made way for "Atoms for Peace" and the International Atomic Energy Agency. Although the hopes then raised have fallen far short of fulfillment, men's minds were changed. Ideas released by that address helped to transform the pursuit of nuclear science from a cloak-and-dagger operation into a field for active and open international cooperation with extensive East-West exchanges.

In September 1961 President Kennedy addressed the United Nations Assembly. He made clear the readiness of this country to join in patient, continuous negotiation for complete and general disarmament, and he strongly endorsed the "statement of principles" agreed on shortly before. This address might have marked an important milestone in progress toward disarmament; but such an effect was counteracted by the closing section of his address, which silhouetted the Berlin crisis against "the flaming pyre" of a world consumed by nuclear war. No connection was made or even suggested between the terror thus evoked and the inspiring vision depicted earlier in the address. For the world audience, the effect that remained was not commitment to the goal of complete and universal disarmament but the nightmare of the planet in flames. A great opportunity was lost to use our enlarged commitment to the cause of disarmament as an instrument for dealing with the Berlin crisis.

3. *Hope versus Fear in the Case for Disarmament.* One final ingredient must be added to the recipe for the public acceptance of any far-reaching disarmament program. The missing ingredient is hope. We need a vision of the world in which (even though nations that call themselves Communist still exist) just rules and procedures replace power politics and friendliness replaces distrust and suspicion, a world in which cooperation can be substituted for dealing at arms' length and for cut-throat competition, and in which freedom becomes a reality.

To motivate public support for disarmament measures of all sorts, the protagonists of various disarmament measures, both in and out of government, have relied on fear. But fear, as we should have learned from the evangelical preachings of hell-fire and brimstone in the war against the devil, is effective only intermittently, and it has damaging side effects. Under the stress of fear brought close to home, people may rush to build fall-out shelters; they are less likely to rush to support measures that will promote lasting peace. Fear makes us hold more tightly to the weapons we have and to call for bigger and better ones—not to lay them down.

Hope is hard to evoke in the light of our past experience in dealing with the Communist states. But the hope we need does not have to concern today, tomorrow, or the day after. We need to see a hopeful goal ahead, even though it may be a distant one. We need to be convinced that people in high places also believe in that goal and are working toward it as best they can. If we can foresee a world without armaments, or nearly without them (and that is our declared goal), cannot we also see a world in which the present struggle has subsided and in which changes in the competing economic and political systems will have so narrowed the gap between them that the incentive of either to destroy the other would have totally disappeared? Then, though competition between the systems continued, it could be pursued on a basis that would permit cooperation in common causes and even friendly interchange.

Our recent relations with Yugoslavia and Poland have amply demonstrated that, in the absence of hostile policies, a Communist government and ideology need not debar reasonably friendly associations. If we can entertain rationally these hopes—and I submit we can—it is high time that we start propagating them. To do so would require us to recognize potentialities for good in our adversaries. This we have been reluctant to do lest, while they remain unregenerate, they make propaganda of our indulgence. We refuse, therefore, to acknowledge that what we are really striving for is a world in which our relations with the Communist states can and will be friendly.

The luxury of concealing this purpose is something we cannot afford if we want to bring the two power blocs close enough together to permit the negotiation, execution, and ratification of a treaty for general and complete disarmament. Under such a treaty both sides would have to accord great power and authority to a body that neither one could fully control. Confronted by this predicament, the separate interests of each require that we and our present rivals learn to plan and work together. Only by so doing can we expect to join in the noblest and boldest adventure in man's political history: the quest for general and complete disarmament.

References

1. David F. Cavers, "The Challenge of Planning Arms Controls," *Foreign Affairs,* October 1955, *34:* 66.

2. My observations are based on the version in which that paper was circulated for comment before publication. The paper, extensively revised but preserving the substance of the original, appeared as "The Role of Deterrence in Total Disarmament," *Foreign Affairs,* April 1962, *40:* 392.

3. Fred C. Iklé, "After Detection What?" *Foreign Affairs,* January 1961, *39:* 208.

LEWIS C. BOHN

Peace with Disarmament—or Without?

An international agreement to disarm has been widely regarded as perhaps the most desirable way to escape from the perils of a nuclear World War III. Impressive pronouncements on the need for disarmament have been made by statesmen in virtually all countries since 1945. Very few political leaders or students of international relations have been willing to go on record as opposing the proposition that an adequately controlled disarmament system would be a very great improvement over the present situation of mutual nuclear deterrence, cold war, and vast national military budgets.

Despite the almost universally proclaimed support for disarmament, however, one can hardly be hopeful that the major governments will agree to it. The record of disarmament negotiations since the early 1920's, especially since 1946, is very discouraging; every effort to achieve a detailed treaty on arms limitation has failed (unless one excepts the "demilitarization" of Antarctica). In the case of the nuclear-test ban there has been no success, despite a number of favorable conditions, including the fact that the inspection problem is technically much simpler than it would be for most other arms limitations, and involves a minimum encroachment on legitimate military secrecy. This discouraging record is made still bleaker by what appear to be serious inherent obstacles to future progress toward agreement—obstacles such as the nature of Soviet and Chinese societies, the political structure of the world community, the ideology of Communism, the rapid progress of weapon technology, the reliance by all major governments on military power to keep the peace and (in some cases) to further political objectives, and intrinsic problems of communication and negotiation in the absence of mutual trust.

If there has been no agreement on international disarmament, there has also been no nuclear war. The many risks in the present situation are very impressive and certainly not to be ignored; but since we have now had some seventeen years without nuclear war, do we really need to continue the search for disarmament? Should we recognize that a diplomatic agreement to disarm is very improbable and devote ourselves to more attainable goals? Should we pursue those measures on which we have reluctantly had to depend since 1945—supplementing these where possible with the relatively modest adjustments attainable through arms control and unilateral initatives such as those proposed by C. E. Osgood,[1] in the hope of gradual reduction in political tensions? The temptation is considerable. It is easy to be discouraged by the many very real obstacles to disarmament. Arms control, new initiatives, and efforts at political settlement may well improve matters, and must therefore be pursued with great vigor; but in my view we dare not settle for such partial measures. To pursue the elimination of nuclear weapons at least from national arsenals remains vital, even though it is obviously true that nuclear war has so far not occurred. The obstacles to an East-West agreement on disarmament call for far more effort to overcome them, rather than complete discouragement.

We shall try first to consider briefly why multilateral disarmament, at least with respect to weapons of mass destruction, cannot be dispensed with as a central and urgent national goal. Then we shall outline some ways to increase the (at present) very small chances for getting acceptable disarmament agreements with the governments of the USSR, China, and other major powers. Finally we shall consider an approach that may indicate new supplementary ways to keep the peace in the armed world with which we are all too likely to be faced—and that may also contribute to changing it into a disarmed world, and a better one.

The Need for Nuclear Disarmament

The reasons for the inadequacy of any situation short of multilateral nuclear disarmament are as follows: unless there is nuclear disarmament of all countries, we shall still be living in a world threatened with the mass extermination of many millions of us, fifteen minutes (or perhaps very much less) after a decision (rational or irrational) for war has been taken in any one of several national capitals. As long as the basis for maintaining peace is a nuclear-deterrence system involving nuclear weapons poised in ballistic missiles, submarines, satellites, or other space-launching platforms, so long will that peace remain an artificial and utterly perilous state that man simply has not the capacity to manage. If nuclear-deterrence systems remain, as they would even under the most advanced "stable deterrence" system, and if nondemocratic regimes prevail in any advanced nations, then all of us who live in the major cities of the potential combatants will be existing from minute to minute at the mercy of a handful of individuals thousands of miles away whose concern for our welfare is considerably less than absolute and whose wisdom in exercising their power is open to question. Moreover, unless the operation of the unilateral measures and arms-control techniques is perfect, there remains at least some chance that nuclear extermination could come upon us accidentally, without the deliberate choice of those in whose hands our lives and futures are now placed.

Nor is this perpetual subjugation of human destiny to chance or alien decision limited to urban residents of the United States or Europe: it adds a further burden for the subjects of authoritarian rule in East Europe, China, and the Soviet Union. Moreover, the many millions in Asia, Africa, and Latin America, for whom a fraction of our military budgets can now make the difference between continued poverty, starvation, and tyranny, on the one hand, or rising living standards, hope, and political freedom on the other—these millions, though perhaps receiving some of our help, are living under the constant threat of the collapse of all their hopes through a nuclear war, one which we are not likely to start but in which a full share of the damage and global contamination would be from weapons "made in U.S.A."

As long as we continue nuclear deterrence, we shall be prolonging the fantastic paradox in which the fundamental instrument for preventing war means that war, if it comes, must be quicker and more dreadful than the imagination can conceive. So long as we continue nuclear deterrence, we shall be pretending that we have so completely mastered the subtle balances of military technology and the infinite variations in human behavior that control these balances that we are willing to wager our own lives and the fate of millions on the absolute perfection of the system.

The elimination of *all* weapons and armed forces from national arsenals should presumably be the ultimate objective of disarmament. It is the objective professed now by the major governments of East and West. But surely it is the mass weapons—chemical, biological, and (above all) nuclear—which pose by far the greatest threat to our lives and all we value. It is the imminent possibility of nuclear war that has made peace so urgent. Therefore, the disarmament approach to peace surely requires above all the elimination from national arsenals of nuclear weapons; and that is what I shall stress. More general disarmament may be more desirable still; but I cannot see that it is so urgent or even indispensable to an acceptable future for all of us. A world without nuclear armaments is not necessarily Utopia. History provides ample evidence of the hells wrought by evil, deluded, or ambitious men; the potentials for destruction that science has created will in any event remain in men's minds; misunderstandings and human imperfections can still produce conflict at every level.

What nuclear disarmament *can* do is to change the human situation from one which man cannot handle to one he can. If an aggressive tyranny plans war, there will be weeks, months, or years in which the prospective victims can take action, instead of mere minutes. When disputes between nations do occur, or even armed conflict, the level of violence will be comparatively moderate, and the danger of uncontrollable "escalation" into thermonuclear disaster in days or hours will be gone. If mental breakdown or failures in equipment occur, the consequences will not include the immediate death of millions, the injury of millions more, and the irreversible pollution of our planet. The defects in the systems to be used to keep the peace can be discovered and handled in a process of gradual evolution, instead of in the universal cataclysm inherent in a breakdown of our present system of mutual nuclear deterrence.

I have asserted that the situation without nuclear disarmament is fundamentally defective. If true, this alone is not reason enough for giving much more serious attention to controlled nuclear disarmament. The question inevitably arises: what new problems might develop, perhaps even worse than the problems already overcome? If there are unacceptable features to a world with nuclear weapons, how can we be sure there would be no equally serious drawbacks to a world in which such weapons had officially been eliminated?

The answer is that we cannot be sure. We do not have enough understanding of the problems that would be raised, or of the ways they might be dealt with, to know for sure that the balance would work out favorably. Indeed, we may never be able to establish this with complete certainty. Yet in my opinion none of the many objections to controlled nuclear disarmament has so far, in the light of what we now know, appeared insuperable. The objections raised include the following:

1. An adequate inspection of nuclear disarmament is technically impossible.
2. Complete nuclear disarmament is intrinsically too unstable.
3. It is so distant from where we stand now as to be almost unimaginable.
4. It would require fundamental changes in human nature, or at least changes in international political structure so drastic as to be impossible.
5. The United States itself would never agree to it.
6. The Soviet and Chinese governments, as long as they are authoritarian and Communist, will never agree to the necessary inspection.
7. If the Soviet and Chinese governments did agree to nuclear disarmament, it would only be in order to violate the agreement or to circumvent it.
8. Nuclear disarmament is militarily too advantageous to the Sino-Soviet bloc, with their inherent advantage in the size of their populations.
9. The necessary international police force or other enforcement agency would be uncontrollable and a hazard to the international community.
10. Communist political-economic expansion would go unchecked.
11. The United States economy would collapse.
12. The task of negotiating a treaty in the necessary detail to ensure Communist compliance is intrinsically impossible.
13. The process of transition through arms-control measures or other stages from our present situation to one of controlled nuclear disarmament would take many decades, if it could be done at all.

This is not the place to indicate how these important objections can be met, though I believe they *can* be met. Let me only emphasize that before we accept controlled nuclear disarmament as a replacement for mutual nuclear deterrence, meet them we must. Some good work has been done to this end; much more remains. There is no guarantee of success in devising solutions; but the prospects do look good.

Improving the Chances for East-West Agreement

One aspect I want to discuss further is the problem of improving the chances for East-West agreement. If the controlled nuclear disarmament of all countries does hold promise and is indispensable to a satisfactory world, we surely ought to do everything we can to increase the chances of bringing it about. While the rising interest in these matters in the United States is extremely welcome, I think it important to appreciate that there is still very much more we can do, not only to find answers to the various difficulties, such as those listed above, but also to make the probability of East-West agreement more than the remote hope it appears to be today.

1. We can influence the various groups in the United States, the USSR, China, the United Kingdom, France, and elsewhere who have a vested interest, real or imagined, in keeping nuclear weapons. These groups may be found in political, military, intellectual, industrial, scientific, and even labor circles. It is necessary to understand the real or imagined interest of each group in keeping nuclear weapons, legitimate and otherwise; to find ways of meeting these needs to the extent this can safely be done; and to find ways of communicating the results to the group in question. With respect to such groups in the United States, to some extent this could be done in a joint research effort with the group members. Some ways of approaching the Chinese and Soviet groups will be mentioned below.

2. We can develop and support groups in the United States (and if possible elsewhere) who have vested interests in the abolition of national nuclear arsenals. These interests may be economic: dairy farmers who meet increased consumer resistance as their products are contaminated by nuclear tests; power companies or financial interests wishing to get cheap "surplus" fissionable material for commercial atomic power plants; manufacturers of data-processing equipment who hope for large contracts for disarmament inspection; merchants whose foreign trade is restricted by cold-war embargoes. They may be geographic: city dwellers in the potentially belligerent powers; people living near military airfields, missile sites, or other wartime targets; those downwind from major industrial, military or population centers; those particularly exposed to fallout from nuclear tests; or even all the inhabitants of the northern hemisphere. They may be social: people who live in apartments without fallout shelters, or who are too poor to build them; those unable to move to safer locations; mothers of young children, who are particularly susceptible to radioactive contamination from nuclear tests; scientists eager for increased international contacts. They may be religious and moral: pacifists of Christian or other faiths; Buddhists or others opposed to taking life in any form; all those unhappy with

United States reliance on nuclear weapons which, if war comes, will kill millions of innocent civilians in many countries.

In many cases, even military men could find an interest in nuclear disarmament: those in the smaller and "neutralist" powers could anticipate positions of influence in an international police force; ground soldiers, marines, and sailors might participate in various inspection and enforcement operations; airmen now watching over missile sites might find it more congenial to be airborne once again as civilian inspectors over former "enemy" territory; strategists and systems analysts might be challenged by the immense task of evaluating inspection and control arrangements, and adapting these to technical advances; lazier military types could anticipate earlier and perhaps especially fattened pensions.

The solidarity, productivity, and political influence of such groups could be increased by research conferences, by regional, national, and international congresses and conventions, the formation of local study groups, national and international centers for research coordination, the publication and (where necessary) subsidy of group periodicals; essay contests with attractive prizes; visits and exchange programs; and (in democratic countries) by the establishment of appropriate lobbies.

3. We can bring to bear on disarmament problems talents and specialties not yet tapped. On the talent side, for example, there are hundreds of able historians in this country and elsewhere. The behavior of peoples in different times and with very different cultures is obviously relevant to man's present problem of surviving his technology; with encouragement, many scholars of history could discover the lessons of the past for reaching a disarmed world and making it work if we can get there. Or again, in this country there are hundreds of individuals with first-hand knowledge of modern China (former missionaries, teachers, merchants, scientists), but at present there is no effort to encourage them to help bring about Chinese support of controlled nuclear disarmament. As for untapped specialties, there are above all the sciences of human behavior. Much able and fruitful research, some of it experimental, is proceeding in these areas, here and elsewhere. It has an obvious relevance to problems of war and peace, in particular to the attainment and successful operation of nuclear disarmament agreements, and it should surely become an area of multiplied activities in basic research, training, and organized application to national security and world peace.

In the past, the number of people involved in full-time research on disarmament in the United States has usually been less than a hundred, and sometimes less than ten. The number of other specialists who have published papers or made other substantial contributions since 1945 is probably less than 200. The caliber of the research has not always been first rate, and the areas of knowledge brought to bear have been relatively limited. It is necessary to involve directly thousands of men of the greatest ability and with the fullest training, and to develop and apply all areas of scholarship, learning, and human experience that are relevant to the problem. As far as I can see, there are no inherent obstacles to doing this. It is just that we have not realized how little we were doing, and have even, I think, lacked the concept of an appropriate and full-scale effort. The current large-scale Vela program (on nuclear-test detection) and the creation of the United States Arms Control and Disarmament Agency are important steps in the right direction. But very much more can and must be done. The situation in the USSR has, if anything, been considerably worse. While we cannot take unilateral action to change this, what we do to multiply our own activities is for various reasons likely to induce an increase in such activity on the Soviet if not on the Chinese side.

4. We can establish the possibility of a respectable and prestigious career in disarmament. Students, college faculties, businessmen, diplomats, military men, and others must take seriously the possibility of devoting themselves full time to disarmament work as they would to another profession. At first the attraction might have to be the prestige of being connected with new disarmament research institutes, the intellectual stimulation of a uniquely creative and interdisciplinary research activity, and the moral satisfaction of working on something so important to human affairs. To the extent that disarmament measures can be implemented (if only on a "field test" basis), there may also be attractive opportunities for travel. University degrees and faculty chairs in disarmament studies would help.

5. We can develop with the Soviet Union, China, and others a common understanding of disarmament. This can be promoted by joint research efforts, by liaison groups such as that proposed under the auspices of the American Academy of Arts and Sciences, by the open publication whenever possible of our own research results, perhaps the exchange of research personnel, and perhaps some changes in our philosophy of disarmament negotiations.

6. We can try to change the ideology of Communist elites. In my view there is no point in pretending that the obstacles to nuclear disarmament will automatically disappear with closer contacts and increased mutual understanding. There exist fundamental differences among the policy-making elites in the present or potential nuclear powers, especially between East and West. A major effort is required to define these differences, uncover their origins, assess their implications for attaining effective nuclear-disarmament agreements, and to discover or invent ways of reducing these differences and avoiding their undesirable consequences.

This is at best a difficult and a long-term undertaking. It may well be that the present rulers of China have a view of the outside world that would not permit the degree of international collaboration needed to get a disarmament agreement or to operate it effectively and safely. It may be necessary to await a new generation of Chinese policy-makers. On the other hand, a major effort recognizing the crucial importance of this problem might have an appreciable effect in a few years, especially if it points out ways to adapt negotiations, inspection, enforcement, and the rest to the remaining fundamental differences in world views, value systems, national objectives, and ideologies in general. In time, important changes might be effected in the ideology of Communist elites by United States invitations to Communist policy-makers and others to visit this country, to argue in person with real United States decision-makers and imagined "ruling circles" (such as Wall Street), to experience the feelings and outlook of ordinary United States citizens, and in many other respects to become acquainted with the realities of our society. Such invitations might sooner or later lead to similar opportunities for American decision-makers, disarmament researchers, and others to obtain a more accurate understanding of the realities of the Communist world than is possible today.

Also called for here is a major intellectual effort to understand fully the official Communist doctrine, distinguish its theory from its practice, show objectively and persuasively where it is anachronistic or otherwise defective, and present the "ideology" of non-Communist alternatives. By merely denouncing Communist ideology or by analyzing it only superficially we shall not do anything to bring its present adherents in closer touch with reality. Rather, we must demonstrate in theory as well as in practice the many ways in which modern technology and Western political and social concepts of the twentieth century offer both theoretical and practical approaches to the legitimate goals of individual and social welfare. We must show the present-day adherents of Communism and potential converts that their societies—and ours—can progress without tyranny, without war, and without the threat of war. This kind of intellectual undertaking is hardly congenial to Americans, but it is nonetheless necessary. Perhaps we can share some of the burden with intellectuals of other democratic countries.

7. We can prepare crisis plans for disarmament.[2] In the event of a nuclear accident, the misfiring of an ICBM, the irresponsible use of nuclear weapons by a small country, or even a limited nuclear war that does *not* escalate, there may be a sudden and transitory opportunity to reach international agreement on some sort of limitation on nuclear weapons. If plans are at hand, preferably discussed at least informally by both East and West, then these crises can be converted into opportunities to make some progress in the direction of nuclear disarmament. Important but short-lived opportunities may also come from sudden political changes, such as a revolution in a Communist satellite, a successful coup by military extremists in France or another Western ally in possession of nuclear weapons, or even a major shift in the leadership in China or the USSR.

8. We can conduct field exercises and other large-scale experimental work on arms inspection and concealment, both unilaterally and in cooperation with our allies or with neutrals. For example, we might "disarm" an entire state, and invite foreign inspectors to come and inspect it. Or, it has been suggested that we might conceal a missile or some (real or dummy) nuclear weapons in a designated area and then try to discover them by physical and nonphysical means.[3] This kind of experiment would allow a test of technical and legal arrangements for inspection and provide invaluable experience and even some useful training for the participants. It would no doubt produce a variety of unanticipated problems and also incentives to devise ways of handling them effectively, before the stakes involved were as great as in a real nuclear disarmament agreement. To the extent that Allied, neutral, or even Soviet governments could safely participate, it might help give them—and us—confidence that the inspection task can be done effectively without excessive interference or disruption of the country inspected. It would demonstrate impressively the seriousness of our interest in effective disarmament.

Perhaps the greatest benefit would come from publicity accompanying such exercises. This could make disarmament theory and practice "newsworthy" and perhaps do more to stimulate wide and constructive attention to the possibilities than anything else. Such exercises might take the subject of disarmament at least partly out of the confines of purely intellectual speculation and diplomatic bickering and provide it with some concrete content.

9. We can make a major effort to get an international agreement to limit regional arms, perhaps in Central Europe, or outside the area of direct East-West conflict, as in Latin America. Besides making some contribution to the political stability of the area concerned, and perhaps to the reduction of some local military budgets, these regional disarmament agreements would present similar opportunities for testing inspection and control arrangements in practice, and for the training, publicity, etc. mentioned above. The incentives for such agreements in terms of the local situation may be small; but, as opportunities to help devise and agree on effective nuclear disarmament, they appear to be worth major diplomatic efforts, research, and financial investment. The recent treaty on Antarctica is in principle an example; but the lack of permanent inhabitants, existing military installations, practical access to ground or air inspection, etc., make it a rather special case.

10. We can reexamine the relation between arms control and complete nuclear or general disarmament. We should attempt to shape research on arms control, the negotiation of arms-control agreements, and the operation of any arms-control systems agreed to, so that their contribution toward advantageous, controlled nuclear disarmament is unequivocal. At the same time we must give special attention to preserving or expanding the chances for more complete arms limitations, even if efforts toward partial ones fail. Efforts should be made to encourage the extension of the present intellectual ferment on arms control into matters of disarmament; and to encourage people dedicated to disarmament at least to keep up with the studies and theories of arms control.

No doubt still other ways to improve the outlook for successful East-West disarmament negotiations can be developed. And every effort should be made to do this, unless we deceive ourselves that we can get disarmament without much additional effort or that to continue indefinitely under the threat of imminent nuclear catastrophe is an acceptable prospect. Yet even if everything possible is done to improve the chances for a major East-West disarmament agreement, one still cannot regard such agreement as certain, or even very likely. Above all, we cannot rely on favorable decisions on the part of policy-makers in Moscow and Peking, even if our own support for a disarmed world becomes faultless.

Personal Deterrence

The cornerstone of our policy to prevent major war is nuclear deterrence. By the threat of devastating nuclear response, we intend above all to deter Soviet and Chinese decision-makers from major aggression or an all-out surprise attack. I propose in this final section to suggest that this basic United States policy is fundamentally defective. It means that we rely primarily on large-scale military techniques for what is at root neither a large-scale nor a military task. This is an unnecessary and dangerous error. It is something we have come to do by a natural and perhaps inevitable process of extending concepts and actions once appropriate into new conditions, technological and political, to which they are not suited. But it is something we can change to our advantage in preventing major Communist aggression or war in the present highly armed world, and ultimately in achieving a disarmed one and in keeping it disarmed.

What are these "fundamental defects" in the basic United States policy of nuclear deterrence? Nuclear weapons by their very nature are scaled to cities, regions, and whole countries. Their action is truly "mass destruction." They represent a greater concentration of energy and power than man had dreamed of. The statistics that can be cited to demonstrate this power are endless and very impressive.

Since it is nuclear weapons that we associate with deterrence, we may come to picture the job of influencing Soviet and Chinese policies as something inherently on the same vast scale. We may lose sight of the fact that while Soviet cities are very real, and the Soviet territory which our deterrence weapons could devastate is certainly vast, and the Soviet nuclear and missile arsenal which threatens us is both real and of dreadful capacity, and our own nuclear deterrence force is at least as huge and powerful, still the basic target of all our deterrence efforts is a handful of Communist decision-makers. It is the minds and emotions of a few individuals in Moscow and Peking that we must influence if we are to keep the peace. The vast array of our nuclear deterrence forces exist basically because of the influence we hope they will have on certain bits of flesh and blood half a world away. Furthermore, the nuclear weapons and the delivery systems on which we rely for nuclear deterrence constitute a *military* capability. We hope that deterrence will work, so that we will not have to use these instruments in war; but nevertheless their nature is military, and they are designed for effective operation as a military system in war.

Though the instruments are military, however, their basic task of influencing Communist decision-makers is not. That influence must exert itself in peacetime if it is to fulfill its mission; at root it is not a military interaction with enemy cities, weapons, or armed forces, but a psychological interaction with the thoughts and decisions of certain men in Moscow and Peking. Military techniques and preparations are one of the means for this peacetime psychological job; but the basic problem is not military in character; and other means besides military ones can be used to tackle it. They may even be far better adapted to the task than military techniques, however impressive and potent.

In the past, the security of the United States and of other countries has depended ultimately on military instruments and capabilities. When efforts to contain Hitler's various aggressions by alliance, diplomacy, appeasement, or threat finally failed, for example, it was the military power of the Allies which ultimately overcame him and his Axis partners, and which protected our own territory from Nazi conquest. Nevertheless, whereas military techniques used in war could formerly protect the national security, they now cannot. They cannot defend any country from devastation by nuclear rockets, for example, once those rockets are launched. No responsible scientist who has looked into the possibilities for antimissile defense has concluded that an airtight defense of our nation is feasible. Protection in our time can only come through effects exerted *before* a major nuclear war. Safeguarding the national security means safeguarding the peace, not exerting military power in war if the peace is broken. While military instruments were once the means of protection to be used first in defense against an aggressor and then in conquering him, there is no reason they should be particularly preferable to other, nonmilitary instruments when national security must be secured before war begins, and cannot be achieved afterwards.

Nuclear weapons, then, are mass instruments, and they are military instruments, but this should not deceive us into supposing that their root purpose has either of these characteristics. To make nuclear deterrence the core of our national efforts to influence Communist governments away from aggression and war has been a natural course for the United States. We have had a very pronounced advantage over the USSR, and even more over China, in nuclear weapons and their delivery systems, at least up to the new era of the intercontinental ballistic missile, while in other military capabilities, and in the political realm as well, we have felt at a pronounced disadvantage. Furthermore, unlike the USSR, we have had extensive experience in strategic bombing in World War II, including the only use of nuclear weapons in war to date. To rely on a nuclear-bombing capability in the postwar period has thus seemed a sensible extension of our own military experience, as well as a utilization of a principal strong point relative to the USSR.

In addition, there is a very attractive logical appeal in exploiting the central truth of the nuclear age which makes it so perilous: namely, the impossibility of an effective defense of cities and national territory. We cannot achieve such defense, but neither can the Soviet Union or China; and the strategy of nuclear deterrence is intended directly to utilize this Communist vulnerability in order to keep the peace.

Like the fact that national security in the past has rested ultimately on military capability, these considerations may be quite valid also. Yet to use a technique because one has more experience with it, or because one has an advantage in the number and quality of its instruments, or because it seems to exploit a new peril, is not necessarily desirable if it is not adapted to the new job one has to do. Because one has more sledgehammers or more practice in driving posts with them, or because one is vulnerable to blows with sledgehammers, does not establish that for keeping hornets away the sledgehammer is the best choice.

Another reason for the appeal of nuclear deterrence is that we project an image of how it might work on us. Since we are a democracy, our leaders, though they do make the immediate decisions for war or peace, can do so only as long as we feel they are truly representing our interests and are giving due weight to our desire to avoid nuclear extermination. Since our preference for peace must so directly affect our own leaders, we tend to imagine that the same is at least as true in other countries, including the USSR and China, and that the sharp memories of the Soviet and Chinese peoples of their suffering in World War II means that their leaders cannot expose them to World War III. But the fact of the matter is that our primary task is to deter not democracies but autocracies. And there it is not the wishes of the people that are the ultimate determinants of policy.

Certainly, if a Soviet ruler has a genuine concern for the survival and welfare of his people, as Khrushchev and some of his colleagues may well have, then the threat of United States nuclear counteraction is likely to deter. In such a case there is a direct relation between the Soviet cities, farms, industry, and population, who would be the victims of our nuclear counterblows, and the Soviet rulers, who are the ultimate target of our peace-promoting efforts; but the direct relation is by chance, according to the internal dynamics of the top-level power struggle, and not by any threats or action of the ballot box.

As a very different example, consider the image that most of us have of Mao today (I lack the evidence as to whether this image is valid or not). He seems to combine some of the characteristics of a tyrant on the model of Stalin or Hitler. He must have had a considerable drive toward personal political power to have attained his supreme position. The only path open to still further personal power is by conquest of neighbors or by direct attack against his major power rivals (as he would picture them). His estimate that he could survive a nuclear war and remain in power might turn out to be mistaken, but he would have taken personal risks before in his career. His physical survival might be guaranteed by a magnificently equipped shelter, to which he could repair in good time in a war he had initiated. The very shock of the swift nuclear counterattack against his country, he might imagine, would unite the survivors against the foreign enemy whom they believed to be the aggressor. The populations of Japan, Germany, and Russia did, after all, rally around their governments in World War II, even under crushing military assault. If such a ruler had more than a pro-forma belief in Marxism or possessed a thirst to rule the world not unknown to autocrats before him, he would regard the destruction of the "capitalist strongholds" in Western Europe and the United States as a very great achievement, alone worth considerable peril and cost. He might well picture the economic, political, and social disruption that would prevail in most of the world following a nuclear war as the ideal soil for a quick global "take-over" by Communism.

Against these anticipated gains in personal power and ideology, such a ruler might regard the anticipated damage to his own country as not unacceptable. Both Stalin and Mao, after all, accepted the direct suffering of many millions of their own countrymen for the sake of remaking their agricultural systems to fit the Communist image of the time. Global victory on either a personal or ideological level might easily appear to be an end that justified still more drastic means. Even our own policy makers—certainly no tyrants—are after all presumably ready to accept tens of millions of American dead, if that is the price of action to support our national purposes.

My contention here is partly that our nuclear threat might completely fail to deter the aggressive tyrant, who after all is most likely to threaten other nations and world peace. More fundamentally, the point is that *every* measure designed to influence other governments away from war and aggression must be evaluated in terms of its ultimate effects on the individual decision-makers. It must be designed for maximum *personal* influence in the desired direction. This does not necessarily mean maximum military effect or even *any* military effect. It certainly does not require a maximum threatening effect on the general Soviet and Chinese populations, who in fact are not at all likely to share ideological or political ambitions for expansion, but instead may long only for a larger apartment or a larger ration of rice, and who by all reports frequently harbor the friendliest feelings toward Americans.

What would be the nature of the United States policies and actions which might better influence Soviet and Chinese decision-makers toward peace? In my view there is no single answer to this critical question. There is no sign of any one policy or action available to the United States that will with certainty reach Communist leaders and guarantee that their decisions will be in the direction needed to prevent World War III. But I do believe on the basis of some study of the problem that, through the fullest possible variety of approaches to this key task, we could develop a degree and direction of influence superior to that now obtained through nuclear deterrence. If we relinquish our present misconceptions and recognize the true nature of this problem as well as its importance, we can develop a combination of policies and actions which would be very much less perilous than our present course.

After all, the problem is not so very different from what we have long faced in a variety of other contexts. What we are trying to do is to influence human behavior, and for this we have over countless generations developed a variety of means. We apply them every day toward members of our families, friends, bosses, business associates, enemies (if any), and even casual acquaintances. Appropriate variants are successfully applied by very small children on adults, and (less successfully) by adults on children of all ages. They have been studied by sages and psychologists, capitalized on by public relations consultants, argued over by everyone, and popularized in best-sellers on how to win friends and influence people. They have been used for good and for evil, in every profession, in every human relationship, and in every walk of life. The task of preventing major aggression or nuclear attack by the USSR or Communist China is in large measure the task of applying similar methods in appropriate ways to influence the men in these countries who determine national actions. This is an age of technology; but this part of keeping the peace happens not to be at root a technological problem, but one of individual human psychology. When we fully recognize this characteristic of the problem, we shall not find it impossible to cope with.

Perhaps it has been natural and in part inevitable, but it is still an amazing fact that, for all the billions we have spent on nuclear deterrence and for all the policies we have built on this cornerstone, we have never paused to scrutinize its ultimate purpose, nor set ourselves to examine how that purpose might be accomplished with other and perhaps less perilous means. What is needed is to discover *all* the measures that are now available or that can be invented or manufactured for this job—psychological, political, economic, military, ideological, moral, or whatever. This requires a major organized research effort, fundamental and applied, not as an amusing diversion nor as a luxurious addition to our present nuclear-deterrence effort, but as a matter of central importance to our national security and to world peace. It requires new institutes, new fields of academic study, the application of a wide variety of experience in related fields, and experimental research in psychology and other fields. It requires the devotion of creative imagination, money, organization, trained personnel, and physical resources in amounts appropriate to the stakes involved.

While it is the policy-makers who must be the immediate focus of our unilateral measures for peace, our actions toward other non-policy elites in Russia, China, and elsewhere, and also toward the general populations, are important as well. For one thing, it is directly in our interest to see to it that these groups have a greater voice in the decisions of their government than now. This is not a matter of idealism or of crusading for democracy, but one of practical and direct importance in preventing nuclear war. For the danger of war is high as long as decisions for or against it can be made without regard for the popular will for peace, and as long as decision-makers can deceive the millions who would suffer most as to what is being done by their governments and by their "enemies." People in all countries now share a vested interest in peace that is perhaps greater than anything they have ever before held in common; but, unless this interest can be brought more effectively to bear on the political leaders of Russia or China (and of all other autocracies), the governments of those countries can too easily ignore or override this interest.

Another policy objective must be to strengthen the contacts between our own country and the nonpolicy elites and the general populations of the Communist bloc. This will not of itself in some vague way bring about peace, since those non-governmental groups do not now determine Soviet or Chinese policies; but it will encourage the ordinary citizens in these countries to strengthen what influence they do have, and to see themselves, not as faced with autocrats at home and enemies abroad, but rather as having powerful and friendly allies in the West, at least in the preservation of peace.

Our present policies frequently undermine this important objective. Although we sometimes profess friendship for the Russian or Chinese people, we often avoid contact with them. In those contacts we do have, we tend to hold them responsible for actions and policies of their governments over which they have no control and to which in their hearts they may object bitterly. Under our basic strategy of nuclear deterrence, we threaten to exterminate these people by the millions, should their dictators choose war—a choice which the population as a whole would certainly deplore and might even actively oppose, if it could know of it. In general, by reacting to Soviet and Chinese policies as if these were the products of monolithic societies, we encourage the people to identify with their rulers, however tyrannical these may be. By opposing whole countries, rather than the few leaders and perhaps the elites responsible for those countries' policies, we make enemies of friends, and we strengthen dictatorship rather than promoting evolution toward democracy. Our actions, in short, tend to make our operating image of political solidarity come true. By ignoring the opportunities in the political realities, we lose the opportunities, and we change the realities to our disadvantage.

One may disagree with specific suggestions of how Communist

decision-makers can best be reached. I can see no room for argument, however, as to these central points: first, since Soviet and Chinese rulers make the decisions for war and peace on behalf of their countries, to influence these decisions requires that we influence these rulers; second, this is a job that is not intrinsically military, least of all susceptible directly to weapons of mass destruction, but one that affects the thoughts and emotions of certain specific individuals in Moscow and Peking, and in this sense fundamentally personal and psychological; and third, only when we have studied the problem in its true light and done our collective best to solve it in these terms will we have done what the situation demands.

No amount of effort or resources devoted to our nuclear-deterrence weapons is any substitute for a hard and honest look at the real nature of the problem and for action in accordance with that reality. It may give us a certain satisfaction to do things that are not directed to the point; we may cling to the former truth that in the end our only protection is our weapons, when today the one thing our weapons cannot do is to protect us; we may find the products of our technological ingenuity fascinating and vastly impressive; our national economy may benefit from all the military activity; mass action, rather than attention to the individual, may be the norm of our society. But better paths are open to us, toward our goals of national security, freedom, and world peace.

Implications for Disarmament

Does all this have anything to do with disarmament? First of all, if we can devise important techniques for influencing Soviet and Chinese leaders away from war or aggression, we can make the armed peace that now faces us less perilous. Without nuclear disarmament, it will never be particularly agreeable; but at least it may be somewhat less precarious than it is now or appears likely to be. Moreover, if we can develop nonnuclear ways of doing the job we have been trying to do by nuclear deterrence, we can reduce our own reliance on strategic nuclear weapons and go further in the direction of nuclear disarmament. If necessary, we can do this by independent steps, perhaps with the intention of getting Soviet and Chinese reciprocation, as proposed by Osgood. Or perhaps we might proceed on our own as far as the effectiveness of personal deterrence, in our judgment, permits us to replace our nuclear-deterrence weapons with these other techniques.

Personal deterrence, however, can also be used to induce Soviet and Chinese disarmament. We can hardly use nuclear weapons to influence Soviet or Chinese leaders to give up their own nuclear weapons; the more we rely on them ourselves, the more certain it is that Communist governments will do likewise. But nonnuclear measures and nonmilitary influence can be used to induce Moscow and Peking both not to use their nuclear weapons and not to keep them. As in keeping the peace, it is a complex question of incentives, deterrents, ideology, values, information, etc. (Several of these matters were touched on in earlier suggestions for improving the chances for East-West agreement on disarmament.) But there is no intrinsic reason why personal deterrence cannot be used to influence Communist governments away from relying on nuclear weapons, especially if they see us succeeding by such methods.

Finally, the concepts of personal deterrence can be very helpful in making agreed disarmament systems operate, once they can be attained. Inspection systems can make good use of the central political role of a few men in Communist societies (and to a lesser extent, in our own). As enforcement is viewed less in terms of pressures on whole countries and more in terms of pressures and inducements on key individuals, it will become easier to devise disarmament systems that are stable, so that the world, once disarmed, will stay so.

REFERENCES

1. C. E. Osgood, "Suggestions for Winning the Real War with Communism," *Conflict Resolution*, December 1959, *3*: 295-325.
2. For this idea I am indebted to Thomas C. Schelling and Herman Kahn.
3. See the important article by Amrom Katz, of the RAND Corporation, "Hiders and Finders," *Bulletin of the Atomic Scientists*, 1961, *17*: 423-424.

LEONARD S. RODBERG

The Rationale of Inspection

Both the United States and the Soviet Union have accepted the principle that inspection must accompany an agreed disarmament program. Nevertheless, the problem of inspection has presented a major stumbling block in the path toward an agreement. This paper will discuss the principles governing the kind and extent of an inspection system that may be desirable and acceptable. The technology of inspection will not be discussed; many specific inspection techniques have been previously identified, and the primary need in that area is to conduct detailed investigations of the feasibility and applicability of each of these methods. The problem to be examined in this paper concerns the use of inspection to provide the necessary degree of assurance. It is the why, not the how, of inspection that interests us here.

The past few years have seen the beginning of a development of a theory of inspection. Jerome B. Wiesner,[1] Donald G. Brennan,[2] John B. Phelps,[3] and others[4] have contributed to this discussion. An increasing sophistication is becoming apparent, though far more analysis will be needed before the requirements for national security can be understood and the foundation of public confidence created. The type of disarmament agreement to be considered here envisages a gradual but general reduction of forces to very low levels. For the most part the discussion will focus on the early stages of this reduction, primarily because we must successfully pass through the early stages before we arrive at the later ones, but also because it is difficult to envisage what the world will be like at that later time. Among the foreseeable elements of that future world may be continuous negotiations on arms and arms reductions, international inspectors, an active and effective United Nations or other forms of peacekeeping machinery, and an international police force. The political and economic environment is impossible to foretell. To make any progress toward that world, we must agree on the first steps which enhance the security of all while leading to the ultimate goal.

Balanced but limited reductions will nevertheless, in this nuclear age, leave an awesome amount of power in the hands of the nations involved. Even after these reductions, the world will remain a dangerous place. It may be somewhat safer, because of the assurance against surprise attack that the inspection system might provide, because of the improved climate which should result from a successful agreement, because of the diversion of national efforts and attention to the process of disarmament, and because of the limited reduction in the ability to cause destruction. In general, though, it may be anticipated that during the early stages of disarmament military considerations will continue to be important, and that military establishments will continue to play a major part in furthering national security.

United States and Soviet Positions

Between June and September of 1961 extensive discussions of the principles governing disarmament were conducted between the United States, represented by John J. McCloy, and the Soviet Union, represented by Valerian A. Zorin. At the conclusion of these talks the Soviet Union admitted to the United Nations a statement[5] describing the Soviet plan for general and complete disarmament and the control procedures to accompany it.

In the Soviet plan, control is viewed as a means of "verifying the implementation by states of the various measures in the field of disarmament. Control that is divorced or detached from disarmament measures would become an international system of legalized espionage." The Soviet disarmament plan provides that "on-site control would be established over the destruction" of agreed types of armaments and would "verify the disbanding of troops." The control organization would inspect "all enterprises, plants, factories, and shipyards previously engaged, wholly or in part, in the production" of armaments and delivery systems. "After the entire program of general and complete disarmament has been implemented, the control organization would continue to operate and exercise continuing supervision in order to verify that no state has resumed, clandestinely, its military production and has not started again to create armed forces." Inspection of retained armaments prior to the completion of disarmament is not permitted.

The Soviet statement provides that "the control organization be given unimpeded access to records pertaining to budgetary allocations of legislative and executive bodies of states." It further suggests that "permanent teams may be established at some plants and installations" and that "the control organization may, when necessary, institute a system of aerial inspection and aerial photography over the territory of states." On the other hand, the Soviet Union insists that, while it favors "strict international control over disarmament," it "resolutely objects to control over armaments."

The United States has proposed[6] that inspection should provide each party to an agreement with reasonable assurance that any commitment that has been agreed upon is being complied with from the moment implementation of the measure begins. A central point in the United States position provides that whenever a measure involves the reduction of armed forces, armaments, or other military material to specified levels, the control machinery must have the right and the ability to verify that such agreed levels have been reached and are not exceeded at any stage. The process of verifying agreed levels of armed forces and the curtailment of arms production should also include a reasonable capacity for dealing with clandestine activities. Thus it is agreed that inspection should verify compliance with disarmament treaties, but there is sharp disagreement over the right of the inspectorate to verify remaining levels and to search for clandestine facilities.

Another area of disagreement which has emerged is the administration of the control organization. The United States wants the day-to-day operation of the inspectorate to be administered by a single impartial administrator. The Soviet Union proposes that the control organization be administered by a council composed of "representatives of the socialist countries, representatives of states now members of Western military and political alliances, and representatives of neutral states." The United States has rejected the concept that the inspectorate should be composed of representatives of a country or bloc, but advocates the establishment of an impartial organization administered by a single international civil servant. Such disagreements may arise owing to the varying requirements that are to be imposed on inspection systems. It is important, then, to examine the roles that might be played by an inspection system.

Inspection as a Source of Reassuring Information

Disarmament is a cooperative or multilateral approach to armaments policy, in which the major military powers move to a lower level of armaments through mutual agreement. Inspection should promote the security of each party during and after the reduction of forces.

Since it will not be feasible to check every factory, warehouse, storage depot, training site, and individual simultaneously, it will not be possible with complete certainty to verify compliance with a disarmament agreement. An agreement may, for instance, fix the number of men in the armed forces of the major powers, and it may limit the number of strategic aircraft and missiles. Even if all the military manpower could be checked, there would still be enlistments, discharges, deaths, and transfers to allied countries which would complicate the census. Even if all arms-production facilities and depots could be checked, there would still be the replacement of parts, dismantling or scrapping, transfers in and out of storage, and loss which would test even the accounting systems of the host country itself. The movement, replacement, scrapping, repair, or destruction of delivery vehicles would prevent a precise count of those vehicles. In addition, there are the difficulties involved in hiring, training, equipping, housing, and transporting the hordes of inspectors needed to accomplish a complete coverage.

The result is that one cannot with absolute precision verify compliance with a disarmament agreement. This does not mean that one must rely entirely on trust; significant arms reductions without some means of reassurance would lead to an unstable, apprehensive, political environment. One must have a more reasonable criterion than absolute reliability by which to judge the adequacy of an inspection system. Such a criterion follows from the requirement that the security of each party to a disarmament agreement, with its associated procedures for inspection, should be greater than in the present competitive, unregulated environment.

There is no international inspection authority today; how then do the major powers determine the level of armed strength they will maintain? Among the factors they consider is the information available to them. This information, obtained from published sources, from the interpretation of the available statistics, and from other intelligence sources, permits an estimate of the arms and armed forces of each nation. This estimate is only approximate, and there are uncertainties as to which may or may not be significant, depending primarily on the openness of the society under consideration and the level of its armed forces. Each side attempts to maintain a sufficient force to deter the opponent, even if the actual forces facing it should be somewhat higher than the estimate. Thus there must be a direct relation between the estimated force of the enemy, the uncertainty in that estimate, and the size of the force which a country must maintain. One's own forces must be sufficiently strong so that any uncertainty in the level of the opponent's forces is not militarily significant.

Under a disarmament agreement a nation would be constrained to hold its arms and armed forces below some maximum level. If it is to abide by this agreement, it must feel that at this level it has adequate security. Its relative military position must not be impaired, and its ability to deter possible armed conflicts must not be degraded, in adjusting its forces to this new level. It may be concluded, by comparison with the present situation, that each nation must have adequate information about the state of the forces of its potential opponents in order to feel secure in maintaining its own forces at the agreed lower level. The primary purpose of an inspection system is to provide this reassuring information.

It has been noted that no inspection system can be foolproof; there will always be some uncertainties and omissions in the information it produces, some delay in the collection and analysis of the data, some ambiguity in the interpretation of the data. One condition to be imposed on any inspection system is that the lack of precision in the information about each nation's forces must not permit militarily significant violations of the agreement. The techniques of strategic and political analysis can appraise the significance of possible violations. For example, statistical analysis can provide estimates of the forces and armaments which could be hidden from a given inspection system—taking into account the portion of the country examined by the system in a given period of time, the possibility of observing men and material in transit to or from the clandestine forces, as well as other indicators of forbidden armament. Using these tools, and adjusting both the arms level and the inspection system, it should be possible for us to find reasonable systems which provide all parties with an assurance that their security is not being endangered by the reduction.

Initial estimates of the capabilities of inspection systems have suggested that a sufficient degree of assurance can be provided during the early stages by an inspection system which is both technically and economically feasible. Such a system would include control over the dismantling and demobilization of forces and would allow limited access to verify with reasonable accuracy the level of existing forces and the absence of clandestine forces or preparations to build such forces.

One possible arms-control measure which has been much discussed is a restriction on the number of strategic delivery vehicles (that is, long-range aircraft and missiles) permitted each nation. In evaluating the inspection requirements for this measure, one should consider the effects of possible violations and ask such questions as: What indicators are available to reveal the production or deployment of a clandestine force of a given type and size? What is likely to be the military significance of such a force? What defensive preparations would be needed to guard against it? At what stage in its development would it be necessary to discover such a force? What is likely to be the political impact if such a force is revealed? What action would the innocent party take if it discovered such a force? What sequence of events is likely to follow if the force is not detected? Are the gains to be achieved by producing such a force commensurate with the risks involved? Are there variations, such as vehicles carrying high-yield weapons, which might have unusually severe political or military impact?

The result of such a study is a series of requirements fixing the "confidence levels" which the inspection system must provide. In this case it is likely that, if the agreed level of delivery vehicles was rather high, only a very large clandestine force would be significant, and a correspondingly small inspection effort would be required.

These results are subject to a further adjustment based on political considerations and on the size and cost of the required inspection system. One obvious political consideration lies in the common assumption that the national security is enhanced by increasing the level of arms. In the present environment, this is far from obvious; President Kennedy has observed that "in a spiraling arms race a nation's security may well be shrinking even as its arms increase. . . . The risks inherent in disarmament pale in comparison to the risks inherent in an unlimited arms race." Nevertheless, this reliance on arms is a fact of today's world. Together with the natural suspicion one feels toward a potential enemy, it provides a checkrein on the pace of disarmament and may also lead to more stringent conditions on the inspection system than purely military considerations would warrant. The inspection system should be able to provide information in sufficient quantity and with sufficient clarity to inspire confidence in the general population as well as in political and military leaders.

It appears then that for a country safely to disarm the inspection system must, by supplementing present information, reduce the uncertainty in the existing knowledge about each nation's forces, so that no force could be built or hidden which would significantly unbalance the military situation. As the size of each nation's force decreases, the significance of any clandestine or undetermined force increases correspondingly. This is the strategic concept behind the idea that the degree of inspection should increase with the degree of disarmament: the uncertainty in force level must be reduced as the force level itself is reduced. The additional information must place closer and closer limits on the possible clandestine forces maintained by a nation's opponents. In effect, a nation is maintaining its security by trading weapons for information. A nation may be willing to give up a superior weapon capability if it gains in exchange sufficient new information to know that its potential opponents do not retain or rebuild forces which can adversely affect its security.

One problem which has perplexed disarmament planners is the asymmetry between the present major powers. The United States has a preponderance of strategic delivery systems; the Soviet Union, on the other hand, has the advantage in "conventional" armaments and installations. These differences exist because the defense needs of the United States and the USSR are quite different; the societies and degrees of openness are very different. As a result, equivalent reductions in forces can have very different effects, and similar inspection systems can be acceptable to one side but completely objectionable to the other. The asymmetry apparent in today's world will be somewhat reduced if the inspection system is considered as an integral part of the disarmament agreement, and the information it provides as an integral contributor to the security of each side. Then the "weapons gap" on one side may be traded for the "information gap" on the other.

The Soviet Union has claimed that the verification of agreed levels of armed forces and armaments is "legalized espionage." The use of this epithet illustrates the fact that all nations must become increasingly sophisticated in their thinking about inspection and national intelligence and the parallelism between them. One may think of national intelligence as one method (but not the only one) of obtaining information about another country. An inspection system provides a legal and regulated method for obtaining and increasing specific kinds of information. The most important distinction is that inspection is regulated and specific, since the host country, by assumption, has agreed on the type and extent of the inspection and is usually participating in it.

Inspection as a Deterrent

Thus far we have discussed the role of inspection in providing reassuring information. From another point of view, the inspection system may also be considered as a means of deterrence, intended to create a risk of detection and make evasion unattractive. Especially since foolproof inspection is impossible and the complete coverage of a nation impractical, the parties to a disarmament agreement must rely on the deterrent value of the inspection system as well as on its actual capacity for detecting violations.

The degree of deterrence can be enhanced by various techniques, including the introduction of an element of randomness into the selection of sites to be inspected. The deterrent value of a system also depends on the supplemental measures each party takes to increase the credibility of its intention to respond effectively if violations are discovered. While the problem of sanctions is beyond the scope of the present discussion, it is evident that the effectiveness of an inspection system depends not only on reducing the incentive to cheat but also on the belief that significant remedies are available to the innocent party, and that he intends to take advantage of them should the need arise.

Both the technical efficiency of the system and the credibility of appropriate countermeasures will contribute to making evasion or violation unattractive. Numerous false alarms will seriously strain the agreement and can cause a breakdown of the disarmament program. Ambiguous indications are also harmful since a nation, though feeling its security threatened, may be reluctant to take action. The same sanctions which inhibit violations also tend to inhibit a nation from reacting to apparent violations. Often these reactions might take the form of violations of the agreement, involving either intensive rearmament or a serious threat to do so. The more severe are the sanctions against such violations, the more reluctant will a nation be to react to minor or ambiguous violations. It follows that a primary technical requirement on the inspection system should be that the data which it yields be as reliable, direct, and persuasive as possible. If it fails in this respect, there are likely to be recurrent periods of suspicion, accusation, recrimination, and ultimately the failure of the system.

During the early stages of disarmament, the primary sanction is likely to be the threat to rearm. How much and what type of warning is necessary for a nation to rearm? In these days of rapid technological advance and of an increasing complexity of arms, a nation cannot mobilize at its leisure after it discovers that another nation has clandestinely rearmed. Any violation must be discovered early enough for the injured party to take corrective measures before its security is seriously endangered. For a democracy, which must mobilize public and congressional opinion and appropriate the funds, as well as reconvert industrial resources, retrain workers, and remobilize troops, this can be a lengthy process.

One criterion for determining the type of inspection is therefore the magnitude of the violation it must be able to detect. If only gross violations can be detected, there may be insufficient time to react. A related condition is the period which can be permitted to elapse between the time that the violation begins and the time when it is detected, evaluated, and recognized by the political heads of the respective countries. This time lag involves the degree of violation required before a reliable "signal" is registered by the system as well as the time required for transmission, collation, and analysis of the data.

Some additional requirements which should be imposed on the inspection system are the following:

1. It must be able to cope with technological change.
2. It must be relatively unobtrusive and unobjectionable to the population within the host country.
3. It should require a minimum release of sensitive information.
4. Its cost should be commensurate with the significance of the measure itself.
5. The parties must be able to provide the trained manpower and technology required.

The Mechanics of Inspection

A major difficulty inherent in most inspection schemes is the need to disclose the numbers, locations, and types of weapons and production facilities prior to the beginning of actual disarmament and inspection. It is this requirement which often causes the inspection requirements to seem out of proportion with the amount of disarmament.

There are at least three approaches which, singly or in combination, can assist in surmounting this problem: (1) the inspection can be introduced in graduated steps, with disclosure of only the information needed at any particular time. One specific means of accomplishing this is the method of zonal inspection,[7] in which successive geographic areas within each participating state are subjected to inspection; such an inspection system has been proposed in the United States Treaty Outline at the Geneva conference on 18 April 1962; (2) the introduction of warning systems and other guarantees against surprise attack can accompany the disclosure and compromise of the locations and types of weapons; and (3) the sequestration and destruction of limited amounts of arms at specified depots, as a sign of good faith and as a concrete arms-reduction measure, can take place prior to the onset of inspection. This represents a feasible approach, if each country has an adequate degree of confidence in its current information, so that it can tolerate limited reductions without feeling its security endangered. One should be able to devise arms reductions which are significant yet which leave residual forces large enough so that the uncertainty in current information is not critical, and which therefore provide an adequate degree of security. If it is found that no reductions can take place without some increase in the information available—or to avoid setting the precedent of reducing arms without some degree of access—some limited inspection might be included to increase the information. This might consist of a specified number of on-site inspections or field trips, or a quota of peremptory on-site inspections to be conducted at the discretion of either party, or an aerial survey.

In estimating the effectiveness of a particular set of inspection procedures, one should ideally take a "systems" approach to the problem. One should consider all sources of information, including those provided by intelligence sources as well as those provided by the system, and attempt to make optimal use of all the kinds of information available in designing the system. To determine the likelihood of detecting a particular violation, one should consider all the changes in the military posture which the violation would entail and examine all the ways in which information about these changes would become available. Different inspection techniques and sources of information will tend to reinforce one another, and related changes in the military establishment will help to expose the violation.

The effectiveness of the inspection system can be enhanced by the use of overlapping inspection techniques. Four general means of conducting inspections are: the physical inspection of forces in being, the inspection of industrial production, "knowledge detection,"[8] and budgetary control. Each of these may be more or less appropriate for particular measures. The overlapping surveillance provided through the use of each technique and the integration of information related to different aspects of the military establishment provide a degree of assurance that is significantly greater than the sum of its separate parts. There has not yet been a satisfactory mathematical analysis of this, but it represents a major consideration in inspection systems. To this analysis must be added judgments about the political environment in which the system will be operating and about the effect that the operation of inspection has on the growth of confidence in the system.

The access required for a physical inspection of the forces in being has presented a major stumbling block in past disarmament discussions. One might conceive of three types of access permitted simultaneously perhaps for different purposes: a fixed and continuous inspection of the major facilities for production, testing, transportation, and storage; mobile inspectors with strictly limited rights of access and areas of circulation; and a limited number of on-site inspections permitted at the request of any party. The first and third were included in the inspection system proposed for the nuclear test ban. (The Soviet Union agreed on fixed inspection stations, but it viewed on-site inspections as purely "symbolic" and would not agree to a substantial number of them.) The second kind might be an extension of practices commonly followed under the military attaché system, in which each country is permitted an agreed number of attachés with limited privileges of access.

In designing an inspection system one must recognize that the actual system will be established as a result of an international agreement, most likely arrived at through difficult multilateral negotiations. A technically ideal system will be modified and distorted by the requirements of political acceptability until the designer may find it unrecognizable. How this would affect the prior analysis of the system is difficult to say, but it is clear that the system should be flexible, have numerous and nearly equivalent modifications, and be relatively conservative in the form in which it is initially presented.

The inspection of any disarmament agreement is likely to involve the continuous interpretation and evaluation of partial or contradictory information, along with continuous negotiation between the powers concerned. For example, the limits on human and material resources will require that only intermittent, sampled checks can be made of most areas and facilities. It will be necessary, on the basis of partial and sometimes outdated information, to determine whether the agreement is being respected to the best of each party's ability and whether any apparent violations are the result of faulty information, errors, or unintentional violations. Regular procedures might be established by which any party could voluntarily provide additional assurance that it is indeed abiding by the agreement. This feature of the system may be important in an international arena, where suspicion is likely to be a continuing part of the political climate but where each party will wish to retain the agreement in being.

It has been pointed out earlier that a serious problem in designing an inspection system is the release of sensitive information, which may be greater than is warranted by the degree of disarmament. In an ideal situation, one might imagine all inspection data being collected by automatic unmanned detectors which transmit their information to an electronic computer, where it is sorted and analyzed. The machine would compare the actual input data with the results which a nonviolating nation should show, and it would determine automatically whether a violation had occurred or where one might look to find a violation. If such an "automatic inspector" were possible, and if confidence in its "judgment" were developed, there would be no release of information to any person, and only the output of the machine (simply "no violation" or "a violation of Agreement X in Region A") would be known. In practice, of course, while each element in this ideal system will probably have some usefulness in an actual inspection arrangement, no such automatic process is possible. The collection of data cannot be made fully automatic, the information received is often ambiguous or qualitative, and the analysis of the data involves a considerable amount of interpretation and intuition. Nevertheless, there may be areas, as in certain industrial processes, where this technique could be used, and the concept of using information which is not released but is part of the evaluation process may be applicable to more general cases. Methods of approaching this ideal may be worth exploring in the quest for an acceptable system.

Regardless of such future improvements, a real inspection system will inevitably yield excess information. Nothing can prevent the inspectors from seeing more than the particular objects they are assigned to see. This could lead to accusations of illegal espionage and charges of bad faith. The use of sampling to reduce the degree of access to information might allay these charges; but the problem posed is also one argument for a broad disarmament agreement. The inspection of a limited agreement may require as great a breach of internal security and as large an intrusion into national affairs as the inspection of comprehensive disarmament would. For example, an agreement providing for the cessation of the production of fissionable materials would require fixed inspectors to be stationed at declared production sites. But there must still be a system of mobile or pre-emptory inspection to insure against clandestine or undeclared facilities. This might be more acceptable, as well as more efficient, if the inspectors were also checking for other forms of clandestine activity. In fact, it may only be possible to gain agreement on the kind of access which is necessary if significant disarmament accompanies the granting of this access.

The composition of the inspectorate influences both the effectiveness of the inspection system and its impact on the host country. An international inspectorate enables all nations to participate in the inspection process and provides an opportunity to train a group of international civil servants who are especially competent in the techniques and problems of inspection. The ultimate composition should certainly be of this type in order to assure permanency, impartiality, and continuity despite changes in national alignments. On the other hand, the presence of all nations on the inspectorate may provide an opportunity for any nation to interfere with the inspection process and, conversely, it may cause a nation to lack confidence in the effectiveness of the system when it is operating in some other country.

The concept of reciprocal or "sides" inspection, in which each "side" in the present cold war inspects the other, has been suggested to avoid these difficulties. While this system has its advantages during the early years of the agreement, it is susceptible to charges of "espionage" and to direct recrimination from one side or the other. In the long run, this arrangement would tend to institutionalize the present division of the world. Nevertheless, one does not survive the long run unless he lives through a series of short runs, so that reciprocal inspection, if it proved agreeable for the present and if it eased the problem of recruiting qualified inspectors, might represent a way of beginning the complex task of developing agreed inspection procedures.

The approach envisaged in this paper, in which military and political evaluations are related to technical analyses of inspection so as to determine the most desirable system, is more complex in concept but simpler in operation than an inspection system which is complete and foolproof. The type of system which emerges seems to be practical in terms of cost and manpower requirements and should be acceptable to nations or peoples in the present environment. While neither aspiring to perfection nor relying completely on mutual trust, it is possible for us to seek an inspection system which will provide a sufficient degree of assurance and make the risks of disarmament smaller than those we face in the present arms race.

References

1. Jerome B. Wiesner, "Inspection for Disarmament," in Louis Henkin (editor), *Arms Control: Issues for the Public.* New York: Prentice-Hall (for The American Assembly, Columbia University), 1961.

2. Donald G. Brennan, "The Role of Inspection in Arms Control," in *Collected Papers of the Summer Study on Arms Control.* Boston: American Academy of Arts and Sciences, 1960.

3. John B. Phelps, "Information and Arms Control," in *Collected Papers;* see Reference 2 above.

4. Seymour Melman (editor), *Inspection for Disarmament.* New York: Columbia University Press, 1958. Bernard T. Feld, "Inspection Techniques of Arms Control," in Donald G. Brennan (editor), *Arms Control, Disarmament, and National Security.* New York: George Braziller, Inc., 1961. Thomas C. Schelling and Morton H. Halperin, *Strategy and Arms Control.* New York: The Twentieth Century Fund, 1961.

5. Statement by the Soviet Government on the Bilateral Talks, 22 September 1961, in *Documents on Disarmament 1961.* Washington: United States Government Printing Office, 1962.

6. United States Declaration Submitted to the General Assembly: A Program for General and Complete Disarmament in a Peaceful World. 25 September 1961 (see Reference 5 above).

7. Louis B. Sohn, "Phasing of Arms Controls: The Territorial Method," in David H. Frisch (editor), *Arms Reduction: Program and Issues.* New York: The Twentieth Century Fund, 1961.

8. Lewis C. Bohn, "Non-Physical Inspection Techniques," in Donald G. Brennan (editor), *Arms Control, Disarmament, and National Security.* New York: George Braziller, Inc., 1961.

LAWRENCE S. FINKELSTEIN

The Uses of Reciprocal Inspection

ARMAMENTS AND the effort to control them have been a central theme in international relations since World War II. From the Baruch Plan of 1946 to today's plans for general and complete disarmament, the negotiated regulation and limitation of arms have most often been seen as a world problem, to be resolved by multilateral agreements and administered by multilateral agencies. The world as a whole is actively and vocally alarmed by the hazards and is uneasy over the cost of the arms array today—and tomorrow. Arms are widely distributed, and with them, the potentiality of their use. Whether the great powers with their big weapons are initially involved in hostilities or not, the risk that an outbreak of warfare anywhere in the world will ultimately involve them is an ever present and ever recognized reality. Thus, arrangements to cope with arms problems seem to involve all or most of the world's powers, large and small, and to require multilateral remedies. Besides, there is by now a considerable tradition of efforts to limit arms by multilateral agreement, going back at least to the Hague Peace Conferences of 1899 and 1907. When we think of disarmament, we tend automatically to think of agreements reached around green baize tables, and of international teams of inspectors supervising the performance of the undertakings agreed on. Finally, disarmament has been intimately linked in peoples' thoughts with hope for a world at peace, regulated by global institutions of law and global means for settling disputes and promoting justice. The aspiration is global, and there is thus a tendency to treat the means to achieve it as global also.

Yet, despite the global characteristics of the arms problem, in significant respects it is a bilateral problem. The main arms to be regulated, reduced, or eliminated under negotiated agreements are those either of the Soviet Union and the United States or of their principal allies. However great the concern of other nations with the arms problem, there is little reason to doubt that they would welcome any arrangements the two great powers and their chief allies arrived at among themselves.

Moreover, to the extent that the arms problems of the two alliances are linked with the world's other disarmament problems (arms races among smaller powers, for example), the solution of the latter is impeded. There are opportunities for progress in arms control that do not depend on the solution of the less tractable problems of the great powers. Treating all arms-control matters in one big general and complete disarmament package makes all the problems more difficult to resolve. If some of the peripheral problems (arms control in Africa is one example) were taken out of the big package, the main issues remaining would unmistakably be the bilateral problems of the two great alliance systems.

The essential two-sidedness of the central arms problem is attested to by many things. Our very vocabulary reflects it. We have become accustomed to speaking of the two sides requiring this or that assurance or having this or that right, even when we are concerned with arrangements that are formally multilateral. We think about and undertake unilateral measures of arms control. There is no doubt that it is with the Communist nations that we seek to communicate tacitly and to reach tacit understandings in this way. To the extent that such understandings are enforced at all, the enforcement is reciprocal. When we insist on guarantees under the proposals for a nuclear test-ban treaty, for example, we are concerned today with a possible violation by a Communist state, even though the proposals contemplate inclusion of many states not allied to the two great powers. The United States-United Kingdom draft treaty proposed in 1961, incidentally, was a quite remarkable example of a bilateral arrangement in multilateral garb. It was permeated by the concept of two adversaries—or "sides"—policing each other's observance of the agreement. This "sides" concept was explicitly expressed in many of its provisions. This proposed treaty was primarily designed to accommodate the problems and interests of the Soviet Union and the United States within a broader framework.

There are relatively few examples of control schemes which expressly acknowledge the essential two-sidedness of the problems they seek to deal with. President Eisenhower's Open Skies proposal of 1955 was one that did. That plan advocated mutual surveillance, designed to deal with the reciprocal Soviet and American fears of surprise attack. Subsequently, consideration was given to some possible measures—avowedly reciprocal in intent and method—to diminish the mutual fear of surprise attack, such as aerial surveillance in the Arctic and surveillance over defined zones of Europe and North America. Mr. McCloy's informal proposal in the summer of 1961 that the Soviet Union and the United States exchange teams of inspectors to ensure that there should be no preparations going on for underground tests in violation of the then existing moratorium was another example of an avowedly reciprocal scheme.[1]

Later on, when the Russians had resumed atmospheric testing, President Kennedy joined with Prime Minister Macmillan in proposing that such tests cease. In their statement the two leaders indicated that their governments were "prepared to rely on existing means of detection, which they believe to be adequate, and are not suggesting additional controls."[2] Thus, without using the term "reciprocal inspection," President Kennedy and Prime Minister Macmillan were nevertheless proposing inspection which, since it relied on the national resources of the two sides without the intervention of any third party, was in fact reciprocal. Not long thereafter the Russians, as might have been predicted, responded with a draft treaty proposing the elimination of tests in the atmosphere, in outer space, and under water, to be inspected by "national systems of detecting nuclear and thermonuclear explosions." In substance, this was the United States-United Kingdom overture expanded to include outer-space and under-water as well as atmospheric tests. The Soviet draft also included provision for an uninspected moratorium on underground tests. The Western powers rejected the entire proposal at the time.

In August 1962, Britain and the United States advanced new proposals. One, for a ban on tests in the atmosphere, outer space, and underwater, made no provision for special inspection arrangements. It thus depends on national means of inspection and fits the pattern of the Kennedy-Macmillan statement. The second proposal, for a ban on tests in all environments, provides for a "mix" of national and international inspection arrangements in the framework of an international organization with "impartial" characteristics. Within the broader framework, however, the draft treaty unmistakably reflects a reciprocal emphasis in many of its provisions.

Overt reciprocity thus seems to command more interest when the powers address themselves to limited arms-control measures of some immediacy rather than to long-range package programs to deal with all arms problems. The primary examples have been the negotiations on surprise attack and the cessation of nuclear testing—both instances of the powers' discussing efforts to do something fairly quickly. In both cases, the problem they addressed themselves to was one which, while it concerned others, was amenable to solution exclusively by the two superpowers and their principal allies.

On the whole, then, we confront the paradox that, while the kernel of the arms problem is the bilateral relationship between the two great alliances, our negotiating efforts have tended to obscure this fact by our seeking multilateral agreements, multilaterally supervised and enforced. If our problem is pre-eminently a bilateral one, why should we not be seeking solutions that are pre-eminently bilateral? The purpose of this article is to examine the advantages and the limitations of bilateral or reciprocal, as distinguished from multilateral, arrangements for the regulation of arms.*

The main difference between the two is that under reciprocal arrangements the parties directly inspect, cooperate with, or enforce compliance on each other. Under a multilateral system, however, third parties are introduced, the parties are expected to cooperate with the "system," and "impartial" procedures for inspection and control are sought. Other patterns for organizing arms limitations are conceivable. The Antarctic Treaty, for example, is multilateral but provides for no special inspection system. Under that treaty, each party is free to inspect all the others in an "open" continent. It might thus be described as a kind of reciprocal system among a fairly large number of parties. It is theoretically possible to conceive of an agreement controlling the arms of two sides—a bilateral agreement, essentially—with control exerted by impartial means. Other variations are conceivable. Moreover, it seems likely that arms arrangements to which serious attention is given in the foreseeable future will in fact involve some "mix" of the two approaches, reciprocal and impartial. For analytical purposes, this article distinguishes between the two, but in doing so it will no doubt exaggerate the differences. For, however much a reciprocal arrangement emphasizes the direct relationship between the two sides, the parties will still have ties to the rest of the world that significantly affect their judgment and behavior. Even under purely reciprocal arms-control ar-

* The analysis which follows owes a great deal to the study by Fred C. Iklé and collaborators, *Alternative Approaches to the International Organization of Disarmament* (Santa Monica: The RAND Corporation, 1962). It is cited hereinafter as "Iklé: Alternative Approaches."

rangements, the great powers would wish to appeal to third-party judgments (world opinion) some of the time. To emphasize the "impartial" features of multilateral systems, on the other hand, presupposes far more agreement between the great powers—as to the rules to be applied and as to who is to apply them and how—than seems likely to obtain for a long time to come. In fact, recent multilateral disarmament schemes relegate to distant stages the introduction of impartial methods of enforcing the agreements, such as a United Nations peace force; in the early stages, enforcement would remain a matter of independent national action. If the experience of the nuclear test-ban negotiations and of negotiations on other disarmament measures in recent years is a reliable guide, the main purpose of "impartial" systems would be to enable the two great alliances to reassure each other—or to fail to do so. "Impartial" systems for some time to come will disguise much reciprocal inspection, cooperation, or enforcement.

Between these two approaches, however, there are important differences of profession and practice, despite the degree to which they overlap. The differences of profession—what the choice of approach seems to say about its assumptions and purposes—may be quite significant. In particular, the reciprocal pattern can be a useful and constant reminder of the adversary relationship between the principal parties. The reciprocal arrangement would have the advantage of making explicit where the emphasis belongs—on the responsibility of the parties to reassure *each other* that the continuation of the agreement will serve their interests even against the background of continuing conflict. Albert Wohlstetter once counseled that "sound arms-control arrangements can be based only on an explicit and precise mutual distrust." [3] Cynical though that prescription sounds, it is a more instructive standard than the apparent expectation of the impartial approach, that the parties will cooperate enough to accept third-party determination of their interests. For this reason, it might be wise to label reciprocal arrangements "adversary" systems. One hopes, however, that the explicit distrust will breed pragmatic cooperation; I will therefore use the somewhat more neutral term "sides" to describe reciprocal systems. Sides can either compete or cooperate, but the word implies that whichever they do it will be with each other.

Governments appear to agree that the purpose of control systems under arms agreements is to provide assurance that the obligations undertaken under such agreements are being faithfully fulfilled. This is one side of a coin, the other side of which is the assurance that violations will be detected. Governments must either be satisfied that their interests are being preserved by the operation of the agreement in question, or they must have a reliable basis for taking remedial action. The better the arrangements to reassure the parties that the agreement is working well and also that they will know it if it is not, the better will the system operate and the greater the likelihood that violations will be deterred. Moreover, the greater the certainty that there will be appropriate and effective responses to violations, the less likely is it that violations will occur.

However the basic purpose is pursued, whether by sides or impartial arrangements, two principles are central to successful arms regulation. The first is that the parties must have access (reliably and without obstruction) to the information they need to enable them to judge whether their interests are being preserved. The mutual reassurance of governments which by inclination and experience are suspicious of each other's *bona fides* is a process that depends on information. Governments need data. They must be sure of having the necessary data if other parties are interested in interrupting the flow. They must be able to evaluate the quality of the data they receive. And they must be able to evaluate the significance of any interruption in the flow of data.

Second, the decision as to what action to take on the basis of the information supplied by the system and the evaluation of the evidence prerequisite to action are functions that governments are likely to insist on exercising independently for some time to come. Arms agreements, if they have any meaning at all, will seriously affect the vital interests of nations. Their governments are unlikely in the extreme to yield to third parties the decisions as to whether their national interests are being served by the successful operation of the agreements, or whether there have occurred violations which seriously threaten the national interest and require countermeasures. For example, the Western draft treaty of April 1961 on the nuclear test ban included a provision (Article 22) acknowledging the "inherent right of a Party to withdraw and be relieved of obligations hereunder if the provisions of the Treaty . . . are not being fulfilled and observed." The 1962 proposals include provisions (Article XIII of the proposed complete ban and Article III of the proposed partial ban) defining the conditions for withdrawal when a party "deems withdrawal from the Treaty necessary for its national security." Even without explicit recognition, withdrawal is a right which cannot be denied sovereign states, either legally (except when they themselves explicitly relinquish it, and dubiously then) or in fact. The 1961 United States-United Kingdom test ban proposal did not clearly provide for evaluation of inspection data by the organization;[4] none of the proposals has made provision for enforcing action by the organization in the event of violation. It is left to the individual governments to decide what to do should the treaty be violated. Even the eight neutral participants in the eighteen-nation conference in Geneva have acknowledged this specifically in their statement of 16 April 1962 on the nuclear test ban, despite their elaborate proposals for a complex system of control by an international commission of scientists.[5] It is very difficult to conceive of any government of a major power relinquishing its freedom to determine where its interests lie under an important arms agreement. In multilateral agencies, that reluctance may find expression in a veto provision, even if the organization appears to have power to decide and to act.

Sides arrangements for collecting information can be of two kinds. The first, such as President Kennedy and Prime Minister Macmillan proposed with respect to the cessation of atmospheric tests, relies solely on existing national means of inspection and does not require negotiation of new rights of access. Such systems, which now operate to the satisfaction of both sides with respect to the arms restraints they tacitly accept, no doubt rest heavily on technological means for monitoring compliance. Such a system operated with respect to the moratorium on nuclear tests. Our means for detecting Soviet nuclear explosions were effective, except for low-level explosions underground. Governments no doubt rely on other sources of information in addition to technological monitoring, including diplomatic and normal channels of intelligence as well as clandestine means. No formal agreement of this *genre* has ever been negotiated, although in November 1961 the Soviet Union put forward a draft treaty proposing that "with the object of conducting reciprocal observations . . . the states parties to the agreement, shall use their national systems of detecting nuclear and thermonuclear explosions." This language appears to rule out espionage, because the "national systems" referred to are no doubt technological monitoring devices. In general, however, this type of agreement would raise nice questions as to whether governments wish to legitimize collecting clandestine information related to the enforcement of arms agreements.

The second kind of sides arrangement is the negotiation of mutual rights of access for inspection purposes. Such rights might involve, among other things, the placing of monitoring devices (seismographs, for example), sea or air patrols, physical inspection by visiting teams or permanently stationed control posts, or access to records and key personnel. Presumably, they would supplement rather than replace existing national means of inspection.[6]

Both variants of the sides approach offer these significant advantages with respect to collecting information:[7]

1. Sides systems are less subject than are multilateral systems to obstruction from within the systems. No system is invulnerable to the determination of a government to deny access to information in its domain. In a multilateral data-collecting arrangement, however, the information-collecting apparatus itself is vulnerable to legal or illegal disruption. Depending on the basic instruments, a political or administrative decision may be required before information can be collected. Under the latest draft proposal for a complete test-ban, for example, the Russians can hamstring the information-collecting system by vetoing the budget. Governments may infiltrate agents into international staffs, thus perhaps introducing with them opportunities to obstruct or distort the data-collecting processes. In the words of one careful student, "It is therefore not likely that national decision-makers will have a high degree of confidence in an international detection network."[8] Under a sides system, such opportunities for interference are minimal.

2. Since the personnel employed in sides systems would be national agents, avowedly and in fact, problems of reliability, loyalty, and technical qualification would be minimized. Governments may well prefer to rely on their own national agents for data-collecting, rather than on international staffs whose loyalty to the control organization in the performance of their duties may be uncertain, and whose reliability and competence may be uneven or, at least initially, unproven.

3. Sides systems may make it more difficult for potential violators to evade their obligations because the violators are less likely to be certain of the limits of the systems. Moreover, technological improvements and other changes proved desirable by experience can be introduced more easily under a sides arrangement than under an impartial one.

4. Since information collected under a sides arrangement is overtly intended to provide the basis for independent national eval-

uation and decisions to act, there is an implication that all available information is relevant. Impartial systems, on the other hand, imply the opposite, in so far as they provide only for admission before the impartial forum of specified types of information which has been collected by the means enumerated in the basic agreement. The distinction should not be exaggerated. Under both systems, the governments will finally decide what their interests are and use all information at hand in doing so. There is in addition the possibility that a sides agreement granting mutual rights of access will appear to limit the sources of information to those specified in the agreement, as would be true under a multilateral arrangement. However, the sides approach seems to accord, more than does the impartial approach, with the concept that all means of collecting information are legitimate.

5. Sides systems obviously involve no inhibition on governmental access to the information collected, whereas the instruments for impartial systems might be obscure on this point. The 1961 test-ban treaty, for example, entrusted the Commission with the function of establishing "procedures for disseminating to all Parties . . . data produced by the system." Thus it implied that such data might not be automatically available. Under the treaty, the Administrator was obliged to forward to the Commission "all reports submitted . . . by inspection teams and special aircraft missions, together with any relevant data and analyses." While the members of the Commission presumably were to have access to materials thus submitted, the reports referred to might not have been the raw data, and the Administrator was apparently allowed discretion as to what "data and analyses" were "relevant." Moreover, the Administrator was allowed discretion as to whether data concerning seismic events met the criteria which obliged him to make the data public. Such obscurities are not necessary ingredients of multilateral agreements, and the 1962 proposal for a complete ban remedies these defects, but it is clear that there can be no such doubts under sides arrangements.

When it comes to providing a basis for effective national responses to violations, sides arrangements offer additional advantages:

1. Obviously, to the extent that sides inspection is more reliable in providing information, national judgments will be facilitated. This is a very important consideration, since one main assurance that a system will operate effectively is the expectation that governments will be able to respond appropriately and efficiently to any violations. Since, as F. C. Iklé has pointed out,[9] governments will at best

find such responses difficult to make, any measure that increases the expectation that they can do so is of cardinal importance.

2. Sides arrangements facilitate national response in a second way by eliminating the intervention of third-party judgments, thus avoiding opportunities for political obstruction and dependence on the decisions of unpredictable governments. Impartial agreements may not provide for collective decisions that are based on the information collected, at least for some time to come. Some proposals, including certain Soviet proposals for an International Disarmament Organization, do make such provisions. Whether these are adopted or not, the existence of collective organs to receive data about the performance of the system's requirements would at least imply national obligation to undergo collective procedures before national action can be taken. In the statement on the test ban already referred to, the eight neutrals acknowledged national freedom to act, but only "on the basis of reports furnished by the international commission." Thus national response will be at least delayed—and time may be an important consideration if some kinds of arms restrictions are violated. The facts and the issues may be obscured by debate, which is likely to reflect political considerations as much as efforts to decide clearly whether a violation has occurred and, if so, what its extent and nature may be. "Truthfinding," it has been said, "is likely to go not by humanity but by nationality."[10] Where the objective should be to provide a clear basis for an effective response by the aggrieved states, impartial procedures will probably emphasize efforts at conciliation and temporization.

There is another facet to this problem. The difficulty governments confront in responding to major violations has been remarked on. It may be that governments would be fortified by having impartial "certification" that violations had occurred and broadly based encouragement to respond vigorously. Third-party judgments have the virtue of legitimizing national action. In some circumstances, governments may find it more difficult to act in the absence of such international approval. The advantage of sides arrangements in providing reliable information and in simplifying the process of national decision in response to a violation may be offset by the fact that the sides approach sacrifices the access that impartial machinery might offer to international moral support of responses to violations. Neutral opinion is important, and its involvement in impartial arrangements, despite the difficulties, is an asset lost under a simple sides arrangement.

It has already been observed, however, that firm conclusions may be hard to come by in impartial forums. And, under sides arrangements, the governments have the option of appealing for international support when they choose to do so. Under a sides arrangement, governments can decide to reveal to the world—through the United Nations or otherwise—the evidence on which they base the conclusion that obligations have been violated. They can display seismic data, photographs, transcripts of testimony, individuals' observations, or whatever evidence they may have. In extreme cases, they can decide to reveal clandestine information, even though they thus risk compromising their clandestine sources. In this respect, the virtue of sides arrangements would be their flexibility. The parties to a sides agreement can act independently or display their evidence to chosen associates or to the world, on an *ad hoc* basis or regularly. It might even be possible to arrange for the participation of neutrals as witnesses to the collection of information by one side or both, thus perhaps making it easier for neutrals to attest to the findings. A sides system would thus not necessarily sacrifice the advantage of having the "certifiers" participate in the task of collecting the evidence, as they would do in an impartial system. The greater flexibility of the sides arrangement may thus strengthen the deterrence of violation.

3. While sides arrangements should facilitate vigorous governmental responses to violations, they should also encourage flexibility where that is appropriate. While governments should be enabled to respond as vigorously as possible, they should not be forced to do so. Any arms-control system is likely to be subjected to friction over interpretation or minor violations for which the seemingly obvious national responses of compensatory violation or withdrawal from the agreement may not be appropriate. For many minor perturbations, the appropriate response is to avoid public agitation over the difficulty in order to negotiate a mutually satisfactory accommodation with the other side.[11] Impartial forums offer some advantages in negotiation, particularly the easy availability of potential mediators. As suggested above, impartial forums will tend to generate pressures for conciliation of differences. It is a moot point, however, whether such accommodation will not benefit more from the direct bilateral confrontation of the sides pattern (emphasizing the parties' need to reassure each other), from the greater opportunities for secrecy in negotiation that the sides arrangement affords, and above all from the flexibility of the bilateral channel as contrasted with the formal

procedures of a multilateral forum. The availability of a bilateral channel—which exists in any case—is no assurance that the parties will not argue their cases before the world rather than seek to resolve their differences quietly. The obligation to deal with minor perturbations in a formal and probably public multilateral forum may well be an almost irresistible incentive to do the former. Finally, under a sides arrangement, nothing would prevent the parties from resorting to outside mediation—via a multilateral organ if they preferred—whenever they chose to do so.

Sides arrangements have limitations which should be frankly faced. First, the sides approach is not much more likely than any other to lead to agreement on arms regulations. No formula can be substituted for governmental willingness to agree. If the degree of inspection required to police any arms agreement is more than governments are willing to accept, the sides approach is no more likely than any other to resolve the dilemma. In fact, to the extent that sides arrangements may be more efficient than impartial arrangements, governments may be more reluctant to accept them. The relative inefficiency of impartial arrangements may be the price that has to be paid to get any particular agreement. If there are other central factors obstructing agreement, sides proposals will not remove the obstructions. The relative simplicity of sides schemes, however, does offer some marginal advantages that may ease negotiations for arms-control agreements. Fewer issues have to be settled in a sides negotiation than in a negotiation for a multipartite agency. Budgets, staffs, organizational patterns and procedures remain matters for independent determination by the sides rather than for mutual agreement. Thus there is less need to become involved in contentious long-term issues not centrally relevant to the arms arrangements themselves. How many hours in international arms-control negotiations have been spent on voting arrangements, for example, more because of their importance to the development of international organization than because of their relevance to arms regulation. The sides approach might help to streamline negotiations and reduce contention. This point is dramatically confirmed by the contrast between the six articles of the recent United States-United Kingdom proposal for a partial test ban, which relies on national means of inspection, and the eighteen articles of the proposed complete ban, providing for a "mixed" system. The former provides virtually no opportunity for controversy over matters which are not central to the prohibitions themselves.

Second, a sides arrangement is useful mainly in situations that are bilateral in structure. Multipartite arrangements are probably necessary to superintend limitations on objects of control that are very widely distributed, although the Antarctic Treaty suggests that multilateral agreements might incorporate a form of sides inspection. Even when the parties are arranged in sides, the utility of a sides scheme decreases as the number of parties goes up. A sides arrangement is most relevant to an agreement between the United States and the Soviet Union to regulate nuclear submarines, for example, or ICBM's, which only they possess. If the agreement to be supervised involves the other members of NATO and the Warsaw Pact, sides arrangements are still relevant, but the difficulties increase. To make a sides system work, when allies are involved, would require either the creation on each side of joint instruments to perform the inspection duties or a fairly careful sharing of duties and responsibilities on the basis of competence. Either arrangement would depend on high mutual confidence among the allies. The sides approach might well be unavoidable with respect to some kinds of agreements affecting the alliances such as, for example, an agreement to restrict armaments on a territorial basis in Europe. The best way to police such an agreement would be a sides arrangement, with some kind of NATO apparatus doing the job for the Western side and either the Soviet Union or a Warsaw Pact apparatus doing it for the other.

Third, sides inspection may be most useful when the functions of inspection can be performed without deep or extensive penetration of the national territory or the national fabrics of the parties. If what is involved is the intimate inspection of the production records of American electronics companies, for example, or the detailed interviewing of Americans employed by the Atomic Energy Commission, the American people and the Congress are likely to prefer impartial international inspection teams to teams of Communists. Agreements providing for such deep penetration will be difficult to reach in any case, and it is the other end of the spectrum that will be more relevant for some time to come. If what is involved is distant monitoring, as of nuclear tests in outer space, sides inspection is clearly applicable. Between the ends of the spectrum lies a range of possibilities, for which sides arrangements may or may not be appropriate. To prohibit weapons of mass destruction in outer space, for example, will require prelaunching inspection of the contents of the vehicles to be orbited. In some ways that may be a fairly far-reaching form of inspection; but, since the launching sites are likely to be clustered in a few areas which are (or can be) fairly isolated, sides inspection should cause no greater problems than impartial inspection. A Russian desire to keep the launching sites secret may be an important obstacle to reaching any such agreement, but the difference between impartial and sides inspection should not matter much, if at all. Agreements which involve sampling of forces stationed in camps or of weapons concentrated in depots may lend themselves to sides arrangements.

Fourth, sides arrangements requiring the deployment of new means of inspection may involve more total cost than impartial systems, because of the duplication that independent national systems may involve. Some duplication seems unavoidable in any case. The United States will not disband the CIA if we participate in an impartial arms-control system. Nor is it likely that all technical monitoring capabilities would be turned over to the international system. Some governments are likely to maintain independent inspection capabilities even under fully elaborated impartial arrangements. However, it does appear that sides systems would involve more duplication than impartial systems and hence greater total costs to all the parties.

Fifth, sides arrangements obviously sacrifice the advantages of having multilateral machinery available. If we assume a progression of arms-control measures, from the simpler to the more difficult, there may well be a value in having machinery in existence to perform new assignments that must be conducted on a multilateral basis, thus avoiding the pitfalls of negotiating from scratch for the creation of new instrumentalities. The existence of working instruments may facilitate later agreements. There would be experienced international staffs to assist in the negotiations, and the basic machinery might require no more than expansion to perform new functions. However, this advantage of multilateral arrangements would be less significant if, as may well be the case, sides and impartial arrangements coexist.

Finally, it is apparent that supervising arms agreements on a sides basis does not emphasize the construction of international institutions as steps along the road to a peaceful, well-regulated, international order. Yet it should be apparent that whatever works best will be most conducive not only to successful arms regulation but also to the emergence of patterns of cooperation and links of confidence. These are the three pillars on which a structure of world order must ultimately rest.

It has been the contention of this analysis that sides arrangements offer advantages over the impartial alternatives with respect to some kinds of arms agreements. The advantages are most marked with respect to an assurance of access to reliable information. In general, it seems likely that most agreements that can be negotiated in the near future will be amenable to the sides approach. The focus of current negotiations falls quite properly on arresting the arms race and turning the curve downward if possible. Thus it is the armaments of the great powers that are emphasized, the Soviet Union and the United States pre-eminent among them. In the general panorama of arms-control possibilities, it is the relationship between the Communist and the Western sides that stands out in sharp silhouette. This relationship, as has been suggested, is essentially bilateral. Moreover, it might be profitable to examine whether some of the arms problems of the lesser powers can be handled on a reciprocal basis. The advantages of the sides approach would be equally relevant to such problems. Because arms-control arrangements among the lesser states are likely to involve a lower level of technological complexity, perhaps requiring less intensive inspection procedures and less depth of penetration, sides inspection may be even more applicable to such cases than to the problems of the great powers.

Given the resistances that have to be overcome before far-reaching inspection will be acceptable to governments, it seems likely that only schemes that do not require a deep penetration of national territory and of national societies can be negotiated in the years ahead. Thus on this ground also the sides approach will be relevant to the kinds of agreements we are most likely to witness soon. However, it is apparent that the sides structure is not appropriate for many kinds of agreements, some of which might materialize in the short term.

Whether the sides structure is employed or not, the approach offers lessons that may be useful in multilateral settings as well. Even in multilateral frameworks, there are opportunities to emphasize the mutual responsibilities of the great powers and of their close allies to reassure each other. The 1962 Western proposal for a complete nuclear test ban calls for a mixed system in which a broader apparatus harbors a reciprocal core; but the reciprocal elements of that proposal only partially respond to the needs of the governments principally interested. In the future we can seek authorization for inspection by trusted agents of the important adversaries, even in an impartial setting. We can make it possible for governments to introduce before an impartial forum any evidence of violation derived by other means than those specifically provided for in the basic instrument of the organization. We can insist on arrangements to give the member governments immediate and unobstructed access to all inspection data collected under the system, recognizing that the important thing about doing so is to make the data available to a few of the many members. We can emphasize the obligation of the principal adversaries to negotiate with one another about minor perturbations in the system. We can seek to drive home the lesson that major violations too are essentially a problem to be dealt with by the two sides, and that the chief function of the organization may well be to facilitate sharp and effective responses by the aggrieved side when the other side violates the agreement. In short, if the cake is to have an impartial icing, we can try to make sure that everyone understands what is cake and what is icing, to increase the general appreciation of cake over icing, and to keep the icing from seeping into the cake. Toward these ends, we should not hesitate to call a side a side.

REFERENCES

1. John J. McCloy, "Balance Sheet on Disarmament," *Foreign Affairs*, 1962, *40:* 342, footnote 2.

2. "Joint United States-United Kingdom Proposal, September 3," Department of State *Bulletin*, 1961, *45:* 476.

3. "National Purpose: Wohlstetter View," *New York Times*, 16 June 1960.

4. On this point, see Iklé, "Alternative Approaches," *op. cit.*, pp. 31-33.

5. *New York Times*, 17 April 1962.

6. T. C. O'Sullivan has dealt with the intimate and intricate relation between arrangements for international inspection and national systems, both open and covert, with respect to the nuclear test ban. See his Nuclear Test Ban, Detection Networks and National Decisions, revised edn., 9 May 1961 (mimeographed).

7. The advantages and disadvantages of reciprocal systems are examined in Iklé, "Alternative Approaches," *op. cit.*, pp. 4-16.

8. O'Sullivan, *op. cit.*

9. F. C. Iklé, "After Detection What?" *Foreign Affairs*, January 1961.

10. Julius Stone, *Quest for Survival* (Cambridge: Harvard University Press, 1961), p. 59. The point made with respect to defining responsibility for aggressive war applies equally to violations of arms agreements.

11. T. C. O'Sullivan has suggested other reasons why the rigidities introduced by arrangements for open international inspection may sometimes be undesirable in The Disadvantages of Reliable International Inspection and the Problem of Evaluating Information Needs (20 April 1962, mimeographed draft).

ROGER FISHER

Internal Enforcement of International Rules

ON ANY AGENDA for a peaceful future there is a topic which may roughly be called, "world law and machinery for peace." It is invariably recognized that in the future there will continue to be rules regulating the conduct of countries and, in fact, that there will be a great number of new rules established by disarmament treaties or otherwise. The existence of such rules, such world law, raises two kinds of problems for the international legal mechanic. First, there is the need for mechanisms to create rules and to interpret and apply them—to determine the obligations of a state when they are in flux or in dispute. Second, there is the need for some mechanism to enforce the rules—to cause a state to do what it is legally obliged to do. This paper is concerned with the second problem.

The first problem is no doubt difficult. The techniques available for developing rules and resolving disputes are subject to significant variations. Rules may be developed through treaties, agreements, and patterns of conduct. The International Court of Justice, the General Assembly, and the Security Council are institutional means for determining what states ought to do. Alterations might be made in these institutions. Additional institutions might be created which would have either the legislative power to declare new rules or the authoritative jurisdiction to decide cases. But a discussion of such changes seems somewhat academic without facing up to the basic problem: Who is going to make the governments of the world comply with the rules and with the decisions? International law has always been considered as something other than "real" law because of the enforcement problem. Before refining the procedures for interpreting and applying international rules to governments, we should consider the process by which we hope to cause governments to obey those rules.

The best sustained consideration of this subject is no doubt Grenville Clark and Louis Sohn's *World Peace through World Law.* That important and valuable books spells out what would be involved in implementing the most widely held theory of how respect is to be obtained for international rules against arms and violence. In essence, the theory is that of the policeman on a larger scale. As stated by Mr. Clark in his introduction,*

> In short, our conception is that if police forces are necessary to maintain law and order even with a mature community or nation, similar forces will be required to guarantee the carrying out and maintenance of complete disarmament by each and every nation and to deter or suppress *any* attempted international violence.

Clark and Sohn propose a full-time, professional United Nations Peace Force of between 200,000 and 600,000 men, plus reserves of between 600,000 and 1,200,000 more. Nuclear weapons would be available to the Peace Force only in extreme emergencies, but the units would be strong and mobile so that they could quickly be assembled in the event of any "serious defiance of the authority of the world organization."

It is fair to say that reliance on such an international police force is basic to most plans for a disarmed world. American thinking has tended in the direction of the superstate. We foresee an international organization which brings about governmental compliance with the rules of international order by threatening action against any country which does not comply.

The present paper emphasizes another theory on which we might proceed. Rather than relying exclusively, or even primarily, on threatening nations with superior force, we might seek to weave international obligations into the domestic law of each country, so that by and large each government enforced the obligations against itself. This technique, used in conjunction with other enforcement techniques, should add strength to the forces for compliance.

As David F. Cavers points out, major changes in the arms race are likely to go hand in hand with major changes in political attitudes. We are seeking to devise machinery which will operate under and help bring about a steadily improving political climate. It is probably more realistic to assume that the negotiation and implementation of a disarmament agreement will produce a world whose

* Grenville Clark and Louis B. Sohn, *World Peace through World Law* (2d edn., Cambridge: Harvard University Press, 1960), p. xxix.

concerns are increasingly directed to other issues than to assume a continuation of the present levels of tension. In such a world the enforcement problem may be a good deal less difficult than now appears. In such a world the techniques here discussed may operate more effectively than they could today.

What follows is not a blueprint of the legal machinery to enforce disarmament. Rather, an attempt is made to consider the general theory of the means by which compliance with rules is sought and to suggest what appears to be a promising approach. One would be unduly optimistic if he thought that by any combination of means he could bring about 100 percent compliance with international obligations. Governments do not always comply with the domestic laws applicable to them. We do not seek, nor can we await, a perfect legal system. If we can devise means which might produce a pattern of governmental compliance with international rules comparable to that now existing for domestic rules, we shall be lucky indeed.

In the international area we are primarily interested in obtaining the compliance of governments, not of individual people. In one respect the task is far more difficult than the task of controlling individuals, since we are dealing with vast political enterprises invested with great power. But in another respect the task may be easier. Big governments like the United States often comply with constitutional restraints and other rules without a bigger force to make them do so. A government is a gigantic and complex machine. As with other such machines, it may not be necessary to have a bigger or a stronger one to bring it to a stop. A monkey wrench may be enough.

In other circumstances, however, even the existence of superior force may not be enough to make a government comply. The armed forces of the federal government of the United States are vastly superior to those of Louisiana, yet years after the Supreme Court's decision in the school segregation cases the government of Louisiana has failed to comply with that decision. The existence of superior force is thus neither a necessary nor a sufficient condition to governmental compliance.

There are two basic ways of bringing about compliance with a rule. The first of these is to make it *unreasonable* to break the rule. This method operates on the hopes and fears of the one whose compliance is sought. The possible consequences of compliance and of noncompliance are arranged in such a way that a rational person will choose to comply.

The second basic way of bringing about compliance is to make it *difficult* to break a rule. Rather than rely on the state of mind of the one whose compliance is sought, we construct barriers, so that even should he decide that he wanted to break the rule (and run the risk of suffering the consequences), he may not be able to do so. In devising the best means of causing governments to comply with international rules, we should consider the advantages and disadvantages of the techniques available. The following sections explore the two basic techniques, first as applied to individuals and then as applied to governments. Against this background the paper considers the method of obtaining governmental compliance with international obligations that is based primarily on national self-enforcement.

Making Noncompliance Unreasonable for Individuals

Individuals obey most rules from habit. When an individual is faced with a conscious choice between complying and not complying with a rule, he weighs the net advantages of following one course of conduct compared with those of following the other. This balance may be affected by a hoped-for advantage from complying or by a feared disadvantage from not complying. In some instances no institutionalized response need be provided. Compliance brings with it its own reward. A rule that persons going to the top floor of an office building should ride the express elevator is "enforced" by the immediate self-interest of the passengers. In other instances a general pattern of compliance may result from an enlightened self-interest—from a realization that everyone is better off with the rule than without it. The generally poor compliance with rules against littering the countryside suggests that in that case the hoped-for reward seems either too little or too unlikely.

Most of our rules, particularly legal rules, are enforced by a threat of punishment for noncompliance. We try to induce compliance with laws against murder by threatening a severe punishment in the event the law is broken. We try to induce compliance with ordinances against parking in certain areas by threatening a five- or fifteen-dollar fine. The effectiveness of a threat is dependent, of course, on how it is viewed by the person whose compliance is sought. If he considers the threat empty or the punishment insignificant, he will not be deterred. Even a mandatory death sentence will be an ineffective threat if one refuses to believe that the sentence would in fact be imposed.

A more important limitation on the usefulness of threats and promises, however, is that their effectiveness may depend on a rational weighing of the pros and cons by the one whose compliance is sought. Crimes of passion are not deterred by threats of punishment. Persons operating under emotional strain or great anxiety are not likely to make an accurate assessment of advantages and disadvantages. Thomas C. Schelling points out that this may cut either way. There will be cases of irrational compliance as well as of irrational disobedience. But man's common failing is to be shortsighted—to give greater weight to the immediate than to the remote—and threatened punishment is always in the future. Unless it can be arranged so that the loss must be suffered before the benefit is obtained, poor judgment is likely to lead to unrestrained conduct.

One factor affecting a rational choice between compliance and noncompliance is that of moral training or indoctrination. The more society's rules are respected because of internalized controls, the easier it is for society and for the individual. To some extent this may be considered as a limitation on rational choice. One complies with a rule because he has been brought up to comply with rules of its type. There is no cold weighing of the pros and cons. On the other hand, training to respect rules may be considered as one way of arranging for unpleasant consequences in the event the rules are broken. By education we condition a person so that he is constantly threatened with a guilty conscience should he break rules which he feels he ought to respect. The potential usefulness of this moral force should be kept in mind in considering alternative ways of enforcing rules against governments. In the long run, education and indoctrination in support of particular rules or particular categories of rules may be a major means of increasing the forces for compliance. In the short run, moral views can probably be considered as fixed. They are important data which should be taken into account in formulating the rules and in devising the procedural means for clarifying and interpreting them.

Making Noncompliance Unreasonable for Governments

To some extent a government can be considered as a unit which will respond rationally to the presentation of alternative courses of conduct. The government of the United States may be induced to comply with a decision of the Supreme Court because of its hope that by doing so it will set a good example for others and because of its fear that if it does not comply it may be difficult to convince others of the importance of respecting the law. Governmental respect for rules may sometimes be caused by fear of what the voters would do if the government did not comply. In international affairs fear of the consequences is a major factor affecting the rational decisions of governments. Every government, irritated at times by the immunity of foreign diplomats, decides nonetheless to respect the international law of diplomatic immunity. The probable consequence of disrespect is reciprocal denial of immunity by other governments, and this may outweigh any immediate gain from noncompliance.

The way governments behave today, compliance with the most important international rules—those against waging aggressive war—is induced at least in part by express and implied threats of retaliation. On political issues such as Berlin, for example, one government may seek to cause other governments to comply with its understanding of the applicable law by threatening dire punishment if they do not. Proposals for the enforcement of a disarmament agreement usually rely on the threat of superior force to cause continued respect for its terms. Once the retaliatory forces of other governments have been reduced beyond the point where they are a serious threat, it is usually contemplated that there will be an international police force strong enough to frighten nations into continued compliance.

There are, however, serious problems involved in this approach. A nation is not an individual, but a collection of a great many individuals. When one seeks to affect a country's behavior by giving it the choice between the advantages of complying with a rule and the disadvantages of not complying, one must consider not how those advantages and disadvantages would appear to us, nor even how they should appear to the other country as a whole, but rather how they appear to the various individuals who will in fact be making the decision.

Most simply stated, an external threat of violence directed toward a country may strengthen the hand of the government, not weaken it. The alternatives that are open, and the probable consequences of each, may look quite different from the personal point of view of an official than they look from the point of view of the country as a whole. Assume, for example, that the United States told Communist China that it must withdraw from Tibet or suffer nuclear attack on one of its major cities. Assume also, that in the best judgment of the leaders of China there was a 60 percent chance that the United States would carry out its threat. For the interests of the country as a whole, it might be wise to leave Tibet; but for the interests of the officials in control, the balance might appear quite different. Perhaps, if these officials thus bowed to a nuclear threat from the West, the army or some rival political force within the country would oust them, whereas a nuclear attack on a city might cause the entire populace to rally firmly behind the regime. It might, in fact, entrench the regime so that it would remain securely in power for years to come. In such circumstances, where a threat of consequences "unacceptable" to the country is not a threat of consequences unacceptable to the officials who make the decision, one could expect the threat to prove ineffective. (On the other hand, a modest threat, appropriately devised and accurately directed at the officials in control might be surprisingly effective.)

Even in our own country the threat of superior force may fail to achieve compliance. For years West Virginia failed to comply with its legal obligation to pay its fair share of the debt of the pre-Civil War commonwealth of Virginia. In theory, the United States army was available to enforce the decision of the Supreme Court ordering payment; but, from the point of view of a legislator of West Virginia, the superior forces of the United States army seemed less threatening than the consequences of an irate electorate should he vote to increase West Virginia taxes in order to pay money to Virginia.

We in the United States often insist that the officials in control of some country are serving themselves and are not really concerned with the welfare of the people. At the same time we may seek to influence that government's conduct by threatening dire consequences for the people. Since an economic boycott, for example, would be hard on "Russia," we tend to assume that "Russia" will not take steps which would result in our imposing a boycott. The two "Russias" here involved, however, are not the same entity. The decision-makers are not the ones directly threatened. A threat to the country affects the decision-makers only to the extent that they truly have the country's interests at heart. And however honestly an official may try, his appraisal of the national interest is likely to be affected by his personal perspective.

In an effort to induce governmental compliance with rules, threats are sometimes directed at the individual officials concerned. To deter the government from engaging in unlawful searches and seizures, we allow actions for damages against the individual officers who engage in such activities. But there is also an opposing interest. In order to have our officials act wisely and free from undue fear, we want them to be immune from liability for their official actions. We want our courts to decide cases according to the law, but we do not want to enforce this rule by making the judge personally liable for his mistakes. Some margin for official discretion is desirable.

The same technique of threatening the individual officer is attempted in the international area with respect to war crimes. We may be able to make it unreasonable for the country as a whole to break a rule, but decisions are not made by countries as a whole. To be most effective, the threatened consequences of noncompliance should be directed not only at the political abstraction that is a country but also at the individual human beings who make the decisions. We must try to make it unreasonable for them to act contrary to the rule. The consequences of noncompliance must appear to *them* to be worse for *them* than the consequences of compliance. Yet the threat of a war-crimes prosecution against individuals has only a limited effect on decisions. This is true not because of any lack of severity in the threat (the death penalty is about as serious a threat to an individual as one can make), but from the lack of certainty that the threat will be carried out. By and large, war-crime trials are carried out only by other governments and only after a war has been lost. Each side usually expects to win. The punishment is severe, but it is neither swift nor sure.

Today the threat of individual punishment by hostile governments seems even less likely to be effective than heretofore. Unconditional surrender would seem a prerequisite to trials by one government of the officials of another for war crimes or comparable offenses. Unconditional surrender is today an unlikely outcome for any but the most catastrophic wars. Any threat that could be carried out only after a major nuclear war is hardly likely to be effective.

Making Noncompliance Difficult for Individuals

The second basic method of enforcing rules is to make it difficult to break them. We may seek to control a horse by a judicious use of the carrot and the stick—or we may build a fence. And there is much to be said in favor of the fence. The technique of inducing respect for rules by making it difficult to break them is frequently used in addition to the method of threatening punishment for noncompliance. We are not satisfied to rely wholly on the fear of punishment to protect the President's life—we make it difficult to kill him. He is provided with secret-service men, cars with bullet-proof glass, and other preventive devices. We not only punish thieves, we use locks and safes.

At the outset one basic limitation on this preventive technique should be noted. The difference between preventing a bad action and requiring a good action is significant. If the rule is that the horse should not leave the pasture, we can enforce it with a fence; but if the rule is that the horse should pull the wagon to market, we must rely on the carrot or the stick. We can make inaction seem unreasonable; we are usually unable to make inaction difficult. If the rule is that young men must report to the draft board (a rule which requires affirmative action), we have no ready way of making noncompliance difficult. We must satisfy ourselves with offering rewards for performance and threatening punishment for nonperformance—and hope that the young men will be persuaded to comply by examining rationally the alternatives open to them.

Precautionary Rules

Up to this point we have considered that the interest of society is that the rule not be broken. In many cases this is true. Where the rule is against murder, any violation of the rule is certain to offend the interest which the rule is designed to protect. Yet in many instances we are cleverer than that. We construct a rule some distance back from the interest we are trying to protect, so that a breach of the rule does not necessarily offend that interest. Creating and enforcing a precautionary rule of this kind is one method of preventing any real injury to the interest which the rule is designed to protect. Having built a house near some dangerous rapids in the Potomac, a friend of mine was worried about the safety of his two young girls. He made a rule that they should not play in the water; but any violation of that rule was likely to be fatal; so he built a fence about fifty feet back from the river and made the rule that children should not cross the fence. By making the rule in this fashion, he allowed for the possibility of some breaches in the rule without any real injury.

By creating and enforcing a precautionary rule, violations of the basic rule are reduced. To some extent this result is simply one of statistical probabilities. If we do not want cars parked in front of hydrants when there is a fire, we draft and enforce a rule to take effect earlier: never park in front of hydrants. Quite a few violations of this precautionary rule can be tolerated without creating much risk of a violation of the basic rule. Violations of the basic rule can be further reduced by combining the precautionary rule with a technique for intervening after it has been broken. In our fire-hydrant case the police might tow away cars parked in front of hydrants. Such police action, occurring after a breach of the precautionary rule, makes it physically difficult to break the essential rule, that cars should not be in front of hydrants when there is a fire.

Other examples of precautionary rules which lay the basis for preventive action include rules against carrying dangerous weapons, against possessing narcotics, and against storing dynamite in residential areas. In each of these cases the breach of the precautionary rule triggers an action which may prevent any real injury from taking place. The dangerous weapon or the narcotics may be confiscated before they are used; the dynamite may be removed before it explodes. Although this technique may not make it difficult to break the precautionary rule, it is designed to make it difficult to injure the community. We are not limiting ourselves to the method of persuasion. By seizing the dangerous weapon we operate on the ability to use it. The preventive technique may also be applied after there has been a real injury in order to avoid its repetition. We may let a dog have one bite but after that tie it up. Some persons are kept in prison not simply to keep the threat of punishment credible but to prevent their committing crimes during the period of their confinement.

There are great administrative advantages in building a rule back from the brink. In the event of a breach the authorities have time to act, and they have a standard by which to act. There is often less incentive to break such a rule. There are also drawbacks to such precautionary rules. One's freedom is restricted even though breaking the rule will not injure society. Innocent acts which cause no direct harm will be punished. Precautionary rules are thus likely to seem arbitrary and to command less popular support than the more basic rules against conduct that is directly harmful.

Preventing Noncompliance by Preventing Cooperation

Another, and for our purposes the most interesting, method of making noncompliance difficult is to construct the situation so that to break the rule requires the cooperation of two or more people. The rule is made to run to the individuals. We seek to induce each individual to comply with the rule by threatening him with punishment or by otherwise trying to make it unreasonable for him to attempt to break the rule. In addition, however, the situation is physically arranged so that it will take joint and simultaneous illegal action to succeed in breaking the rule.

The simplest example is that of the grocery-store safe which requires two keys to open it, each key being given to a different employee who is supposed to keep it always by him. Compliance with the rule against embezzling funds is thus made increasingly likely. To embezzle the money will require the joint illegal conduct of both trusted employees. Either employee, in suggesting embezzlement to the other, runs a substantial risk. Neither has it in his power to break the rule. Another example is that of a policeman directing a crowd. The crowd respects the orders of the policeman not because he is more powerful than they are taken as a whole. On the contrary, taken as a whole they could easily overpower him. But probably no one individual by himself is physically able to ignore the policeman's commands, and it is difficult to organize a crowd to take joint and simultaneous illegal action.

Making Noncompliance Difficult for Governments

Governments are legally bound by many provisions of domestic law, and in general they comply with them. Some of these domestic rules (as discussed above) are enforced by a fear of the consequences to the government if they are broken, a fear held by officials who have the ability to break the rules if they want to. But perhaps the most important factor tending to cause compliance is that noncompliance by a government is often difficult to bring about.

Governments are rarely restrained from breaking domestic rules by simple physical limitations such as locks and fences. To be sure, it was early proposed that the federal government be prevented from usurping powers reserved to the states by not allowing it to have a standing army. To some extent the locks on our doors prevent illegal entry by the police as well as by burglars. But the basic method used to prevent the government from breaking rules is that of the two keys to the grocery-store safe. We establish subsidiary rules which run to the individuals whose conduct is involved and then we arrange matters so that it will require the joint illegal action of many people to break the big rule with which we want the government to comply. It is largely by such means that the United States government is prevented from violating the Constitution. By such means general governmental compliance with court decisions is obtained.

The government is big and has a vast army. The Supreme Court is weak and has no army; it has no more soldiers at its disposal than does the International Court at the Hague. General compliance with the decisions of the Supreme Court and with the Constitution and statutes of the United States is not simply the result of a conscious weighing by the government, as a unit, of the pros and cons of compliance and noncompliance. That question, in fact, rarely arises, because the government is not a unit: it is a lot of individuals, each of whom regards it as his duty to comply with the law. For the government to take any major action requires the cooperation and participation of a large number of individuals. There is a personal risk to any officer who suggests to others that they jointly undertake a course of illegal conduct. Every government officer has not only a loyalty to his superior but a loyalty to the system and to the rules. Every government, even the most dictatorial, tends to establish loyalties to programs and principles, loyalties to the system. Those rules which hold the system together and which are the product of the system cannot easily be broken by any one individual, even an individual on top. Obviously some governments are domestically more law-abiding than others; but every government of size is an institution which operates according to set rules. The functions of government cannot be carried on in a state of anarchy, nor by a wholly *ad hoc* series of decisions. To the extent that governments do comply with rules relating to their domestic order a major factor appears to be a form of institutional inertia—the practical difficulty of suggesting, reaching agreement on, and carrying out an institutional decision to violate the rule.

The separation of powers is thus a far more basic phenomenon of government than the division between the executive, the legislative, and the judicial. To achieve maximum governmental compliance with a rule it is desirable to establish subsidiary rules which run directly to the many individuals who make up the government and to induce individual compliance with these rules by all the normal means at one's disposal. In these circumstances it will be more difficult for the government to bring about and execute a collective decision to break the rule.

In the light of the foregoing discussion, what are the best means of enforcing international obligations, particularly those relating to disarmament? First, it is apparent that there is no necessity that one means should be used to the exclusion of any other. In fact, quite the contrary. The chances for compliance with any given international obligation will in large part depend on the extent to which a combination of forces can be marshaled in its support. Yet running through the various techniques suggests that in marshaling the forces in support of compliance we should place less emphasis than is currently proposed on international armed forces and a greater emphasis on the national enforcement of international law.

Making Noncompliance Unreasonable

A nation may be deterred from breaking an international obligation by fear of such unorganized responses as an adverse world public opinion. We are here concerned, however, with the institutionalized threat, the organized deterrent. We are interested in designing appropriate legal machinery, which would, among other things, tend to make public opinion part of an organized response. The basic deterrent suggested for a disarmed world has been a United Nations peace force, stronger and more powerful than the remaining international forces of any one state. There are serious initial problems of getting the nations of the world to accept the idea of a superior international army. As the prospects come closer to realization, the difficulties will become more apparent, and the objections can be expected to increase. The large role which armies have played in overthrowing political authority in one country after another through the course of history will cause many governments to worry about a United Nations army. But however big or small it may be, we will want some standing United Nations force.

An international army, once established, should be able to make it unreasonable for any government with weaker arms to engage in open military aggression against another country. It should also be a useful instrumentality for pulling apart opposing forces and preventing the continuation of hostilities that may have broken out. In such cases there would not only be clear grounds for international action; the appropriate responsive action by the United Nations forces would also be apparent. However, it would appear to be no easier for a United Nations force to deal on a governmental level with many breaches of international law than it is now for the United States. A threat of punishment is both difficult to make and difficult to carry out. To seek to deter governmental action by threat of punishment to the nation raises all the problems inherent in massive retaliation, as well as the problem of threatening the nation rather than the decision-makers. To make a threat credible and moral, it must be appropriate to the offense. It is difficult to devise national punishments that are appropriate for various assumed national actions. As suggested by Clark and Sohn, the most promising appropriate actions by an international force consist of measures such as the confiscation of prohibited weapons and the destruction of prohibited facilities. The fear of such actions might act as a deterrent, but the actions are primarily effective because they make it difficult for a government to continue to break a rule.

Turning from international to national threats, we find that the one most basic to a disarmament agreement is the threat of reciprocal noncompliance: "If you rearm, so will we." As with other threats, the ability to discover violations is required for the threat to be made effective; but inspection does not necessarily produce compliance. To a country that now thinks disarmament unwise, a threat of reciprocal noncompliance is no real threat at all. The only enforcement action which other countries threaten is to participate in tearing up the rule. This is hardly an effective deterrent for a state that wants the rule abolished. National retaliatory action of a more drastic sort involves the full range of problems involved in current military deterrence, among which the problem of making the punishment fit the crime is perhaps the most difficult.

Making Noncompliance Difficult

Perhaps the oldest means of trying to bring about compliance with international rules against waging war was that of trying by physical means to prevent a successful violation from occurring. To the extent that defensive weapons like the Maginot Line and the antimissile missile are designed to prevent attack, these are international versions of the lock on the door.

Rules against aggression leave no margin for safety. In international affairs even more than in domestic there are great advantages in moving the rule back from the edge of the water. The entire movement for disarmament can be viewed as an effort to make the international situation less precarious by moving the rules further back from the vital interests they are designed to protect. Just as in the domestic community we outlaw the carrying of concealed weapons or the possession of narcotics, so in the international community we seek to outlaw the possession of the major weapons of war. Unless such rules create instability, they increase our margin for safety. They give us time and a situation in which we can tolerate some violations. By having rules against possessing arms rather than against waging war we do not need to have 100 percent compliance in order fully to protect the interests at stake. Disarmament itself is thus a means of securing compliance with rules against waging big wars by physically preventing countries from being able to do so quickly.

By creating precautionary rules against possessing arms—by moving the rule back from the brink—we not only make some violations tolerable, we make it possible to prevent violations of the basic rule (against *using* weapons) through techniques of intervention. Here is where an international police force might be extremely useful. The task of confiscating or destroying particular weapons involves far fewer problems than the task of punishing a nation. There is no need to determine what action is appropriate to the violation. There is no need to determine responsibility or guilt. Just as narcotics are confiscated without determining ownership and just as the car in front of the hydrant is towed away regardless of how it got there, so weapons might be confiscated and removed by an international police force. Major difficulties might exist, particularly if the local government presented organized opposition; but an international force would appear to have greater chance of success where it is taking preventive action than where it is making deterrent threats.

Although disarmament moves the rules back from the brink, there remains the basic problem of preventing breaches of the precautionary rules. One cannot go back indefinitely by having rules against possessing the machines which can make the machines which make arms, etc. At some point we must stop trying to prevent a breach of the rules by physical means and try other techniques, including the method of the two keys to the grocery-store safe. With governments, as with individuals, the merits of internalized controls are great. It would seem that we have been too quick to reject such controls for the enforcement of international obligations and, in particular, for the enforcement of disarmament. Internal controls by themselves are not likely to be enough but when supported by a modest amount of international machinery they may well be able to carry the bulk of the load.

The object would be to weave the international rules into the domestic-law system of each government. As suggested above, every government must act according to some book, and the goal of the promoter of international law would be to have his rules written in *that* book. In some countries this may be the constitution or the statutes at large. In other countries it may be the precepts of the party constitution as elaborated by the current party line. But wherever the rules are that are taken as authoritative or binding by government officials as well as by the man in the street, that is where the terms of a disarmament agreement should be incorporated if one wants the highest probability of compliance. In the United States a treaty can be repudiated by the President, but a statute cannot. For greater durability a treaty should require the United States to adopt comprehensive legislation at both the federal and state level to implement its provisions. (If one wished to minimize the chance that the United States would break a disarmament treaty, one might incorporate the basic terms of the treaty in the United States Constitution). The rules should be mingled with the regular domestic law to the point where they became indistinguishable. Rather than have a separate disarmament statute which pulled together all the terms (and which could thus more readily be identified as a statute to be ignored), the new provisions should be scattered throughout the existing laws. The Interstate Commerce Act might be amended to regulate the shipping of arms by railroads. Statutes might authorize the recovery of one's land plus triple damages for anyone whose land was taken by the government for an illegal purpose. The Criminal Code could be amended to include a great variety of crimes dealing with the design, construction, or interstate transportation of armaments. To the extent possible, each rule should be one of domestic law, which would be enforced as a matter of course, as are other provisions of domestic law.

In addition one would seek to create groups and individuals who would acquire vested interests in the carrying out of the disarmament program. Government agencies should be established, at the federal and perhaps at the state level, charged with implementing the agreement and working out appropriate administrative regulations—getting Parkinson's Law on the side of disarmament. The general techniques of inspection by the people should be aligned not only on behalf of collecting information but also on behalf of the domestic enforcement of the rules.

This paper has avoided the problem of the mechanisms for determining what are the obligations of a nation when they are in dispute, and has concentrated on the problem of enforcing the obligation once it has been determined. To a large extent such separation is unrealistic. The incorporation of the substantive provisions of a disarmament agreement into the domestic law of each nation necessarily would mean that problems of litigating facts and interpreting the provisions of law would come up first in the national courts. All in all, this seems wise. In the first instance, local courts should be used to the maximum extent, both for criminal and civil actions. Where possible, civil actions should be directed against an individual officer, on the theory that he is acting improperly. The technique of litigating against an officer rather than against the government itself—a technique used widely here and used, to some extent, in the Soviet Union—has distinct advantages. It saves face. It tends to narrow the question to one which a court can properly and more easily decide. And a specific judicial command against an officer is more likely to be complied with than a general decision that the government ought to do something.

One way of modifying municipal procedure to make it more certain that cases would actually be brought would be to give representatives of foreign governments, international inspectors, and perhaps private citizens the standing to initiate judicial proceedings for injunctive relief against government officers or others. Truly international judicial machinery could be limited to courts which would review the decisions of the national courts at the request of an aggrieved state or at the request of the international disarmament organization. Presumably there might be enough judicial business to require using panels of the International Court of Justice or otherwise to increase the capacity of that court.

To the extent that decisions would be directed at individuals, the only physical force one would contemplate using would be the force necessary to arrest an individual and either to punish him or to hold him in contempt for failure to respect a judicial command. Most such operations would be done by the local judicial machinery itself. Even should the political branch of a government reach a collective decision to resist a decision, further efforts through the local courts might still be worth while. The courts themselves might not be involved in such a political decision and might see the national interests differently. The Virginia Supreme Court owed much to the major political forces of Virginia, and it generally shared their views on the racial integration of the schools; nontheless, this court held unconstitutional the Virginia "massive resistance" laws. The collective political decisions of Louisiana to try to frustrate compliance with the constitutional requirement of unsegregated schools become somewhat fractured by judicial action taken against individual officers when such actions achieve ultimate success in the Supreme Court. Rather than defying openly any specific judicial order, collective action is limited to seeking other "legal" means of accomplishing the result desired. One advantage of having the rules back from "the brink" is that there may be time for such methods. If a nation should effectively organize noncompliance, the "two-keys-to-the-safe method" would have failed (just as it would have had the two employees got together and used both their keys) and other techniques would have to be used.

The Acceptability of Self-enforcement

An obvious question is whether any such domestication of international obligations would be acceptable to Communist countries. Would they agree to incorporate the disarmament rules into their internal system and to enforce them? One cannot know for sure. Probably the Communist leaders themselves will not know until they are confronted with particular proposals in a particular context. In general, the Soviet Union would seem far more likely to accept such self-enforcement of international obligations than to accept the establishment of a world peace force with an army stronger than their own. In June 1946 the Soviet Union proposed the outlawing of nuclear weapons under a convention which would have included some explicit self-enforcement provisions. Under Article 3 of the draft convention, each nation, within six months of the entry into force of the convention, was required to pass legislation providing severe penalties for violators of the terms of the convention. Difficulties would no doubt arise over the measures necessary to satisfy other nations that each country was in fact enforcing such local legislation as was adopted. But there is no reason to suspect that the verification of enforcement measures would be more objectionable than the verification of compliance.

The more critical question is whether self-enforcement would work. As one moves from the domestic analogy of the United States enforcing the Constitution against itself to the immediate problem of the Soviet Union enforcing disarmament against itself, there are a number of differences which may be crucial. One issue is whether international obligations are inherently different from domestic ones. The superficial suggestion that it is to our self-interest to enforce domestic obligations but not international ones must be dismissed.

Once an international obligation is incorporated in our domestic law it becomes a domestic obligation, and we tend to comply with it, no matter who benefits directly and no matter how remote might be the indirect benefit to this country. The United States pays just compensation to aliens as required by the Fifth Amendment. Government officials comply with the terms of foreign-aid legislation for the benefit of foreign governments. The laws against counterfeiting foreign currency and stamps are enforced. The Government regularly enforces the statutory standards for the export of apples and pears, dairy products, and livestock, and the labeling requirements of other goods being shipped abroad. The fact that the immediate beneficiary of one of our laws is a foreigner or a foreign government does not appear to be significant. In fact, laws against the manufacture or possession of weapons in this country would in many ways seem more of a truly domestic matter than many statutes now on the books.

Another question is whether countries like the Soviet Union have a stable core of domestic law which in fact limits the freedom of action of the government. Certainly they have no such system of checks and balances as do we. Soviet experts will have to appraise the degree to which the man at the top has complete freedom to change the rules of the game. Some points stand out. The role of dogma and party line seems large. If nuclear weapons were once firmly labeled as immoral and contrary to party policy, there would apparently be risks for any leader in trying to reverse the position. There are others who might like to be on top, and being a "deviationist" is risky. In any regime there are some checks and balances which tend to favor the existing rules of the game. At the present time, Mr. Khrushchev is apparently seeking to make coexistence (a rule of international behavior) a matter of Communist party doctrine. Here is an attempt to weave into the domestic fabric of rules the international obligation to refrain from at least some kinds of aggressive war. Should coexistence be accepted as party doctrine, we might expect some lasting effect. Any government which devotes as much attention to doctrine and propaganda as does the Soviet Union must to some extent become the victim of its own words. The government buys popular enthusiasm, conviction, and support for its present policies at the cost of limiting the freedom with which it can change them. The importance of doctrine to the Soviet Union is demonstrated by the fact that the current controversy in the Communist world is apparently not over proposals for immediate action (as might be expected in this country) but over doctrine. The strength of the felt necessity to conform to such doctrine is suggested by the efforts repeatedly made to demonstrate that current actions are consistent with past doctrine.

A major difficulty in internalizing the control over disarmament is the ease with which government officials assume that they are above the rules. In this country, and presumably elsewhere, the government official is all too ready to break the law in order to carry out what he believes to be wise government policy. Officials of the Central Intelligence Agency lent support to a military attack on a country with which we were at peace, in violation not only of international law but of the apparently plain language of the Criminal Code of the United States. State police regularly tap wires and disclose information in violation of the Federal Communications Act and go unprosecuted. The history of unlawful searches and seizures by federal officers in violation of the Fourth Amendment suggests that they might also think it their duty to violate a disarmament agreement. This matter of the erroneously implied exception to the laws for official acts poses a most serious threat to the self-enforcement technique.

The first essential to lessening the problem lies in knowledge. In secret much can be done, but if the facts can be disclosed by inspection and verification techniques, the forces for compliance are greatly increased. The more quickly and more widely the data can be disclosed, the more chance there will be to bring local self-enforcement into action. Often the alleged "official exception" will not be able to stand the light of day. Where the rule is one directed primarily at government officials, as is the case with disarmament, it is more difficult to imply an exception for government officials. Also, a careful drafting of the statutes can make it difficult indeed to read in any exception.

In considering the effectiveness of internal checks and balances as a way of enforcing disarmament it is important for us to remember that we are seeking to prevent action, not bring it about, and that the kind of action we are seeking to prevent is large-scale action involving a great many people. Some governmental obligations, whether they are domestic, like integrating the schools, or international, like allowing ships to go through the Panama Canal, in fact require affirmative governmental action of a substantial sort. As pointed out above, it is easier to prevent the manufacture of weapons than to require their disclosure and destruction. Once a state of disarmament has been reached, the enforcement should be facilitated not only by the political atmosphere which one would hope would accompany it but also by the nature of the involved and complicated rearmament process which is barred.

In order to rearm, a government would not simply need to reach an agreement between two key holders to break the rules. Significant rearmament would be a "mega-key" project requiring the united and affirmative cooperation of a great many people, many of whom would undoubtedly be opposed to it and also feel that they had the law on their side. Rearmament operations would be likely to come to light at a fairly early stage, when they were under discussion or were first being organized. The difficulty of secretly recruiting and training a comparatively small band of Cuban refugees suggests the magnitude of the problem with which a government would be confronted, at least in an open society. Increasing the number of people who could start a case in court increases the chances that the issues will be raised. Providing an institutional framework of law within which the issues can be raised gives the forces of restraint a better chance of prevailing than they otherwise have. A prosecutor might use his discretion not to prosecute a CIA official for conducting enlistment and training activities in apparent violation of the Neutrality Act. If the Fair Play for Cuba Committee is given standing to initiate litigation, however, a court might well enjoin such activity. In the face of an adverse court decision either by its own courts or, under our hypothesis, by an international appellate court, the government might well quit doing what it set out to do.

It may be said that such a system for the national enforcement of international obligations as is suggested in this paper requires the constant consent of the governments involved. Yet it is not foreign to our thinking that a government should rest upon the consent of the governed. We cannot contain violent forces by paper rules, whether those rules limit the way in which a government is supposed to behave or the way in which an international police force is supposed to behave. The best we can do is to look to experience and see what can be done to structure forces so that those forces in support of respecting rules have the maximum opportunity to be effective. It is suggested that a promising way to do this is to try to weave the international obligations into the domestic rules in each country, and to rely in the first instance on national enforcement. International judicial machinery and an international police force should supplement such internal enforcement, rather than having to carry the full burden by themselves.

Such a combination of domestic and international legal machinery would not guarantee compliance with a disarmament agreement. One can be confident that there would be continuing problems, repeated violations of rules, and many difficulties. The question is not what will assure us of a peaceful world. There can be no assurance. The question is rather what approaches may offer us a good chance of survival. Examination suggests that a combination of domestic and international enforcement techniques would be better than relying exclusively on enforcement by a superior international armed force. The comparatively strong and effective national governments now existing may be our best means of controlling human conduct for the preservation of peace.

LOUIS B. SOHN

Progressive Zonal Inspection: Basic Issues

On 18 April 1962 the United States presented an "Outline of Basic Provisions of a Treaty on General and Complete Disarmament in a Peaceful World" to the 18-Nation Disarmament Conference in Geneva.[1] The treaty proposes three methods for verifying disarmament measures: the verification of the destruction of armaments or of their conversion to peaceful uses; the verification of the cessation or limitation of production, testing, and other restricted activities; and arrangements for ensuring that the agreed levels of armaments and armed forces are not exceeded and that activities which are prohibited or limited by the disarmament treaty are not being conducted clandestinely.

Except for some details, there seems to be a general agreement between East and West on the first two types of verification methods. Ever since the Soviet Union presented its proposal for general and complete disarmament in 1959, it has emphasized its willingness to accept complete controls over "disarmament," that is, the process of destroying weapons and eliminating the production of armaments. The Soviet proposals of 15 March 1962, for instance, provide that the "States parties to the Treaty shall in good time submit to the International Disarmament Organization such information about their armed forces, armaments, military production, and military appropriations as are necessary to carry out the measures of the corresponding stage," and that the "Inspectors of the International Disarmament Organization shall verify the implementation of" such measures as the elimination of rockets capable of delivering nuclear weapons and the dismantling of enterprises engaged in the production of such rockets.[2] These provisions seem to indicate that the Soviet Union would submit an inventory of the weapons to be destroyed in each stage and a list of the production facilities to be dismantled, and that it would allow international inspectors to be

The views expressed in this essay are those of the author and do not necessarily reflect the views of any agency of the United States Government.

present at the places where the weapons would be destroyed or adapted to peaceful uses, where the troops would be disbanded, and where enterprises producing weapons would be dismantled.

The Soviet Union, however, insists that any measures going beyond these steps would constitute "espionage," and would represent, not control over disarmament, but control over armaments and prying into military secrets. As long as some nations retain armaments sufficient to inflict tremendous damage on their enemies, and perhaps even large enough to destroy by a sudden attack another nation's capacity to retaliate, the Soviet Union does not consider it possible to open its territory to foreign inspection teams. It is often implied that only the mantle of secrecy thrown around large areas of the Soviet Union has saved it from an attack by its enemies. If those enemies discovered Soviet military secrets at an early stage of disarmament, they would immediately abandon further disarmament, which they use only as a wedge to pry open those secrets, and they might even launch an attack at the Soviet rocket bases which they will have discovered through the inspection process.

Assuming that Soviet military secrecy is as important as this argument suggests, and that there may also be other reasons (political, economic, and sociological) for restricting the access of foreigners to certain parts of Soviet territory, a complete acceptance of this point of view would make it impossible to devise any method for ensuring that the Soviet Union has not hidden a significant number of important weapons or is not engaging in the clandestine production of such weapons. A nation's declaration that it has only a specified number of various types of weapons and its list of enterprises engaged in the production of such weapons would have to be taken at its face value. The Soviet proposals provide no means for checking on any information, whether acquired through intelligence channels or from private informants, that in other locations weapons are hidden or are being produced.

When verification is permitted at only a few locations selected in advance by the inspected state, the possible margin of error is so large that no nation can be expected to enter into an agreement for disarmament which would leave it exposed to a devastating attack that utilized undeclared or clandestinely produced weapons. In a period of grave international tension, an agreement on disarmament, however desirable and necessary, is not possible if it has to be based on trust alone. Therefore, a system of verification must be devised which would, on the one hand, take into account the legitimate Soviet fear of suddenly losing all military secrets, and, on the other hand, provide sufficient assurance that no significant amount of major armaments has been hidden or is being produced.

To achieve this result, the Western powers would also have to make some concessions from their original positions. It has often been argued that national security is so important that there must be complete assurance about the accuracy of initial declarations concerning the quantity of armaments and the number and location of the facilities for the production of armaments. This approach has led to an insistence that such declarations must be followed by a period of one or more years, during which their accuracy would be thoroughly investigated. Only if such investigation should establish positively that no nation has made an attempt to hide any important weapons or factories, would the disarmament process actually start. While the Soviet approach has been sometimes characterized as involving 100 percent disarmament without any inspection, the Western approach has been criticized as involving 100 percent inspection without any disarmament.

It is obvious that the solution would have to lie somewhere in between. As the latest United States proposals put it, the "extent of inspection during any step or stage [of disarmament] would be related to the amount of disarmament being undertaken and to the degree of risk to the Parties to the Treaty of possible violations."[1] There should be some proportion between the amount of verification and the amount of disarmament. Such a proportion might be a direct one, for example, an agreement to disarm by 10 percent might be accompanied by a 10-percent increase in the amount of inspection. Or, the relationship need not be exactly the same, for example, in the early stages each 10-percent cut in armaments might be accompanied by a 5-percent increase in the amount of inspection, while in the later stages the proportion might be changed to a 10-percent cut in disarmament and a 15-percent increase in inspection. Finally, under either system, the goal of 100 percent disarmament and 100 percent inspection would be reached.

The Soviet Union seems to accept this final goal, but under its proposal this goal would be reached suddenly, by some magic or miracle. On some specified day all armaments would be destroyed, and free access would be provided for international inspectors. Before that day no search for clandestine armaments would be permitted, and any nation disarming in good faith would be exposed to the grave danger that one of its possible adversaries might have hidden a sufficient amount of armaments to assure its domination of the world. The current United States proposal, on the other hand, contemplates a gradual approach to this final goal, and the Western powers have repeatedly shown their willingness to investigate various methods for establishing a proper relationship between the extent of inspection and the amount of disarmament. Tentatively, more as an example of what could be done rather than as a definitive proposal, the United States suggests this arrangement for solving the problems of proportionality:[1]

(1) All parts of the territory of those Parties to the Treaty to which this form of verification was applicable would be subject to selection for inspection from the beginning of Stage I as provided below.

(2) Parties to the Treaty would divide their territory into an agreed number of appropriate zones and at the beginning of each step of disarmament would submit to the International Disarmament Organization a declaration stating the total level of armaments, forces, and specified types of activities subject to verification within each zone. The exact location of armaments and forces within a zone would not be revealed prior to its selection for inspection.

(3) An agreed number of these zones would be progressively inspected by the International Disarmament Organization during Stage I according to an agreed time schedule. The zones to be inspected would be selected by procedures which would ensure their selection by Parties to the Treaty other than the Party whose territory was to be inspected or any Party associated with it. Upon selection of each zone, the Party to the Treaty whose territory was to be inspected would declare the exact location of armaments, forces and other agreed activities within the selected zone. During the verification process, arrangements would be made to provide assurance against undeclared movements of the objects of verification to or from the zone or zones being inspected. Both aerial and mobile ground inspection would be employed within the zone being inspected. In so far as agreed measures being verified were concerned, access within the zone would be free and unimpeded, and verification would be carried out with the full cooperation of the state being inspected.

(4) Once a zone had been inspected it would remain open for further inspection while verification was being extended to additional zones.

(5) By the end of Stage III, when all disarmament measures had been completed, inspection would have been extended to all parts of the territory of Parties to the Treaty.

This proposed arrangement constitutes a modification of the proposals for territorial disarmament which were developed in private writings in 1959 and 1960.[3] While several of the early proposals combined zonal disarmament with zonal inspection, the official proposal of 18 April 1962 imposes no obligation to disarm the selected zone. This would allow each state the option of utilizing its armaments in the selected zone for fulfilling all or some of its obligations of disarmament and of satisfying the remainder of its obligations by destroying additional weapons, at supervised locations of its own choice, in other areas. The early proposals might easily have created a dangerous military vacuum, especially in crucial border areas, while the new proposal would permit a state to keep some armaments of its own choice in the selected zone, provided it destroyed equivalent amounts in other zones up to the point required during a particular step of disarmament.

The official proposal also seems incompatible with the idea that Soviet secrecy might be safeguarded if the selected zone were at first only surrounded by international inspectors and if the nation to be inspected were permitted to destroy all its armaments before the inspectors entered that zone.[4] In such a case the purpose of inspection would be merely to ascertain that no armaments are left. On the other hand, the main object of zonal inspection in the official proposal is to provide assurance that the initial declaration of armaments is correct, that the armaments declared to be located in the zone are actually there, and that no other armaments have been hidden in it. The idea of destroying all armaments in the zone before inspection also creates the same difficulties concerning a military vacuum as are created by destruction of armaments in a zone after it has been inspected.

The proposal made by the United States at the Geneva Conference is a tentative one, and various aspects of it are being studied further. It is quite possible that in the light of these studies some amendments will be made in the text. In addition, the special annex on verification which would probably be appended to the final text of the disarmament treaty would contain more specific provisions implementing the necessarily sketchy principles embodied in the present outline.

The basic feature of the proposed arrangement resembles a method employed sometimes in private affairs. A farmer leaving his land to two sons often provides in his will that one of them should divide the land into what he considers to be equal parts, and that the other should select the part he prefers. Similarly, if two museums are left a set of pictures, one might be authorized to divide them into two groups, while the other would be given the right to select one of these groups. Sometimes parents use this method in dividing a cake among a group of children. In an analogous manner, the United States proposal provides that each party to the disarmament treaty divide its territory into an agreed number of zones, and that the other parties to the treaty be authorized to select one or more of them for inspection during each step of the disarmament process.

While it is suggested that the division be according to "appropriate" zones, there is no further indication of a criterion for such appropriateness. Each state might apply a slightly different criterion, though its chief component is likely to be the element of military significance. Some states might prefer to divide their territories in such a manner that each zone would contain an equal number of military forces, or of launching pads for long-range missiles, or of factories producing certain types of armaments. Others might draw the boundaries of the zones so as to ensure that only a minimum of military secrets would be lost because of the selection of any one zone.

It is proposed that the "zones to be inspected would be selected by procedures which would ensure their selection by Parties to the Treaty other than the Party whose territory was to be inspected or any Party associated with it." For instance, it might be provided that the zones in the territories of the states which are parties to the Warsaw Pact be selected by a committee appointed by the members of NATO; and vice versa. Alternatively, the selections might be made by the Control Council of the International Disarmament Organization, but it might be provided that in each case the state to be inspected and its associates should not take part in the decision of the Council. It has also been suggested that many difficulties in selecting the zones might be avoided by using a random system such as drawing lots. Such a system, however, would make it impossible to base the selection on available intelligence data or to check a particular zone because of a suspicious concentration of events which seem to indicate the possibility of a violation. These objections to a random selection of the zones to be inspected would lose their importance if provision were made elsewhere in the treaty for the investigation of alleged violations, for the punishment of violations (for example, by increasing the number of areas to be inspected in the violator's territory) and, to even things up, for the punishment of unjustified accusations (for example, by decreasing the number of areas to be inspected in a state whose innocence has been established by the investigation). In the absence of such provisions, there might not be any other alternative to leaving the selection of the zones in one group of states to the other group of states directly concerned with the adequacy of inspection in the first group.

The United States proposal envisages the inspection of one or more zones in each country during each step of disarmament. The principal problem involved here relates to the size of the zone. Should there be a large number of small zones, or a small number of large zones? Assuming a ten-step disarmament plan, if each country were divided into ten zones, only one of these large zones would be inspected during each step. If, however, each country were divided into five hundred zones, fifty of these small zones would be inspected during each step. Of course, any number between ten and five hundred might be used. For instance, if it were decided that in the early phases only five percent of each country should be inspected, while in later phases this would be compensated for by inspecting fifteen percent of the territory, a division into twenty zones would thus be possible.

A map of the economic regions of the Soviet Union, published in *Pravda* on 23 February 1962, shows a division into nineteen regions; if one of these (for example, the tremendous Region 9 embracing almost half of Siberia) were divided into two, this map could be used as a temporary basis for evaluating the feasibility of a twenty-zone system. Naturally, any such evaluation would be purely hypothetical; the Soviet Union would probably divide itself in a different fashion, as the economic regions do not always coincide with zones of military significance. Nevertheless, the *Pravda* map could be used provisionally to explore the problems of the large-zone approach.

Any plan for zonal inspection would require a prior inventory, by zones, of the major weapons and of the enterprises engaged in the production of such weapons. Only numbers, not locations, would be disclosed. As long as the number of regions is relatively small (ten or twenty), important military information would not be disclosed by this process. The more the number of regions is increased, the more significant is the information that, for instance, twenty launching pads for missiles are located in a particular one. Even this is not too dangerous, as modern methods of protecting missile sites require pinpoint accuracy in any attempt to destroy them. In large countries, such as the United States and the Soviet Union, such targeting information could not be acquired even if the number of zones were increased to 100 or more.

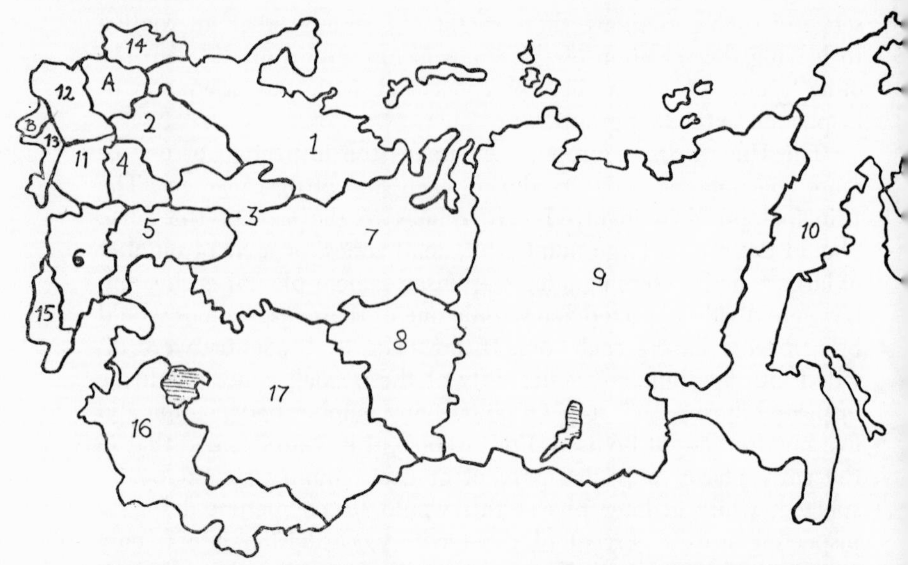

Figure 1. Economic Regions of the Soviet Union. Map published in *Pravda*, 23 February 1962.

There is, however, another relevant consideration. A division into a large number of zones implies that during each disarmament step several zones would be selected for inspection, either simultaneously or consecutively, while the large-zone method would require the selection of only one during each step. If a group of states (for example, NATO or the Warsaw Pact) were entitled to select ten or twenty small zones in each of the territories of the other group of states, they might be able to pick out in the first period the most significant areas and gain a disproportionately large amount of military information. If, however, the number of zones were small, the country to be inspected would be able to draw the boundaries of those zones carefully, so as to minimize the disclosure of military secrets. The process of "gerrymandering" (drawing the boundaries of election districts in such a way as to maximize the opportunities of a particular party) is well known in many countries; it can easily be utilized to balance the military risks involved in selecting one zone rather than another.

The small-zone approach has nevertheless certain other advantages which need to be considered. If one zone only were to be selected during each step, adequate arrangements would have to be developed to provide assurance against clandestine removal of armaments from the zone being inspected in the period between the selection of a zone and the sealing of its borders by the inspectors. In the case of a small zone, the borders can be sealed much faster, and the fact that a neighboring zone might be selected simultaneously or soon after makes the shifting of armaments among the zones more easily detectable, without a need for other arrangements.

The acceptance of the large-zone concept, which might be preferred by some states, would depend primarily on the development of such arrangements for sealing the borders as would present less intrusion into the affairs of the inspected country than the multiple inspection of several zones during each disarmament step. Some early proposals have envisaged stationing inspection teams on the boundaries of all the zones and at principal rail and road centers and airfields at the time of the selection.[3] The following arrangements might accomplish the same object and also lessen the risk of acquiring military information outside the zone chosen for inspection:

1. A few days before the selection of a zone, inspection teams would be transported by the inspected country, by means of its own choosing, to the major airports in each zone, as well as to the principal railway and highway centers which are situated, on the one hand, near zonal boundaries and, on the other, on important railways or highways crossing from one zone into another. While in transit to their destination, the inspectors need not see anything that the inspected country does not want to show them. Similarly, while the inspectors are waiting for a zone to be selected, their freedom of movement might be restricted. In a manner analogous to that applied to certain visitors to the headquarters of the United Nations, the inspectors would be permitted to stay only in a clearly defined area in which there are no important military objects; they would be permitted to use only certain specified roads; and for visits to other places they would require special permits which the inspected country would have no obligation to grant.

2. Immediately after the inspectors had been notified of the selection of a zone, the inspectors stationed in that zone would be given complete freedom of movement in it. Using the fastest means of transportation, including planes and helicopters, they would proceed toward the borders of the zone and establish control posts sufficient to prevent the removal of armaments. They would be entitled to check the contents of all road vehicles and railroad cars crossing the boundaries of the zone in order to ascertain that they do not contain any weapons subject to disarmament limitations.

Similarly, all air traffic to and from the zone might be temporarily suspended until controls are established at all airports in the zone from which military planes or planes transporting major armaments could be flown. Thereafter, the inspectors would be entitled to check the cargoes of all planes leaving the zone and, in specified circumstances, even of the planes arriving in the zone.

3. Simultaneously, as soon as a zone has been selected, the inspectors located in the neighboring zones, at rail and highway centers which are near the boundaries of the selected zone, would be authorized to proceed from those centers toward the boundaries of the selected zone and would check all the vehicles and railroad cars which might have left the zone after its selection but prior to the establishment of inspection posts on its boundaries. It might also be necessary to check the contents of neighboring depots, warehouses, and cars in railroad yards which might have been utilized for storing armaments removed from the zone after the moment of selection. This supplementary investigation of roads and railroads leading from the selected zone would be strictly limited in time, and after a day or two all the inspectors thus engaged would arrive in the selected zone and augment the inspection group already functioning there.

4. The inspectors located at airports outside the selected zone and those located at railway or highway centers not situated near the zone would perform no verifying functions at the places where they were stationed. As soon as possible, and subject again to such restrictions on the means of transport used by them as the inspected country might find necessary, these inspectors would leave their temporary posts and would be transferred either to the selected zone to help inspect it or to some other country to participate in inspection activities there.

5. In countries in which water transport of armaments might be significant, controls similar to those on roads and railroads would be established on major rivers and canals. Special controls would have to be devised also for maritime ports.

6. To facilitate the inspection of each zone, each state might be required, as soon as a zone has been selected, to submit a detailed list of the armaments and facilities subject to control which are situated in the selected zone. The inspectors would check both the accuracy of the list and the existence in the zone of armaments and facilities which have not been listed. If the inspected country chose to take most of the cut in its armaments it had agreed to for

the disarmament step then in progress within the selected zone, the inspectors would watch over the actual destruction of weapons. On the other hand, if the inspected country preferred to destroy its weapons in some other zone, special inspection teams would be dispatched to the place of destruction. Similar procedures would be applied to the dismantling of military production facilities or to places where limited further production was allowed. If those facilities were located in the selected zone, they would be supervised by the inspection group functioning there; if, however, they are located outside that zone, separate inspection teams would check on compliance with the disarmament obligations.

These arrangements would apply principally to large zones, but some of them might also be used for the small zones. In general, however, this second approach might not require the stationing of any inspectors at road and railroad junctions, as the problem of removing armaments could be handled through the simultaneous, or nearly simultaneous, selection of neighboring zones.

Even a division into only ten zones might be difficult in some countries, especially in such small ones as Luxembourg, Albania, or El Salvador. It has been suggested, therefore, that instead of division by countries there might be division by military blocs. Thus, the territories of all the European members of NATO, taken together, might be divided into ten zones cutting across national boundaries. One region might include, for instance, southern Denmark, northern Germany and the northern Netherlands. Similarly, ten zones might be established in Eastern Europe (including perhaps the Ukraine and Byelorussia, or all the Soviet Union west of the Urals). The Asian part of the Soviet Union (or all areas of the Soviet Union not included in the Eastern European region) would also be divided into ten regions, as well as the North American countries of NATO (the United States and Canada). If this approach should be accepted, instead of a zone being selected in each country, four zones only would be chosen, one each in the four areas outlined above—in Western Europe, Eastern Europe, Soviet Asia, and North America. Analogous procedures might be applied in South America, Africa, Asia, and Australia (including New Zealand and other Pacific islands), unless the countries of these continents should prefer the establishment of separate zones in each country. The European neutrals might be considered also as a separate region.

The approach here discussed should be distinguished from various proposals for disengagement in Central Europe. While the zonal approach would involve disarmament and inspection in both Eastern and Western Europe, no discrimination against the Europeans would take place. Any steps taken with respect to the European countries would also be taken simultaneously in North America and the Soviet Union, and probably also in the other continents. Nevertheless, it might be desirable to consider whether, in the light of the special situation in Central Europe, the zonal approach should not be modified in order to permit a simultaneous inspection of the zones facing each other across the East-West boundary. This exception should not cause any difficulties as long as other zones in other countries were subjected at the same time to an identical amount of inspection.

Whichever zonal approach is selected, all measures of verification authorized by the disarmament treaty would be applied in the selected zone in order to ascertain whether some nonlisted armaments had been hidden in the zone and whether some nondeclared facilities were continuing to produce weapons clandestinely. Both aerial and mobile ground inspection would be permitted; public and private buildings would be open to inspectors to the extent sanctioned by the disarmament treaty; and the interrogation of public and private persons would be allowed, subject to such restrictions as the treaty might contain. It may be expected that the special annex on verification which will accompany the disarmament treaty would contain exact provisions on the extent and limits of the inspection process. In preparing that annex, it is necessary to keep in mind that the arrangements must be sufficient to minimize the possibility of evasion and, at the same time, should not impinge unduly on the normal life and customs of the country being inspected. This difficult balance would have to be found, however, in any case, whether the zonal inspection plan is adopted or not. The zonal approach would create no special problems in this area.

Progressive zonal inspection is but one method for implementing the principle that "the extent of inspection during any step or stage would be related to the amount of disarmament being undertaken and to the degree of risk to the Parties to the Treaty of possible violations."[1] The Western delegations at Geneva modestly presented this proposal only as a suggestion to be studied and did not ask the Soviet delegation to accept it on a take-it-or-leave-it basis. If the Soviet Union should abandon its negative approach to the whole subject of inspection, a subcommittee might be established to draft the necessary detailed arrangements. It is quite likely that in the process of such discussions the proposal here outlined will be considerably modified; the present proposal already bears only a family resemblance to the early suggestions which started this chain of studies. If, however, the Soviet Union should reject this approach, it would be incumbent on its delegation to present an alternative method for achieving proportionality between inspection and disarmament. It is obvious that the current Soviet proposal, which permits no inspection outside the listed arms depots and factories, does not fulfill this requirement. Until a better idea is proposed by somebody else, the concept of progressive zonal inspection within the framework of progressive disarmament by stages deserves further study and exploration.

REFERENCES

1. "Outline of Basic Provisions of a Treaty on General and Complete Disarmament in a Peaceful World," 18 April 1962. Published in *Blueprint for the Peace Race,* United States Arms Control and Disarmament Agency, 4 May 1962; and in the Department of State *Bulletin,* 1962, *46:* 747.

2. *Treaty on General and Complete Disarmament under Strict International Control* (Draft of the U.S.S.R.). United Nations Document ENDC/2.

3. Louis B. Sohn, "Territorial Disarmament," a privately circulated memorandum (2 November 1959), cited in Jerome B. Wiesner, "Comprehensive Arms-Limitation Systems," *Dædalus,* Fall 1960, pp. 930, 950; "Problems of Arms Control," *Harvard Law Record,* 4 February 1960; "Phasing of Arms Reduction: The Territorial Method," in D. F. Frisch (editor), *Arms Reduction: Program and Issues* (New York: The Twentieth Century Fund, 1961), p. 123; "Security through Disarmament," *The Nation,* 25 February 1961, p. 159; "Disarmament and Arms Control by Territories," *Bulletin of the Atomic Scientists,* 1961, *17:* 130, reprinted in E. W. Lefever (editor), *Arms and Arms Control* (New York: Frederick A. Praeger, 1962), p. 209; "Zonal Disarmament and Inspection: Variations on a Theme," *Bulletin of the Atomic Scientists,* 1962, *18:* 4. For a partly different but otherwise parallel development of the same idea, see also Melvin Mooney, "Total Disarmament by Territorial Divisions," a privately circulated memorandum (29 January 1960); and his *Total Disarmament Now,* privately published (Melvin Mooney, 44 Melrose Road, Mountain Lakes, New Jersey), July 1961. See also Evan Luard, "Conventional Disarmament," in *Studies in Disarmament and Arms Control* (London: Institute for Strategic Studies, n.d.), Adelphi Papers, vol. 4, no. 2, p. 14.

4. Betty Stone, "Regional Disarmament," *Bulletin of the Atomic Scientists,* 1961, *17:* 295.

EMILE BENOIT

The Economic Impact of Disarmament in the United States

THE QUESTION of what might happen to our economy if we could ever get a Russian agreement on a sensible plan for disarmament may seem rather academic in view of the repeated failure of disarmament negotiations over the last two decades. This is a picture, however, that could change rather suddenly. The first nuclear test in mainland China, which may occur quite soon, will probably bring about a discernible rise in the international temperature and inspire some rethinking of policies, both in Moscow and in Washington. With additional nations achieving a nuclear capability and with the rapid spread of "small-yield" tactical atomic weapons, the already significant risks of war by accident or miscalculation are mounting geometrically. The possible benefits from continuing the arms race may soon come to seem trivial in relation to the appalling risks it incurs.

In his speech to the United Nations last September, President Kennedy placed in the record the official United States acceptance of the goal of general and complete disarmament. A draft proposal embodying this goal was presented at the Geneva Disarmament Conference on 18 April 1962. The Russians, in the McCloy-Zorin agreement on disarmament principles, have made major concessions (at least on paper) with respect to the inspection and enforcement of a disarmament agreement. Congress has backed up the Administration by establishing the United States Arms Control and Disarmament Agency for research, planning, and negotiation, and this should markedly improve the chances of finding a workable solution. While we may be no closer to an agreement than we were, we are at least clearing the decks for the strenuous thinking along fresh lines which probably must precede a meaningful agreement.

Once we begin to make progress on the political issue, the latent fears about the ability of our economy to withstand the shock of disarmament and to prosper without defense expenditures may become an important issue. The stock market has already shown occasional signs of jitters at talk of a *détente;* and the public discussion and political repercussions created by defense cutbacks in particular localities (as in the case of the Republic Aviation Company on Long Island) suggest that a serious disarmament proposal might encounter considerable opposition for essentially economic reasons—even though they are not always explicitly recognized as such. Although Premier Khrushchev (at some sacrifice of Marxist-Leninist orthodoxy) disagrees, much of the world (including Communist China) still believes that the United States cannot be sincere in its disarmament negotiations, because its economy is chiefly sustained by the production of war materials and because disarmament would be economically ruinous for it. This stereotype might itself become a serious source of distrust and an obstacle to an agreement. Moreover, there may be those in our own country who fear that without defense orders our economy will be outdistanced by the collectivist economies, and who cling nervously to our atomic armaments as a protection against the diffusion of revolutionary ideologies. The time is therefore ripe to examine with some care what substance resides in the idea that the United States could not "afford" to disarm.

The chief conclusions to which a year's research on this subject has led the present writer may be summarized here for the convenience of the reader.

1. The economic burden of armaments has been considerably exaggerated in popular thinking. While burdensome to a degree, defense expenditures have also made a substantial contribution to the world's economic progress.

2. Since World War II, there has been an apparent relationship between the size and build-up of defense activities and the level of United States industrial activity and general prosperity. This does not mean that defense spending is necessary for prosperity, but only that the economy has been stimulated by defense expenditures when they expanded, and that we have had inadequate compensatory programs to replace defense expenditures when they have been curtailed. European countries and Japan, with far smaller defense expenditures than ours, have considerably outstripped us in rates of growth.

3. Disarmament, under reasonable assumptions as to its scale and timing, might cause some real economic problems—though not of a catastrophic nature. A depression is less likely to be the out-

come than a dangerous slow-down in our growth. Problems such as shifting people and resources from defense-oriented industries and communities would inevitably arise.

4. Such problems are entirely capable of solution, and the real issue is not *whether* they can be handled, but *how best* to handle them.

5. Whether well- or ill-handled, the disruptions would be a relatively small matter compared to the long-term economic benefits we may expect if we pursue sensible economic policies. With such policies, the resources released from the defense program might further contribute to our prosperity, and to that of the countries we might be better able to help.

6. What is most likely is that disarmament would accentuate some of the economic problems of growth and flexibility we already have. If we can solve these, then the additional problems of disarmament will be less formidable. But even at the worst, the economic problems of disarmament are not so grave that they should be allowed to influence our attitude toward armaments.

This last point cannot be too strongly emphasized. Disarmament relates to the physical survival and political security of a nation, and economic adjustments connected with it are trivial in relation to issues of that magnitude. The real reason for disarmament is not that modern armaments are so expensive but that they are so *dangerous*—that the classic unilateral defense system no longer can provide the basic security that was its only possible justification and that a collective-security system under enforceable international law would better preserve our physical security and our essential freedoms. Within very broad limits, this nation can afford to spend as much or as little on defense as its genuine needs require. To determine the nature and size of our security program by the incidental economic hardships or benefits of armament-spending or of variations in the amount of such spending would be a bad case of the tail wagging the dog. These six conclusions will be elaborated in the remainder of this paper.

The World's Burden of Armaments

Whether we call defense spending a "burden" or talk of the "dependence" of the world's economy on armaments, the main facts are roughly as follows. The world as a whole spends approximately $115 billion a year on defense programs—equal to about two-thirds of the incomes of all the underdeveloped countries of the free world. Probably over three-fourths of the world's spending on defense is by the United States and the USSR. United States defense expenditures at $47 billion represent about 9 percent of our national output of goods and services, or, in the economist's vocabulary, of our gross national product (GNP). Probably the arms expenditures of the Soviet Union are in real terms a little less than ours, but because their total output (or GNP) is only about half as large, the burden on their economy is almost twice as great. (If the Communists are, as they claim, the camp of peace, they are certainly an armed camp—and in recent years they have shown an alarming tendency to rattle their arms to attain diplomatic objectives.)

In other countries the burdens are smaller absolutely and, with a few exceptions, are also smaller in relation to total production. In Europe only Yugoslavia, England, and France have defense burdens as high as 7 percent of national production. In the more common European case, the burden is around 4 or 5 percent, and this is true also for Canada and mainland China. In a few Asian countries (South Korea and Vietnam in particular), United States aid permits the assumption of an exceptionally heavy defense burden, but normally in Asia (for example, in India) defense expenditures run no higher than 2 percent of the GNP.

Another index of the burden a nation may feel is the number of men under arms relative to the population. The ratio for the United States is 1.4 percent and for the Soviet Union about 1.7 percent. The four nations whose armed forces exceed 2 percent of the total population are Yugoslavia (3 percent), and France, Greece, and South Korea (between 2 and 3 percent).

Do these figures reveal a "crushing burden of armaments"? That depends on the point of view. The burden is, of course, only a fraction of what it was during World War II or the Korean War. While defense expenditure absorbs resources which would otherwise be available to the civilian economy, it also contributes importantly to that economy. Some of the defense budget is spent for food, clothing, housing, and medical services, and it contributes to consumption, even though our national accounts do not indicate this. In some countries, members of the armed forces do public work of a civilian character, such as the engineering and construction of highways, dams, harbor and airport facilities, and emergency transport. A great deal of technical training is also given by some defense forces, and in the less developed countries the army may be a lead-

TABLE 1

Projected Primary Impact on Employment of a Reduction in National Defense Expenditures[1]

Industry	% Output used by military 1958	Defense employment (000) 1965	Decrease in defense employment (000)[2] Stage I 1965–68	Stage II 1968–71	Stage III 1971–74	Stage IV 1974–77	Total
Chemicals	5.3	62.7	23.4	15.1	9.3	8.8	56.6
Fuel & power	7.3	85.8	28.7	20.2	13.4	11.2	73.5
Petroleum	10.4	51.7	15.9	11.8	9.3	6.6	43.6
Primary metals	13.3	198.1	81.5	50.6	22.1	27.4	181.6
Iron & steel	9.8	90.5	35.5	23.5	11.0	11.7	81.7
Fabricated metals	7.9	149.8	53.6	35.2	23.6	20.0	132.4
Non-elec. machinery	5.2	91.8	29.9	22.2	18.1	12.3	82.5
Elec. machinery	20.9	376.4	126.5	85.3	68.2	61.5	341.5
Radio, commun.	38.0	279.4	100.0	64.4	43.5	47.8	255.7
Trans. equipment	38.5	1302.2	504.7	375.6	145.9	173.1	1199.3
Aircraft & parts	93.7	739.4	361.5	192.9	35.9	114.8	705.1
Ships & boats	60.7	238.6	87.1	123.2	4.6	2.9	217.8
Ordnance	100.0	290.6	45.3	51.8	96.8	51.6	245.5
Instruments	20.1	66.8	30.5	17.2	4.5	10.9	63.1
Transportation	5.9	128.7	44.6	29.5	18.6	15.9	108.6
RR & trucking	5.4	101.1	36.6	23.3	14.2	12.1	86.2
Trade	1.4	159.5	60.4	36.3	24.0	16.2	136.9
Services, etc.	1.3	260.3	85.4	59.7	40.0	33.5	218.6
Business services	3.8	105.1	36.5	24.9	16.5	13.3	91.2
Prof. & ser. ind.	1.9	129.3	39.2	28.6	20.3	17.1	105.2
Construction	2.1	81.8	37.2	7.5	0.0	0.0	44.7
Other industries[3]	2.4	228.8	84.8	52.7	31.4	26.4	195.3
Total Industry[4]	5.6	3192.7	1191.2	807.1	419.1	417.2	2834.6
Government							
Armed Forces		3000.0	500.0	500.0	1000.0	500.0	2500.0
Civilian		1171.0	327.0	270.0	179.0	178.0	954.0
Total Government[5]	85.2	4171.0	827.0	770.0	1179.0	678.0	3454.0
Total Industry & Government[4]		7363.7	2018.2	1577.1	1598.1	1095.2	6288.6

[1] "Primary Impact" refers to direct and indirect effects as measured by input-output analysis but ignoring possible multiplier effects or final demand offsets.

[2] The assumed reductions in expenditures are in accord with the hypothetical

ing center of national education and training, and a prime factor in developing administrative ability and technique—in short, an important modernizing force, as well as an essential support for the maintenance of public order and the deterrence of insurrectionary regionalistic and other divisive tendencies.

In underdeveloped countries with large-scale unemployment and even more concealed "underemployment" (relatively unproductive waste of manpower in agriculture and unnecessary services), the use of manpower for defense is a less serious waste than it would be in the developed countries—and this is the main type of defense expenditure out of domestic resources in these countries, most of the weapons now being obtainable free under military assistance programs. Military assistance programs, in turn, may involve little real economic cost to the donors, since the weapons transferred are largely from surplus stocks of weapons viewed as obsolescent in the producing country.

Even more important, a substantial part of defense expenditures in the United States (and in other industrial countries) goes to support research and development, and a quarter of all pure research is now financed directly or indirectly by the defense program. While most of this is immediately directed toward developing weapons, the indirect stimulus to the civilian economy is often profound. Most of the important technological breakthroughs of recent years have originated in defense research, including radar, atomic energy, jet engines, and space exploration. These in turn have had important effects on the development of new civilian products and services. For example, space research has yielded improvements in basic

---

model of general and complete disarmament as follows: Stage I, $17.2 billion; Stage II, $11.9 billion; Stage III, $9.7 billion; Stage IV, $7.1 billion.

[3] Food and kindred products, apparel and textile-mill products, leather products, paper and allied products, rubber and rubber products, lumber and wood products, nonmetallic minerals and products, and miscellaneous manufacturing industries.

[4] Totals not exactly equal to the sum of the parts because of rounding.

[5] Federal purchases of goods and services for national defense as percent of total federal purchases of goods and services.

Source: Leontief-Hoffenberg 1958 matrix, adjusted to 1965. Table prepared by READ (Research Program on Economic Adjustments to Disarmament), with minor adjustments on the basis of discussion in Panel on Economic Impacts of Disarmament, *Economic Impacts of Disarmament,* United States Arms Control and Disarmament Agency, (Washington: U. S. Government Printing Office, January 1962).

materials, in water purification, and in techniques for the automatic measurement of body changes. A major drug for the treatment of emotional depression was developed from one component of a rocket fuel.

Indeed, it seems entirely likely that the heavy defense programs of recent years will in time more than pay for themselves in the indirect effects of the new products and improved technologies which they will provide for the civilian economy—assuming, of course, that they do not finally blow it all up. It is the threat to this creative, innovational element in our life (rather than the simple problem of replacing defense activities with others) that may constitute the chief economic hazard of disarmament.

Something less than a tenth of the output of the United States economy is now devoted to defense, around $52 billion out of a total production (or GNP) of $550 billion. A somewhat similar proportion of our employment is now absorbed in defense activities. Out of a total labor force of around 75 million, around 6.5 million people are employed directly or indirectly in defense work—about 2.5 million people in defense industry, some 3 million in the armed forces, and over 1 million as civilians in the Department of Defense and defense-related agencies. With a continued buildup of the defense program, the number of people dependent on defense expenditures may reach 7-1/3 million by 1965, which is the earliest date by which disarmament might realistically have been negotiated and be ready to start.

Defense-industry employment is heavily concentrated in particular industries. About 95 percent of the employment in aircraft and missiles, 60 percent of the employment in ship and boat building, and 40 percent of the employment in radio and communications equipment is directly or indirectly dependent on defense expenditures. In other industries, such as primary metals and fuel and power, the numbers are substantial, although the proportion of the industry dependent on defense expenditures is much smaller, and most of this dependence is indirect (for example, steel is not directly purchased, for the most part, by the Defense Department but enters into the production of components which are ultimately assembled into weapons). Substantial numbers of people are similarly linked, many in an indirect way, to the defense program in transportation, trade, and services. (For details, see Table 1, page 138.)

The dependence on defense production is also concentrated in certain areas of the country. As indicated in Table 2, a good num-

TABLE 2

States Likely to Experience a Relatively Heavy Economic Impact from Disarmament

	Employment in Major Defense Industries,[a] April 1960, as percent of:		*DOD Payrolls[b] as percent of:*
	Total manufacturing employment	*Total non-agricultural employment*	*Personal income 31 Dec. 1960*
Kansas	30.2*	6.2*	4.1
Washington	28.6*	7.6*	4.9
New Mexico	23.8*	1.7*	9.0
California	23.3	6.3	3.7
Connecticut	21.1	9.5	0.5
Arizona	20.6*	3.0*	4.2
Utah	20.4*	3.6*	6.7
Colorado	17.8	2.9	4.7
Florida	14.1	2.1	3.8
Maryland	12.2	3.5	5.2
Missouri	10.3	3.0	2.0
Texas	10.0	1.9	5.5
Massachusetts	9.5	3.5	2.3
Oklahoma	8.2*	1.2*	5.9
National Average	*7.3*	*2.2*	*2.9*
Virginia	7.0	2.2	10.2
New Hampshire	5.0*	2.2*	7.4
Georgia	4.3*	1.4*	6.8
Alabama	3.9*	1.2*	6.1
Alaska	2.1*	0.2*	26.5
District of Columbia	1.5*	0.6*	10.8
South Carolina	1.1	0.4	7.6
Hawaii	0.4*	n.a.	18.2
Nevada	**	***	6.5

[a] Ordnance, electronic components, aircraft and parts, ship-building and repairing. Not all employment in these industries (except ordnance) is on military production. Employment in these industries and total employment in manufacturing include only employment in firms covered by unemployment insurance, but in practice most of such employment is covered.

[b] Military pay and allowances, and civilian DOD wages and salaries.

* Incomplete because it excludes employment which, in one or more of the industries, was not given by state, since that would disclose information about particular firms. For the whole country, the total excluded from the state-by-state distribution amounted to 13,900 or 1.1 percent of the total. For an individual state, of course, the exclusion might be much more important.

** Between zero and one percent.

*** Less than ½ of one percent.

Sources: Employment in defense industries and the total covered employment

ber of states are particularly dependent on the procurement of defense items for employment in manufacturing especially in relation to other employment opportunities. Thus, in Kansas, Washington, New Mexico, California, and Connecticut, from 20 to 30 percent of all manufacturing employment is based on major defense procurement. In other states a large proportion of personal income is generated by Defense Department payrolls (for personnel in the armed forces, civilian employees, the operation of bases). Thus, from a tenth to a quarter of the incomes of Alaska, Hawaii, Washington, D. C., and Virginia depend directly on defense payrolls. Moreover, some states like New Mexico and Utah, and also Kansas, Washington, and California are not only heavily dependent on defense contracts for employment but also on Department of Defense payrolls for personal incomes.

The common stocks of firms heavily engaged in the defense program have in many cases been very highly capitalized, reflecting anticipated payoffs arising from intensive research and development. In the event of disarmament, the value of these securities may be extremely vulnerable. Thus there is a probability of a stock-market break in the event of disarmament.

The defense industry has been changing in ways that may accentuate the problem of reconversion. In World War I most defense industry was essentially civilian industry which had converted, often quite reluctantly, from the production of civilian items, to which they were impatient to return. During the Korean war the production of items similar to, or readily converted to, civilian items (for example, planes and tanks) still accounted for the bulk of defense expenditure. Today, however, the heart of the effort in defense production is in the creation of highly specialized military equipment which bears little resemblance to any civilian production. A good share of defense production is in the hands of highly specialized defense contractors who have little or no experience with civilian production and for whom disarmament would imply not reconversion but a radical diversification into types of production in

in manufacturing from the United States Department of Labor, Bureau of Employment Security, *Employment and Wages*, Second Quarter 1960, pp. 22, 30, 73, and 74. Total nonagricultural employment from the Department of Labor, Bureau of Labor Statistics, *Employment and Earnings*, June 1961, p. 18. DOD payrolls are from the Department of Defense, Office of the Secretary of Defense, Directorate of Statistical Services. Personal income for 1960 from *Survey of Current Business*, August 1961, p. 13.

which they are inexperienced. Unfortunately, most of the attempts of these firms to diversify into civilian lines have so far been financially unsuccessful.

There are also some indications that our economy has become less resilient since the 1945-1953 period; it has shown higher levels of employment, a higher level of consumer debt in relation to disposable income, and lower utilization of industrial capacity. Unless these trends are reversed, the economy will clearly be more sensitive to the deflationary effects of defense cutbacks, and less capable of easy and automatic readjustment than in the past.

In this connection it would be unwise to draw too much reassurance from the success of our economic adjustment to demobilization after World War II, since its relevance to present conditions is very debatable. Between 1944 and 1948 expenditures on consumer durables tripled, and there was a ten-fold increase in non-farm residential construction. This was made possible by the $255 billion of wartime deficit financing, as reflected in an accumulation of personal savings of over $160 billion. Savings, which had soared to over 25 percent of disposable income during the war, dropped to an abnormal low of 2.8 percent. Moreover, consumer debt at the end of the war was at the extraordinarily low level of 4.5 percent of disposable personal income. In recent years consumer debt has risen to around 15 percent of disposable income and the savings ratio has shown considerable stability at levels between 6 and 8 percent. Another such burst of consumer expenditure and housing construction financed by already existing pools of liquid consumer savings or by increases in consumer debt could hardly be anticipated, although there is no reason to doubt that consumer expenditure would rise if disposable income were increased by tax cuts.

Finally, as has already been indicated, defense expenditures have been particularly important in stimulating research and development. This has been true in the electronics, nucleonics, and aerospace industries, which constitute the most fundamental element in modern defense industry and which have provided the most rapid pattern of growth and the most dynamic applications of science and technology.

What Pattern of Disarmament?

The first essential for projecting the economic impact of disarmament is to have a clear idea of what concrete steps disarmament would involve. Many of the disagreements about economic impacts are traceable to divergent assumptions as to the concrete content of disarmament. On the one hand, Thomas C. Schelling and others argue that the heavy inspection costs and the need to increase our stock of low-yield weapons if we reduce our nuclear deterrents might result in no reduction, or even an increase, in defense expenditures in the event of an arms agreement. They are explicitly or implicitly talking about limited arms-control rather than a true disarmament program—that is, a repatterning of national defense systems in the interest of greater stability, rather than the virtual replacement of national defense systems by a system of collective security.

On the other hand, those who predict dire economic results if we eliminate defense expenditures overnight, or within a few years, are talking of what I call "bilateral disarmament"—a parallel reduction of national forces without the creation of effective supranational inspection and peace-keeping machinery. This seems to me an impractical concept which would offer no genuine security to the disarming nations. If the proper machinery is to be established, the process could not, in my opinion, be accomplished in less than twelve years, and even this is optimistic. Moreover, while it allows for the necessary time to negotiate and to obtain political acceptance of the disarmament treaty, the model utilized assumes that the disarmament process does not begin until 1965. The model also assumes a continued build-up of defense expenditures until the disarmament program begins. This is predicated on the belief that the arms race is probably irreversible until some crisis gets us close enough to disaster to shake national governments out of their complacency and to generate a willingness to accept the fundamental political changes involved in the establishment of an effective world security system.

Our disarmament model involves a reduction over the full twelve-year period of United States defense expenditures from $56 billion estimated for 1965 to $10 billion estimated for 1977. Offsetting this would be a rise to $7 billion for the United States contribution (assumed to cover one-third of the total) to the annual current costs of the judicial, administrative, inspection, police, and deterrent functions of a World Peace Authority (many of the capital items are assumed to be obtainable free by transfer from national defense systems). It is also estimated that the NASA space program, and the civilian Atomic Energy programs (both of which have been closely associated with the defense program) will rise from $4 billion to about $11 billion over this period. Thus the net cutback of all security expenditures (taking account of these offsets) would be from $60 billion to $28 billion—or about $32 billion. Of this total, however, over $21 billion is estimated to occur in the first three years. It is during this period that the maximum economic impact will presumably be felt.[1] (These figures are at annual rates.)

The Danger of Depression

Would a defense cutback of $5 billion a year risk putting the economy into a depression? The answer is "probably not," but it does depend somewhat on the adjustment policies we follow. An initial reduction of $5 billion of expenditures, if not offset by compensatory programs, would lead, through the action of the multiplier, to a decline in aggregate demand of between $10 and $12 billion a year—this despite the built-in stabilizers. It seems most unlikely, however, that we would be foolish enough to allow the multiplier to exercise this effect without intervening to take some compensatory action. There would be a strong public and Congressional interest in tax reduction and presumably some willingness to expand public-service programs which have been held back because of the heavy burden of defense expenditures. It is hard to believe that we would again make the same mistake that we made in 1953-1954, when federal nondefense programs were cut by $2 billion at the very time when defense expenditures were being reduced. While immediate offset programs might be insufficient to prevent some decline, it seems most unlikely that we would let ourselves in for a severe downward spiral.

The most serious danger, however, might arise from the psychological effects of changes in the business community. We have never before faced a situation in which a long series of deflationary stimuli stretching over a number of years could be foreseen, and it is hard to know just how much discouragement this would create. A major break in the stock market, which, as indicated above, should be anticipated at this time, would undoubtedly intensify a general mood of pessimism. In such a situation everything might depend upon the attitude and programs of the government itself. If the government were ready to move promptly with adequate offset programs, and could convince business and consumers that there was no need to fear any significant letdown, then a depression should be fairly easily avoidable. The credibility of government policies and proposals, however, would be markedly affected by the success of the government's economic policies in the years immediately prior to disarmament. If the government succeeds in restoring high levels of employment and rapid growth, there will be greater public faith in the government's capacity to protect prosperity. On the other hand, an economy that already has a high level of unemployment and a serious underutilization of industrial capacity will be far more vulnerable to the additional deflationary stimuli arising from defense cuts. From this point of view it might be said that the time to start preparing our economy for disarmament is immediately, since a healthy, vigorous, rapidly expanding economy would be highly resistant to a depression in the event of disarmament.

We have already had some foretaste of the kind of problems we may encounter in the economy's rather lame adjustment to the post-Korean defense cutbacks. If we discount price increases, real defense expenditures declined by 30 percent between 1953 and 1960. Resistance on the part of the conservative coalition to providing adequate offsets was soon encountered. Between these dates, Federal nondefense expenditures for goods and services, instead of being expanded, were also cut in real terms by 30 percent and, despite a small reduction in tax rates in 1954, tax rates were held high enough to provide a rise in federal cash receipts of about 37 percent by 1960—of which no more than 16 percent could be attributed to increases in the price level. By reducing expenditures and holding up taxes, the Federal government, in four out of the seven years from 1954 to 1960, inclusively, took more purchasing power away from private consumers and businesses than it restored to them by its own expenditure and benefit programs (that is, it ran a "budget surplus on income and product account"). With the resultant deflationary impact, unemployment more than doubled, and the industrial output rose only 18 percent in the period between 1953 and 1960—in marked contrast to the 54 percent rise in industrial output and the reduction in unemployment achieved in the seven preceding years.

There is good reason to fear that a similar resistance to the provision of adequate offsets may afflict us again in the event of disarmament. One source of such opposition is Congressional antipathy to federal expenditure programs other than for defense purposes. (These are, in real terms, still about a fourth below what they were before World War II, notwithstanding a 40 percent increase in the population, the growth of urbanization, and the complex demands made on government in the modern world.) Another source of this resistance is the fear of inflation (coupled with an oversimplified mechanistic theory of it) which seeks to combat rising costs by inappropriate restrictions on final demand. But perhaps an even more fundamental source of resistance is a naive opposition to unbalanced budgets and a quixotic determination to reduce the national debt as soon as the pressure of defense requirements on the budget is relaxed.

The propensity to reduce the national debt may well be the chief potential danger to a successful disarmament readjustment. A recent survey conducted by the University of Michigan Survey Research Center, on behalf of the Research Program on Economic Adjustments to Disarmament, found a strong public attitude favoring the use of defense savings for national debt reduction, with 20 percent of the respondents choosing it as the best use for such savings and another 15 percent naming it as their second choice. This use of defense savings was far more popular than an expanded foreign-aid program, and just as popular as a reduction in income taxes. Respondents with a college education were particularly strong for debt reduction.

Such attempts to obtain a budget surplus would clearly have a deflationary effect, even though a partial offset might be provided by increased loan expenditure out of the replenished bank reserves created by debt retirement.[2] The dangers of such attempts at debt reduction may be particularly serious if, as Paul McCracken suggests, structural factors may occasionally require an increase in national debt to make possible continued economic growth.[3]

There may also be difficulties in having offset programs approved quickly enough to neutralize the effect of defense cutbacks. This is important because our economy responds sharply, not only to declines in defense expenditure, but also to declines in defense *orders*. To be most effective, therefore, offsetting measures should, if possible, be implemented at the very time that defense contracts are being canceled, and before the ensuing decline in defense expenditures. This kind of anticipatory response is, however, difficult or impossible to achieve with the complicated and slow-moving machinery of Congressional hearings, authorization, and appropriations. Clearly, what is needed is some degree of administrative flexibility, authorized by Congress, or stand-by public works, or tax bills, as recommended by the United States Monetary Commission.

While in principle adequate offsets to defense cuts could be provided either by expansion of public programs or by tax cuts leaving larger amounts of purchasing power in the hands of businesses or consumers, additional difficulties may arise if the tax-reduction device is given the main emphasis. Because of what economists call the "balanced-budget multiplier," tax reductions may generate a smaller amount of activity than is lost by equivalent cuts in government expenditures.[4] Hence, to provide adequate offsets, tax cuts would have to be even more sharp than the reduction in budgetary expenditures, and would therefore encounter the political taboos against deliberate deficit financing, not to mention the legal obstacle of the national debt ceiling.

A more subtle difficulty associated with exclusive or heavy reliance on tax cuts is that it would reduce the protection against cyclical instability which the greatly enlarged budget now gives us. The high tax rate required by existing heavy defense budgets has been an important automatic stabilizer, permitting declines in the private economy to be absorbed by declines in taxes rather than in disposable income. With a smaller public sector we would have a smaller amount of protection of this type.

To mention all these difficulties is not to assume that they are insuperable, or even to imply that we will not somehow summon the intelligence and mental flexibility required to overcome them. There is, after all, no basic difficulty of an economic sort to prevent us from maintaining a rapid rate of growth without any defense program. The difficulties are those of public ignorance and institutional inflexibility. Presumably, a president who really understood modern economics and who was inspired by a sufficient sense of urgency could rally sufficient public support to prevent the needless waste of our resources and the unnecessary deprivation and suffering that have accompanied our economic blunderings in the past.

This point may have particular importance in a postdisarmament situation, since international rivalries between free and regimented societies might have a much greater importance than at present. In such a setup a continued failure to eliminate excess unemployment and the underutilization of capacity and to restore rapid growth rates could gravely lower our national morale and weaken our international prestige and our capacity for world leadership.

Which particular offset programs deserve priority is clearly a matter to be decided by the electorate. We have numerous pressing "needs" of a collective sort, especially in the fields of urban renewal, public health, commuter transportation, etc. Moreover, despite much talk about the "affluent society," average consumer incomes are far from princely. Our average spendable per-capita income of $40 a week—luxurious as it might seem to an African or Indian farmer—does not permit much self-indulgence in a typical American city. And a substantial fraction of our population, perhaps a sixth, continues to live in severe (and anachronistic) poverty.

Ending such pockets of poverty may have particular strategic significance for the moral and physical strength of the nation. Other programs of exceptional strategic importance include: the continuous strengthening of our education and research potentials, the modernization and improvement of our industrial plant, and the provision of adequate resources and leadership for world economic development.

In the event of a failure of government policy to provide the sufficient aggregate demand to utilize our full resources, one may anticipate rising pressure to "take up the slack" by reducing working hours, increasing the length of vacations, imposing earlier retirement on our older citizens, and discouraging the entry of women into the labor force. Such policies would be at odds with the continued preference of most of our citizens for more goods rather than for more leisure—as is clearly demonstrated by the eagerness of most workers for overtime work and the growing amount of "moonlighting" (double or triple job holding). Such policies—if they were made effective—would also help the Soviets in their declared aim of overtaking the United States industrial output.

In any case, controversy over the best use of the resources released from the defense program and the far greater resources which will be made available through the growth of our productive capacity should not be allowed to obscure the more fundamental problem of assuring that our resources are used in one way or another. It is less important that we agree on the *best* uses of our resources than that we make sure that nothing we have is wasted.

Because of the peculiar strategic importance that research and development have for the nation's progress and survival, some mention must be made of the potential effects of disarmament on this area of the economy. About half of our research and development effort is financed by the defense program, and while not much of it goes to basic research, a far larger part of defense-supported than of private industrial research and development goes into efforts to achieve major breakthroughs. Although, since the mid-1950's, non-military research and development have been growing about as rapidly as the military variety, there can be little doubt that disarmament would bring about a very heavy slash in our total activity in this field—despite a minor offset from the employment of United States personnel on R and D programs of the World Peace Authority—unless some special offset program on the national level were prepared in advance and ready to go into effect immediately.

The special R and D program sketched here would provide alternative opportunities of a constructive nature for a large part of our human and physical scientific resources that otherwise would be forced into lower-grade uses. Other special programs could undoubtedly be developed, working in the same general direction. Whatever the methods employed, there can be little doubt of the need to develop some type of program to conserve these precious resources. While the continued growth in the demand for research and development would seem to assure the ultimate re-employment of an even greater number of scientists and engineers than are employed today, a number of years' potential could meanwhile be wasted. Even worse, the temporary redundancy of R and D personnel might cast a damper on the academic preparation of the enlarged flow of students and teachers required to maintain our scientific and technological preeminence.

None of the above is intended to deny that a defense cutback might provide a suitable opportunity for a reassessment of our R and D resources and goals and, in many cases, a redesign of our R and D activities. For example, an increased emphasis on the biological and human sciences, as opposed to the physical sciences, would appear to be inevitable as one result of disarmament. Here again, our concern for an improved utilization of our resources should not be allowed to obscure our primary concern for the full utilization of these resources. Most important of all is the encouragement of the most rapid possible increase in these resources. In a wider sense, this includes the strengthening of our whole educational mechanism—in particular, that phase of it which deals with the selection and stimulation of our most talented individuals. If disarmament involved a slackening in this effort, we should have had to pay a heavy price indeed for whatever defense savings we achieved.

Individual, Company, and Community Adjustments

One class of problem with which we will inevitably be faced in connection with disarmament is the problem arising out of the concentration of defense activities in particular industries and areas and also in certain vocational groups. Even if we can assume that an adequate aggregate demand is maintained, we will still be faced with the problem of shifting these highly specialized human and material resources from defense to nondefense activities. It will not be necessary, however, as some people have assumed, to plan in advance exactly how these shifts are to occur, where each worker will go, and to what type of production each factory will convert. In our type of free market-directed economy, many of these shifts will be easily and automatically made through the spontaneous activities of businesses seeking to obtain new markets, and workers seeking to obtain new jobs, wherever the new opportunities are to be found. It is a serious mistake to underestimate the flexibility of our economy in regrouping its resources to meet new patterns of demand as they arise. Such shifts, of course, are much more easily made if an adequately high level of aggregate demand is maintained.[5] There is more difficulty and less incentive in making the necessary shifts in resources if there is a substantial excess unemployment—society derives little benefit from adjustments which provide jobs for some people only by taking jobs away from others. However, even under the condition of an adequate aggregate demand, a disarmament program would involve such sharp and major changes in the pattern of output that many individuals, companies, and communities would find it impossible to make the necessary transitions expeditiously and without severe losses, unless with outside assistance—particularly in view of the previously mentioned demographic and technological forces which will make for increased unemployment during the 1960's, even in the absence of disarmament.

One group that may pose special problems of satisfactory reemployment may be found among the permanent members of the armed forces. Some of them may lack traditional civilian industrial skills, or they may be in age groups difficult to place; further, some are accustomed to relatively high levels of real salary (taking into account the imputed values of the food and dwellings provided) and in some cases may not be well adapted to routine civilian employment. Other cadres of course may be highly skilled and adaptable.

Readjustments will also undoubtedly be required for workers in defense industries who, in some cases, have acquired specialized skills for which there may be little requirement in civilian industry. Our experience with retraining programs has not been overly encouraging; the experiments along these lines which have been studied, such as those by the Armour Company and those in the Belgian coal mines, have indicated that the number of workers willing and able to benefit by retraining is limited, and that the expense of such programs may be excessive in relation to what they accomplish. On the other hand, programs which have been more successful, such as those of the vocational rehabilitation centers, suggest that improved teaching methods and the provision of adequate incentives may give better results in the future. Much probably depends on restoring a full-employment level of opportunity, so that people will be confident that the new skills, once acquired, will find employment.

A more fundamental kind of difficulty resides in the regional concentration of much of our defense activity. As indicated in Table II above, certain states (and this is even truer of particular towns and communities) have an excessive concentration of defense-dependent economic activity in relation to other available opportunities. While in theory such difficulties might be met by a relocation of excess workers, this is not likely to be an alternative favored either by the workers concerned, by the local businesses who depend on their patronage, or by their political representatives. Moreover, recent developments in the economics of industrial location begin to throw additional doubt on the wisdom of such a course. With the rapidly rising cost of housing, roads, schools, hospitals, shopping centers, and other community facilities—relative to the cost of factories, and with the relatively lower costs and increased diversity of transportation and power, and also with the increased rate of obsolescence in plant and equipment—the advantages of moving new industry into areas where a skilled labor force and community facilities already exist begin to outweigh the advantages of moving unemployed workers to other areas where there may be idle industrial facilities. It is interesting to note that most of the European programs addressed to the problems of the areas of excess unemployment or stagnation have concentrated on stimulating the entry of new industry rather than on trying to disperse the unemployed workers to other areas. A similar approach is now embodied in the United States legislation on depressed areas; the experience gained under this program should prove valuable in helping to develop appropriate regional adjustment policies in the event of disarmament.

The most stubborn adjustment problems of a structural character are likely to be found in connection with the highly specialized aerospace-nucleonic-electronic industrial complex, which is also highly concentrated in particular geographic areas, and which also, because of its heavy emphasis on research and development, will contain a good share of the most serious vocational readjustment problems. The difficulties here may be so great and the potential contribution of this sector so important that it may be considered advisable to treat this as a special case warranting separate treatment—for example, the development of new kinds of programs for research and development which might make contributions of an exceptional character to the nation's growth and to long-term strategic objectives, programs which this industrial complex might be particularly well equipped to undertake.

In this connection certain peculiarities of this industrial complex should be borne in mind: (1) it employs an exceptionally high ratio of skilled workers, scientists, and engineers; (2) it is highly specialized in research and development, particularly in highly sophisticated research aimed at fundamental breakthroughs in system development; (3) its organizational and business management is specialized in large projects and in getting its business by obtaining government contracts rather than by traditional merchandising techniques in competitive civilian markets; (4) it is generally less cost-conscious and more quality-conscious than most industries; (5) it has often proved quite unsuccessful in its attempts to diversify into the traditional markets for civilian goods.

Among the special programs which might well be developed and to which these industries could make a notable contribution are the following: (1) disarmament-inspection technology; (2) a civilian space program going beyond even the present ambitious plans (considerable expansion in these plans is already under active consideration in Washington); (3) the development of atomic energy for power—particularly if, in the meantime, a major breakthrough in atomic-fusion processes has occurred; (4) the development of other unconventional energy sources; (5) industrial exploitation of our ocean resources (to which our naval research people could undoubtedly contribute a great deal); (6) a renewed attack on major health problems, centering on cell chemistry and possibly including determined efforts to improve the electron microscope (the benefits of which might be astonishing); (7) a new research-and-development effort aimed at technological breakthroughs in the field of world economic development.

The last point is sufficiently unfamiliar and sufficiently promising to deserve some further explanation. It is my own view that present aid programs in support of international economic development are only partly effective, and that important technological breakthroughs are required for a sufficiently rapid progress in this area to meet our fundamental political objectives. Large research-and-development programs addressed to these technological problems might therefore make a much greater contribution than would ever-increasing expansion of aid programs along present lines. Among the projects that might be included in such a new program are: the development and mass production of teaching machines and other communication equipment; solar engines; water purification, climate control, and other techniques for combating aridity and restoring desert areas; the elimination of tropical and other endemic diseases; population control; the mass production of nutritional supplements; the mass production of simplified standardized components for houses, factory buildings, schools, hospitals, etc., and even certain basic types of farm instruments and industrial equipment.

Establishing a major research and development program along these lines would not only help solve what seems likely to be a major structural problem connected with disarmament, but would also fulfill the very strong expectation of the underdeveloped countries that the resources freed by disarmament would to a substantial degree be devoted to the support of world economic development.

Such programs as the above would presumably be handled by means of government prime contracts to present defense contractors, as well as to universities, to research organizations such as RAND, the Stanford Research Institute, and the Center for Research on Conflict Resolution, and to new institutions which may be set up for channeling government R and D funds to the most likely places. A large backlog of such contracts in the hands of our major defense contractors would do more than anything else imaginable to allay anxiety and reduce latent opposition to defense cutbacks. This is something which we could start preparing immediately, and which could start well in advance of any disarmament agreement. Certain of these contracts, particularly in the field of disarmament inspection, are already badly needed.[6] Such contracts would not only create an atmosphere of greater realism about disarmament, but, if they led to technological breakthroughs in inspection techniques, might bolster the prospects of disarmament's being achieved in time.

Immediate Steps

In addition to such bold specialized measures, there are numerous other more limited measures designed to facilitate structural readjustments. Clearly, a great deal of what may have to be done in the event of disarmament follows the lines of what would be highly desirable right now, since the economy already suffers from structural maladjustments arising out of technical changes, population shifts, and alterations in the weapons "mix." Listed below are the specific measures which might begin now and which would lend themselves to further adaptation:

1. The system of United States employment offices might be strengthened to provide a more complete, accurate, and up-to-date body of knowledge about job openings.
2. At the same time, the unemployment-insurance program should be strengthened to assure adequate minimum standards and a greater degree of uniformity between the states.
3. The government should encourage workable retraining schemes and recognize the fact that such retraining will often require the inclusion of elementary education—as in literacy and elementary arithmetic.
4. The value and costs of a relocation program should be explored. This might play a considerable role in highly specialized defense communities which either have no worthwhile potential for nondefense production or will take a fairly long time to develop alternative industrial opportunities.
5. Open-minded study should be given to the means of encouraging defense industry to adopt more liberal provisions on severance pay, even to allowing such programs as a legitimate cost in defense contracts. Naturally, the government should consider extending such benefits to its own defense forces and civilian employees.
6. The government should encourage industry to provide more liberal and flexible pension practices, group insurance, hospitalization, and similar benefits, with company-wide rights of transfer and seniority. Measures of this sort help to strengthen worker mobility.
7. Defense contractors should be encouraged (possibly by sub-

sidizing their research along these lines) to begin making their own studies of postdisarmament adjustments. Included in these studies would be such questions as the types of civilian production to which they could convert with the least difficulty; the types of alternative employment available in their vicinity; the grades of manpower and kinds of skills now used which would probably be redundant in a civilian economy; the new type of research and development programs to which they might hopefully contribute; their financial requirements in the event of a sudden cancellation of defense contracts; and the most practicable types of financing.

In summary: our approach to the reconversion problems of disarmament is likely to be more successful if we emphasize the tremendous positive opportunities which the release of these resources provides, rather than the difficulties in merely finding some place where such resources can be reapplied. If we succeed in mantaining an adequate demand and opportunity for employment, we shall be much more alive to this positive aspect of the structural and reconversion problems, and we can then enjoy the challenge it poses.

REFERENCES

1. This conclusion rests heavily on the assumption that cutoffs in the production of bombers and liquid-fueled missiles, and of nuclear fuels and warheads, would occur early in the disarmament program—since the destruction of such weapons while we continue to produce new ones would make little sense, for the existing supply of these items will presumably be so large by 1965 that the cessation of production would not seriously weaken the defense capabilities of the major nuclear powers. Some positive measures of disarmament will be required, since to begin inspection without any concrete measures for disarmament is clearly not a negotiable proposition. This model also makes the more controversial assumption that a significant cutback in the armed forces from an estimated 3 million in 1965 to 2.5 million would occur in the first three years. Even more controversial perhaps is the assumption that the inspection function would remain under national bilateral or multilateral control for the first three years and that it would be transferred to the World Authority only after that time. Thus inspection measures would be limited during the period when limited disarmament measures were being taken.

2. See Emile Benoit, "The Propensity to Reduce the National Debt out of Defense Savings," *American Economic Review, Papers and Proceedings,* 1961, *51:* 455-459.

3. See Paul McCracken, "The Debt Problem and Economic Growth," *Michigan Business Review,* 1956, *8:* 11-15. The total debt may have to rise, since

commercial banks, trust funds, life-insurance companies, and other institutional channels for investing personal savings are by law and custom restricted to the investing of most of these savings in debt instruments (for example, bank loans, secured by notes and receivables, mortgages, bonds, etc.) rather than in equities. Moreover, a *part* of the rise in debt may have to be in the *public* debt sector (roughly a third of the total), since if all the debt increase is in the private sector, private debt would be required to rise faster than private income, and the rising burden of private debt-servicing might ultimately inhibit any further willingness to assume debt, resulting in restraining effects on income growth. This sequence of events is as yet far from demonstrated, and its substantiation needs further research, but the possibility should be held in mind.

4. This effect of tax reductions would be attributable to the fact that a portion of the additional disposable income of the recipient of the tax cut will be "saved," and, for the time being, will raise the total value of financial claims, rather than immediately increase the total of expenditure and production. On the other hand, there is some possibility that additions to consumption—at least when there is a close-to-capacity utilization of the existing plant—may provide a greater stimulus to new investment than would an equal amount of defense expenditure. In that case, smaller tax cuts might suffice.

5. It is mainly because the Soviet economy lives continually under conditions of excess demand and in a state of "suppressed inflation," rather than because it has a planned or socialistic economy, that it would probably find adjustment to disarmament considerably easier than we would—just as we in 1945-1947 under conditions of suppressed inflation found the adjustments to demobilization surprisingly easy.

6. An example of the need for such programs was a promising research lead by a scientist, employed by a major defense contractor, for a new method of locating buried objects—it was not followed up because there was no official indication that such a device, if proved feasible, would find a market.

RICHARD C. RAYMOND

Problems of Industrial Conversion

INDUSTRIAL CONVERSION is a change in the types and quantities of goods and services provided by industry in response to customer demands. It is made possible by the manpower, facilities, information, and other assets which are available to industry. Conversion is influenced by many decisions on the part of all the groups and individuals involved. Government decisions make new risks seem more, or less, attractive and make the mobility of the needed resources increase or decrease. Owners and managers of industry devise new products and services and new ways of doing business, and decide whether to risk the assets of their businesses on the new items. Engineers, salesmen, and manufacturing experts make many choices regarding detailed designs, production techniques, and channels of distribution. Labor negotiates conditions which have a strong influence on the costs of the new items. Customers decide whether or not to buy at prices which make the production possible.

Conversion has been going on ever since industry became identifiable as a form of human activity. The rate of conversion has increased to a very high level because of rapid changes in population and technology. The rate will increase further in the future whether we disarm or rearm. Industry in the United States has shifted from peace to war and back again several times in the current century. The exact problems which a new disarmament would raise depend mainly on the rate of disarmament and the international forces which might be established to inspect and police it. Input-output econometric analysis can give only a few leads to the principal effects on industry.

There are many unfilled human wants which demand industrial attention. Increased service in many areas would be made possible by disarmament. Among the possibilities lie energy, education, transportation, recreation, water, food, air, construction, information, medicine, space, and weather.

To try to direct any large part of a conversion process centrally would raise severe problems. The theoretical tools for such direction are very poor, and the process of central direction would deprive us of many of the individual freedoms for which we have long fought. The proper role of government in conversion includes negotiating dependable disarmament agreements, providing those social facilities which lie outside the reach of private enterprise, and making labor and capital as mobile as possible. The owners and managers of industry must recognize the changing nature of the world in which they operate and make bold decisions so as to take advantage of conversion opportunities as they arise. It is through the early recognition of wants and prompt service that a free industry deserves and preserves its freedoms. Labor must make conversion easier by understanding that conversion will call for more of some kinds of work and less of other kinds. People with an interest in education and in moving into new employment can contribute greatly to the speed and ease of conversion.

A successful industrial conversion requires a myriad of individual choices on the part of all the people concerned. Experience has shown that many of these decisions will take unpredictable twists, even in a highly authoritarian, centrally controlled community.[1] The complexity and unpredictability of the total situation suggests that no individual or small group can assume responsibility for planning the whole process in advance.

To regulate all these decisions by the action of any of the groups of people involved poses many problems even in a slave society. In an open society where competitive enterprise is valued as a key to progress, it is impossible. Each independent decision has an effect on all the others. To make the conversion process as effective as possible, we must broaden the understanding of all of the decision-makers in government, industry, labor, and the public. We must strive for an atmosphere which promotes responsible decisions on the part of all the many individuals involved.

Conversions often serve as forcing factors in social and political changes. Social and political changes force conversions. The world contains examples of cultures in which industry as a specialized activity is still not known and examples in which industry is a social institution with a profound effect on the daily life of every person. Between these extremes are cultures in which the ferment of change owing to contact with the industrialized cultures is violent.

Perhaps the most significant pacing factor, both at home and abroad, is the rapid growth of the population. The vast increase in the total number of people and the internal dynamics of the population boom are having a wide impact on markets for all kinds of industrial goods. Between 1950 and 1960 the United States population grew both older and younger.[2] While the markets for such things as appliances have temporarily ceased their rapid postwar expansion, markets for education and for items of use to older people have increased considerably. Further changes in this distribution will extend over at least the next two decades.

We are in the midst of great changes in technology. Products, services, and industrial processes which a short time ago existed only in science fiction are being produced and used. As a result of the tremendous increase in expenditures on research and development in the last two decades, further changes are inevitable. At the turn of the century there were at most a few ways of doing almost any industrial process. By the mid-1950's there were so many that engineers and managers were on the point of nervous breakdown.[3]

The forcing effect of shifts in military expenditures over this century has not been small. President Theodore Roosevelt's Great White Fleet required a considerable proportion of our industrial output in its time. In World Wars I and II, again in the Korean incident, and later as the cold war intensified and the race for space began, we saw sharp increases in the fraction of industrial output going to government uses. There have also been sharp declines. Many conversion problems can, of course, be attributed to all of these changes. In general, we can expect that the effects of a future disarmament would be noticeable, but we are faced with so many opportunities for conversion already that it is really a matter of the specifics, not an abrupt shift in conditions, that we must consider chiefly.

Our tools for gathering high-level information on conversion and for estimating the effects of a large change in demand on the part of any large customer are not precise. The input-output analysis used by Wassily W. Leontief and Marvin Hoffenberg,[4] however, illustrates two very important points about any industrial conversion. First, the effects of a sudden shift in customer demand are less drastic in a particular kind of industry than might at first be imagined. Second, the effects reach much farther into related industries than it is obvious they should. Industry is so complex in its internal relationships that a severe disturbance in any sector is likely to be felt in all the others. When we ask what kinds of industrial conversion might be occasioned by disarmament, we must deal not only with the clearly identifiable producers of military hardware; we must also consider the producers of milk, gasoline, shoes, clothing, transportation, entertainment, and a host of other things which are purchased in large quantities by companies in the military business and by the military forces. We must work through the maze of the suppliers of intermediate equipment and materials who provide the goods and services which are converted by the end item suppliers for military use. To solve this analytical problem for any specific case requires many assumptions concerning the exact nature of the shift in industrial demand which would accompany disarmament and also the speed with which the changes would occur.

There is an infinite set of circumstances under which disarmament might force industrial conversion. The factors most important are the speed of disarmament, the kind of international-security forces which might be established to inspect and police disarmament, and the short-term effects of a disarmament decision on the over-all economy.

The short-term economy changes we might expect probably depend primarily on the rate of disarmament. In the case of slow disarmament, the required rate of industrial conversion will not be much larger than the rates now anticipated without disarmament. Conversion does, however, entail time lags for the steps outlined at the beginning. It is quite probable that a four-year disarmament would bring about a considerable amount of industrial dislocation. It might easily trigger an economic recession. Similarly, a one-year disarmament would probably lead to a depression. In the case of either a depression or a serious recession, the problems of industrial conversion would be made more difficult by tightening the supply of risk capital.

A cautious disarmament, carried out over a reasonable period of time and accompanied by the establishment of international forces for inspection and policing, might force another kind of conversion from the one normally considered in discussions like this one. Even for the relatively simple task of detecting clandestine nuclear explosions, fairly large forces equipped with sophisticated detection and communication systems would be needed. Broadening the inspection problem to include the detection of carefully concealed modern weapons of many kinds and adding a properly equipped international police force might require an expansion of some parts of the arms industry, especially during the period when the new international forces were being organized and equipped. Beyond the initial equipment period, a continued program for the development and re-equipment of the international force would probably be necessary to prevent technical surprise.

A more rapid disarmament, even if it involves the establishment of large international forces, will be more difficult to manage. It is important to note here the recent establishment of the Arms Control and Disarmament Agency in the United States Government. This agency is growing in stature and competence. A great deal of the success in a rapid conversion might well depend on its wise leadership in sponsoring the development of needed equipment and the intelligent planning of its forces and operations. It might for example plan to use personnel released from the armed forces and many products and services from industry not essentially different from many of those now provided to the military.

Unfilled Wants

If we are successful in some way in reducing the amount of our industrial talent applied to arms, we will have assets in the form of manpower, facilities, technology, and inventories to apply to other human wants. Some of these will be applied to expanding the existing products and services to meet current changes in demand; some will be available for many kinds of new items.

The equipment of inspection and policing forces has been mentioned above as a business area to which much of the defense-related industry could easily turn. There are many other wants deriving from the very rapid rise in world population as this population interacts with the changing political map and with the new ideas being developed in many places. Let us ignore for a moment the destabilizing influence of this interaction and look at some of the areas where industrial ingenuity could make large contributions in a peaceful and disarmed world. This will necessarily be a very broad treatment; the amount of information needed for a detailed plan in any one of these areas is far beyond the scope of this paper, and many specific assumptions would be needed.

Some estimates of the over-all size of the potential demand have been collected by Harrison Brown.[5] He states that to bring the entire population of the world up to the United States standard of living overnight would require the instantaneous investment of about one hundred times the annual world production of most of the metals. The resulting culture would require about ten times the current rate of energy input. Clearly there is a basic volume of human want which challenges the technologist and the businessman as well as the politician.

The population explosion is increasing the total volume of want at a rapid rate. In many areas of the earth people are being added to the population faster than the local economy is expanding to support them. The available goods and services per person are actually decreasing. In most of these areas, the introduction of industry as we understand it creates not only great opportunities but also great problems. The education, folkways, mores, and other cultural institutions of the peoples involved are not compatible with an industrial society. Peter F. Drucker[6] points out that we cannot expect the people of Latin America to convert to an industrial society without social and perhaps political upheaval.

Some of the challenges to industrial management arising from population dynamics may be inferred from the age distributions of the United States population in 1950 and 1960. There was a very large increase in school-age population as well as an increase in the number of persons beyond retirement age. Knowing approximately the age-specific fertility rates of our females and observing the strong present tendency toward early marriage and large families, we can see that the population boom in the United States will probably increase its rate in the next twenty years. The labor force, drawn from the center of the population distribution, will increase slowly in the next ten years. Beyond that a very rapid increase will begin. Let us look more specifically at some of the things this growing population will want, both here and abroad.

Energy

The energy industry is basic to all other industrial processes as well as to a wide range of other human activities. The sources of energy available for industrial exploitation include direct solar radiation, solar energy converted into falling water through natural processes, solar energy converted into carbohydrates by growing plants, energy in hydrocarbon fossil fuels stored in previous ages, energy in fissionable nuclei such as uranium, and energy in fusible nuclei such as hydrogen. Considered broadly, the energy industry involves the recovery or extraction of the naturally occurring forms, conversion of these forms to forms more useful for other processes, distribution of energy to users, and the manufacture and distribution of equipment for use in the over-all process. In an exhaustive treatise for the Atomic Energy Commission, P. C. Putnam[7] has related the basic sources of energy to anticipated human wants.

The scale at which the many extraction and conversion processes of the industry must be carried out if energy is to be made available at low cost dictates that the businesses in this field be big. The technologies are simple in most cases, but the problems of reliability, safety, and cost which must be solved result in a considerable complexity. Very high skills are needed in the design and manufacture of all of the items of equipment which are used, whether automobiles, turbine alternators, aircraft engines, or nuclear reactors. There is little sign that these technologies will become less demanding in the future.

Although few realize it, there is a fairly rapid industrial conversion going on in this field at present. The decision not to build a nuclear-powered airplane, the shift in emphasis from aircraft to missiles, the rapidly developing nuclear-power technology, competition between oil and coal, the developing science of nuclear fusion, the growing demand for electric power in all areas—all are leading to many changes in the products and services of the entire industry. It is quite clear that disarmament would not only lead to many changes in the demands felt by the energy industry, but it would also make available valuable resources which might change and expand the industry considerably. One factor which inhibits economic growth in the newly emerging nations is the lack of a reliable energy industry as a basis for improvements in their agriculture, transportation, manufacturing, and other processes. United States companies in the energy industry have shown technical leadership throughout the world. If conditions are made easier for service to the world market, this industry can expand considerably.

Education

If we are to achieve a peaceful and disarmed world, the education process will be fundamental. Even at present the unfilled demand for education on a world basis is hard to imagine. The need for fourth-grade achievement in reading, writing, and arithmetic is felt by hundreds of millions of persons. At higher levels persons desiring education are somewhat less numerous, but the problem of providing it is nearly as large. Even in the United States our universities face a serious crisis in the next ten years. Reasonable predictions show that there will probably be at least twice as many students in 1972 as there are today. This means that unless there are fundamental changes in the processes of education we shall have to duplicate our existing facilities and faculties.

At the same time, human knowledge is expanding so rapidly and changing so quickly that the problems of choice of curricula, design of courses, lengths of terms, standards of achievement, and selection of faculty members are much more severe than ever before. The costs of higher education are not high in terms of the long-range benefit to the individual, but an increase by a factor of two in these costs over a decade may be very difficult for the economy as a whole to adjust to.

All these problems, from the basic one of world-wide literacy to the somewhat smaller one of higher education in our own country, suggest that the time is ripe for innovations in the whole educational process. Many of the needed innovations are unpredictable, but in one area they can be described, at least in quality. A review of the ways in which education has been performed over the last few decades shows that in general the productivity of the personnel who carry out the work has not increased anywhere nearly as rapidly as the productivity of most other professions, in spite of the prolific growth in information technology. If we view education as a process largely concerned with information, we see that there is at once a great need, a growing technology, and also adequate resources. We can expect that the information technology will be invoked to a large extent in the next decade to increase the productivity of the scarce professional personnel in the field. Many are already at work on various phases of the problem. The release of additional resources from the arms industries would permit a much faster development.

Transportation

The growth of the megalopolis has already made personal travel from place to place an exasperating experience. The railroad, automotive, and aviation industries have provided partial solutions, but there is no evidence of a well-thought-through system. If we are successful in building a supersonic transport airplane, it will mean that the future traveler from Los Angeles to New York will spend about one-half of his elapsed time in transit in a $20-million airplane skimming along at 2,000 miles per hour and the other half in a $2,000 car fighting traffic at 20 miles an hour. If we add enough roads to eliminate the urban bottleneck, a large fraction of our city space will be surrendered to traffic and parking. I believe that we now have at work in the defense industry the skills in engineering, analysis, information, and management to solve some of these problems. It will take strong leadership willing to take large risks to make any real progress.

As population densities increase in both rural and urban areas, we shall probably find it economical to carry transportation routes much further into the third dimension than now. Subways have long been used to expedite urban transportation, and these can be expected to increase, as will the number of elevated and depressed roadways for rubber-tired vehicles; but we can also expect more practical aircraft to be developed for local service. The technology of short or vertical take-off and landing aircraft has been advanced considerably in recent years. This technology is likely to be pursued more vigorously, combined with more accurate and higher-capacity navigation, control and communication technologies. Certainly such devices would make much more sense as connections for long-range aircraft than our present buses and taxis. Roadways in dense urban areas could be improved very considerably by double-decking, so as to separate truck traffic from passenger-car traffic. The whole subject is closely linked with the design of urban communities, the relations between dwelling areas and working areas, provisions for education, entertainment, recreation, and essential services. Very little has been done toward planning many of these relations. For a glimpse of the earth with a population of 50 billion inhabitants, see Richard L. Meier's study.[8]

Recreation

Economists differ on the amount of leisure time we may have if rapid economic growth continues. My own view of the internal dynamics of the United States population leads me to believe that at about 1970 we shall find it desirable to reduce the work week and leave even more time to spend in recreational activities. Products as diverse as pleasure boats and television have shown phenomenal growth since World War II, and many more opportunities will appear for new kinds of industrial goods and services in this field.

Water

California voters last year approved a plan to spend $2 billion on a water system for the state. This system will collect water in the areas where nature provides it and deliver it to areas where people want it. The service will be expensive in comparison with less comprehensive systems, but it will still cost far less than water from the most optimistic process of converting sea water now known. In many areas of the world the entire problem of political stability hinges on water supplies. As the population increases in density, a specific solution to the water problem in each area will become essential.

The thermal efficiency of devices for purifying water has been improved somewhat in recent years and not much more is possible in this direction. If energy were free, however, there would still be large capital costs associated with the purification facilities. In some places we still see large volumes of natural water being allowed to flow into the oceans. In others we are still throwing away large amounts through sewage systems. Recovery from these sources will probably be economically more feasible than sea-water recovery for some time to come. The byproduct recovery of minerals from the sea is often mentioned as a cost-reducing factor, but it is far too small at present to pay the capital costs for the additional equipment needed, let alone the costs for the primary process.

Some imaginative thinking[9] has dealt with rearranging the earth's topography to take much better advantage of natural fresh water. Even fantastic schemes of this nature will probably turn out to be more economical in many cases than the erection of the required industry for large-scale processes.

Food

If populations continue their rapid growth and even if all the potentially arable land of Asia is farmed by Japanese standards, still the peoples of China, India, Japan, the Philippines, Southeast Asia, and Indonesia will be unable to feed themselves beyond about 1970 without imports. The entire world may face a similar situation by about 2000. The solution of these agricultural problems is conditioned by solutions to the water problem. By thermodynamic standards, agriculture is only about one percent efficient. There is room for much improvement from a technical standpoint, but the investment in a chemical-process industry to take the place of any significant fraction of agriculture will run into hundreds of billions of dollars. It is not too soon to start working on some of the possible processes, because the provision of food is essential to world peace.

People have discussed "farming the oceans" by a variety of techniques, even including the use of submerged nuclear reactors to bring up the deep mineral-rich water and thus promote the growth of plankton and fish. Numerical studies of the relationships involved tend to show, however, that no very significant contribution can be expected from this source. The output of sea food can be increased somewhat, but the amount to be expected is small in comparison with that provided by farming the land. As the British found out in their African "ground-nuts scheme," many of the soils which appear fertile are quickly exhausted. The chemical-fertilizer industry must be expanded considerably and diversified somewhat if many areas are to remain arable. At present this is not done for reasons of cost. The costs may not be prohibitive when people are willing to pay more for food, and these same price rises will also make a direct chemical-process industry more attractive.

Air

Air was once regarded by economists as free goods. More and more we confront the situation of having to spend money to process air before we can use it in such activities as assembling vacuum tubes and building precision gyroscopes. In some places normal meteorological conditions concentrate the pollutants released by our factories and automobiles. A few people have been killed by such concentrations and many more are uncomfortable and perhaps endangered.[10] Processes which stop the release of pollutants from automobiles are being developed and will be required as standard equipment in California within a few years. Larger-scale processes to promote air mixing or to wash out some kinds of impurities appear impractical at present,[11] but they may appear more practical in the future.

Shelter

As urbanization grows and population climbs, so does the demand for new structures. Accelerated rates of change cast doubt on the wisdom of building "permanent" structures for many purposes. Those who have had the misfortune to use the LaGuardia air terminal in the last few years will recognize the desirability of building some structures to facilitate change rather than to endure. Before that terminal was ten years old, many makeshift alterations were needed; when it was twenty-four years old, it had to be destroyed completely. The whole field of architecture, community planning and construction is on the verge of great change.

The construction of Pittsburgh's new sports arena which can be enclosed and air-conditioned leads to speculation about the possibility of enclosing entire communities so that not only the air but other factors such as weather could be controlled within the structures. Such roofed communities would permit many changes in materials, in design, and in other features of the facilities inside. Even without going that far, there are many new materials and structural concepts which will bring us more effective and cheaper structures for many purposes. Metals, plastics, glass, concrete, and new forest products processed and assembled by new techniques promise to take building construction out of the massive, expensive, permanent capital-investment area and into the area of expendable commodities. Much of our defense-oriented industry has learned to use these materials and processes.

Information

The United States has benefited from one of the best operated and most aggressively developed information technologies in the world. The press, the broadcasting industry, the telephone and telegraph industries, and motion pictures have made a wide variety of information instantly available to anyone. I recently had occasion to estimate for one of our executives the quantity of information which he receives on a typical day and which might conceivably affect his decisions. He has only time enough to give attention to less than one percent of the available material. Ellis Johnson describes the information crisis of the scientist and engineer even more forcefully. New knowledge is being developed in all our fields much faster than we can assimilate it. There is some hope in the fact that almost all the work of military electronics is in collecting, processing, transmitting, and using information.

While there are still many deficiencies of logic and performance in our military electronics, we have nonetheless built quite a few large-scale information systems, and we may have learned enough to apply some systems to nonmilitary areas. It will take time, courage, and perseverance to cope with the risks involved in any large-scale nonmilitary system, but the conditions are ripe for success for firms that can assemble large-scale information systems which take advantage of the peculiar skills and properties of both men and machines. The basic theory of such systems remains to be developed, but work is being done toward such a breakthrough.

Medicine

Developments such as the heart pacemaker, the artificial kidney, and the heart-lung machine open a considerable field of conjecture about future surgical techniques and development of prosthetic devices. Continued developments in analytic and diagnostic techniques accentuate the need for better systems of handling information. The extension of medical services to elements in the population which are now poorly served is a considerable challenge to management, and there is room for many labor-saving inventions.

The great strides made in public health during this century are dramatically illustrated by the lengthening of the average life span and the rapid increase in world population. There is still more to do in this field. At the same time there is the whole host of new medical problems which have become important as the older ones were solved. Chief among these are cures for cancer, heart disease, and mental illnesses. Controversial yet vitally important is an economic approach to birth control. In part these problems are chemical and biological, and in part, informational and educational.

Space

There are many who question the real need for space flight, and there are many who would stand in line for tickets. If our major opponents abandon space as an area of political self-expression, we may lose some of our interest in it, but our scientific-research program in space has been very fruitful, and we can soon answer many new questions about the feasibility of space travel. After a few trips, we should know much better some of the things which we can expect to gain there. The program will be large, and it might be even larger if some of the personnel and facilities now involved in weapon development could be made available.

Weather

One of the more promising early space vehicles has been the

weather observation satellite. It has contributed more to our knowledge about the circulation of the atmosphere than any other tool of meteorology. When the instrumentation of these vehicles is brought up to its potential, and when the needed information system is installed, we can improve our forecasting and our understanding of the complex thermohydrodynamics of the atmosphere. We may be able to find mechanisms to make important changes in some situations. To speak of controlling a hurricane is perhaps a misnomer, because the energy release in a hurricane is so great that it is difficult to visualize an artificial energy mechanism for real control. It may be possible, however, to provide triggering devices of relatively low energy which can shift the course or alter the lifetime of a storm. If these techniques can prevent one or two destructive storms each year or if they can add any reasonable quantity of water to our reservoirs, they will be worth truly large expenditure. Everyone who has examined these matters can add many examples to this type of list.

How to Encourage Industrial Conversion

There is a popular tendency to look to a higher authority for solutions to a problem which appears insoluble by immediate local action. In some cases this is productive, but if so, the higher authority must have both the wisdom to select the right courses of action and the power to order and enforce them. Let us consider how an industrial conversion made possible by disarmament might be managed by a central authority.

If there were an up-to-date, highly detailed, econometric model of world industry and a precise schedule for reallocating the demand from military goods to demand for other kinds of goods and services, the central authority would compute the demand for all kinds of industrial output. It would make a complete plan for worldwide industrial conversion. The plan would interfere with the sovereign powers of all the nations to regulate their own economic affairs. To implement the plan, the authority would dictate choices to the management of every business in the world and to labor and customers alike.

Whatever the likelihood of our seeing general and complete disarmament in any near period, it seems even less likely that the treaties and agreements needed to set up an operating World Economic Authority with powers of this sort could be concluded. Further, it is unlikely that the crude theoretical tools now available could be refined sufficiently to make such an authority truly effective in less than a few decades. In the final analysis the impact of such an authority on individual freedom everywhere would take us in the United States farther from our major objective of individual freedom.

The problems of central planning in a single nation such as the United States are somewhat less difficult, but they are still formidable. It may be argued that the total foreign trade of the United States is somewhat smaller than the military budget, so that to neglect foreign trade in planning the domestic economy would have effects small enough to be disregarded. While this might be true from a gross standpoint, the foreign trade in particular industrial sectors is much larger than the military trade. Shifts in foreign industry would thus have very sharp effects on particular industries in the United States. Some estimate of such shifts would be a necessary part of an over-all economic plan.

Perhaps a more fundamental objection to central planning is the fact that the tools at our disposal would not permit a simple deductive logic to set goals for future economic output. Innovation and inductive logic are also needed. The needed inventions would not all be forthcoming from a central planning group of any manageable size. Central planning would either waste the ingenuity and inventiveness of a large fraction of our business and professional leaders or it would turn this great force to seeking techniques of avoiding the personal consequences of the central plan. Central planning may attain reasonable success in backward areas where the goal of catching up to the advanced industrial cultures can be clearly defined, but it is doubtful that the innovation needed to secure effective leadership can be developed when individuals of all classes are not allowed to act on their own initiative and ideas.

The detailed central planning of the world economy, or even of the national economy, appears impractical for our objective of individual freedom, if we consider the theories, the information processes, and the authorities needed to make it a success. What then are the proper roles and responsibilities of the groups which must take part? Many groups and many different kinds of people with different backgrounds and outlooks are now making choices daily in the conversion process. Conversion is a process of change. It connotes mobility of resources, shifts in technology, and modifications in many aspects of all the processes of production and distribution. The principal problems of a rapid conversion are connected with the need for rapid changes. Many people are required to make many decisions, some of which lead them into unexplored fields. We can list a few of the things in which each group must take initiative if rapid conversion is to take place.

Governments

Beyond the negotiation of dependable international agreements, the proper responsibilities of government lie in two major areas. Government must provide those social facilities and operations which are recognized as good but which cannot be provided in other ways, either because they lie outside the reach of other groups or because the benefits and the operations are not closely enough related to permit industry to continue operation over a reasonable period of time. Government must further establish, as an objective of laws and regulations, a high mobility of both capital and labor in the economy. Laws under which industry-wide control of labor comes into the hands of a single labor leader do little for mobility. They work against it. Laws and regulations on the depreciation of all kinds of industrial facilities are in many cases seriously out of date with the mobility requirements of advancing technology. They must be brought up to date if we are to change more rapidly in the future. A move in that direction is under discussion in Congress.

As recent experience with international trade and money has shown us, we are no longer free in the United States to inflate our currency as we please. Government action to reduce the effects of the unbalanced budget and the effects of the unbalanced bargaining positions of labor and management could do a great deal to reduce inflation. Combined with actions favoring world trade, they could provide a great boost to mobility.

Education is a social good which has long been predominantly in the area of government responsibility. We can improve the mobility of personnel at all levels in industry by improving adult education, so that all those whose skills and trades are threatened by change may have their horizons broadened and may acquire new skills, new trades and new basic knowledge.

Owners and Managers

As Benjamin M. Selekman and Peter F. Drucker[12] point out, industrial leadership is in a position of power in many aspects of world and national economics. This power is exerted through decisions to allocate the resources of industry toward the attainment of selected goals and the selection of strategies for competition in particular situations. Decisions regarding new products and services have a strong bearing on the success of conversion. Here owners and managers must consciously take risks on new products and services. In a period of rapid conversion, the magnitude and extent of risk must be increased. The opportunities for new kinds of businesses must be exploited. In some areas positive long-term decisions must be made to provide products and services which may strain the resources of the industry or take its management into previously unexplored fields.

If industry does not rise to fill expressed human wants, there will be strong pressure for government to do so. Through positive movement into new fields, private industrial management can show its ability to lead its share of industrial conversion and make it unnecessary for governments to enter these areas. While the variety of things which might happen in a disarmament conversion is so great that specific planning for conversion is just as impractical for industry as for government, it must be a regular part of industrial management to keep awake to the range of possible situations and to explore continuously new ways of serving society. Planning effort is a good way of keeping alert, even though specific plans may not prove very useful.

Engineers

As the group primarily responsible for the detailed design of a new product or service and the machinery which may produce it, engineers have a considerable responsibility for the success of each item offered. They often have a role connected closely with the ownership and management of the industries they serve, and thus they may greatly influence decisions as to which of the great variety of possible products and services will be offered. Engineers have an opportunity in any conversion to match new technologies with their understanding of wants.

Salesmen

This group bears the responsibility of demonstrating to potential customers the value of the new products and services being offered and of persuading the customers to support industrial conversion by paying fair prices for the values offered. Through extensive customer contacts, the salesman can also reflect to his management and his colleagues in engineering and production the kinds of changes in strategy, design, and other features which will make the item more attractive to customers and therefore worth more to all concerned. In making rapid conversion possible, it is the salesman's job to seek new areas of industrial service and to devise positive techniques for making the connection between user and supplier. A broad understanding of current social and political changes is helpful here, as is an intimate and detailed understanding of the function which the product or service may perform for the customer.

Labor

If a conversion is to be accomplished at all, it means inevitably that there will be more of some kinds of work to do and less of other kinds. Changes in demand for all kinds of goods and services, as well as technological changes in the methods of producing them, call for differences in the way work is done. A willingness to accommodate to change, to accept retraining in different skills, and to move from one location to another can be of great value to all in any kind of conversion. A refusal to understand and participate in conversion can seriously impede the process, to the detriment of all. Even without the rapid conversion which might be caused by disarmament, there will be many other rapid conversions owing to foreign competition, technology, style, and other factors. If labor participates in these changes through education, reasonable mobility, and a willingness to do fair amounts of work in exchange for fair compensation, the whole process is carried out much more readily. If labor regards its continued performance of the same amount of work, using the same processes in the same place for a continually increasing compensation as a vested political right, then conversion is made much more difficult. The industries in which this kind of labor relations are practiced tend to die out. Everyone suffers.

Conversion and Freedom

The most valued aspect of life in a free society is the freedom of each individual to decide on his own course of action. This freedom is subject to many constraints; it also imposes many responsibilities. The process of converting our industrial structure to provide new kinds of products and services in response to any kind of change in customer demand requires a large number of choices for each individual in the whole society. If we call on higher authorities to make all these choices, we give up freedom in many ways. If we are to succeed without calling on higher authorities, we must make them ourselves. Each of us has a responsibility here for understanding as much of the total situation as possible and for making the choices we face in a constructive way. Only through responsible individual action can we prove our right to make our own choices. If we give up our responsibilities, we must also give up our freedoms.

REFERENCES

1. Joseph S. Berliner, *Factory and Manager in the USSR.* Cambridge: Harvard University Press, 1957.

2. Philip M. Hauser, "The Census of 1960," *Scientific American,* July 1961, *205:* 39.

3. Ellis Johnson, "The Crisis in Science and Engineering," *Operations Research,* January-February 1958, *6:* 11.

4. Wassily W. Leontief and Marvin Hoffenberg, "The Economic Effects of Disarmament," *Scientific American,* April 1961, *204:* 47.

5. Harrison Brown, *The Challenge of Man's Future.* New York: The Viking Press, 1954.

6. Peter F. Drucker, "A Plan for Revolution in Latin America," *Harper's,* July 1961, p. 31.

7. Palmer Coeslett Putnam, *Energy in the Future.* Princeton: D. Van Nostrand, Inc., 1953.

8. Richard L. Meier, *Science and Economic Development.* New York: John Wiley & Sons, Inc., 1956.

9. James C. DeHaven, *A Brief Survey of the Technology and Economics of Water Supply.* Santa Monica, Cal.: The RAND Corporation, 1958. Also, *Water Newsletter,* Water Information Center, Inc., Port Washington, New York, many issues.

10. "Lung Cancer Is Linked to Auto Fumes," *Philadelphia Inquirer,* 9 June 1962.

11. Robert L. Daugherty, "The Control of Air Pollution," *Engineering and Science,* April 1960, p. 16.

12. Benjamin M. Selekman, "Businessmen in Power," *Harvard Business Review,* 1961, *39:* 95; Peter F. Drucker, "Big Business and the National Purpose," *Harvard Business Review,* 1962, *40:* 49.

ROBERT W. KASTENMEIER

United States Machinery for Disarmament

SINCE THE unleashing of nuclear energy in the summer of 1945, the problem of the arms race has challenged the major powers with inexorable force. During this period, civilization has made the most terrifying progress ever known in developing and perfecting both conventional arms and weapons of mass destruction. The complexity of the problems of disarmament has correspondingly increased. To solve such onerous and urgent problems as face the nation today, the highest skills must be brought to bear, not only on diplomatic and military issues, but on the whole complex of the scientific, technical, legal, and economic structure as well. Disarmament planning is today our foremost and most pressing intellectual problem.

In recent years there has evolved a growing consensus that governmental disarmament machinery is lacking in adequate organization and is inadequately staffed. In 1959, the legislative and executive branches of the government launched a concerted effort to assess the existing machinery and estimate the needs, in an endeavor to determine how best to organize an effective administration for focusing on disarmament matters. The result of this effort is a new executive agency, the United States Arms Control and Disarmament Agency (ACDA), established in September 1961 by Public Law 87-297. The new agency is intended to be the focal point in government for the planning, negotiating, and execution of international disarmament agreements. Overwhelming votes—73 to 14 in the Senate and 290 to 51 in the House—for the legislation demonstrated the widespread awareness that a new approach to disarmament is needed.

The scope of ACDA's functions and responsibilities, an evaluation of the structure that has been set up, and some of the intricate questions of government coordination will be discussed in what follows. As a prelude to an evaluation of the administrative machinery created by the recent legislation, however, a look at the past may be in order. During a period in which disarmament negotiations have become more frequent, problems have grown more technical, and proposals become more complex, what kind of governmental machinery has the United States had with which to handle these problems and challenges?

Organizing for Disarmament: 1945-1961

In the past sixteen years, the United States has been represented at seventy international meetings and conferences at which disarmament has been discussed. Some of these meetings involved serious and prolonged negotiations. The Geneva Conference for the Discontinuance of Nuclear Weapon Tests, for example, ran to three hundred and forty sessions over a period of nearly three years. On the Soviet side, the principal negotiator at major disarmament conferences invariably has been one of a highly trained and experienced group: Vyshinsky, Gromyko, Malik, Sobolev, Tsarapkin or Zorin. On the American side there has been no similar continuity of representation. During the sixteen-year period United States delegations to international disarmament conferences have been led by some sixteen different officials. Too often these officials have been forced to meet Soviet professionals with a staff recruited only a short time before.

The lack of continuity in the United States representation at the negotiating table is a reflection of the general inadequacy of our organizational machinery for disarmament for most of the postwar period. Until 1955, with the appointment of Harold Stassen as Special Assistant to the President for Disarmament, there was no centralized direction of the various governmental activities concerned with disarmament nor any sizable staff regularly assigned to the disarmament function. Even the famous Baruch proposals for the international control of atomic energy stemmed from the work of a temporary committee. For the development of policy, and sometimes for technical studies as well, the government has been largely dependent on *ad hoc* committees, and this has been true even with the expansion of staff that occurred after 1955. In the Department of State, where the primary responsibility for policy lay, the permanent disarmament group during this period seldom comprised more than four professionals.

Stassen's appointment marked a step forward in the United States' preparation for disarmament. For the first time a centralized organization came into being. Concerned with the danger of the arms race, President Eisenhower gave full recognition to the importance of the problem by allowing Stassen independence from the often inhibiting controls of the Department of State. By May 1957, Stassen's disarmament staff comprised only fifty-four clerical and professional personnel. However, there were assembled in one place under unified direction the beginnings of a secretariat, a library and documents center, a consultants' liaison staff, a research staff and a formal interdepartmental group. The coordination of policy was handled through the President's Special Committee on Disarmament Problems, with Mr. Stassen as chairman.

The disarmament organization enjoyed this improved status only until February 1958. By then, Stassen's independence, his access to the President, and his new power inevitably led to conflicts with Secretary of State Dulles. As Sherman Adams has documented, Dulles never believed in disarmament and eventually moved to control and finally to eliminate Stassen. With the latter's resignation, the White House Disarmament Staff was disbanded and the function returned to the Department of State. At first the staff assigned was minimal, but it was evident that even minimal responsibilities could no longer be handled on the basis of improvisation. In 1958 two highly technical international conferences opened, one on surprise attack and the other on the suspension of nuclear-weapon tests. Negotiations got down to the hard specifics of the contents of a treaty, and for this task technical experts were required as an integral part of the staff. In the following two years, the State Department staff for disarmament showed a small but steady increase. However, it numbered only twenty in 1960.

Looking back over the disarmament record of the years since World War II, it is easy for us to discern occasions in which careful policy planning, a permanent, experienced body of negotiators, and better coordinated policy guidance might have resulted in a more serious negotiating position for the United States. Whether any one, or all three together, might have won a disarmament agreement from the Soviets cannot be known. But to paraphrase the remarks of George Kennan in connection with the question of arms control and security in Central Europe, "We know the Kremlin will not walk through a door obviously closed by inadequate United States proposals; we will only learn whether they will walk through a door opened by serious proposals if we have the men and will to make them."

It would be misleading to overlook the fact that mistakes were made on our side, that often we could have been clearer and more specific in our proposals, stronger in our defense of sound positions, more politically realistic in our requirements. In evidence of our past weakness, Henry Cabot Lodge, former United States Ambassador to the United Nations, recently testified before Senate and House committees that United States negotiators have often been under a serious handicap when they have been unable to get quick policy decisions from authorities at home. United States representatives have gone to disarmament negotiations with a prepared opening position, but have been unable to make prompt and (if necessary) flexible responses to Soviet proposals because of delays in reaching a consensus within the United States government. At moments we have been unable even to establish our initial position in time because of the many delays in clearance with several government departments. When Frederick Eaton, United States representative to the ten-nation disarmament talks in 1960, opened discussion with our allies prior to the Geneva meeting, he was unable to convey to them the United States position because the Department of State and the Department of Defense had not been able to resolve their differences. At that time, Senator John F. Kennedy pointed out:

> We are meeting next week in Geneva with nine other nations in an East-West Disarmament Conference, but (except to the extent we will accept the broad British proposals) we have prepared no plan for our conferees. We are meeting the Russians at the summit this spring to discuss among other things, presumably, disarmament, but we have no idea what our stand will be.

On other occasions difficulties have been created not by problems of policy coordination but by a basic shortage of information and by the inevitable weakness caused by insufficient knowledge. The State Department had no authorization to conduct the scientific and technical research necessary for the development of sound proposals. There was no extensive planned program of research to test adequately even those proposals already advanced. The difficulties created by this kind of unpreparedness were clearly demonstrated when the technical criteria for a treaty on a nuclear-test ban agreed upon by American and Soviet scientists in 1958 were thrown open to question by research subsequently undertaken by the Atomic Energy Commission. Although the United States experts had not been allotted sufficient funds to conduct fully adequate research on the issue of a nuclear-test ban, they were called on to meet the Soviet experts to work out the technical requirements for an effective inspection system. On the basis of the meager experimental data on hand, United States technical representatives reached conclusions with regard to the principal features of an inspection system. On the basis of their report, political negotiations to conclude a treaty ending nuclear tests were initiated. It should be pointed out in this connection that the Soviet side contributed even fewer data.

Subsequent research by the AEC revealed that there were possible, although extremely difficult, ways of hiding underground tests by reducing the seismic signal from a nuclear-test explosion to a fraction of the original size. As a result, possible inadequacies of the detection system agreed on by the experts came to light. Mr. Eisenhower accepted the AEC view, and the United States awkwardly revised a position previously taken. This revision was not only due to the facts of new data on test concealment but was also the direct result of a situation in which expertise lay in the hands of only one insistent group within the AEC and not in the hands of the evaluating group—the disarmament negotiating staff. This group had little serious opposition when it presented its case against a test ban to the President. From beginning to end, this episode demonstrated the weakness of any policy formation by those having inadequate resources to present and advocate a seriously conceived and well-informed judgment.

As Saville Davis, managing editor of the *Christian Science Monitor,* wrote of this situation in 1960,[1] "The President and Mr. Dulles were unwitting prisoners, in their lonely isolation at the top of the government pyramid, of the special selection of knowledge and attitudes which came to them through official channels and especially through Admiral Lewis Strauss." Davis shows that with the appointment in late 1957 of James R. Killian as Science Advisor to the President "a new weight was added to the balance" by creating a scientific group independent of the interests of another agency.[2] But expert scientific opinion, while useful, must relate more directly than this to the formulation of policy in order to exert sufficient leverage to alter the flow of events. The Killian group, conscientious and hard-working as it was, was never sufficiently integrated into the policy-making machinery of the Eisenhower administration to be a suitable match for other informed and especially interested advocates less concerned with a new approach to disarmament.

William C. Foster, the new director of ACDA, later summed up the general resultant of this basic situation when he returned from the last Surprise Attack conference at Geneva. "I doubt," he said, "that we have really given the intense study to the kind of measures which will make this [prevention of surprise attack] possible and which we would have to do before we go back into these further talks." It was a superb understatement.

From 1959 until the enactment of legislation establishing the ACDC, study and public discussion increasingly pointed to the inadequacies of the United States position and the need for a more effective organization to deal with problems of arms control and disarmament. During the 1960 presidential campaign, both Senator Kennedy and Vice-President Nixon supported an expanded effort to cope with these problems. For a number of years, especially during 1960, Senator Hubert H. Humphrey, the chairman of the Senate Disarmament Sub-Committee, had laid the factual groundwork for these demands, and had continually advocated an increased disarmament effort. It was only during the 1960 campaign, however, that the Department of State responded to this pressure with the establishment of the United States Disarmament Administration.

Seemingly an afterthought of the last administration, the Disarmament Administration is responsible only to the Secretary of State and is staffed with personnel drawn from the State Department, other government agencies, and from outside the government. The press statement released at the time stated that the Disarmament Administration was being established as a result of a study initiated in the autumn of 1959 by the Secretary of State (at the request of the President) "to investigate arrangements which would provide the United States with the most effective means of dealing with the increasingly complex disarmament problem."

This tardy establishment of the Disarmament Administration only highlighted the growing awareness that the United States had not conducted serious research on disarmament since 1946. More and more it was realized that for every $50,000 spent for armament less than $1 was being spent for disarmament. The public debate and the growing attention to the problem revealed a number of difficult areas requiring serious government consideration and action. The key problem centered around the need for establishing an authority to direct and contract a full-scale research program. This was but the first and most glaring weakness in the program. Next it became clear that some central body was needed to reconcile the great divergencies of opinion about disarmament that exist in the government. The Pentagon and the AEC, each honestly and patriotically committed to their own tasks, have not often received disarmament programs with open arms. In the past they have stalled negotiations and even openly sabotaged proceedings by revealing to the press glamorous new weapons that "demand" testing and "forbid" agreements on arms control. While it was generally agreed that the views of these agencies required careful consideration, it became clear that a trained and skilled evaluating team must be given final authority for recommendations to the President on disarmament. Only if a central body were established could decisions be reached, views be reconciled, and progress made.

This need for a coordinating agency was clearly related to the work of the existing policy-making section of the State Department, which also bore responsibility for conducting negotiations. Although it was realized that the coordinating and negotiating functions had to be performed, it was not originally clear that the research agency necessarily would have responsibilities in these areas also. Initially, the problem seemed to be the absence of adequate research. Later, the intimate connection between research, policy, and negotiations became clearer. Studies of the complicated issues involved in the relationships between these functions were undertaken both in public and in Congress. Out of these studies came a series of proposals. The present Arms Control and Disarmament Agency incorporates many features of the ideas put forth both by government and private officials. A review of some of these proposals demonstrates the evolution of our understanding and how areas of weakness were differently approached in various studies and by different groups.

Proposals for Disarmament Machinery 1959-1960

A proposal that a National Peace Agency be established was made in December 1959 by the Democratic Advisory Council. The new agency, while it was to be independent and was to report directly to the President, was to work in close collaboration with the Department of Defense and the Department of State. It was to have a director, a deputy director, and the "necessary organization to administer and support a peace program." There would be a permanent "Laboratory for Peace" to conduct research and study programs.

The agency, primarily designed to undertake research on various aspects of disarmament—inspection and control systems, and the effects of radiation on man—was also to conduct research relating to underdeveloped countries, in such areas as scientific and technical problems, the improvement of food production, the conservation of water and mineral resources, the development of power-generating systems for agricultural and industrial needs, and the reduction of the technological dependency of the underdeveloped countries.

While holding to a broad concept of how peace must be approached, the basic objectives of the agency were limited to carrying out the research aspects of a certain range of problems. The agency was to contract with both domestic and foreign educational and research institutions. In so far as possible, all research was to be performed on an unclassified basis for the better promotion of the free flow and exchange of information.

The December statement of the Democratic Advisory Council was adopted from a proposal originated by the Council's Science and Technology Committee in October 1959. The Science and Technology Committee included two Nobel Prize winners—Dr. Polykarp Kusch and Dr. Harold C. Urey—and other leading scientists. Much of the inspiration for the proposal stemmed from the work of Trevor Gardner, former Secretary of the Air Force. Congressman Charles Bennett of Florida introduced the first bill to create a National Peace Agency on 6 January 1960. The agency was to be established by the President, who was also to "establish procedures designed to insure that the agency will carry out its functions in close collaboration with other agencies, but without duplicating the efforts of any such agency." The director was to act "under the supervision and direction of the President." The purpose of the bill was not only to "deal with problems related to achieving peace through arms limitations agreement," but also to apply "scientific and technical resources to promote peace by eliminating or reducing the economic causes of war."

The bill provided that the director establish a "Laboratory for Peace," through which the agency would develop and administer its research and study programs. In addition to research and the development of programs relating to the over-all problems of disarmament, the agency was to conduct the broader research and development suggested by the Democratic Advisory Council, that is, problems of underdeveloped countries in such areas as food production, conservation, health, and education.

In 1960, Senator Kennedy also borrowed some of the essential features of the report for his proposal from the Democratic Advisory Council Statement. He proposed that an Arms Control Research Institute be established under the immediate direction of the President to "undertake, coordinate, and follow through on research, development and policy planning needed for a workable disarmament program." The director was to be directly responsible to the President. The institute again aimed primarily at the research question. It was to conduct a broad study and development program on various aspects of arms control and disarmament, and on inspection and control systems. It was also to carry out research on the economic and political problems involved in converting an arms economy into a minimum-arms economy, and in adjusting from a defense-oriented economy to an economy of peace. Studies of economic, social and political factors related to preventing war and to establishing a lasting peace also were to be undertaken. The institute was to cooperate with other government agencies, though the exact process of cooperation was not spelled out. It was to make the results of its research and development programs, as well as its recommendation, available to the Secretary of State and to Congress on request.

My own bill for a National Peace Agency was introduced on 18 February 1960. I drew on earlier proposals but rewrote and added certain specific provisions I considered essential. Focused also at the research question, my bill clarified some aspects of the problem by proposing that:

(a) The ultimate goal, as expressed in the statement of purpose, should be disarmament, not merely arms limitation.

(b) Certain topics should be added to the list of research subjects, including the means of controlling and eliminating chemical, biological, and radiological weapons, and the feasibility of a United Nations police force.

(c) A training center for peace should be established to produce personnel for inspection and other functions necessary to the disarmament process.

(d) An advisory council, composed in large part of distinguished private citizens, should be established to advise the director on the performance of the agency's functions and to generate public understanding of disarmament.

In order to move forward in the legislative process, I sought the cosponsorship of a large number of members of the House for my own version of the peace agency bill. By early 1961 there were more than thirty Representatives who joined in sponsoring bills embodying my approach to the problem.

While this brief review of the actual proposals for a research agency for disarmament stresses the developments of 1960, it must be pointed out that the key facts needed in formulating these proposals were developed chiefly by the work of the Subcommittee on Disarmament of the Senate Foreign Relations Committee. Under the dynamic leadership of Senator Humphrey, the weaknesses in our disarmament approach were thoroughly probed. Humphrey himself took leadership both in this exploration and in the legislative drive for a new agency, and deserves recognition as the most prominent spokesman for a new disarmament approach.

The United States Arms Control and Disarmament Agency

These various proposals brought forward in 1960 by Mr. Eisenhower, together with the establishment of a minimal United States Disarmament Administration within the State Department, provide the materials from which further and more detailed analyses and proposals can be made. On 2 January 1961, the appointment of John J. McCloy as adviser to the President on Disarmament was announced. McCloy was charged with the responsibility of making recommendations to the President on the formulation of United States policy on disarmament and also on the organization of the staff within the government having primary responsibility for disarmament. The staff of the USDA, as well as personnel from other agencies, was made available to him for this work. McCloy presented proposals on organization and recommendations for an independent and enlarged disarmament agency to the President on 9 May 1961, and finally to the Congress on 23 June 1961.

McCloy followed the idea of a peace agency in concluding that a separate agency with broad powers, assigned by Congress, should be established. His reason was his high estimate of the importance of the task to be performed. McCloy recognized that the problem of disarmament was of such pressing international consequence, and the formulation of a national policy on disarmament and the conduct of negotiations were of such complexity, that a separate and independent agency within the government with primary responsibility to carry out the proposals was essential if not crucial. Past failings—especially in the area of coordinating and reconciling divergent viewpoints within the administration—could, in his opinion, be corrected only by establishing a single focal point where all research on arms control and disarmament would be centralized. He concluded that a separate agency should be established at an authoritative level, with exceptionally broad competence, powers, and resources. For the new agency to be effective, it could not be merely another bureau or division of an existing department or agency, but must be rather a separate entity staffed by officers skilled in research, in policy planning, and in negotiations; and it must be supported by sufficient funds to carry out its important functions. Accordingly, it would have its own morale and prestige and would possess the status necessary to carry out its tasks and to attract the high level of the personnel needed, and it would be able to deal directly and authoritatively with all other government agencies.

Because of the magnitude of the research task, and because of the need to coordinate and reconcile different opinions, the McCloy recommendation emphasized the original peace-agency concept of independence; but his approach was not limited to the conception urged by earlier advocates. Rather, it added the new function—not dealt with in earlier proposals—of conducting disarmament negotiations. This addition was made for two reasons: it became more and more apparent that research without a direct and explicit relationship to negotiation might easily wither on the vine; more importantly, McCloy and his staff came to understand the power potential of the negotiating function.

An idea of this shift in concept can best be understood by realizing that some of the sponsors of the peace agency had spoken of their concept of a research agency in terms of a new "national institute of health" devoted to the problem of the disease of war. Research and the academic approach would provide a "tool" for the President which might give him some new ideas, although the agency would not directly enter the arena of daily policy. Not only was this more abstract idea of the relationship between research and policy abandoned as unrealistic; it was seen to reduce research and the new agency to a subordinate position in the executive branch. McCloy realized that the man who directs the negotiations and answers the cables is the man with his hand on power. The sheer pressure of events forces him to be in close contact with the

President, forces him to make decisions, requires him to obtain a reconciliation of viewpoints, and puts him in the center of what I call the "focal point of urgency"—a position in which daily necessity makes him the chief adviser on disarmament.

In real terms, the negotiating function gave leverage to the agency and to the research it performs. The added function, however, inevitably meant that the fully independent status of the agency would be altered. Some of its prerogatives had to be yielded in the negotiating area to the Department of State. Seeking to head off the kind of difficulties that Stassen and Dulles had encountered, McCloy proposed that the agency be closely coordinated with the Department of State. In recognition of the dual status of the proposed agency, he recommended that its director be under the direction of both the President and the Secretary of State.

When the Senate Foreign Relations Committee considered these proposals, it was much concerned with this question of power and dual direction. Although the Committee—as expressed in its report on the agency bill—was anxious to grant the new agency the authority necessary to fulfill its role as the central body within the executive branch for dealing with disarmament matters, it was also concerned with two other factors.

First was the fear that the proposed independent agency might encroach on the activities of governmental departments and agencies already established. Second was the firm belief that disarmament was so intimately related to foreign policy that the relationship of the agency director to the Secretary of State should be more closely integrated. The Foreign Relations Committee therefore proposed that the agency be established *within* the Department of State under the direction of an Under-Secretary of State. The Senate bill further reduced the status of the agency by providing that the new Under-Secretary serve as the principal adviser to *both* the Secretary of State and the President. On 8 September 1961 the Senate passed a version of the bill slightly modified by the Foreign Relations Committee.

The House Foreign Affairs Committee sided with the McCloy recomendation, however, and the House passed a bill setting up an independent agency on 23 September. A conference committee resolved the issue in a compromise that favored greater independence: the director of the agency was not to be an Under-Secretary under the supervision of the Secretary of State, but was to be independent of the normal State Department organization. He was, however, still to serve as the principal adviser to both the Secretary of State and the President on arms control and disarmament matters. Similarly, in carrying out his duties under the act, the Director was to follow the "direction" of the Secretary of State, but it was no longer stipulated that he be under his "supervision." The President signed the final legislation establishing the USACDA on 26 September 1961.

Prospects and Perspective

The immediate problems facing the new agency are to determine organizational structure and to recruit qualified personnel to carry out its mandate. Table 1 shows the main components of its organization.

TABLE 1

Office of the Director	
Office of the Deputy Director	(authorized by law, it acts for the director when appropriate)
General Advisory Committee	(this committee, authorized by law, shall not comprise more than fifteen members. It will be appointed by the President, with the consent of the Senate, to advise the director on arms control and disarmament policy and activities)
General Counsel	(chief legal officer, authorized by law)
Public Affairs Adviser	
Secretariat	
Executive Staff	
Disarmament Advisory Staff	(a policy planning and recommending group)
Reference Research Staff	(performs research in support of all offices of the agency)
International Relations Office	(to be headed by an assistant director; conducts disarmament negotiations and carries on a program of political research)
Science and Technology Office	(to be headed by an assistant director; conducts scientific research)
Weapons Evaluation and Control Office	(to be headed by an assistant director; conducts research in this area)
Economic Office	(to be headed by an assistant director; conducts economic research)

Reflecting the emphasis on research in the earlier proposals for a peace agency, more than half of the current budget of the agency (at present about $2,000,000 for the fiscal year 1962) is allocated to purposes of research and study. Over the past months agency officials have given considerable thought to a comprehensive plan for research. Existing studies have been assessed to determine where gaps exist. Panels of government and nongovernment experts have given recommendations and advice on the studies to be pursued. Priorities are now being determined and terms of reference framed.

Studies can be either contracted outside or carried on within the government. The choice depends to a large degree on the subject matter of the study and the availability of research personnel with the appropriate expertise. Since the agency now has only a small research staff, it is anticipated that the majority of the research initially will be contracted. However, it is contemplated that the in-house research capacity of the agency will be built up as rapidly as possible, because some types of research, especially those of a political nature, can most satisfactorily be carried on within the government. In addition, it is difficult to organize and manage a contract program to optimum advantage without the aid of a staff that is itself skilled in research and in active contact with the developments in the field.

Thus it is obvious that a large segment of the agency's attention and resources will be directed toward basic research. Since the number of problems (political, scientific, technical, military, economic, etc.) that must be explored in the areas of arms control and disarmament is extremely large, there is little likelihood that the agency will exhaust existing research possibilities in the foreseeable future. One special problem on which research will be begun, extended, and expanded when progress on disarmament is made will deal with methods to ensure that the United States economy can adjust to the impact of reductions in defense expenditures.

Ultimately, the participation of the agency in negotiations depends on international developments, particularly on the willingness of the Soviet Union to negotiate on reasonable terms. It is anticipated that negotiations on disarmament will be resumed in some form as a result of the decisions approved at the current session of the United Nations General Assembly. In the meantime, the agency is providing support and guidance to United States Representatives regarding those items relating to arms control and disarmament on the agenda of the current session of the Assembly. Consequently, it appears that the agency will be directly involved in negotiations for some time.

Summary

In fulfilling all these functions, there is no doubt that the new Arms Control and Disarmament Agency will do much to solve the basic problem of inadequate disarmament research. It should also act as a powerful counsel for a new approach to peace within the executive branch of government. Its resources and expertise will give it a new status and a new force in policy-making. It is by no means certain, however, that other basic weaknesses in organization have been corrected.

The two most important points to watch involve the problem of coordination and the problem of perspective. The first is one problem which the new agency has been designed to solve. The legislation established an instrument intended to bring together the varying opinions of the armament and diplomatic agencies in the government. Whether or not the director has been given sufficient status to do the job—or indeed, whether it is possible to achieve a new approach and new reconciliation at all—will be tested in the months ahead. As new disarmament proposals are brought forward, it is a fair assumption that sincere and dedicated men in the Department of Defense and in the Atomic Energy Commission will judge that given proposals are dangerous or that they conflict with their own views of how American security can best be protected. When these conflicts occur, the agency will have to withstand both a great deal of internal pressure and—if the future follows the past—a great deal of external pressure.

This is to be expected, however. A more subtle and difficult problem involves the very nature of bureaucracy and negotiation. The personnel of the new agency is charged with both a day-to-day negotiating responsibility and a more abstract research responsibility. In melding the functions of the disarmament negotiations and of disarmament research, two conflicting pressures have been built into the very core of the agency. The power that its negotiating function adds carries with it a new danger. Men faced with the details of specific proposals, with the need to maintain face, with the necessity of formulating instructions under pressure, become imbued with a more narrow and limited view of problems than do those able to think and study the situation from outside the area squeezed by the heavy pressure of events. The new agency is the marriage of a negotiating and a research agency. Ideally, it will take the best of both worlds and blend the two viewpoints to produce practical proposals that are confident and bold, with the understanding that comes from expert knowledge and perspective. Inevitably, however, and despite new research, the danger exists that the agency will be dominated by men whose views are formed and narrowed under pressure. If this happens, the challenging new "agency of peace" may become just another negotiating arm of the executive. The problems of overcoming these and a myriad other obstacles in the path of a new approach to peace and disarmament now rest on the shoulders of McCloy's eminently qualified successor, William C. Foster.

REFERENCES

1. Saville Davis, "Recent Policy Making in the United States Government," *Dædalus,* Fall 1960, p. 959.

2. *Ibid.,* p. 957.

ARTHUR I. WASKOW

The Evolution of American Military Doctrine

THREE MAJOR CHANGES in world political and military relations since 1945 have given enormous power to the American armed forces. The United States emerged from World War II with a greatly increased role in world affairs; military technology developed a weapon immensely more destructive than those of the recent past; and the Department of Defense drew from both World War II and the Cold War increasing influence within government and society. For the first time in American history, therefore, the officers of the armed forces have come to regard themselves as makers, rather than instruments, of policy. It is scarcely surprising that the officers have felt an urgent need to develop new military strategies.

In their new pre-eminence, the armed forces have been able to call on intellectuals to work with them in exploring the possibilities of revising military doctrine in the atomic age. The techniques of "gaming," "operations research," and "systems analysis" have been applied to questions of military strategy. Thus the tools of mathematics and controlled small-group experimentation have been brought to bear on the problems of complex social systems. Yet for most of the period since 1945, the questions posed have been asked by the armed forces: the officers, rather than the intellectuals, have defined the issues and determined the problems to be studied.

The Department of Defense, far from being monolithic, contains a number of interests that are partly or entirely opposed to one another. The resulting struggles, coalitions, and compromises have developed in such a way that not one but three basic strategies have evolved. Two assumptions are common to all three: they presuppose the continued relevance and usefulness of the United States' possession of armed forces and they look toward the use of such a force to "deter" other nations from using their military forces in certain ways.

Though one of the goals of any army has always been to deter the opponents from fighting, since 1945 it has become paramount for American military planners. The reason is not hard to find. Before 1945 the American armed forces assumed that a war could be won if the United States fought well enough, or that it could be fought to a stalemate (as in the War of 1812) if the enemy were quite strong, or—at the remotely conceivable worst—it could be lost with honor. Military men, therefore, could think in terms of victory, defense, and (though never seriously considered) surrender.

Because of the new technology, the situation has changed since 1945. Military men have come to realize that it is possible to conceive of some wars that could not be fought to either victory, stalemate, or surrender. Because of nuclear technology, one can imagine a war after which the nation itself would not remain. Such a war would absolutely have to be deterred. American military power must be so disposed as to prevent such a war from even beginning.

All strategists seem to agree that the kind of war that must be deterred without fail is the all-out thermonuclear war: by H-bombing the entire American population, it would leave virtually every American dead or dying of blast, fire, radiation, or the starvation and disease that would follow the total disruption of our society. At that point, agreement stops. Whether other kinds of wars must also be deterred in order to prevent the all-out war, and how this can be done, are questions that divide military men into three schools of strategy.

One cluster of opinions in the present debate on deterrence centers around a major distinction between fighting a thermonuclear war against a population, and fighting one against the enemy's atomic forces. The strategy of deterrence built on this distinction argues that it is possible to fight a "counterforce" thermonuclear war in which much of the populations and the social fabric of the warring powers would remain intact: only military targets would be struck.

If such a war were fought, the counterforce strategists argue that it would be an "acceptable" war, in the sense that American society could face its survival and renewal after the war as a grim but "acceptable" prospect. These strategists agree that to prevent a counterforce war from taking place at all would be preferable, and that the most likely way of preventing it would be to prepare to win it. They admit, however, that in such a war the damage to the United

States would be unprecedentedly high, and therefore they sometimes refer to "prevailing" rather than winning it. To prevail would mean the defense of vital American interests and the destruction of the enemy's capacity to interfere with those interests; depending on the way the war went, it might mean accepting the enemy's surrender, or our simply surviving as a nation while the enemy nation had its military teeth drawn.

In counterforce thinking, it is important to note the relation between the "likelihood" and the "acceptability" of thermonuclear war. Most counterforce strategists believe, now that the knowledge behind the H-bomb and the actual possession of it has spread to a number of antagonistic powers, especially to the Sino-Soviet bloc, that some kind of thermonuclear war is quite likely. Since they consider that an all-out war with H-bombs raining on great cities and a thick fallout poisoning the countryside might well demolish the American state, they have tried to conceive of and prepare for a thermonuclear war that would not be so universally destructive. Since they regard some sort of thermonuclear war as likely and a controlled counterforce version of it as "acceptable," they insist that a military system capable of winning or at least prevailing in such a war must be built.

Counterforce strategists apply the view that war must without fail be deterred and that "defense" is meaningless to only one kind of war—a total thermonuclear catastrophe. For all lesser forms of war, including a counterforce thermonuclear war, they believe "defense" is still possible and necessary. In a sense, counterforce strategy comes nearest to the classical American assumption that a war can be won, even one kind of thermonuclear war. Counterforce strategists are sometimes charged with making thermonuclear war more likely by making it more "acceptable," but their belief that such wars would be likely anyway arms them against that charge.

Neither the historical roots nor the concrete proposals of counterforce strategy can be understood without reference to its flesh-and-blood supporters in the Defense Department. The theory is most strongly affirmed in the Air Force, though some officers in the other services accept it. In a historical sense, the connection of counterforce theory with the Air Force may seem surprising, since from 1945 to 1958 the Air Force argued that its atomic capability should be ready for "massive retaliation" against enemy cities. But both positions are explicable in terms of the weapons systems available to the Air Force, changes in world military relationships, and

Air Force expertise in atomic strategy. From Hiroshima on, the Air Force held control of American atomic capability, which was concentrated in the Strategic Air Command, a fleet of bombers ready to drop atomic weapons on enemy cities. After 1958, the Air Force had to face a new factor: the Soviet Union's possession of hydrogen weapons, a bomber fleet capable of delivering them, and an even more frightening potentiality in the field of missiles.

Air Force strategists* by 1958 had become habituated to the concept of atomic warfare, inured to its likelihood, and skilled in its potentialities. They reacted to the Soviet capability, not by deciding it meant that thermonuclear war was too dangerous for the United States to consider, but by working out a refinement of thermonuclear war which they hoped would not be too dangerous. Thus counterforce theory was born, from consultation among Air Force officers, some scholars on contract to the Air Force through the RAND Corporation, and officials in industries serving Air Force needs. The theory was tailored to fit the characteristics of weapons the Air Force either already had or was looking forward to having: the B-58 and B-70 bombers, Atlas, Titan, and Minuteman missiles, the U-2 and reconnaissance satellites, and an atom-powered plane.

From its insight into the possibilities of these weapons, the Air Force has constructed several models of what several wars might be like. The dominant characteristic of all the models is that, in such a war, they assume an intense self-control on the part of both sides, a self-control based on a coldly rationalistic analysis of self-interest.

The Air Force suggests that war is most likely to start through the Soviet bloc's launching a major atomic strike at the United States and attempting a maximum destruction of the American atomic striking force. With what was left of its atomic forces, the United States would have to return the blow. The major decision would be whether to retaliate against Communist cities or Communist forces. An attack against cities would leave enemy atomic forces intact for a second blow, and this blow would retaliate on American cities for the annihilation of Communist cities. Since American cities cannot be adequately protected from H-bomb attack, such a return blow would destroy American society. For that reason, the Air Force would aim the American retaliatory attack at

* When "Air Force," "Navy," or "Army" is used to describe a particular strategic opinion, it should be taken to mean, not that the service adopts the opinion as its official view, but that the view dominates the thinking of the officers of that service.

Soviet atomic missile and bomber bases, with the aim of smashing as much as possible of the Soviet thermonuclear capability without destroying Soviet society.

The hope is that this American return strike would reduce the enemy atomic forces below the threshold of their continued capability to act effectively. If there remained enough American atomic capability to threaten enemy cities effectively, the United States could demand and receive a surrender. If the American atomic force were also knocked out of commission, the war would end in a stalemate that would preserve a continuing, if somewhat damaged, American society. But if the enemy by striking first had incapacitated the American atomic force while preserving its own effectiveness, the United States might have to surrender.

Counterforce strategists argue that the initial Communist attack would be directed at American forces, not cities, for reasons that are a mirror image of American reasons for striking back at forces, not cities. In other words, the Communists would fear that an attack on American cities that left our forces intact would be punished by a direct attack on their cities that would destroy their society. Counterforce theorists therefore argue that each side would find it in its own interest to take extreme care to restrict its attack.

This belief in self-control leads counterforce strategists to insist that American society would not be irreparably damaged by such a war. These strategists estimate that up to 30 million Americans might die, but they regard this as an "acceptable" blow. They believe that after absorbing such a blow the United States (and Communist governments also) would still be able, by carefully rationalistic calculations, to attempt to minimize destruction. They believe it likely that neither side would try to destroy the other's capital and its government, since each side would want to have the other's authorities intact, able to negotiate or surrender.

What basic requirements would our weapon systems have to meet, in order to be able to fight such a second-strike counterforce war? American thermonuclear weapons would have to be made relatively "invulnerable" in order to survive the first enemy attack. American weapons would have to be powerful enough to destroy enemy atomic forces even if they were heavily protected so as to make them invulnerable. The American population would have to be actually separated from the American forces, so as to sustain as little damage as possible. This separation would involve a physical distance between cities and missile or airplane bases, but it would also require protection against fallout for the city populations.

The Air Force has yet another model of the kind of war it might be called on to fight. It might begin with a major Communist attack on some area only slightly less crucial to American defense than the United States itself—for example, an invasion of the industrial centers of Western Europe or Japan. Or the Communists might provoke an American response in some lesser way—for example, the occupation of West Berlin or a Communist revolution in a strategic Latin American country. In such cases, the Air Force argues that the United States should use its thermonuclear striking power first to try to make the Communists back down, and then punish them if they refuse. The Air Force argues that the American thermonuclear threat or attack might be scaled according to the size of the Communist provocation. The United States, not the Soviet Union, would be the first to use thermonuclear weapons; but it would carefully control the size of the attack, ranging from a large-scale punishment for a Russian invasion of Western Europe to a threat against a single city as punishment for their capturing Berlin.

As in the case of the American second strike, this American first strike with the H-bomb would have to be directed against the enemy's atomic forces. In addition, enemy cities, or a few of them, might be attacked, to punish the enemy for his earlier provocation. But the United States could not afford to attack one of the enemy's cities in punishment for his attack on West Berlin, or ten of his cities in punishment for invading Western Europe, yet leave all the enemy's own thermonuclear striking force capable of striking back. Such a course would invite the retaliatory destruction of some American cities.

In this "punitive" or "counterforce-plus" war, since the United States would be the first to use thermonuclear weapons, not all its weapons would have to be invulnerable; many of them would be fired first, and would not need to survive an enemy first strike against them. At the same time, provisions for protecting city populations would be more urgent than in counterforce-only war. Although the first-strike attack on Soviet forces would aim to eliminate them, the United States could not be sure that no enemy forces whatsoever would remain. Soviet plans for weapon invulnerability would of course have been directed at ensuring the survival of some atomic capability. Thus the United States, even after a first strike, would have to fear that a desperate retaliation against some of its own cities might take place. Fallout shelters would be no protection against direct H-bomb attack, and therefore, if this model of war were to be made possible, the United States would have to go much further in protecting its population. For this reason, a punitive war would require preparation for a pre-attack evacuation of Americans from the large cities into huge blast-proof shelters previously dug under rural areas. Counterforce-plus war would presumably make it unnecessary for the United States to possess a large limited-war army, since the attacks such armies are meant to repel would be punished instead by thermonuclear means.

There is a pervasive belief in all counterforce strategy that certain sorts of thermonuclear war can be fought on the nineteenth-century assumption that wars can be won; that a predominant fighting force is necessary to win the war; that fighting forces can be kept distinct from the nation; and that with self-control the nation can parry with its fighting forces, as a dueler wields his sword.

In these nineteenth-century assumptions, counterforce strategy seems not to take into account certain special characteristics of thermonuclear weapons. The assumed separation of people and forces is unlikely to be maintained, since thermonuclear technology makes the weapon revolutions that would make war "total" and destroy even "protected" populations both cheap and easy. The extreme self-control and extreme rationality that are presumed are unlikely to be maintained, since thermonuclear technology destroys communications, prevents the assessment of one's own or the enemy's damage, and possibly even breaks down the command processes that preserve the nation-state. Finally, the potentially decisive character of a first strike with thermonuclear weapons against forces is likely to press any nation that sees another in a counterforce posture to pre-empt the enemy's first strike.

The second major strategy of deterrence is built on the belief that any thermonuclear war may easily become a total thermonuclear war, and that all thermonuclear wars must therefore be prevented. Supporters of this view have decided that "to win" or "to lose" any thermonuclear war is inconceivable, and that any such war will end in the destruction of American society. They believe that there exists no alternative to deterring all thermonuclear war, and they do not believe that preparing to fight such a war to a mythical "victory" will in fact prevent it.

Having accepted the idea that any thermonuclear war will be a total disaster, these strategists believe in deterring it by making absolutely clear to all the world that such a war could not possibly have any result but total disaster. They propose to do this by deliberately increasing the terror of such a war to the *n*th power, thus making it as nearly unfightable as possible. These strategists hope that making thermonuclear wars unfightable will result in the elimination of all but limited wars fought with "tactical" atomic weapons or conventional weapons. They believe that in the classical sense such wars can be won, and that they can be deterred by preparing to win them. In order to do this, they regard the preparation of American and Western capabilities for fighting limited wars as necessary.

Because this program requires the creation of an extremely powerful thermonuclear deterrent on the one hand and of a limited-war capability on the other, it is often called the balanced deterrent. Strategists of the balanced deterrent hope to rule out the more fantastic developments of mid-twentieth century war, and thus to return to the military situation of 1945. The strategy of the balanced deterrent appeals to the officers of the older services, the Army and Navy. It is in those two services that the strongest attempt has been made to restrict war to traditional naval and military actics. But the Army and Navy believe that keeping war restricted now requires that one kind of war be clearly recognized as unrestricted and unrestrictable. Balanced-deterrent strategists therefore believe that the United States should deliberately direct its thermonuclear power in such a way as to threaten the destruction of the whole society of any enemy. They argue that our H-bombs and missiles should be aimed directly at the cities of the Sino-Soviet alliance.

This argument is especially interesting in the historical context, since for many years after 1945 the Navy argued that it was immoral to plan a war that would kill hundreds of millions of civilians; but the Navy now holds that only by planning such a war can this kind of war be deterred, and the original moral intention carried out. This shift in opinion is traceable to the period around 1958, when several factors led the Navy to re-examine its position. First of all, the Soviet Union came into its own as a thermonuclear power capable of destroying the United States. The Navy responded by envisaging the possibility of a mutual stalemate in which neither side could afford to use thermonuclear weapons for fear the other would retaliate. Second, the Navy itself began to grasp the possibilities in the possession of its own thermonuclear weapons. Like the Air Force when it first held control of atomic weapons, the Navy regarded its early thermonuclear missiles as usable only for destroying cities. This reaction was based on the limited power of the Polaris missile, which as a half-megaton weapon could be effectively used only against cities.

Thus, almost simultaneously, the Navy first learned that it would soon possess a city-killing missile, and the Soviets first achieved their status as a thermonuclear power. The Navy saw that it could effectively function as the key deterrent service, if American strategy were directed at preventing the Soviet use of thermonuclear weapons by threatening a retaliatory use of the Navy's city-killing thermonuclear weapons.

Meanwhile, the Army had been rethinking the role of limited warfare. During the late 1940's, the Army had reluctantly begun to accept the idea that atomic weapons made the foot soldier obsolete, but the experience of Korea had shaken that assumption and provoked a re-examination of strategy. The Army came to the conclusion that during the Korean war the existence of the atomic deterrent, then in its period of Air Force city-busting, had served as an umbrella under which the limited Korean war had been fought. The Army concluded that, during a period when both alliances were equal in thermonuclear deterrence, it would be even more certain that ground warfare would come back into its own. By 1958, therefore, the Army's views approximately dovetailed with those of the Navy. Under an umbrella of thermonuclear deterrent supplied by the Navy's Polaris, the Army's ground soldiers and the Navy's marines could defend Western interests in limited wars.

Strategists of the balanced deterrent therefore examined first how to make the deterrent to thermonuclear war virtually absolute. They concluded that if both the United States and its chief enemies should have great masses of populations open to atomic attack—in a sense, being held as hostages—and if on both sides the atomic forces to mount such an attack should themselves be invulnerable, the attack would never be mounted. Their argument is that any nation which struck first in such circumstances would be condemning to death its own population, its economy, its government, its very existence. For its attack would not have been able to destroy the enemy's invulnerable atomic force, and that force would then be used to destroy its own cities and society.

The strategists of balanced deterrence argue that the existence of such an invulnerable striking force would bring all the pressure of hope and fear to bear against any idea of a first atomic strike. They thus argue that the invulnerable deterrent, with vulnerable populations, would stabilize the international situation. Instead of pressing both sides toward a pre-emptive attack, the invulnerable deterrent would impel both sides to think long and hard before attacking. In addition, the argument runs, this situation would constitute a plateau in the arms race. It is suggested that, when both sides reach the level of the invulnerable deterrent, they can tacitly agree to arrest the arms build-up while they attempt to negotiate outstanding difficulties.

The Navy believes that the "invulnerable deterrent" is its Polaris submarine, driven by atomic motors and armed with thermonuclear missiles. The argument is that the Polaris can cruise the oceans of the earth in secrecy, invulnerable to enemy attack, itself ready to strike but with every incentive not to do so, unless the United States is struck first. By its very separation from the land masses and population centers of America, the Polaris would avoid attracting an attack against the continental United States, for such an attack would have no purpose if it left the Polaris still capable of striking. While the Polaris guaranteed a weapon invulnerability, the vulnerability of populations would be assured by avoiding any program of valid civil defense.

To deter or answer a provocation less than an all-out war, strategists of the balanced-deterrent viewpoint look to tactical forces. The wide range of possible provocations on the one hand might include an invasion of Western Europe by the Soviet Union, and on the other, military aid to Communist or pro-Communist rebels in the Middle East, Africa, or Latin America. Naturally, differences of this size would necessitate a similar range of replies. Between them, the Army and Navy believe they can supply so wide a range that a provocation could be resisted without involving the world in thermonuclear war.

What strategists of the balanced deterrent are looking for is a modernized ability to fight comparatively limited wars, ranging from the scale of World War II to that of the Lebanese intervention or even to something like a Laotian-style infiltration. For deterring or winning such limited wars, the Army and Navy look to the historic models of the foot soldier on the spot and the fleet in being, but both the Army and the Navy believe that these models need modernization because of four important factors: (1) the dominance in numbers of the Sino-Soviet bloc as against the populations of the United States and its effective military allies; (2) the totalitarian organization of the Communist states, which permits them to conscript greater proportions of their men and resources for military uses; (3) the far-flung frontier from which Communist tactical attack might come at any moment; (4) and the development of a new Communist combined tactic of infiltration, subversion, and guerrilla warfare.

The Army and Navy have long argued that these four factors require that the mobility and the fire-power of Western tactical forces be increased, and that the numbers of these forces be increased as well. Army strategists in particular have recently added a new suggestion: that the United States develop "sublimited," commando-style capabilities to combat the guerrilla tactics of the Soviets and their allies.

On the question of mobility and numbers, there is a general agreement among the strategists of the balanced deterrent. They believe that what is needed is an airlift capability that would transport a sizable force of infantrymen to any part of the world within hours. They believe that large fleets off the shores of critical areas must be ready to land American marines at a moment's notice. They further believe that every attempt should be made to increase the numbers of allied soldiers available to integrate Western commands. It is this last requirement that has emphasized the need for building a strong German army and for increasing military aid to nations on the Communist periphery that cannot afford to support substantial armies of their own.

Both the Army and Navy have believed that increased tactical readiness would not only deter actual military invasion by Sino-Soviet forces, but also that it could deter internal subversion and revolution. The presence of the fleet "showing the flag" all across the globe, the availability of air-borne infantrymen, and the existence of powerful indigenous armies—all were thought to work against the possibility of internal Communist revolutions. The three techniques of intervention to stop invasion, intervention to halt subversion, and aid to strengthen an indigenous army against either subversion or invasion have been given concrete demonstrations in Korea, Lebanon, and Greece. In each of these cases the Army and Navy believe that they prevented Communist aims from being achieved and, by demonstrating their capacity to win, that they reduced the chances of similar Communist action elsewhere.

Recent Communist successes in areas like Northern Laos, however, have persuaded some strategists of the balanced deterrent that a new component is needed for our limited-war arsenal. They argue that the United States should train commando fighters, specialists in infiltration, for use in combatting internal subversion and revolution wherever the presence of conventional infantry or Marine battalions does not work. There is also some thought of using such especially trained personnel for carrying the attack into Communist-dominated areas, as in Eastern Europe, for example. It would be expected that such para-military fighters would make contact with disaffected elements and try to create trouble for Communist governments.

The one area in which there is considerable disagreement among strategists of the balanced deterrent is that of increased fire-power for tactical forces. Some strategists believe that the West will find it extremely difficult, despite added mobility and increased military aid, to catch up with the Sino-Soviet bloc in the number of available soldiers. They therefore believe that the West's presumed technological superiority must fill the gap and that, if it is impossible to match man for man, each Western soldier must be made the equal of several Communists. These strategists therefore believe that atomic or chemical or biological weapons must be placed in the hands of Western armies to be used against "hordes" of Sino-Soviet invaders. If this is done, they believe, the Sino-Soviet bloc will ultimately cease to be deterred from starting limited wars.

On the other hand, some strategists of the balanced deterrent believe that atomic, chemical, and biological weapons could only spread tactical war into general war. These men argue that the only observable limits are defined by the so-called conventional weapons, that once beyond this limit there is no way of stopping one side or the other from employing still more powerful weapons, up to and including the H-bomb.

With this exception on the question of fire-power, strategists of the balanced deterrent are fairly well agreed on their system. They believe it would be virtually infallible in preventing the thermonuclear war that they believe is absolutely unacceptable to mankind. They believe it can probably prevent both tactical wars and guerrilla-style subversion. Even if it fails to prevent these lesser conflicts, they argue that it will make American or Western victory possible in such situations.

The strategy of a balanced deterrent, instead of applying nineteenth-century rules to thermonuclear war, tries to return to nineteenth-century warfare by nullifying thermonuclear weapons. Nevertheless, balanced deterrence, like counterforce strategy, seems not to take into account certain characteristics of modern war. The idea of weapon invulnerability is basic to the strategy of a balanced deterrent, but technological advance is sure to destroy the invulnerability of weapons by devising new systems of detection and attack. Once invulnerability is pierced, a crucial component of balanced deterrence disappears. The other component (readiness for a limited war) forces that strategy into a dilemma. If the limited-war forces include nuclear weapons, the escalation of war to thermonuclear levels will be entirely likely. If only conventional weapons are used, the West cannot compete with populous totalitarian states without adopting totalitarianism. Thus the strategy of a balanced deterrent is unable to deal with the acceleration of modern military technology, the nature of totalitarian organization, and the problem of escalation in nuclear warfare.

The third deterrence strategy has only recently begun to be elaborated into a coherent doctrine. This third deterrent, "The Mix," demands the simultaneous possession of all the weapons proposed by the other two strategies, and argues that both the other strategies ought to be held ready for use.

"The Mix" can be most easily understood, not as a carefully reasoned doctrine, but on the basis of its origin. Officers who must try to understand and reconcile the conflicting claims of Air Force, Army, and Navy strategists often come to the conclusion that all the services are partly right, and that all their strategies and weapons deserve support. The duty of reconciling the interservice conflicts is placed squarely on the officers and civilian officials connected with the Joint Chiefs of Staff or with the central organization of the Defense Department. "The Mix" is therefore most strongly supported in these higher levels of defense planning, among the military statesmen of the Department. In addition, some officers in each of the particular services actually believe in either the pure counterforce theory or the pure balanced-deterrent theory, but think they must support "The Mix" in practice. They feel compelled to support it because they fear the effects on their careers and their ideas of demanding exclusive support for their own position. Such a demand would jeopardize the institutionalized prerogatives, the industrial allies, and the political supporters of the opposite theory. The interests jeopardized would fight back. Thus, to demand that a choice be made between the two theories might backfire. Many officers therefore publicly support "The Mix," while working to incorporate in it as much of their own program as they dare.

The supporters of "The Mix," however, have not rested content with political arguments for it. They have begun to work out a strategic theory for justifying it. Their rationale suggests that the existence of potentially unstable situations may actually guarantee stability. They hold that a defense so constructed that the results of an attack would be unpredictable is the defense most likely to deter attack. If a would-be aggressor does not know what might happen, he will stay his hand and nothing will happen. If all the capabilities —first-strike and second-strike, counterforce and countercity, tactical nuclear and conventional, limited-war and "sub-limited" guerrilla —were to coexist, this "Mix" would presumably deter attack at any level from subversion to all-out thermonuclear missilry.

In addition, supporters of "The Mix" believe that an extremely diversified ability to strike back is an excellent way to achieve invulnerability. In other words, the more wide-ranging and variegated the American military capacity, the less likely that a first strike by the Communists—even an all-out first strike—could knock out all forms of retaliation. The likelihood of retaliation would deter attack.

Finally, strategists of "The Mix" argue that it would benefit the United States even if deterrence failed and some kind of attack were mounted by the Sino-Soviet alliance. They believe "The Mix" makes possible a continued ability to choose the American response, even in the midst of war. It is this doctrine of choice that has become the major intellectual argument inside the Kennedy administration for keeping "The Mix" of weapons and strategies. The possibility of choice is enhanced by new techniques of "command and control," which would presumably allow the United States to continue the process of deterrence even after the war had begun. For example, by threatening to use a city-killing weapon system, the United States could try to force an enemy to keep its attack restricted to the counterforce level. Effective command and control might allow the use of directed and controlled punishment, rather than a "spasm war" of total retaliation.

"The Mix," like the other two strategies, seems not to take into account certain characteristics of modern war. Not only would it involve the same difficulties as its two components; it would also have some major difficulties of its own. Each component would actually destroy the advantages claimed for the other. Balanced deterrence claims the advantage of making pre-emptive attack unlikely; but the simultaneous existence of a counterforce capability would make the enemy fear that a pre-emptive strike remained possible, and it would therefore force the enemy toward pre-emption. On the other hand, counterforce strategy claims the advantage of directing the enemy's attack against American forces instead of American cities; but if the United States possessed a countercity capacity that would be hard to use against forces, the enemy could only conclude that the United States might intend to strike his cities, and his reaction would be to attack populations instead of forces. Thus the coexistence of counterforce and balanced-deterrence strategies and weapons would mean that each nullified the claimed benefits of the other.

"The Mix" is in fact a disguise behind which adherents of counterforce and balanced-deterrent strategy continue to battle. "The Mix" blurs any public understanding of the two pure strategies; it also hides the fact that they are actually not alternatives but only alternate steps on a rising escalator of destructive capacity. This escalator to oblivion is powered by the automatic pursuit of research into new military technology. The first step on the escalator is a period of high instability tied to a counterforce strategy. Then, as one side or the other catches up in the techniques of making its weapons invulnerable, there would be a second period of moderate stability and the dominance of balanced-deterrent strategies. During this period research would continue on ways to nullify weapon invulnerability, to increase the power of the weapons, and to make populations less vulnerable. When one side or the other had achieved a breakthrough in one of these techniques, a new period of extremely high instability would result, and again the counterforce strategists would dominate. But in the third period the destructiveness of the weapons, the hostilities of the peoples, and the speed of reaction would all have been heightened.

All the strategies claim to provide a deterrent that is either "stable" or "rational"; but the "stability" claimed by balanced-deterrent theorists and the "rationality" claimed by counterforce theorists are only on a superficial level. Short-run stability would lead to long-run increases in the chances of war. Short-run rationality would accomplish its own replacement by an irrational spiral. Why have the strategies failed to guarantee the deterrence at which they were aimed?

The reasons for this failure can be found in the incompatible assumptions made by both the military men who ask strategic questions and the scholars and scientists who try to answer them. The questions the military men ask have assumed the continuance of thermonuclear force as a workable part of deterrence. The analytical tools the scholars use have assumed great rationality and great self-control on the part of the nations being deterred; but these two assumptions contradict each other. So long as thermonuclear weapons exist, all major national decisions will be made in an atmosphere of crisis, under the threat of national extinction. The scholars have depended on mathematics and small-group experimentation to analyze such situations. Neither technique can help in understanding or predicting almost instantaneous decisions made under conditions of extreme emotional stress, with values at stake that are not merely high but total.

The effect of using such specialized tools is that many strategists have thought of deterrence as if it were a game; but the stakes in deterrence are the physical survival of whole peoples, the continuity of their societies as going concerns, and their nations' political independence. Will those who play for such stakes remain immune to the enormous pressures of hope and fear? In the real world, frightened by unprecedented catastrophe in the offing, men and nations may not react in any rationally predictable way. What is likely to happen at the height of an extreme and vital international crisis?

At such a moment, when deterrence is most needed, there is some evidence that deterrence disappears. As is generally recognized, deterrence exists in the minds of the major policy-makers of the nations deterred. There is evidence that under conditions of extreme and growing tension, the major decision-makers in every great power become unable to pay attention to the warnings, the threats, the deterrents of their potential enemies. That was what happened in the summer of 1914, when the Allies and the Central Powers tried by mobilizing their full strength to deter each other from going to war. In 1914, however, the only information that officials had enough time and energy to accept was information about their own nation's capabilities and preparations. When their attention could no longer be fixed on the threat of retaliation, deterrence failed. In the game model, it is unnecessary to face this problem of the height of the crisis, because the crises in games do not drive the players to irrational acts or to acting as if the other players had disappeared.

The game atmosphere has also made it seem to defense theorists that both sides must be "playing" the same version of Deterrence. One does not expect that one's opponent in chess or poker is playing on different premises, with different rules, and with different goals; but in the real world of Deterrence, a number of very different societies confront each other on the atomic frontier. What seems rational to one may not be at all rational to the others. A capability that in Soviet hands deters us would not necessarily deter the Soviets if it were in our hands. Yet the three deterrents depend essentially on the premise of symmetry. In actuality, one side may not respond as the other side expects.

Might there occur responses that did not obey the "rules" of Deterrence? If they did, this might indicate irrationality in the leadership of another state. None of the three strategies could prevent a war if the leadership of an atomic power were to become irrational. In a sense this problem of deterring all forms of rational and irrational violence is the problem of "trust." The three deterrents are built on an enormous trust in the intentions of any opponents. Trust is not surprising in the context of a game. In a game a player does not expect his opponent to "cheat," and if he does, one simply stops playing. But to stop playing Deterrence is to go to war. The three strategies assume that the opponent will play according to the rules; that he will not respond to an attack on his atomic forces with an attack on cities; or that some astonishing development in his government will not lead him to use his arms regardless of the threatened retaliation with invulnerable weapons. In none of the three deterrence strategies is there any proposal for enforcement, other than dependence on what is presumably the self-interest of the other parties. In a game that is sufficient, since the parties are playing more for the sake of playing than to win. But when the stakes are extremely high—in other words, in the real world of Deterrence—trust must be avoided as far as possible.

All three strategies assume that decision-making processes inside each nation are reasonably simple and that governments competing for high stakes in periods of great crisis would remain rational. All three trust all the governments to react "rationally"—that is, as we want and expect them to act—to control their own reactions, and to abide the arms race without growing impatient, unstable, or irrational. Nevertheless, these assumptions, reasonable as they may have been under the nineteenth-century conditions when no nation was staking its existence, are incompatible with thermonuclear technology. Questions asked by military men who assume the continued existence of the H-bomb cannot be answered by research in the game model.

The presuppositions of those seeking a new military doctrine for the atomic age have frustrated the search for new doctrine. As frequently happens in intellectual development, however, the ideas have begun to develop a head of steam of their own. Scholars who have been using the various new techniques have themselves begun to question the assumptions under which they were working and to define strategic problems without regard to those assumptions.

Three major directions of recent research suggest the possible fruitfulness of digging beneath these assumptions. The first direction makes the least break with military presuppositions, since it proposes the preservation of military force under controls. Although the label "arms control" covers a multitude of different ideas, in general it means some version of the balanced deterrent, together with some level of international inspection, to prevent either side from taking an escalator-step up from the balanced deterrent to counterforce strategy. By preserving the weapons (which could still be used by desperate or irrational men despite the inspectors), "arms control" would still assume a rational self-interest on the part of governments even during crisis. But by setting up inspection systems, "arms control" would somewhat reduce the amount of trust each nation would have to place in its enemy.

The second direction of recent research has been the serious examination of total disarmament and the "systems analysis" of what would be necessary to bring it about and to keep it stable. This new strategy avoids the game analogy by accepting human irrationality and lack of self-control. It insists that these facts of life require the elimination of thermonuclear weapons, and it suggests that the elimination of the weapons, by reducing the proportions of crisis, would reduce the amount of government irrationality. Total disarmament with inspection virtually eliminates the necessity of trusting the enemy.

Finally, out of concern with military strategy there has grown an interest in the basic theory of conflict. Recent examples of this kind of research are Kenneth Boulding's investigation of the pure theory of the defense of systems (biological and political) and Anatol Rapoport's discussion of the similarities and differences between games and fights as special areas of conflict. This development of a theoretical concern with conflict and its resolution offers a long-term hope for a more adequate understanding of effective deterrence and of other possible strategies aimed at eliminating war.

REFERENCES

N. B. This paper is based on a series of interviews with military and civilian officials of the Department of Defense.

For a more detailed exposition and critique of the three strategies, see Arthur I. Waskow, *The Limits of Defense* (Garden City: Doubleday, 1962). For defenses of each particular strategy, see the following: for counterforce, Richard Fryklund, *100 Million Lives* (New York: Macmillan, 1962); for balanced deterrence, see Oskar Morgenstern, *The Questions of National Defense* (New York: Random House, 1959); Henry A. Kissinger, *The Necessity for Choice* (New York: Harper, 1960); and George E. Lowe, "Balanced Forces or Counterforce—Does It Make a Difference?" *United States Naval Institute Proceedings,* April 1962, *88:* 23; for "The Mix," see Herman Kahn, *On Thermonuclear War* (Princeton: Princeton University Press, 1960), and Robert S. McNamara, Secretary of Defense, Address to the American Bar Foundation, (mimeographed), Chicago, 17 February 1962.

For a discussion of the "gaming" approach to strategy, see Thomas C. Schelling, *The Strategy of Conflict* (Cambridge: Harvard University Press, 1960), and for critiques of that approach, see Sir Solly Zuckerman, "Judgment and Control in Modern Warfare," *Foreign Affairs,* 1962, *40:* 196-212, and Michael Maccoby, "Social Psychology of Deterrence," *Bulletin of the Atomic Scientists,* 1961, *17:* 278-281.

For examples of the systematic-strategic approach to arms control and disarmament, see Donald Brennan (ed.) *Arms Control, Disarmament, and National Security* (New York: George Braziller, 1961); Seymour Melman (ed.) *Inspection for Disarmament* (New York: Columbia University Press, 1959); and Amitai Etzioni, *The Hard Way to Peace* (New York: Collier, 1962). The books referred to as explorations of the pure theory of conflict are: Kenneth Boulding, *Conflict and Defense* (New York: Harper, 1962), and Anatol Rapoport, *Fights, Games, and Debates* (Ann Arbor: University of Michigan Press, 1960).

HERBERT RITVO

Internal Divisions on Disarmament in the USSR

SPEAKING TO the new graduates of the Soviet military academies (8 July 1961), as has been his wont in recent years, Nikita S. Khrushchev, the head of the Soviet Party-State, announced that the 1961 defense funds would be increased by 3,144 million rubles. This sudden escalation of budgetary military expenditures by one-third, from 9,255 million to 12,399 million rubles, in the final six months of the year was coupled with the suspension of the reduction in the armed forces begun in January 1960. The Supreme Soviet, which met on 6 December, less than a month before the fiscal year closed, then granted post *de facto* approval to the additional disbursement and hailed the cessation of demobilization as unanimously and as enthusiastically as it had confirmed the highly publicized cuts of 1960-1961.

For the First Secretary-Chairman of the Council of Ministers, who had identified himself first as the proponent of lower military spending and less manpower in 1960, and eighteen months later as the herald of large increments, the belated consent of the nominally necessary legislative assembly was hardly more than a parliamentary formality. Khrushchev, as could have been safely predicted, received the same "prolonged applause" from the predominantly civilian deputies in December as he had obtained from the officer graduates six months earlier. For the latter, the funds already expended without legislative consent meant more "guns" for their soldiers, although Marshal Malinovsky subsequently set limits to their expectations:

> I declare with a full sense of responsibility as Minister of Defense of the USSR . . . that we are at present stronger . . . and we are not going to stand still. We have no special need for increasing the numerical strength of our rocket forces and our weapon stocks. The next stage is no longer the stockpiling of weapons, but their routine perfection and renewal of stocks [*Pravda,* 24 January 1962].

To the deputies, who confirmed the slightly higher 1962 military budget (13,410 million rubles), the heavier investments in armaments were tantamount to a renunciation, partial at least, of promises of "butter" for their constituents, despite Khrushchev's assurances six months earlier that the 1962 expenditures would not exceed the upward revision of 1961:

> Soviet citizens might be interested in the question of whether it is necessary to allocate even greater funds for strengthening our armed forces. . . . According to the preliminary opinion taking shape in the Central Committee and the Government, this is unnecessary. The funds already appropriated for the strengthening of the defenses of our homeland and the armaments already built or being built are sufficient for us [*Pravda*, 7 August 1961].

In the same speech in which Khrushchev explained the strategic concepts underlying demobilization (14 January 1960), he had proclaimed to the Supreme Soviet—and to a world-wide audience—that the leaders of the first nation to resume nuclear tests "will cover themselves with shame and they will be condemned by the peoples of the world." Less than two years later, at a time when President Kennedy was under increasing pressure from protesting scientists and military advisors, Khrushchev announced the unilateral cessation of the 36-month moratorium, one of the most successful Soviet propaganda initiatives of the postwar period. The resumption of tests, which followed immediately over an 8-week period, was climaxed by the explosion of a 55-megaton bomb; but instead of bowing contritely to his own sense of shame, Khrushchev boasted, at the XXIInd Congress on two occasions (17 October and 27 October) of the success of Soviet nuclear weaponry.

Although the Soviet public was not informed of the progress of the testing, there is no doubt that the highly propaganda-conditioned masses had understood the announcement of 31 August of the end of the moratorium as the beginning of the tests. Thus even in Smolensk letters were already being published the next day from workers, who recognized that "in the name of peace on earth, we are carrying out experimental explosions of nuclear weapons," and from peasants, who had as speedily comprehended "that in the name of peace, experimental explosions of nuclear weapons are being carried out" (*Smena*, 1 September 1961). Within days, in the words of *Izvestia* (3 September), "a wave of enthusiastic meetings has swept the country from the Baltic to the Pacific . . . [as] the working people in all parts of the Soviet Union have been unanimously approving the timely and indispensable decision on the temporary deferment [of demobilization] . . . and on the staging of nuclear weapon test explosions." From the factories where workers appealed to their trade-union leaders to seek permission to return to an eight-hour work day (*Trud*, 3 September) to the barracks, where soldiers "warmly approved" the indefinite extension of their service (Radio Volga, 2 September), the propaganda chorus resounded without a single discordant note.

By the end of the Congress, the Soviet people had been informed in gruesome detail about the crimes of Stalin and some of their other former leaders; they had learned nothing (except from foreign broadcasts) about the extent of the series of nuclear-bomb explosions which had poisoned the atmosphere and had shaken the whole world. Those in the West, who write an "open letter to the Russian people," calling on them "by whatever means to make your wishes known to your government in the interests of a common humanity and the cause of genuine peace," have failed to realize how completely controlled public opinion has remained under Khrushchev—despite his reliance on incomparably less coercion and terror than Stalin exerted to induce conformity.

It is therefore not surprising to learn that in the first publicized poll of the newly organized Public Opinion Institute (Institut Obshchestvenogo Mneniya) 968 of the 1,000 persons interviewed gave an affirmative answer to the question on which all disarmament discussions depend: "Will mankind succeed in averting a war?" Only slightly less than the percentages obtained in Soviet-style elections, this response should perhaps be regarded merely as the propagandistic projection of the universal hope of the Soviet people, rather than as their realistic appraisal of the present and the immediate future. Exploiting these fervently held desires (if not expectations) for peace, the Soviet leadership from Lenin to Khrushchev has waged what it calls a "relentless struggle against war," while creating in a remarkably short period of time one of the world's most powerful military machines. From the Soviet masses who, the poll states, "unanimously support the foreign policy of the Communist Party and the Soviet government aimed at the affirmation of the ideas of peaceful coexistence," there will be no overt dissent to proposals for disarmament, general or partial (see the Appendix); but, whereas their almost universal approval can be taken for granted, their influence on political decisions is practically nonexistent.

At the other extreme, the summit of the Party-State hierarchy, where all powers of deciding policy are concentrated under the Soviet system, substantive disputes, directly and indirectly related to the struggle for personal power, are the rule. In fact, the history of the post-Stalin period, as now presented in the victor's version, has been an uninterrupted series of violent controversies covering every aspect of Soviet society, from agriculture and industry to art and ideology. The methods employed to resolve these controversies range (again according to Khrushchev) from permanent solution by shooting on the spot (Beria; see the *New York Times,* 19 November 1961, and *Atlas,* March 1962) to an unprecedented appeal to the Central Committee to prevent "a temporary majority" in the Party Presidium from removing the First Secretary in June 1957. Because disarmament as a specific issue of intra-Party dispute had not been mentioned previously, the following long excerpt from Mikoyan's attack on Molotov at the XXIInd Congress warrants careful consideration:

> These differences with the conservative-dogmatist group were not just differences on some particular organizational or separate political questions. No; they concerned the definition of the party's entire policy at the new stage of historic development—in fact, its basic policy line.
>
> . . . under present conditions we were concerned not merely with organizational measures but with evolving a policy which could insure a successful building of Communism in our country and which would make it possible to avert a world war.
>
> Indeed, before the XXth Congress [7 February 1955] Molotov, in a report at a session of the USSR Supreme Soviet, openly cast doubt on the fact of the building of a socialist society in the USSR.
>
> Under the influence of criticism in the Central Committee, Molotov was forced to justify himself in the pages of *Kommunist,* reducing the question to mistaken formulation. But it was not a matter of mistaken formulation. It is clear that, if only the foundations of socialism have been built, the question of transition to the comprehensive building of Communism cannot even be posed. If only some people's democracies have taken the first steps toward socialism, this means that the world socialist system has still not been formed, and consequently one cannot speak about its growing influence on the course of public development.
>
> This was a basically mistaken, un-Leninist appraisal of the distribution of the class and political forces in the modern world. By minimizing the forces of socialism, and thereby exaggerating the forces of imperialism, Molotov was led to serious mistakes in questions of international development, of peaceful coexistence, of the possibility of preventing a world war, and of the diversity of the forms of transition of various countries to socialism.
>
> Molotov altogether rejects the policy of peaceful coexistence, reducing

this concept merely to a state of peace, or rather to the absence of war at a given moment, and to a negation of the possibility of preventing a world war. In substance, this view was close to that of the foreign opponents of peaceful coexistence, treating it as a variant of the cold war, as a state of armed peace. A concept of this sort contradicts the Leninist concept of relations between two systems; it would lead to a rejection of the extensive development of economic relations between them, to decreasing contacts and cultural ties. Finally, this would be a factual acknowledgement of the unavoidability of war, a repudiation of active efforts at reaching agreement, directed toward easing international tension and to disarmament. And it is not accidental that he rejects the historic tenet of the XXth Congress on the possibility of preventing a world war in the modern era [*Pravda,* 24 October 1961].

Molotov's long-time Politburo comrade was not the only speaker at the Congress to attack the already defeated ideological spokesman of the "anti-Party group." A less known contemporary, the present head of the Marx-Engels Institute, P. Pospelov, also added some virulent supplementary remarks:

Molotov had opposed the extremely important principle of the XXth Congress on the possibility of averting a new world war in the contemporary epoch. Molotov is against the idea expressed in the final section of the Party Program that Communism will triumph not through war but by the form of example. . . . According to him Communism can win new followers by war, but this is precisely what our greatest enemies impute to us. This is exactly the "big lie" of imperialist propaganda about the Soviet Union's alleged intention of promoting the spread of Communism in other countries by war and not by the force of example. . . . This is clear dogmatism or ignorance. . . . This is obtuse, factionalist obstinacy . . . his own putrid anti-Leninist line [*Pravda,* 26 October 1961].

Almost immediately a junior member of the Central Committee, the editor of *Pravda,* revealed that in a letter Molotov had branded the new Party program "antirevolutionary, revisionist, and pacifist in spirit," because it included new theoretical principles which took into account a rapidly changing world situation (*Pravda,* 27 October 1961). On the same subject a functionary of the Agit-Prop Department of the Central Committee in a post-Congress commentary furnished a few more details:

Molotov and others . . . cannot or do not wish to understand the most profound shifts which have taken place in world affairs, and they seek to push the Party on to an adventurist path. . . . Hopeless dogmatists like Molotov recognize . . . only one kind of bond . . . armed outside intervention in the developing class struggle in the capitalist countries . . . [which is] an appeal to unleash a world war [T. Timofeyev, *World Economics and International Affairs,* 1961, No. 11].

Although it must be assumed that Molotov's views—no others are usually named in this context[1]—are distorted and oversimplified, there can be little doubt that Khrushchev's reinterpretation of Lenin's and Stalin's doctrines on temporary "peaceful coexistence" and "the inevitability of war" became the core of the intra-Party ideological debate, an integral part of the struggle that also involves the question of the revelation of Stalin's crimes and the responsibility of some of his accomplices which had simultaneously formed the crux of the personal struggle for power. This revision, under way as early as 1954 (see A. Leontiev, *Kommunist,* No. 13, September 1954), received its formal theoretical refurbishing at the XXth Party Congress in February 1956, *after* the conclusion of the protracted debate in the military press in which the primacy of nuclear weapons in Soviet strategic thinking was established (see Herbert Dinerstein, *War and the Soviet Union,* New York, 1958; and Raymond Garthof, *Soviet Strategy in the Nuclear Age,* New York, 1958). Its extension from the formulation used in 1956 and in 1957 ("It is now realistically possible to prevent war") to the formula introduced at the XXIst Congress in 1959 ("It is possible even before the full victory of socialism in the world, while capitalism continues to exist in part of the world, to banish world war from the life of society") brought this critical issue into the arena of international Communism, where the 1959 wording was firmly rejected by the Chinese and Albanian parties (Richard Lowenthal, "Diplomacy and Revolution," in *The Sino-Soviet Dispute,* New York, 1961, p. 13). Its connection with disarmament is best shown in the violent reaction of the Albanians to the Khrushchev-inspired proposal for the Balkans:

> . . . let us take the problem of disarmament. It is known to all that our government has supported the USSR proposal for general and complete disarmament, because as long as weapons exist and the arms race continues, as long as general and complete disarmament has not been achieved, peace will not be assured.
>
> Our government has wholeheartedly supported and does now support the decision of the Soviet Government to resume nuclear tests as a very important step indispensable to the security of the USSR and the whole socialist camp. We realize that the problem of disarmament is a delicate one, requiring great efforts and also a resolute and uncompromising struggle on the part of socialist countries and all peace-loving forces to impose it upon imperialism. Instead of following this correct path, N. Khrushchev seeks to disarm a socialist country surrounded on all sides by enemies, as Albania is.

By weakening the defensive force of Albania, he harms not only the interests of our country but those of the whole socialist camp.

And all this is happening when the United States Sixth Fleet comes and goes in the Mediterranean like a dragon, while United States rocket bases are installed in Greece and Italy, while NATO forces feverishly continue the arms race, while West German revanchists rattle their sabres and seriously threaten world peace.

The Albanian Government was neither at fault nor responsible for this. In any event, N. Khrushchev should in no way have reached the point of openly inciting the imperialists and various reactionaries against a socialist country such as Albania. Nevertheless, the defense of Albania's frontiers is completely assured [Radio Tirana, 8 November 1961].

The Chairman of the Danish Communist Party (*Land og Folk*, 20 December 1961) has provided the following version of this argument:

The Albanians accuse the Soviet Union of not living up to its international commitments because it does not want to give in to Hoxha's demands that rockets and atomic weapons be put at his disposal: "We [the Albanians] are entitled to these weapons because we are surrounded by hostile and capitalist countries."

He then places the Soviet refusal in direct quotation as follows:

Our rockets are available for the defense of your borders should the imperialists violate them. We have always been prepared to uphold our international solidarity and our commitments to the Warsaw Pact, but to turn over atomic weapons to you, we will not and cannot.

The categorical refusal by E. Hoxha to permit Albania (together with Bulgaria and Rumania) to serve as a laboratory for Khrushchev's experiment with localized disarmament is circumstantial evidence, at the very least, of the pressures which the Soviet leader had sought to exert upon an erstwhile ally in connection with his disarmament proposals of 1959 and 1960. The efforts to persuade Hoxha to participate in the project, already accepted by the Rumanians and Bulgarians, had apparently continued even after M. Shehu had provided the first public indication of Albania's unwillingness to comply with this particular aspect of bloc policy (Report on the 1960 United Nations General Assembly to Albania Parliament, Radio Tirana, 25 October 1960). In their polemics with the Soviet propagandists, the Albanians explain their position by seeking to establish a clear distinction between their acceptance of an atom-free and nuclear-free zone in the Balkans and the Adriatic, and their rejection of the 1960 Bulgarian proposal for disarmament in the Balkans only, which did not, therefore, include Italy (*Zeri i*

Populit, 2 March 1962). As a unique instance of documentary proof of the "sincerity" of Khrushchev's disarmament scheme, the Albanian defiance in practice, despite its relatively narrow geographical limitations, is as significant and as relevant to any disarmament discussion as the more highly publicized Sino-Soviet theoretical controversy on the "inevitability of war."

There is perhaps no more accurate indicator of Khrushchev's intentions toward the problems of disarmament than his readiness to risk the obviously serious intra-Party and inter-Party-State repercussions of opposition to his radical scheme. Nevertheless, only two years after he had finally overcome (July 1957) the domestic foes of his extensive reform program, including disarmament, as revealed by Mikoyan and others, Khrushchev presented his plans for general and complete disarmament to the United Nations (September 1959) in the face of overt and covert Chinese objections. Perhaps made overconfident by his success in repulsing the challenge to his power and authority at home, the First Secretary-Chairman of the Council of Ministers has not flinched before the consequences of disrupting the socialist camp in pursuit of his foreign-policy goals as he understands them—peaceful coexistence and disarmament. On the eve of the XXIInd Party Congress, the resumption of nuclear testing and the deferment of demobilization again created the illusion that either external influence (Chinese) or internal pressures (military) had compelled Khrushchev to modify his basic policies. The course of events at the Congress, where the Party leader's three major speeches clearly dominated the proceedings, furnished an unambiguous answer concerning Khrushchev's uninhibited control over domestic affairs, not excepting the military; with equal clarity, however, the Chinese and the Albanians have demonstrated within the bloc the existence of division and dissension on foreign policy, including disarmament.

Only the Albanians, however, continue to be mentioned by name, as in an election speech by Mikoyan, who stressed that the Soviet program for disarmament had been opposed within the Communist camp by critics taking "allegedly left-wing positions." Rejecting the Sino-Albanian line that disarmament would hinder the movements for national liberation, Mikoyan said: "Such 'clever' pronouncements can be heard in particular from some Albanian 'theoreticians' who have a confused knowledge of Marxism" (*Pravda,* 15 March 1962; see also pp. 220 below).

Nevertheless, it remains impossible to establish any details of the relationship between the Sino-Albanian open dissent and an identifiable opposition within the present Soviet political or military leadership. In only one case at the Congress was there even an indirect reference to a tenuous tie which might have extended from Peking or Tirana to Moscow. Once more it was Molotov against whom O. Kuusinen (member of the Party Presidium and the Secretariat) brought the following accusation: "He was determined to . . . fish in muddy waters; probably some bony little fish would bite, if not here in native waters, then somewhere in a foreign pond" (*Pravda,* 27 October 1961). Defeated and discredited, yet still stubbornly defiant, Stalin's closest associate has been selected as the incarnation of the ideological opposition which has been isolated at home (if not abroad) and reduced to absolute impotence—in spite of recurrent rumors that "Molotov's 'hard-line' views might find a sympathetic reception in Communist China and Albania" (*New York Times,* 27 October 1961). Not until 30 January 1962, however, did a Prague broadcast in Arabic indicate a direct association between the opposition groups:

> The Albanian leaders have become official spokesmen and ardent supporters of a policy inimical to the CPSU, a policy advocated by the Molotov clique. . . . The cornerstone on which these misconceptions are based and which are embraced by the anti-Party clique in the Soviet Union and ardently defended by E. Hoxha, M. Shehu, and other Albanian leaders—this cornerstone of the erroneous thinking asserts that war is inevitable.

This digression in the search for documentation on internal dissent from Khrushchev's disarmament proposals is justifiable primarily by the absence of any comparable evidence in Soviet publications. To the above-mentioned implications may be added a vaguely worded attack against "shortsighted people who have lost touch with reality [and] . . . fail to see the insistent need for the complete disarmament of all states . . . [and] fail to believe in the possibility of achieving disarmament," and a briefer criticism of those who labeled the official Soviet policy as "a pacifist illusion" (*Pravda,* 13 June 1960, and *Kommunist,* August 1960, p. 12; see also Richard J. Barnet, "The Soviet Attitude on Disarmament," *Problems of Communism,* May-June 1961, p. 37). Since these quotations appeared at the height of and in the context of the Sino-Soviet polemics of that period, even such faint traces of internal resistance also lead back to an identification of Peking's doctrinal divergences with Moscow.

Although the Sino-Soviet ideological dispute with its clearly delineated implications for policy must be constantly kept in mind, it throws no direct light on past or current discussions of disarmament within the Soviet Union. In Soviet publications one rarely finds even the slightest doubt of the desirability of the goal of "general and complete disarmament," let alone any meaningful critical analysis of the subject based on ideological, political, economic, or military arguments. In the 1960 edition of *Fundamentals of Marxism-Leninism* (O. Kuusinen, editor), for example, the word disarmament is mentioned in only four sentences, each time in connection with "peaceful coexistence" and without additional comment. That the most important ideological textbook of the post-Stalin period has not dared to bring this explosive subject within the range of its nearly nine hundred pages is a pertinent reminder that Khrushchev's doctrinal innovations on the "noninevitability of war" have not yet become absolute dogma or an "irreversible commitment." Similarly, in the new Party program there is only a routine reference to disarmament.

Nevertheless, so much has been risked—and perhaps lost, from the Soviet point of view—in the inter-Party dispute with the Chinese, so prolonged a propaganda effort has been concentrated on Khrushchev's coexistence campaign, and so great is the fear of war among the Soviet population that there would seem to be little likelihood of another sudden ideological zigzag which would revive the former unequivocal thesis of the "inevitability of war." Thus, at least during "the Khrushchev era," the most significant doctrinal adjustment concerning Communism and war, without which Soviet participation in disarmament discussions would be meaningless, may be expected to remain valid.

With similar reservations, another important doctrinal modification may be recorded. In his speech of 14 January 1960, Khrushchev adopted the strange un-Marxist procedure of quoting Western businessmen to convince all doubters in the capitalist—and Communist—camp who held bearish views of the West's capacity to cope with disarmament:

> Some people in the West assert that disarmament threatens grave consequences for the economy of capitalist countries. They say that if the production of bombs, guns, submarines, and other means of destruction were stopped, ruin would result and hundreds of thousands of people would be deprived of work. . . . However, only people who see no other way of developing the economy than by subordinating it to the interests of preparing it for war can reason this way.

> The least which can be said about such assertions is that they are completely unsubstantiated. I have had occasion to talk with many representatives of American business circles, and the most reasonable of them have nowhere so gloomy a viewpoint but are confident that United States industry is fully capable . . . of shifting the entire economy to the production of goods for peaceful purposes [*Pravda*, 15 January 1960].

This significant shift in the classical Communist view of the role of armaments in capitalist economies is the necessary complement to the concept of the "noninevitability of war"; and both are intimately associated primarily with Khrushchev—and Mikoyan. As long as the standard Communist argument consisted of the double-barreled prediction of an unavoidable military conflict arising from the classical armaments race necessary to maintain the capitalist system, all disarmament negotiations were destined to be fruitless. The logical inconsistency between proclaiming that capitalism is doomed and incapable of survival without tremendous military expenditures, while advocating "complete and total disarmament" as the panacea for the world's economic woes, had become too blatantly obvious to be ignored as the "peaceful coexistence" campaign reached its climax with Khrushchev's visit to the United States in 1959. Although nearly all Soviet economists had for years propagated the orthodox line, they have now completely shifted—without any notable exceptions or any visible effects on their standing in the scholarly community—to the opposite and currently favored official version.

It is impossible to separate the lasting and completely genuine elements of this latest reasoning from the temporary and opportunistic accommodation of dogma to some inescapable post-World War II facts of life. Thus in Eastern Europe E. Molnar, a Hungarian economic historian, prematurely included among his challenges to the classical Marxist-Leninist doctrine on the intensification of capitalist crises a "denial of the important role of armaments" in averting chronic depressions and unemployment (*Tarsadalmi Szemle*, No. 12, 1959; see also the *New York Times*, 10 January 1959). While in Hungary the Party propagandists rejected—at that time—Molnar's arguments based on his study of the successful transition from wartime to peacetime economies in the West, the Soviets had already begun a limited revision of the "crisis theory" (see L. Mendelson, *Kommunist*, No. 11, August 1959) to prepare the ground for the more reassuring theses propagated by Khrushchev in the United States in 1959 and in his subsequent major policy pronouncements.

In step with the leader since then, Soviet theoreticians and propagandists have turned to such varied sources as the statement by the National Planning Association (4 January 1960) and their own optimistic calculations as to the ability of the United States economy to master the problems of demobilization and disarmament (see the speech by M. Rubenstein, in *Conference of the Soviet Society for Disarmament*, Moscow, 1960, pp. 72-74). Early in 1961 in an East-West conference in Germany devoted to the "discussion of the economic effects of disarmament," there was still no evidence of a return to the former prediction that militant imperialism would collapse without armaments. To the contrary, in perhaps the most definite public modification of this theory to date, the representatives of the Soviet-bloc at the meeting in Kiel unanimously agreed with the Westerners that the "often-held view that high military expenditures are necessary for the elimination of mass unemployment and that low military expenditures are a cause of mass unemployment is fallacious" (quoted from *The Times* (London), 15 March 1961). A year later the signatures of the Soviet, Polish, and Czechoslovak representatives to the United Nations report on the economic consequences of disarmament (*New York Times*, 12 March 1962) confirmed the current validity of this revision.

Yet only a short time before the Kiel conference, Professor I. Glagolev, one of the Soviet participants, had published a study which argued that monopoly-capitalists have a vested interest in arms because: (1) military force provides the best means of expanding their rule; (2) armament production yields large profits; (3) the capitalist economy can be kept at full capacity only through militarization. Which of the Soviet spokesman's commentaries on capitalism, Communism, and disarmament really represents his own views is immaterial; at Kiel—as on any other similar "official" occasion—he and his colleagues could only speak according to scripts approved by the Party leader, who, it must be stressed, has presented a logically consistent doctrinal line on disarmament since mid-1959. Despite the frequently flagrant disparity between Khrushchev's protestations of peace and his threats of violence, he has tentatively developed—with the thesis of the "noninevitability of war" and a slightly modified view of capitalism—an ideological framework into which disarmament could be fitted without undue violence as an example of the "creative development of Marxist-Leninist theory." As noted earlier, these changes, which nevertheless remain vaguely formulated in the Party program, have allegedly drawn from Molotov the epithets of "pacifist, revisionist, and anti-revolutionary"; on the basis of those of Khrushchev's actions which can be documented since 1954, these charges would be exceedingly difficult to prove.

Disarmament as an aspect of internal affairs is everywhere closely connected with the military establishment—the armed forces and the defense industries. For Khrushchev the dilemma of disarmament lies in the problem of reconciling his radical proposals for eventually eliminating weapons and war as instruments of policy with the necessity of projecting an immediate image of the Soviet Union as the possessor of the most powerful military force in the world. As the sole high-level Soviet political leader who has promulgated policy pronouncements on military matters, he has been identified with many (at times sharply modified) views. In the words of a specialist on Soviet strategy, writing in the summer of 1960:

> In the past Khrushchev has made radical and too sweeping statements about the decisive importance of weapons which he claims the Soviets have in superior numbers. In each case he himself has later offered slight modifications of his thesis, his service chiefs have modified it a little more, and low-ranking officers writing in the military press have occasionally exhibited decently veiled but unmistakable resistance to it. As time passes the modifications become slighter and increasingly unimportant. Khrushchev's political predominance in his own country ensures that his theories are accepted as true. Subsequently when theory is translated into practice, his theories become a true reflection of the real situation. . . . For these reasons we can accept Khrushchev's enunciation of the Soviet theory of nuclear war as an authoritative one with practical consequences for the future [H. Dinerstein, "Current Soviet Strategic Doctrines," *Soviet Survey,* October-December 1960].

At the XXIInd Party Congress Khrushchev once again, as he always has in his published speeches since 1953, stressed that the "Party . . . constantly bears in mind the necessity of strengthening [the country's] defense capacity." In an aside, departing from the text of the "report of the Central Committee" in a manner which clearly demonstrates his control over that body, the First Secretary gave the first "official" report of the recent nuclear-testing series and the planned 55-megaton explosion (*Pravda,* 18 October 1961). With these remarks serving as the preface to the boast of the 100-megaton bomb, Khrushchev underlined his concepts that any nuclear war would be an all-out effort with disastrous consequences to both sides.

There are, however, changes in the Congress speech which, no doubt, reflect the continuous process of adjustment to which the Soviet leader subjects his subordinates' estimates and evaluations of their military requirements. Thus he justified the expansion of the Soviet submarine fleet and its equipment with "both ballistic and target-seeking rockets" by noting that "those who wish to unleash war against [the Soviet Union] will be compelled to have supremacy of the sea." Although this reflects a somewhat different appreciation of the value of a modern navy for a hostile power than he previously admitted (in his speech of 14 January 1960), Khrushchev nevertheless deprecatingly referred to "aircraft carriers . . . as quite good targets for our rockets launched from submarines." Similarly, the Soviet leader has applied an apparent corrective to his January 1960 comments that military aviation had been nearly replaced by rockets, that the production of bombers was being cut, and that they *might* become obsolete. However, it was not much more than a sop to the wounded pride of the fliers to be reminded at the very end of his extemporaneous remarks that "we are not leaving the air force out of our reckoning, we are continuing to develop and improve it."

These shifts from the January 1960 speech did not come as a complete surprise. With respect to aircraft there have been no slighting remarks since July 1960, while the denigration of carriers has appeared as recently as the eve of the Congress (*Izvestia,* 10 October 1961). Perhaps the first revision of the January 1960 line came in Khrushchev's summer 1960 meeting with Soviet writers, when he noted that "all service branches are necessary and important" (not published until nearly a year later in *Kommunist,* May 1961). The new type of long-range bomber which made its first appearance at the 1961 May Day demonstration is certainly proof of qualitative improvement, whatever quantitative changes have been introduced to "reconcile" Khrushchev's earlier conditional prediction of obsolescence and Marshal Vershinin's subsequent statement on the significance of the continued production of "new aircraft which were still to be phased into the forces" (Dinerstein, "Current Soviet Strategic Doctrines," *loc. cit.*). It is only necessary, however, to recall the relationship between the Party-State leader, now officially referred to as the "Supreme Commander-in-Chief of the Armed Forces" (Marshal Malinovsky, *Pravda,* 23 October 1961, and Marshal Varentsov, *Red Star,* 18 November 1961), and the Commander-in-Chief of the Soviet Air Force to realize how slight are the latter's chances of imposing a change of policy on his political superior. The subordination of the military to the Party has rarely been more starkly expressed than in Khrushchev's admission to Vice-President Nixon that he had ordered Marshal Vershinin from Moscow to Sochi and then dictated to him an article which appeared in *Pravda*, 8 September 1957, under Vershinin's signature; this was wryly referred to by Khrushchev as "Marshal Vershinin's famous interview on Soviet capabilities of destruction" (*New York Herald-Tribune*, 14 September 1960).

The case of Marshal Zhukov is even more instructive for those in search of indexes for divergent views on disarmament within Soviet society. Since the Marshal's return to prominence in the post-Stalin period is generally attributed to his support for Khrushchev—and some of the present members of the anti-Party group—in the 1954-1955 conflict with Malenkov over the rates of development of heavy and light industry, it is enlightening to read (in an article which argues that the days of battleships and aircraft carriers are numbered) the following belated accusations against the popular marshal:

> We shall not conceal the fact that . . . fundamentally wrong views were . . . circulating among our military staffs. G. Zhukov denied the significance of technical progress, the development of technology for the army and the navy. He asserted that rockets were foolish and that the bayonet was just the thing; he thought the navy archaic, outworn and needed only for parades.
>
> "Those were hard times for the men of the submarine fleet," an admiral stated. . . . The Presidium of the Central Committee and N. S. Khrushchev personally intervened. He wisely defended the place of submarines in the armed forces as a whole. He pointed out that the main feature in the development of our submarine fleet should be the building of fast long-range atomic-powered submarines armed with modern atomic thermonuclear weapons. That is why our sailors call N. S. Khrushchev the father of the atomic fleet. . . . On the instructions of N. S. Khrushchev, Soviet designers have built new types of submarines and produced powerful atomic-powered engines for them [*Izvestia*, 11 October 1961].

It is patently an insult to the intelligence of any Soviet audience, even the readers of *Izvestia*—as well as to that of any Western observer—to expect this absurd retroactive rewriting of Soviet military science to be taken seriously. Whatever Zhukov's shortcomings as a Party politician may be, it is ridiculous to caricature the soldier, who contributed greatly to the revision of Soviet military doctrine for the nuclear age in the debates between 1954 and 1955, as an ignorant opponent of advanced technology in tanks, rockets, bombs, submarines, and planes. On the other hand, there can be little doubt that Zhukov did oppose, as almost every career officer in East and West invariably does, the personnel reductions which began in 1955-1956. Moreover, he very likely differed with Khrushchev, not only on the role of the Party organizations in the armed forces as was charged in October 1957, but also on some of the strategic and tactical principles involved in the complicated process of reorganizing the Soviet army into the most modern and powerful instrument possible to serve the political aspirations of the Party-State. Yet, as early as the summer of 1957, Zhukov, in one of the Leningrad speeches in which he attacked the "anti-Party group" for having sought "to weaken the defensive capacity of the Soviet state," made a strong plea for reducing international tension through disarmament (*Pravda,* 5 July 1957). Four years after his ouster, the real reasons were still a matter of conjecture, but the meaning of the shortest Presidium (Politburo) tenure in Party history should be abundantly clear.

The words and deeds of the present Minister of Defense, Marshal Malinovsky, have shown how fully the implications of the Zhukov case have been absorbed. On no occasion has the present Soviet Minister of Defense deviated in oratory or action from the policies advocated by the First Secretary; his support of the cuts in manpower in January 1960 in no way differ from his approval (at the XXIInd Congress) of the need to halt this reduction of the armed forces for an indefinite period. Still the best overt example of dissatisfaction with the measures inherent in any future Soviet implementation of disarmament plans, the demobilizations of the past five years are extremely important as demonstrations of the relative ease with which the Party leadership has implemented a policy obviously contrary to the interests and privileges of a relatively large and highly favored category of the Soviet elite structure. No better examples of the inefficacy—if not the impossibility—of dissent from official policy are available than the minor mumblings which were allowed to make their way into the press from some of the 250,000 disgruntled officers who had been herded into premature retirement. As late as the spring of 1962 there was evidence of continuing propaganda pressure on demobilized officers to seek work in state and collective farms, indicating that the temporary end of demobilization has not completely solved the employment problems of those already released. Not many of those who have successfully resisted the exhortations of their own local Agit-Prop recruiters are likely to succumb to these entreaties of an ex-Major in remote Siberia:

> The need for cadres in the East is great. We would like to appeal to reserve officers through the *Red Star*—"Come to us in the Far East, particularly to our vegetable-producing state farm in Khabarovsk. Do not fear the difficulties, but be assured that today's state and collective farms are far different from those of 10 years ago" [*Red Star,* 16 March 1962].

Since the quiet (but extensive) purge of the officer corps was followed in May 1960 by the promotion of more than 300 general officers in a decree signed by N. S. Khrushchev as Chairman of the Council of Ministers (*Pravda,* 9 May 1960), the identity of the man responsible for advancing the few as well as releasing the many is readily established. For him it would seem that the danger from the unorganized discontent of thousands of demobilized officer cadres is more than balanced by the gain from dispensing promotions to those selected to remain.

As a trial run for some of the problems to be faced, should disarmament ever move from discussion to deeds, the experience of the series of demobilizations has given an unequivocal answer. Despite the "temporary" difficulties and dislocations experienced in the 1954-1959 demobilizations, frankly described by Marshal Malinovsky in his report to the Supreme Soviet (*Red Star,* 20 January 1960) and acknowledged to foreign audiences (at the East-West Conference in London, 1960, and at Kiel, 1961) as well as at home (the Moscow Conference in February 1960), the limited scope of the problems in manpower and employment suggests that the redeployment of labor and the reallocation of resources could be relatively easily managed by the Soviet economy on a much larger scale. The March 1962 report to the United Nations, for example, states simply that "there is little problem for the centrally planned economies . . . since they can plan and direct the conversion of their industry and placing of manpower."

Although extensive shifts in the top leadership of the Soviet army followed the announcement of the January 1960 demobilization, the promotion of Marshals Grechko and Zakharov to replace Marshals Konev and Sokolovsky provides no clear proof that these changes reflected policy differences. It is of course interesting to note that in January 1960 at the session of the Supreme Soviet which approved the demobilization measures, none of the veteran marshals of World War II (Konev, Sokolovsky, Rokossovsky) appeared as adherents of Khrushchev's proposals. Only Marshal Malinovsky, seconded by the group of district military commanders (Zakharov, Grechko, Chuikov, and Moskalenko) soon to be advanced to the top staff posts, provided "parliamentary" support for the Party leader. Similarly, in the propaganda follow-up in press and radio, the absence of the more famous marshals may be regarded as an indication of opposition to partial demobilization in particular and to any form of disarmament in general.

Certainly one might suggest, as B. Nicolaevsky has done, that Konev, formerly Khrushchev's strong supporter, had joined forces with "members of the high command who condemn the Army cuts as a blow to the country's military potential and who are closely allied to those of Khrushchev's foes within the Party who have from the very first disagreed with his foreign policy" (*The New Leader*, 30 May 1960). Whether Konev's brief return from an assignment in the Ministry of Defense to the post of commander-in-chief of the Soviet forces in Germany (from August 1961 to April 1962) can then be interpreted as a resurgence of these "oppositional forces" is doubtful, even in the context of the end of demobilization[2] and the resumption of nuclear testing. In the interim, there had been other facts which pointed to a further downgrading of the career officers: the increased importance of the military councils in which regional Party secretaries participate, the promotion of the Chief of the Political Administration (F. Golikov) to the rank of marshal, and the replacement of the latter by A. A. Yepishev, a Party functionary associated with Khrushchev in the Ukraine since 1939 (*Pravda*, 22 May 1962).

There is, to be sure, ample evidence of chronic controversy among the military. For example, the *Military-Historical Journal* (May 1961) raised the following complaint:

> It must be noted that in working out the military-technical part of our military science, there are still many disputed and unclear propositions. Evidence of this is given by the discussions which have broken out in the military press and within the walls of the General Staff and the Frunze Military Academies. Unfortunately, no unity has been achieved in these discussions.

Another military journal which admits the usefulness of this kind of theoretical dispute attacks the dogmatists in the army in these terms:

> . . . Partisans of the old . . . did not recognize the change in the role of the various kinds of armed forces and the service branches dogmatically interpreting the well-known tenet of Soviet military theory regarding

> their proportional development.... This tenet never signified that proportional development should be an even development. Our military theory, relying on the Marxist dialectical method, has always considered the development of one or another kind of armed forces or service branch from a specifically historical viewpoint, singling out the main link at each stage, taking account of the need to give scope to the development of the new, the most progressive, that which has a future.
>
> ... some comrades [have] dogmatic notions as to the conditions of preparing for the emergence of war, the nature of the initial period of war, the possibilities for and the time limits of mobilization, the strategic development, and the organizational forms as well as the methods of administering the forces [*Communist of the Armed Forces,* May 1961].

It is therefore no secret that, under the Khrushchev system of rule, sharp debate continues on many key issues of military strategy and tactics in the nuclear age. Although some efforts have been made to identify among the dogmatists in the army the recipients of promotions such as Grechko and Zakharov (see Victor Zorza, *Manchester Guardian,* 25 October 1961), this search is likely to prove as fruitless as the long quest to prove M. Suslov a "Stalinist." Even more difficult is it to single out the genuine proponents of disarmament in that sector of the Soviet power structure where opposition to Khrushchev's scheme may be considered as nearly total, regardless of how often it makes formal declarations of approval.

Thus disarmament is almost invariably mentioned as an ultimate goal in any introduction to a discussion of the nature of the next conflict:

> In its struggle to prevent war and to solve the problem of universal and complete disarmament, the Soviet Union has frequently carried out unilaterally considerable reductions in its armed forces. Yet, as long as no agreement has been reached and no universal disarmament implemented, the Soviet Union and all other countries of the socialist camp are maintaining and will continue to maintain their defensive might at the necessary level. The numerical strength and the firepower of their armies must be that necessary to ensure our decisive resistance and the full rout of any aggressor.... It must not be believed that in a war victory will be won merely by means of rocket troops [Col. A. M. Iovlev, *Red Star,* 5 April 1961].

A somewhat different situation emerges if one transfers the question of the "harmonious development" of the armed forces into the economic sector, where a chronic controversy is reflected in the planning for the rates of growth of heavy and light industry. Here identification is at times easier; Mikoyan and Kosygin come to mind immediately as top Party spokesman for a "consumer goods" course, and Suslov as an adherent of unchallenged priority for heavy industry and defense. Yet there is no real indication that Mikoyan's attitude on the relative rates of increase of producer and consumer goods necessarily denotes an unconditional acceptance of Khrushchev's disarmament proposals; nor is there proof that Suslov's emphasis is equivalent to unqualified opposition to his superior's radical scheme. From the goals fixed for the seven-, fifteen-, and twenty-year plans there is little reason to anticipate any marked shifts in the Soviet investment pattern to the cost of heavy industry or defense, although much more will be done than under Stalin. A recent reminder was furnished by Khrushchev, who concluded the March 1962 plenary session of the Central Committee with a firm rejection of any diversion of investments in agriculture "to the detriment of [either] industrial development or the strengthening of the country's defense"; he described the producer-goods sector and military preparedness as the "bedrock of the existence of our socialist state, of its development and its success" (*Pravda,* 11 March 1962). Moreover, if one looks at the personnel of the new committee created to guide scientific research, the preponderance of specialists from military research (specifically, rocket and space technology) is immediately apparent (Nicholas DeWitt, *Aviation Week and Space Technology,* 11 September 1961). While waiting for disarmament, the men who are now responsible for guiding Soviet science will certainly not neglect their own familiar fields of military and space research.[3]

For years the Soviet press has been talking of the bounties which would accrue to the Soviet consumer—and his brothers throughout the world—if agreement on general and complete disarmament could be reached. Never has there been the slightest publicity given to the problems of maintaining Party power and rule, whether at home, in the international movement, or on the world scene, under such changed conditions. Those near the apex of authority in the CPSU must have fought as bitterly over this issue as they have over many others that have potentially far less consequences for the system which has produced the world's second greatest industrial power. At the present time only this small group, in which the person of N. S. Khrushchev overshadows all the rest, can know with any degree of certainty how much or how little meaning his disarmament proposals have. In the rest of Soviet society the range of hopes and fears may well be as wide as elsewhere. As long as all decision-making powers are concentrated at the top and policy battles fought in the manner described at the XXIInd Congress, these divisions of opinion will have little or no impact. For propaganda purposes, Khrushchev can still count on the total conformity of the views published; for the true story of any internal dissension on disarmament, the outside world—and most Soviet citizens—must wait for Khrushchev's successor.

Since the conclusion of the XXIInd Party Congress, there has been little further clarification of the question of possible ties between the internal and external opposition to Khrushchev and his publicly proclaimed policy on disarmament. The unanimous domestic approval and the successful suppression of all signs of dissent at home on this sensitive issue have not, however, prevented the dispute between Moscow and Peking (particularly as reflected in the continued attacks against and by Tirana) from poisoning the atmosphere at recent meetings of Communist-sponsored international organizations. What is at stake is not, for the moment, the leadership of these groups still securely in the hands of the Soviet supporters, but the degree of influence and pressure which the Chinese can exert today and tomorrow on Soviet foreign policy in general, and to what extent Peking's propaganda and deeds can in particular affect Soviet relations with the West (that is, the United States) in the missile and thermonuclear age.

At the Stockholm session of the World Peace Council (16-19 December 1961), the disagreements between the Soviets and the Chinese (as usual, backed most strongly by the Albanians) were obvious from the opening session to the final communiqué. The ostensible argument (the designation of the World Congress planned for the summer of 1962) was seemingly trivial. The Soviet-led majority proposed a "Congress for General Disarmament and Peace"; the Chinese and their followers, Albania and some of the Afro-Asian countries, insisted that the meeting be named a "Congress for National Independence, Peace, and Disarmament." This quarrel over nomenclature actually revealed, according to an Italian delegate to the Stockholm meeting, "a basic conflict . . . between those who firmly believe . . . in the existence of real conditions which make it possible today to realize general disarmament . . . and those who have less faith in peaceful coexistence and disarmament and therefore put the accent on the . . . struggle against imperialism" (V. Spano, *L'Unità*, 23 December 1961). In the decisive vote, 166 delegates aligned themselves with the Soviets for a "Disarmament

Conference," and 23 remained in opposition, "the first time in the history of the World Council that the unity of the movement could not be established"[4] (Spano, *ibid.*). The compromise solution—the decision to convoke both a world disarmament conference in Moscow (9-14 July 1962) and a second conference of African, Asian, and Latin American countries to deal with national liberation and colonialism at some other date—demonstrated clearly the existence of open dissension over the role of the disarmament campaign in the international movement.

Reduced to its essentials, the Russian argument stresses disarmament as the "most pressing problem of our time." It considers disarmament *propaganda*—with or without practical results—as a most effective method of identifying Soviet aspirations with the hopes and fears of peoples throughout the world. A similar priority for disarmament has, on the other hand, been given no place in the Chinese conception since 1958. For Peking the struggle against imperialism (United States) and colonialism must take precedence over the issue of peace and disarmament. Thus in his speech at Stockholm the Chinese delegate, Liu Ning-I (*Peking Review*, 29 December 1961) firmly rejected the "subordination of the national independence movement to the movement for general and complete disarmament . . . as [an] erroneous and most harmful view." Later the Soviets, according to the Albanians (*Zeri i Populit*, 2 March 1961), cited this as an example of "orators using shameful methods" to confuse the issues of disarmament and national liberation. With the acclamation of the Albanians and the approval of the North Koreans, the North Vietnamese, and the Guinean delegates, Liu argued that the

> . . . most important issue [for Laos, Algeria, Angola, or Kamerun] is definitely not the disarming of whatever small forces they have, but the building and strengthening of their own armed forces to defend themselves. . . . Whether in Cuba or in other newly independent countries, what they need today is definitely not the reduction of the armed forces which they have just built up, but the strengthening of their armed forces for the defense of the independence of their countries.

The Soviet rebuttal (*Kommunist*, No. 2, 1962) to this battle cry insisted that

> . . . contrary to some "theories," disarmament will not weaken the forces struggling against colonialism . . . it will consolidate their position. . . . The military resources of the underdeveloped countries are so insignificant in the general balance of the world's military forces that they

can be practically neglected when the problems of disarmament are solved, at least in the preliminary stages. . . . General and complete disarmament means breaking the backbone of the system of imperialist domination and control over the economy of the underdeveloped countries. . . . To oppose the national liberation movement to other aspects of the revolutionary process weakens the liberation struggle of the enslaved peoples and is harmful to the anti-imperialist front.

The conflict between these opposing views was continued at the Afro-Asian Solidarity Committee meeting in Gaza (December 1961) and at the Afro-Asian Writers Conference in Cairo (February 1962). According to Colin Legum (*The Observer*, 11 March 1962), the Chinese at the latter gathering derided the Russians as having come out "for peace at all costs." This challenge immediately provoked an outburst from the Soviet delegate, Mirzo Tursun-zade, who warned that "only madmen and inciters of another world war do not understand that nuclear war is the only alternative to coexistence." Although at this meeting the Soviet disarmament proposals were presented for inclusion in the final communiqué by the Turkish writer, Naxim Hikmet, the editorial commission, changing its draft twenty times (*Vjesnik* [Zagreb], 22 February 1962) in the face of stubborn Chinese—and other—opposition, finally gave more than "semisatisfaction" to the Chinese by calling for an intensification of the struggle for national liberation and omitting any reference to disarmament. The same Yugoslav newspaper also quoted the delegate from Southern Rhodesia as saying: "What good is disarmament, if we all want guns."

The direct relevance of such skirmishes in the World Peace Council and other front organizations to the Soviet internal scene remains, nevertheless, impossible to establish. It is, however, more than a mere conjecture to state that the Chinese and Albanian objections to the absolute propagandistic priority given disarmament by the "Khrushchev group" may reflect the repressed views of some members of the Soviet party leadership. Although the verbal "war in the peace council" has not yet reached the stage at which the sharp dissension within the international organizations can be related to personalities or factions in Moscow, the relatively open debates in this hitherto completely controlled forum may yet provide some insight into the alignments in the Kremlin.

In conclusion, another possibility should be mentioned. Although Chinese spokesmen continue to warn that Peking will not be bound to any disarmament agreements concluded without its participation

(*Peoples Daily*, 3 April 1962)—a position supported by Khrushchev at the United Nations and in Peking during 1959 and again at the United Nations in 1960—there has been at least one significant indication of a partial reconciliation of Sino-Soviet views on disarmament. Thus, shortly after the conclusion of the National Peoples Congress, the leading Chinese newspaper accepted the "struggle for peace as the general line of socialist countries"; it passed over the earlier dichotomy attributed to disarmament and national liberation by stating that the two "struggles . . . sustain each other"; it described disarmament as "the most radical way to remove war from society," and even recognized that the imperialists might be "compelled" to approve some "partial measures of disarmament" (that is, nuclear) because of the "superior strength of the socialist camp" (*ibid.*). Since the Soviet press (*Izvestia*, 4 April 1962) immediately reprinted the section of the *Peoples Daily* article containing these approximations to Soviet views while omitting most of the more aggressive attacks on the United States, the development of a mutually acceptable Sino-Soviet position on disarmament cannot be excluded.[5] If this is achieved, if only for propaganda purposes, the voices of the "foreign foes" of disarmament (Albania) and the internal opponents will have lost their most effective sounding board.

Appendix

Enough of covering ourselves with sputniks and airliners. Let us come down somewhat lower—to the most ordinary shoes. I have one pair, but I have been walking in them for four years now. And why? Because they are Western; a foreign trademark is on them. Personally I don't need a TU-114, I will get by with the trolley, but I want to live and dress well. [Letter to the editor in *Sovetskaya Rossiya*, 4 October 1959.]

If you told any worker, "Look, Ivan, if we did not launch this rocket, your Vovik (Bobby) would have a yard to play in, a meter of serge wool would not cost four notes but would be only half as expensive, and you could buy an electric iron in a store," he would say, "For God's sake, don't launch that rocket."

Rockets, rockets, rockets! Who needs them now! For the time being, to Hell with them and the moon; give me better things for my table. After that you can play with the moon. [*Komsomolskaya Pravda*, 11 June 1960.]

During the break the young people showed each other verses by a beginner from Dnepropetrovsk: "Rockets with sunset-hued manes, like evil ships of the sky. . . ." This poet thought himself an innovator. More than that, people say that "friends" apparently put this idea into his head. A poet is no gullible butterfly. And if people praise you for one or another poem, it will never do harm to ponder about who praises you and why, and for whose mill your work is grist. There certainly are wise friends, too, but also people for whom the important thing is not literature itself, but scandal in literature." [*Komsomolskaya Pravda,* 4 October 1961.]

It is no secret that the works where the carrier rockets of cosmic ships are made are closed ones. And they will remain closed until that day when the threat of war has been fully liquidated, when the Soviet proposals on full and general disarmament have been accepted. Then the red-starred rockets will serve only peaceful aims. From the gates of the works will begin the exploration of the great beyond of the universe, and new, daring cosmonauts, taking into their hands the controls of the interplanetary ships, will guide them to other worlds.

But until then, while weapons are being rattled beyond the ocean, while our country is surrounded by bandit nests of military bases, not only the glory of space victories will be forged here, but also the grim power of the Soviet armed forces. . . .

Once again one remembers how Nikita Sergeyevich Khrushchev, at the reception of Soviet journalists in the Kremlin, spoke about a visit to one of the works which made rockets. Acquainting one's self with their manufacture, said Nikita Sergeyevich, one experiences contradictory feelings. Here the most death-bearing, most destructive of weapons are manufactured; on the other hand, one is proud that we do have them. In one year this plant which we are visiting sent off the production line 25 rockets with hydrogen warheads. While possessing such crushing weapons, the Soviet people threaten no one, and are consistently defending the cause of peace in the world. [*Komsomolskaya Pravda,* 26 August 1961.]

NOTES

1. An exception appears in the widely publicized article by N. Inozemtsev (*Pravda,* 17 January 1962), who also identifies Malenkov and Kaganovich as "dogmatists" opposed to peaceful coexistence. In this article Molotov is moreover singled out for "having gone so far as to assert that Lenin has nowhere and at no time spoken about the peaceful coexistence of states with different social systems." A few months later this charge was repeated by three noted Soviet authorities on international law who, as in the case of Inozemtsev, were unable to document their refutation of Molotov's statement with any direct quotation from Lenin's voluminous works (*Izvestia,* 18 April 1962). Western scholars would support Molotov's "dogmatic obstinacy" on this point. (See, for example, L. Pistrak, "Lenin and Peaceful Coexistence," in *Problems of Communism,* 1959, No. 6, p. 55.)

2. On 9 February 1962 the Presidium of the Supreme Soviet abolished, effective with the school year 1962-1963, "military training prior to draft . . .

for pupils of secondary schools and of secondary specialized educational establishments" (*Bulletin of the Supreme Soviet,* No. 7, 1962). There is some question concerning the practical effect of annulling this section of the 1 September 1939 decree on conscription because compulsory military training in secondary schools had not been in effect for some time. Even as a step which eliminates outdated legislation, the formal erasure from the law has both psychological and political significance in the context of Khrushchev's disarmament campaign (Soviet Military Developments [by R. R. G.], Background Information—USSR, Research and Evaluation Department, Radio Free Europe, Munich, 29 March 1962).

3. Among the delegates to the XXIInd Party Congress was I. D. Serbin, listed as head of the Central Committee Department for the Defense Industry, the first time such a department has been recorded (*Stenographic Report of the XXIInd Party Congress of the Communist Party of the Soviet Union,* vol. 3, p. 519).

4. The Italian delegate had either unconsciously or intentionally forgotten the World Peace Council meeting in Stockholm, December 1956, which failed to agree on a statement approving Soviet intervention in Hungary.

5. This seems to have taken place in a meeting of the Presidium of the World Peace Council in Vienna where V. Spano reported on a partial reconciliation as follows:

   "It is true that in Vienna our Chinese friends have once again underlined —and they have every right to do so—the problem of national liberation . . . in particular in our memorandum to the Geneva disarmament conference. . . . Yet while the Chinese were firm in their proposals, they advanced them in a spirit of seeking unity. This made possible the unanimous approval of all resolutions, [a unanimity] not reached during the Stockholm meeting" [*L'Unità,* 27 March 1962].

CHRISTOPH HOHENEMSER

The Nth Country Problem Today

IN THE LAST few years the "Nth country problem" has become a permanent part of the vocabulary of the disarmament literature. It is a convenient shorthand for the factors influencing the spread of nuclear weapons to additional countries, and it carries the implication that this is an undesirable development. The letter "N" is borrowed from mathematics, to describe the indeterminate number of countries which may in future unlock Pandora's box of atomic plenty.

A great variety of conclusions have been drawn about the Nth country problem. Some writers have warned of imminent international instability resulting from the diffusion of nuclear weapons.[2-5] Others have seen the acquisition of nuclear weapons by additional countries as either partly or wholly beneficial.[6-8] In the middle ground, some authors have conceded that nuclear weapons will ultimately lead to political instability, but that nuclear explosives must be viewed together with delivery systems in order to get a meaningful picture of Nth country capabilities.[9-11]

My own efforts have been aimed at setting forth technological conditions, rather than political consequences.[1] The discussion of the former, however, suffered by the omission of a discussion of delivery systems. I therefore propose to redefine the problem of the diffusion of nuclear weapons explicitly as the diffusion of nuclear explosives plus delivery systems, keeping in mind, of course, that in certain circumstances extremely primitive delivery systems may be significant, while in other circumstances only the most advanced will be important.

With these considerations, this paper is divided into the following parts: (1) various paths toward the independent production of nuclear explosives are described, and their relative likelihood is assessed; (2) the present and future world-wide distribution of nuclear technology is indicated, and related to capacity for producing weapons; (3) the problems of nuclear delivery systems are described in general terms, and on this basis the two types of "nuclear powers" in the political-military sense are discussed; (4) the requirements and prospects for stopping the diffusion of nuclear weapons by controls and other measures are discussed in the context of past efforts.

Parts one and two will be to some extent based on the earlier study,[1] an attempt to estimate the technological requirements for independent Nth country developments, using data available in 1958. It contained a list of "12 countries which can obtain the bomb in five years." The development of 2-4 plutonium-type weapons was taken as the goal, and the list was compiled on the basis of several simple indices of industrial and technological capability. In the present study, not only the program for plutonium-based weapons will be discussed but some alternatives as well. The process of separating uranium isotopes by gas centrifuges (which received considerable attention in the press in 1960) is given special attention.[12]

In treating nuclear-weapon capability in Section 2, direct indications of nuclear technology around the world will be emphasized, rather than the more general capability (measured, for example, by indices like the levels of steel production) described in the previous study. The present approach is possible now that more countries have constructed reactors and made plans for future nuclear power programs. Not surprisingly, the same countries emerge under both approaches as leaders in nuclear-weapon capability. As before, the big gap in the estimates of capability is the question of Red China.

In the discussion of delivery systems in Section 3, an attempt will be made to define the role of delivery systems in the making of a "nuclear power." Nuclear powers are divided into "greats" and secondary powers. Each case involves a basically different delivery capability. The discussion of Nth country controls in the last part will include a description of past efforts to achieve controls, as well as some suggestions for future control plans directed at the spread of nuclear weapons.

1. THE PROBLEM OF NUCLEAR EXPLOSIVES

How a Bomb is Made: Fissile Material

Two heavy-element isotopes, uranium-235 and plutonium-239, are used for nuclear weapons. The bomb on Hiroshima utilized the former, while the bomb on Nagasaki utilized the latter. Uranium-235 is the only naturally occurring fissile material,* but its low isotopic abundance in naturally occurring uranium metal requires that it be enriched before its application to weapons is possible. Plutonium-239 does not occur naturally but can be produced by conversion of uranium-238 (99.3 percent natural isotopic abundance) in a reactor fueled by natural uranium. The conversion in the reactor depends on the .7 percent uranium-235 in natural uranium as a neutron source. Thus, both types of weapons applications depend directly or indirectly on the only naturally occurring fissile material. While a third fissile material, uranium-233, has been identified and proposed for weapons application, it too depends on uranium-235 for its production.

To produce enriched uranium (higher than .7 percent uranium-235), some process of isotope separation must be employed. The separation of two elements can usually be accomplished by a comparatively easy and cheap chemical process, whereas the separation of isotopes of the same element must make use of nuclear properties exclusively (nuclear mass differences, nuclear magnetic differences, etc.) since there are no chemical differences by definition.** The dependence on nuclear properties makes the process of isotope separation a difficult one. To date, the only large-scale isotope separation has been produced by gaseous diffusion, which in the case of uranium makes use of the gaseous compound uranium hexafluoride

* Fissile material means here an isotope capable of being fissioned by neutrons of any energy. Such isotopes can sustain a chain reaction and release large quantities of nuclear energy in either an explosive (bomb) or controlled (reactor) fashion. There are other elements which may be fissioned by fast neutrons only. Because fast neutrons rapidly slow down in matter, such elements are not capable of sustaining a chain reaction, and cannot by themselves release macroscopic quantities of nuclear energy. They are excluded from the class of fissile materials, even though they can undergo fission under suitable circumstances.

** Elements are distinguished by different electron structures, and hence different chemical properties. Isotopes are the different possible forms of the same element, and differ only in the nuclear properties (in particular, the weight of the nucleus).

(UF_6), and the difference in diffusion rates between molecules containing uranium-238 and molecules containing uranium-235.

For producing plutonium-239, the only method open to a country not possessing enriched uranium-235 is a natural uranium-fueled thermal converter reactor. Such a reactor depends on the sequence of events shown in Fig. 1 for the production of plutonium-239. Triggered by neutrons occurring at random, a sustained (and controlled) chain reaction converts part of the 99.3 percent abundant uranium-238 into plutonium-239. The source of neutrons for the continued operation of this process is the naturally occurring fissile isotope uranium-235, present in .7 percent abundance in natural uranium.*

The construction of a converter reactor for the production of plutonium is much less difficult and costly than the construction of isotope separating diffusion plants (see Section 2.4). France's plutonium producing reactors, which produce enough plutonium for several bombs a year, involve a total investment of only about $90 million. The converter reactor must be accompanied by a plant for chemical separation from spent fuel elements; but this adds only a few percent to the cost. Aside from low cost, and additional and most important advantage of a plutonium program is that converter reactors may be designed for electrical power production, so that the plutonium is produced essentially as a *by-product*. In fact, many countries which have no known active weapons program today are producing significant quantities of plutonium in their electrical power reactors (see Section 3).

How a Bomb is Made: Detonation

The detonation of a bomb depends on building up an unstable (explosive) chain reaction similar to that pictured in Fig. 1. The important difference is that the reaction must be maintained by fast neutrons because of the limited time available, and the rate of fissions occurring must multiply rapidly in time. To attain this condition, large concentrations (several kilograms) of pure, unmoderated fissile material must be present. Because stray neutrons could

* Plutonium can in principle be more efficiently produced (higher rate of conversion from uranium-238 to plutonium-239 per uranium-235 fission). A fast neutron reactor, without a neutron slowing moderator (see Fig. 2.1) would be employed. The construction of such a reactor, however, is possible only if enriched uranium is available as fuel.[13] For this reason the method is not available to a country lacking an isotope separation plant.

Figure 1
Chain Reaction*

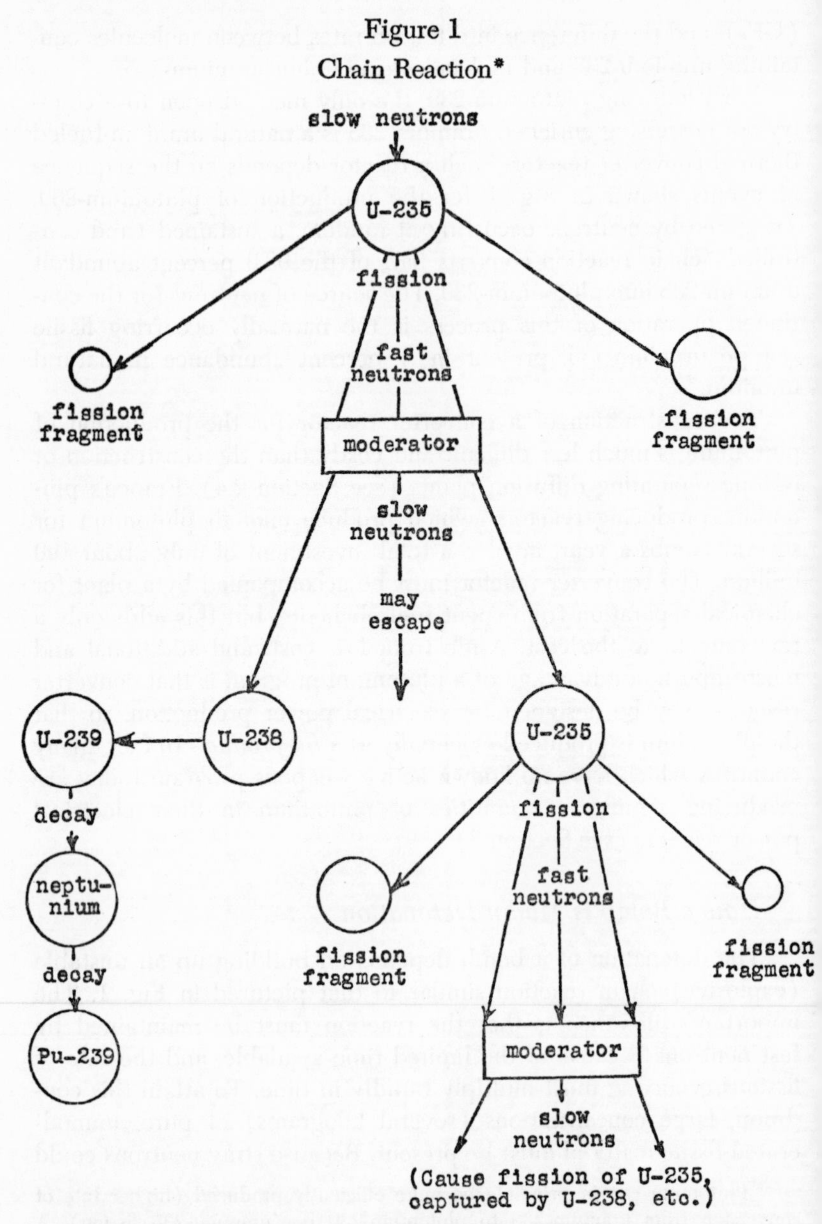

* This schematic representation of the fission of uranium-235 and the capture of neutrons by uranium-238 leading to plutonium-239 is adapted from S. Glasstone, *Sourcebook on Atomic Energy*, Van Nostrand Co., Inc. (Princeton), 1958, p. 432.

start an explosive reaction at any time if enough material is present, the mass of fissile material must be in a subcritical configuration before the explosion. The problem of detonation consists in producing a supercritical (or simply a critical) configuration and in obtaining enough release of energy from fission before the reaction stops.

In detonation, uranium-235 offers distinct advantages over plutonium-239. A uranium-235 device may be detonated by firing two pieces of fissile material into one another to initiate the explosive chain reaction. For plutonium, this simple (ballistic) technique is not possible, and the process of implosion must be employed. In this process, a single piece of subcritical fissile material is compressed to considerably smaller physical size in order to make it supercritical. While the ballistic technique requires some variant of an ordinary gun, the implosion technique necessitates the development of a specially shaped chemical charge of considerable magnitude. Uranium-235 offers the additional advantage that it is a more suitable material for the construction of a fission-trigger for an eventual thermonuclear device, though both uranium-235 and plutonium-239[14] appear to have been used.*

Plutonium: The Most Likely Path

Having indicated the nature of possible materials and ways of constructing a bomb, the question arises: which path will be used by newly emerging nuclear powers? In the previous study,[1] the authors gave three reasons why, despite the greater difficulty in detonation, the path of plutonium-239 would be the first choice. With modification, these reasons are still valid today: (1) plutonium is an unavoidable by-product in production of nuclear power using natural or slightly enriched uranium as fuel; (2) the cost of the installation required to produce plutonium is at present less than that involved in the production of weapons-grade uranium-235 (80 percent enriched) by isotope separation (gaseous diffusion implied); (3) the present nuclear weapons program of France was initially based on plutonium.

It is clear that the uranium-235 isotope separation at a cost comparable to the plutonium program would upset the above reasoning. While there is a renewed interest in the separation of uranium-235

* For a more detailed discussion of bomb design, see Appendix A (available from the American Academy of Arts and Sciences).

by gas-centrifuge, it appears that this is a long-range possibility depending on further technological development. For the above reasons, and for others that will become apparent, plutonium appears as the most likely program for the near future.

1. While plutonium may be considered as a by-product of the production of electrical power, the production of weapons-grade plutonium requires certain additional special measures. One requirement is short fuel cycles, with the removal of spent fuel elements every month or two. The economical operation of a power reactor requires fuel cycles of from two to three years. For the present it is sufficient to note the following: (a) on the basis of the length of the fuel cycles, we may deduce whether weapons-grade plutonium is being produced; (b) consequently, if we wish to prevent the production of weapons-grade plutonium, an effective safeguard is to monitor the length of the fuel cycles.

2. The critical size per nominal bomb (20 kilotons TNT), and the cost of the required production facilities can lead to a cost estimate for a primitive plutonium-based program. From the available unclassified sources cited in detail in the previous paper, the following conclusions are reached: after a period of five years, with an initial capital investment of $50 million and an annual operating cost of from $10 to $20 million, a country with a sufficient industrial base and skilled manpower can produce from two to four nominal bombs per year. It is important to keep these approximate data in mind in comparing this program to alternative ones leading to a few primitive nuclear weapons.*

Uranium-235 Isotope Separation: An Alternative Path

As mentioned, the only method successfully used for separating the isotopes of uranium in quantity has been the gaseous diffusion process. Despite the fact that the first three members of the nuclear club have used it, and that the fourth is taking steps to use it at least for low-enrichment separation, the method must probably be ruled out as a realistic choice for Nth countries with limited resources.

High-enrichment gaseous diffusion plants involve some 4000

* The reader interested in a more detailed, technical discussion of a primitive plutonium program is referred to Appendix B (available from the American Academy of Arts and Sciences).

separate stages, each stage requiring a pump facility and sizable porous diffusion barriers. Acres of barriers and many thousands of pumps are required. Because of the many stages, large quantities of uranium hexafluoride gas must be present, and refined methods of automatic production control are required to stabilize the system. To avoid wasting considerable quantities of uranium, material must be recycled as many as fifty times. The mass production of high-grade, noncorrosive barriers and pumps is a necessity. The consumption of electrical power is high. In a word, the simplest possible design of a gas-diffusion plant consists of such a great number of individual high-grade components that high initial capital investments for even a minimum size installation are unavoidable.[15, 16]

While the details of the United States diffusion facilities have not been revealed, its output and costs are at least approximately known. The United States facilities are quite obviously not of the minimal size needed for the production of a few weapons. The cost and output figures are nevertheless an interesting and impressive example:[17]

Initial capital investment	$2,300,000,000
Yearly operating cost	634,000,000
Yearly feed material (natural uranium)	20,000 tons
Yearly uranium-235 production (weapons grade)	75 tons
Electrical power consumption	6,000 megawatts
Cost per kilogram uranium-235	$17,000

It would, of course, be desirable to estimate the cost of a plant having an output equivalent to a few nominal weapons a year. Such an estimate has not been possible for the author for a number of reasons. Therefore, in substantiating the rejection of gaseous diffusion as a first step in a weapons program, reliance must be placed on such qualitative information as has been presented and on such guarded official statements as: "Gaseous diffusion plants are inherently of substantial capacity, and require very large amounts of electrical power. For various reasons, it is unattractive to many countries to proceed with the necessary effort to build even small diffusion plants."[15]

As already mentioned, the difficulties of gaseous diffusion can perhaps be circumvented if the gas-centrifuge method of isotope separation proves successful for large quantities. In a general statement issued in 1960 the United States Atomic Energy Commission said:[15]

> Even after substantial improvements have been made, thousands of gas centrifuges probably would be required to produce enough enriched uranium for one crude bomb a year. Including auxiliaries, a plant of this type might cost several thousand dollars per centrifuge. . . .
>
> General areas in which problems still must be solved before a satisfactory process is possible with current centrifuges include:
>
> 1) Reliability of the present experimental machines for continuous, long-term service with uranium hexa-fluoride must be proved out.
> 2) A model of the machine satisfactory for mass production of identical units must be developed.
> 3) A method must be developed to provide for introduction and removal of gas when the machines are grouped as would be necessary in a production plant.
> 4) The auxiliary process, services and instrumentation necessary for plant operations have to be determined.
>
> None of these problems is simple to solve. Excellent technical and industrial talent are required. . . .
>
> The technology of centrifuge separation is not now developed to the point where this process can produce uranium-235 at a cost competitive with the product from the A.E.C.'s current gaseous diffusion plants. On the other hand, projections of possible gains in the gas centrifuge process indicate the possibility that the process may become attractive from the economic standpoint.

From these guarded statements we can conclude: (1) The present centrifuge technology has progressed to the point where only the design of a production facility remains before the method may be usefully applied; (2) Even with further improvements, the method is at least as expensive as an equivalent plutonium facility, and does not offer the added advantage of being intimately related to the peaceful production of electrical power. Thus, even though successful, the method appears to have no particular effect on the Nth country problem.

Yet the A.E.C. has classified the United States work, and has asked the Germans and Dutch to classify theirs because of the potential use for weapons. This may be owing to the general conservative attitude in the matters of classification, but it may also mean that the A.E.C.'s only public statement does not tell the whole story.

The general statements by the A.E.C. can be evaluated to some extent through the open literature, which may be sketched as follows. Gas centrifuges for isotope separation were first suggested by Aston and Lindemann in 1919.[18] The first successful experiments (though not with uranium) were conducted in 1934.[18] Some limited success was recorded by the United States' Manhattan project during the years 1940–1943.[18] The theory of isotope separation, including centrifuge applications, has been extensively discussed.[19-21] Postwar work has been reported from Germany and the Netherlands. In 1958, Groth of Germany reported on successfully operating countercurrent gas centrifuges (a type capable in principle of greater separative power than any other kind).[22] An article on the economics of low-enrichment (not suitable for weapons) uranium production by gas centrifuge plants was presented by the Netherlands group, giving the conclusion that A.E.C. gas-diffusion prices could be undercut by a factor of 2 or more, and European gas-diffusion prices by a factor of almost 10.[23] At least one United States company is setting up the operation of German-built centrifuges for producing low-enrichment uranium, so as to undercut the A.E.C. prices.[24] The A.E.C. has cut its price for enriched uranium.[25]

Some general remarks significant for the Nth country problem may be made on the basis of a survey of the literature.

1. Gas centrifuges are limited in the size and speed of rotation by the properties (strength and elasticity) of presently available alloys (the peripheral velocity of present ultracentrifuges in Germany is about 300 meters per second.) The enrichment attainable by a centrifuge varies with the fourth power of the rotor peripheral velocity. Therefore, small increases in rotor speed imply large increases in separative power. A production facility will in general consist of a cascade of centrifuges, with a series of stages feeding into one another. A typical cascade will have 4 machines in the first stage, 2 in the second, and one in the last. Present centrifuges would necessitate about a thousand machines in the first stage, and would require ten or more stages to reach weapon-grade concentrations of uranium-235. An increase of 10 percent in rotor speed may allow the elimination of one or two stages of a typical cascade and lower the number of machines required for a given production by a factor of 10. It is therefore clear that the cost of operation is very sensitive to the future development of special materials for centrifuge rotors. The development of such materials is a typical example of a problem that has no immediate theoretical limitation, and is almost certainly going to be solved with sufficient effort.

2. The cost of a production plant is quite uncertain not only because of the possibility of grossly reducing the number of machines required, but also because the state of present laboratory research

cannot be a reliable basis for judging the cost of mass-producing centrifuges. It is possible to cite cost-per-centrifuge estimates ranging from several hundred to several thousand dollars.[15, 23] The A.E.C., while giving the figure of several thousand dollars, in a sense admits these uncertainties when it says: "As technology advances, it will be possible to make more realistic appraisals of economic attractiveness of the method of separation of uranium-235."[15]

In conclusion, even though gas-centrifuge technology may in the future be a simpler and cheaper method than plutonium production, the present distribution of actual experience and knowledge of plutonium facilities is much greater than is the case with centrifuge facilities. Thus, in the absence of controls, one can expect that the next few Nth countries will travel the proven road of plutonium. In the more distant future, in the absence of controls, the centrifuge method will probably pay off and offer a country an easily concealed, low-cost plant, in comparison to the equivalent plutonium facilities.

Uranium-233, a Third Alternative

Uranium-233 is a third (artificial) fissile material. If it could be produced, it would be useful for weapon production as well as for reactor construction. To date it has not been produced in large quantities even by the great powers. Uranium-233 can be obtained from the naturally occurring fertile material thorium-232, which has an almost 100 percent natural abundance. The production of uranium-233 follows a path similar to that of plutonium-239, (see Fig. 1). Any fissile material may be substituted for uranium-235, thorium is substituted for uranium-238, and the product uranium-233 is substituted for plutonium-239.

Thorium ores are 3-5 times more abundant than uranium ores, and generally in a naturally occurring concentration that is 50-100 times greater. The present cost of thorium on the world market is equal to that of uranium only because no large-scale production has been undertaken. Because of higher thermal neutron capture probabilities, thorium can be converted to fissile uranium-233 at a greater rate than can uranium-238 to plutonium-239.[26] Finally, uranium-233 can probably be detonated by the simpler ballistic technique. Thus at first it would appear that thorium as fertile material for the production of fissile material would offer distinct advantages over uranium.

The difficulty comes in the initial supply of fissile material necessary. Unlike uranium, thorium contains no naturally occurring fissile isotope which can yield fission neutrons for sustaining a controlled chain reaction. Therefore, a converter reactor using thorium as fertile material must have one of the three fissile materials added to it in order to begin operation. The added fissile material must be highly enriched before it is combined with large quantities of thorium.[26] Therefore, it is clear that either a large-scale isotope separation of uranium-235 or plutonium production must precede the use of thorium. This rules out the production of uranium-233 as an initial step.

As an example, India, now in the first stage of her nuclear power program, is building large natural uranium reactors, even though she has thorium reserves equal to the world's supply of uranium. In the second stage, she plans to use the plutonium produced in these reactors as the necessary fissile material to start breeding uranium-233 from thorium. In the third stage, having uranium-233 available, she will be able to use thorium exclusively.[27]

Other Roads to Nuclear Weapons: Controlled Fusion

In the previous sections we have described the methods for obtaining the three fissile isotopes suitable for weapons production. Of these, plutonium-239 and uranium-233 must be artificially produced by neutron irradiation of fertile material. While at present the only neutron sources strong enough for this process are powerful reactors, other neutron sources that may become available in the future could perhaps be used in the production of isotopes and, in particular, fissile materials. It is possible that the controlled release of energy from fusion would provide an equivalent neutron source.

Fusion research is extraordinarily expensive. Because of its implications for weapons, the work was partly classified in the past, and until 1956 it was confined to the United States, Russia, and Great Britain. Since then, the hope of early practical use and commercialization has faded, and today the work has been fully declassified and is being conducted in nineteen countries.[28] The future shape of controlled thermonuclear devices is far from clear, as exemplified by the recent abandonment of a fairly large-scale experiment in Great Britain.[28] It therefore appears that the road to nuclear weapons by way of neutrons from controlled fusion, though conceivable, is not of practical interest in the near future.

Other Roads to Nuclear Weapons: Uncontrolled Fusion

It is well-known that an H-bomb, utilizing large quantities of light elements such as tritium, can be set off by means of an atomic bomb or a fission trigger. The advantage of H-bombs is that they can be made of virtually unlimited size, and that the light elements used to release nuclear energy by fusion are cheap.* The recent debate in the United States on neutron bombs has been interpreted widely as meaning that fusion explosions could be produced without the use of a fission trigger.** If this is indeed so, then it is perhaps possible for small countries to obtain thermonuclear explosives without needing to develop fission devices first.

The most powerful argument against the development of fission free fusion weapons by Nth countries is that the nuclear powers have tried for years without success to do it. The problem is one of sustaining temperatures of the order of tens of millions of degrees over an appreciable volume filled with light material. To do this with a fission explosion is surely not a trivial task. Yet to do the same with chemical explosives is extraordinarily difficult. In not using the fission trigger, one sacrifices approximately eight orders of magnitude (a factor of 100,000,000) in the energy released per atom. It is quite certain, therefore, that the problems of fission free detonation of a fusion explosion far outweigh the problems of producing a simple fission bomb, and that for Nth countries this path to nuclear weapons is not a reasonable first step. H-bombs, on the other hand, can be quite easily obtained as a second step in weapon development. The only critical material that is probably necessary is deuterium, which can be obtained on the world market for $60 per kilogram.***

* The cost of a thermonuclear device is largely due to the fission trigger, and to the amount of fusion material present. This is indicated by the fact that the U.S.A.E.C. gives prices of thermonuclear devices for Project Plowshare that are largely independent of explosive power: a 20-kiloton device costs nearly the same as does a 20-megaton device.[29]

** It is doubtful whether a neutron bomb would necessarily be a fission-free device. Inglis, for one, has argued that a small fission device, whose neutron radiation would exceed its blast radius, would be a method of producing a bomb which "kills but preserves property"—a way which incidentally is available now.[30, 31]

*** For a more detailed description of thermonuclear weapons, the reader is referred to Appendix C (available from the American Academy of Arts and Sciences).

2. WORLD-WIDE DISTRIBUTION OF NUCLEAR TECHNOLOGY

The various approaches to nuclear-weapon production have been outlined. It is now of interest to examine the distribution of nuclear technology in the countries of the world.*

Key Index of Nuclear Technology: Reactors

Nuclear reactors are perhaps the single most important sign of nuclear technology. All in all, there are some 201 reactors built, building, or planned. Of these, 119 are nonplutonium producing research reactors, of which 99 were operative in 1961. The remaining 82 are plutonium producers, and of their number 38 were operative in 1961. The reactor survey cannot be considered complete for the Soviet bloc, since only limited information is available.

It is noteworthy that many of this large number of reactors exist because of the extensive export activities of the United States and Russia, and to a lesser extent Great Britain and Canada. The United States, for example, has to date exported more than 56 reactors and numerous special materials through its bilateral agreements for peaceful cooperation with 42 countries.[32] It is equally noteworthy that for the United States and (presumably) British and Canadian exports, provisions exist for safeguards to prevent the diversion of materials for weapons purposes. In 1961, the United States had applied safeguards to 63 installations in 23 countries.[33] On the other hand, the Soviet Union has said it places no safeguards on exported nuclear facilities.

Such over-all statistics as the above are important in themselves, but not very meaningful for assessing the nuclear-weapon capability of each individual country. In the following list, countries are arranged in various categories of development on the basis of their reactor programs. Particular emphasis is given to the plutonium producing potential, since this, it has been concluded, will be the basis for an initial nuclear weapons program in the near future. The effects of the United States safeguard provisions are also noted where possible.

* A tabulation of the world's reactors, with cost, plutonium production capability, and other data, has been used to reach the conclusions in this section. The tabulation appears in Appendix D (available from the American Academy of Arts and Sciences).

Levels of Nuclear Capability

Some nuclear research: 43 countries possess or will possess at least one research reactor. They are:

Argentina	Hungary	Rumania
Australia	India	Spain
Austria	Indonesia	Sweden
Belgium	Iran	Switzerland
Brazil	Israel	Taiwan
Bulgaria	Italy	Thailand
Canada	Japan	Turkey
China	Korea, S.	Union of South Africa
Congo	Netherlands	United Arab Republic
Czechoslovakia	New Zealand	United Kingdom
Denmark	Norway	Venezuela
France	Pakistan	Vietnam, S.
Germany, E.	Philippines	Yugoslavia
Germany, W.	Poland	
Greece	Portugal	

Some nuclear power production: 18 countries have built, are building, or are planning to build some nuclear power stations. Of these 8 had operative power reactors in 1961 (indicated by *).

Belgium*	Germany, W.*	Poland
Canada*	India	Rumania
China	Italy	Spain
Czechoslovakia*	Japan	Sweden*
France	Netherlands	Switzerland
Germany, E.*	Norway	United Kingdom*

Building their own reactors: 12 countries have built or are building at least one reactor primarily with their own technological efforts.

Argentina	India	Netherlands
Belgium	Germany, W.	Sweden
Canada	Italy	United Kingdom
France	Japan	Yugoslavia

Building their own power reactors: 7 countries have built or are building at least one power reactor primarily through their own technological efforts.

Canada	Italy	United Kingdom
France	Japan	
Germany, W.	Sweden	

Present plutonium production: 10 countries are capable of producing significant quantities of weapon-grade plutonium today. In most cases, the weapon-grade plutonium would have to be diverted by running electrical-power stations on short uneconomical fuel cycles. In only 3 countries is there positive evidence of weapon-grade plutonium production. In addition, 5 countries are affected, and 4 are eliminated altogether by United States safeguards against the diversion of weapon-grade materials. The available information is summarized below, with parentheses indicating that United States safeguards apply.

TABLE 1: APPROXIMATE PLUTONIUM PRODUCTION, 1961

	Production/yr.		Equivalent No. of nominal (20 kilotons TNT) bombs if:	
Country	Total plutonium kg.	Plutonium known to be a weapon grade-kg.	All the plutonium is diverted for weapons use	Only known weapon-grade plutonium is used
Belgium	(12.5)	—	(1–2)	—
Canada	81	10	8–16	1–2
Czechoslovakia	150	—	15–30	—
France	358 + (4)	92	36–72	9–18
Germany, E.	60	—	6–12	—
Germany, W.	(18)	—	(2–4)	—
India	10	—	1–2	—
U. K.	660	200	66–132	20–40
Sweden	(15)	—	(1–3)	—
Switzerland	(5)	—	(0–1)	—

Future plutonium production: in most of the 18 countries which are building power reactors or have plans for them the future plutonium production (without regard to safeguards or fuel cycles) can be estimated on the basis of expected power levels. The available information is summarized below.

TABLE 2: APPROXIMATE FUTURE PLUTONIUM PRODUCTION

Country	Expected plutonium production in kilograms	
	1965	1975
Belgium	142	1500
Canada	261	?
China	?	?
Czechoslovakia	400 +	5000
France	750 +	8000
Germany, E.	300 +	3000 +
Germany, W.	100 +	6000
India	260	?
Italy	500 +	?
Japan	130 +	7000
Netherlands	120	3000
Norway	25 +	?
Poland	200 +	1800
Rumania	?	500
Spain	?	1800
Sweden	45	2000
Switzerland	32	?
United Kingdom	3200	6000 +

Over-all independent capability: since the effects of the extensive importing of reactors and special materials, both today and in the future, tend to blur truly independent capability, it is important finally to ask what countries are capable of producing significant results without the help of others. This was the approach taken in the previous paper,[1] and it is the only approach which will be more or less independent of future political rearrangements in the world. Without repeating details of the previous analysis, countries having the necessary economic base, industrial capacity, and skilled manpower for at least a primitive program for nuclear weapons in the near future are (two have succeeded, of course):

Belgium	China	France
Canada	Czechoslovakia	Germany, E.

Germany, W.	Japan	United Kingdom
India	Sweden	
Italy	Switzerland	

With further industrial and economic development, many others will of course follow.

The Question of China

What about Communist China? Clearly, not much can be said from the above. Reports from China are scanty and contradictory, and perhaps the things we "hear" are in part influenced by the intense fear of a nuclear China which exists in the Western countries. About the only hard information is that China intends to obtain its own nuclear weapons. Two additional statements can probably be made:

1. If the Soviet Union had given China substantial help (for example, a plutonium-producing reactor), the first Chinese nuclear test would have already occurred, or should occur very soon; for China qualifies industrially, economically, and by its manpower, according to the conclusions in the previous paper.[1]
2. China's determination to enter modern (Western) science came in 1949,[34] and for this reason it is wholly unfounded to assume that her nuclear-weapons potential today is in any way comparable to that of the Soviet Union when it stood on the threshold of the nuclear age. The latter, while hindered by the unproductive economic system prior to 1917, was nevertheless an important contributor to Western science one hundred years earlier, even before the United States. China, on the other hand, relies today for her scientific leadership on a handful of Western- or Soviet-trained people, and has not been able to produce first-rate contributors to the frontiers of science in her own universities for a variety of reasons. This is not to deny the great devotion and enthusiasm undoubtedly present in Chinese education today, nor to deny that China soon may produce primitive nuclear explosives wholly independently.

3. THE PROBLEM OF DELIVERY SYSTEMS

It may be argued that, of the two ingredients for making a nuclear power, the acquisition of nuclear explosives is more difficult to achieve than *some* means of delivery, and that for this reason a discussion of delivery systems as part of the Nth country problem is not of primary importance. It is indeed the case that any country having sufficient resources to build nuclear weapons will, within important limits, be able to obtain the necessary delivery systems under present circumstances.

This argument, which will be expanded here, may sound at first strange in the face of the widely acknowledged fact that the present nuclear powers are lagging in delivery systems and rather than in nuclear warheads. However, it is hoped that the necessary distinction can clarify the situation.

Nuclear "Greats" and Secondary Nuclear Powers

The distinction to be made is between what one might call the "nuclear greats" and the secondary nuclear powers. The only true nuclear greats today are the Soviet Union and the United States, for only they are able to approach "credible" deterrence through second-strike capability, that is, the ability to absorb the first blow and still hit back with devastating force. All other powers, whether nuclear or not, must be classed as secondary, because they cannot by themselves muster a second strike capability against one of the nuclear greats.

The basic cause of secondary nuclear status is that the entrance fee to the club of nuclear greats must be paid on a continuing and accelerating basis in *delivery* systems costing an exorbitant price: the mere possession of nuclear explosives means nothing in this situation. The great cost of delivery systems necessary to maintain nuclear-great status is well illustrated by United States expenditures. Despite a stockpile of nuclear explosives of an estimated 50,000 megatons,[17] the annual United States expenditure on first-rank long-range delivery systems is about twenty times the annual cost of manufacturing nuclear explosives. The 9 or more billion dollars spent annually by the United States for long-range delivery systems is roughly equivalent to the cost of keeping up a 2½ million-man army.[35-37] Clearly, this kind of effort is impossible for a country of considerably less wealth than the United States.

The situations in the two countries closest to the status of nuclear great is interesting in itself. In 1960, Great Britain dropped out of the missile race and scuttled the goal of an independent deterrent, after having spent at least $308 million on the development of an obsolescent missile.[38] Despite her nuclear-weapon stockpile of not inconsiderable size, she now describes her goal as a "contribution to the Western deterrent." France, on the other hand, has not given up, but lags so much in the development of advanced delivery systems (and nuclear explosives, for that matter), that it appears that her development serves only to inflate French notions of status,[39] but not as a military deterrent against a nuclear great. By an expenditure of over $500 million a year, France hopes to attain a small (and already obsolescent) Mach 2 bomber force by 1965, and some solid fuel IRBM's by 1968.[40, 41] At least one nuclear submarine is also planned, though its reactor will depend for fuel on an as-yet-incomplete gaseous diffusion plant. Even nuclear-weapon production appears to be lagging, and it is probable that France will not have a stockpile large enough to supply her anticipated bomber force in 1965.[41]

The important point is not that secondary powers like France and Great Britain are inherently incapable of obtaining nuclear-great status and the credible second-strike capability against other nuclear greats that necessarily goes with it. It is that, under present circumstances, the arms race between Russia and the United States shows no sign of stabilizing by itself, and that it requires continued improvement in delivery systems by each side in order to match improvements by the other. Only if the arms race should come to the point where no further significant improvements in delivery and counterdelivery systems are possible will smaller countries be able to gain equality. Other authors have come to similar conclusions.[5, 10]

Nuclear Sharing

Many countries, such as India, have accepted their status as non-nuclear powers. As for Communist China and Western Europe, the situation has not been as simple. China has announced her intention to obtain nuclear weapons and, in fact, nuclear-great status. In Western Europe, the vanishing credibility of strictly British or French deterrents, or of the "conventional" German forces (with American nuclear warheads in the closet), has led to a long debate about "nuclear sharing."

The various degrees of nuclear sharing, as well as the underlying assumptions, have been discussed elsewhere by Raymond Aron,[42] P. M. S. Blackett[5, 43] Alastair Buchan,[7, 44] A. L. Burns,[45]

Klaus Knorr,[46] and Albert Wohlstetter.[9] It will be of interest here to look at the development of the problem, as an illustration of the difficulties which arise out of the instability of the race in delivery systems.

One might start in the early 1950's. At that time, America was trying to achieve a policy of containment through a system of foreign bases. The bases were needed because the shortcomings of available delivery systems prevented the establishment of an adequate force on American soil. Thus, if for no other reason, NATO was formed, and because of her geographical location, West Germany was persuaded to rearm and to accept nuclear weapons on her territory. Meanwhile, Great Britain and later France proceeded in the development of their own delivery forces and nuclear weapons.

By 1958, NATO was firmly established, and for lack of the promised contributions from Britain and France, Germany became the key European member of the alliance. By this time the evidence that Britain and France could not achieve credible deterrence by themselves was beginning to collect. In her famous White Paper on Defense of April 1957,[47] Great Britain, five years after her first bomb, tacitly admitted her loss of deterrent power by her decision "not to defend the whole country, but to defend only . . . bomber bases." This was also the time when significant political forces in Great Britain began to argue that unilateral nuclear disarmament was a logical and militarily sound step for Great Britain under the circumstances.[5, 43, 48, 49]

At the same time, America's interest in NATO had grown from her need for bases to her explicit commitment to defend Europe with her nuclear arsenal. In order to enforce this commitment, she found it necessary to argue at times for a European deterrent—NATO as a fourth nuclear power—because of the oft-expressed fear that a mere promise to defend Europe with nuclear weapons made the American deterrent incredible. During these discussions, the system of joint control of the nuclear triggers with an American veto was established. No one was quite sure who would control the weapons in a crisis, and when Secretary Herter said in 1959 that he "cannot conceive any President engaging in all-out nuclear war unless we are in danger of all-out war ourselves,"[50] there was consternation among some Europeans because this statement appeared to undermine the very credibility that was to be achieved by the sharing of the nuclear triggers.

Meanwhile, France, consistent with her go-it-alone policy, refused to cooperate with the NATO deterrent altogether, and refused explicitly to accede to American nuclear bombers in France, to joint control of IRBM's, or even to the integration of her Mediterranean fleet with NATO.[51] With the stimulus of the Berlin crisis, a new ingredient in the European situation is the threat by some in West Germany to seek nuclear weapons elsewhere if they are not supplied by the United States.[52] In short, West Germans distrust the American promise. With the further development of delivery systems, on the other hand, the original American interest in bases has dissipated; and while America still stands committed to Europe's defense, she is now pressing for greater conventional strength in Europe. The cause of this appears to be the fact that the various proposals for nuclear sharing, after prolonged debate and several years of a two-headed policy, appear unworkable. Simply stated, it appears that the principle of "too many fingers on the trigger" has outweighed the principle of "greater credibility." In any case, at the end of its first year, the Kennedy administration had dropped plans for five NATO controlled Polaris submarines and one hundred NATO IRBM's, and was willing to rely on a conventionally armed NATO force.[53] The apparent retreat from nuclear sharing might indeed explain in part the unusually strong and repeated assertions by the administration in summer 1961, proclaiming that the United States itself will use nuclear weapons in the Berlin crisis, if necessary. Today, in a manner characteristic of the NATO sharing debate, the United States government is again in a sharing mood, as is illustrated in the recent proposal to "turn over" the entire Polaris force to NATO—with American commanders of course.

It would be interesting to know the parallel to the NATO difficulties in the Communist world. The situation reportedly is fairly similar. China certainly feels the need for nuclear weapons, and has said so. The Soviet Union is reluctant to share its status as a nuclear great with China. And, as with the West, the Soviet Union's guarantee to China probably consists of bold words (especially to the West) without a commitment of nuclear delivery systems to Chinese military forces.

A basic conclusion from the efforts of nuclear sharing would be the following. The nuclear greats are in a position of such preponderant delivery power at the present moment in the arms race that one should not expect it to be in their national interest to dilute this power by sharing it on an equal basis with their allies. Since the allies (with the possible exception of China) can achieve nuclear-great status only through borrowing, it is unlikely that new powers with a second strike capability against the nuclear greats will arise. In fact, those secondary powers who choose to align themselves with either of the nuclear greats in the East-West conflict will have to rely on the verbal promises of the nuclear greats for their national "power." This is not to say that there will not be more nuclear powers in the future, but only that they will be secondary nuclear powers. It is also not to deny that secondary nuclear powers could cause nuclear war between the nuclear greats by accident, misinterpretation, catalysis, or irrational action in a manner that has been described by many writers.

The Secondary Nuclear Powers Among Themselves

The nullification of the secondary nuclear powers in rational opposition to the nuclear greats leaves us with the question of delivery systems in conflicts in which secondary nuclear powers oppose other secondary powers. Here the requirements for a useful delivery system are greatly reduced. Without attempting to go into details of military delivery systems, one can see that relatively primitive ones will be sufficient. Just as it was possible to deliver the first atomic bomb with a 300 mph aircraft, so it will be possible to do this today with the same equipment against equivalent air defenses. Unfortunately, no detailed information about air-defense systems around the world has been discovered by the author. On the other hand, some considerable evidence of a widespread distribution of aircraft can be given.

First, even though the United States and Russia far out-produce all other countries in advanced military aircraft, at least ten other countries have an aircraft industry capable of producing at least one model of advanced fighter aircraft. These countries are:

Australia	France	Japan
Canada	Germany, W.	Sweden
China	Great Britain	Switzerland
Czechoslovakia	Italy	

Most of the aircraft produced by these countries are short range, defense-oriented aircraft. However, many of the modern interceptors and fighters are so heavy that they can carry nuclear weapons for distances of from 1,000 to 2,000 miles. France and Great Britain are the only countries among the above which are known to be producing modern medium-to-long-range strategic bombers.

Second, with thousands of obsolescent military aircraft cast off by the great powers each year, almost every country in the world can buy an air force equipped with United States or Soviet (and some British) military aircraft which were first-line aircraft for the great powers some five or ten years ago. At the moment, the standard United States export is F-86 Sabre Jets of the Korean War vintage, and some slightly more advanced models dating back to as late as 1958. The standard Soviet export is the Mig-17, which is also of the post-Korean War vintage. Transport aircraft, reconnaissance aircraft, light bombers, and helicopters are exported to almost all countries in addition to fighter aircraft. The price paid for these obsolescent models is not great, and poor allies frequently receive them as outright gifts. Thus it should not be surprising that some poor country will find itself with an airforce of from 50 to 100 jet fighters, but no pilots to fly them.

The result of the widespread independent manufacture of aircraft and of the even more widespread export of aircraft is seen in a survey of the world's air forces. From the most detailed work available on these air forces,[54] we may abstract some cumulative statistics: (1) at least 56 countries are equipped with some model of jet fighter aircraft; (2) at least 24 countries have post-World War II model bombers; (3) the total operational military aircraft exceeds

(a) 100 in 44 countries
(b) 300 in 27 countries
(c) 600 in 9 countries
(d) 1000 in 6 countries.

Since even the extensive United States and Soviet air defenses and radar warning lines are by no means one hundred percent effective against the penetration of single aircraft, it is probably correct to conclude that the balance between air-defense and delivery capability leans heavily to the latter in the case of secondary-power conflicts. This state of affairs means that almost any country can deliver the bomb against a secondary power, even though only some countries can make the bomb. The nuclear club as such is therefore limited by the ability to manufacture nuclear weapons, and not by the ability to deliver them. Finally, it is of interest that even a restriction of the widespread trade in military aircraft would not change this state of affairs. For the group of independent producers of military aircraft is also roughly the same group that is most likely to achieve an independent nuclear-weapon capability in the near future.*

4. NTH COUNTRY CONTROLS

As already noted, discussions of the Nth country problem have always contained the explicit or implicit assumption that some manner of control to halt the spread of nuclear technology will eventually be desirable. Even those who argue that the spread of nuclear weapons is not necessarily an undesirable step would agree with this. The governments of the United States, the Soviet Union, and Great Britain are all on record as favoring halting the diffusion of nuclear weapons. In fact, the underlying principle of the International Atomic Energy Agency (IAEA), with over seventy member nations, is that the development of weapons by additional countries must be stopped.

Thus everyone is agreed. We might then naively ask, why has no progress been made? There are many answers. Some would argue that there are no controls technologically available to ensure that new countries will not utilize atomic energy for military purposes. This, however, is not a serious objection, for it can be shown, even if the spread of nuclear weapons capability cannot be 100 percent controlled, that it can be severely dampened by such measures as a universal test ban and a variety of controls over the production of fissionable materials. Others would argue that Nth country controls, even if technically possible, go against the interests of national sovereignty everywhere, and would point to the example of India, who has refused to accede to the modest control system of the IAEA.

In the author's view, the real difficulty, though mentioned by some,[10] has not often been emphasized. It is necessary to distinguish between two types of solutions to the problem of nuclear-weapon diffusion: (1) solutions that involve equivalent sacrifices on the part of the nuclear powers as well as the nonnuclear powers; and (2) solutions that involve marked restriction on the nonnuclear powers alone. Only the first type can be expected to succeed. Yet no at-

* The reader interested in a tabulation of independent aircraft manufacture around the world, as well as a country-to-country survey of aircraft strength is referred to Appendix E (available from the American Academy of Arts and Sciences).

tempt has been made in that direction, while a lot of effort has been wasted on the second approach. In the following sections, these assertions will be enlarged and various measures for control discussed, with the indicated distinction in mind.

The Baruch Plan

It is instructive to recall the first attempt at the international control of atomic energy when only N = 1 had materialized, and N = 2 was in the making. In the United Nations in 1946, the United States, under what has come to be called the "Baruch Plan," proposed to the Soviet Union that all aspects of atomic energy, including military aspects should come under the international ownership of an International Atomic Development Agency (IADA). The IADA would be charged with the further development of the beneficial aspects of atomic energy, and would enforce strict prohibitions on military production. The authors of the plan, recognizing the purely negative aspect of control, put great emphasis on the developmental aspects of the proposal. They also strongly emphasized the need to control *every* step in possible production processes. They envisaged 300 inspectors, for example, to guard a gaseous diffusion plant.[55]

For reasons now widely recognized as understandable, the Russians refused to cooperate. Negotiations during 1946-1948 were marked by disagreement on almost everything except the principle that some kind of safeguards with inspection were desirable. In particular, while Americans proposed that the atomic weapons they held be relinquished and destroyed as one of the last steps in the plan, the Soviet Union insisted that the bomb be outlawed and destroyed as the first step. With all the goods on the American side of the table the Russians had in fact no bargaining power.[56, 57]

Without denying the importance of the truly revolutionary idea of international ownership or the sincerity of the American scientists and businessmen who formulated the plan, it must be concluded, in retrospect, that the Baruch Plan was decidedly of the second type, involving marked restriction on the nonnuclear powers alone, and that it failed primarily for this reason.

The Grand Plan of the IAEA

The Soviet Union and the United States carried on a fruitless battle of words on nuclear disarmament throughout the 1950's. The next development related primarily to Nth country controls came in 1956 with the founding of the International Atomic Energy Agency (IAEA). Like the Baruch Plan, the Agency was an idea spawned among the scientists and politicians of the West, and it drew its specific impetus from President Eisenhower's famous speech, "Atoms for Peace."[58] The first purpose of the IAEA was to promote the peaceful uses of atomic energy, and to act in particular as a distributor of nuclear materials and installations. A second purpose was to set safeguards on nuclear materials and to prevent their diversion for weapon purposes.

A comparison with the Baruch Plan is interesting. Unlike the Baruch Plan, the Statute of the IAEA[59] recognized the need for some national control over nuclear development and the unacceptability of international ownership. Like the Baruch Plan, the program of the IAEA would depend for its nuclear materials on the nuclear power(s), and would prevent applications of this material to weapons. And unfortunately, unlike the Baruch Plan, the program of the IAEA did not even take note of the existing stockpiles of weapons of the nuclear powers.

What has been the result of the Agency's five years of existence? In brief, the plot has failed despite all good intentions. And it has failed for other reasons than the fact that the plan contained no major concessions on the part of the nuclear powers. The first purpose of the Agency (to distribute nuclear materials and installations) has gone forward very slowly. While useful work has been performed on setting standards, distributing limited quantities of isotopes, and serving as a center for the exchange of technical information, the job of large-scale distribution of atomic installations has been done by the nuclear powers outside the Agency. As already noted in Section 3, the United States has contributed to at least 63 reactor installations around the world, yet only 3 reactors have been channeled through the Agency.[60] One reason for this is that large private companies in the West have been able to do the job more efficiently than the Agency at less cost.[61] Also (so far at least) the United States has absorbed the cost of the safeguards it applies, while under the Agency the not trivial cost of the safeguards is borne by the receiving country. The Soviet Union has bypassed the Agency as well, and in its numerous bilateral agreements it has supplied many countries with reactors without safeguards. The inactivity of the Agency to this date is not, however, due to fundamental flaw in its structure. The bypassing of the

Agency merely reflects the confused policy of the nuclear powers. In fact, to correct her policy, the United States has belatedly proposed to put all her bilateral agreements under the jurisdiction of the Agency.[60]

A more serious question is the matter of the safeguard system of the Agency. From the beginning, the subject of safeguards has been a source of disagreement, and when the Statute of the IAEA was passed in 1956, the Soviet bloc and a group of neutral nations led by India opposed the majority decision on safeguards. In January 1961, when a more detailed document on the Agency safeguards was approved, the same division existed in the IAEA Board of Governors.

The Safeguard Debate in the IAEA[62]

Because the IAEA safeguards debate illustrates the basic difficulties encountered in establishing Nth country controls, it will be of interest to examine the main arguments.

The majority share the United States' view, supported by nearly all her allies in Europe, Asia, and America, and by a few unaligned countries including Sweden, Switzerland, the Union of South Africa, Iceland, and Israel. In this view, safeguards outlined in the Statute and in more detail in the document of 31 January 1961[63] should be adhered to. These safeguards include the following major points:

(1) Agency approval of the design of reactors and other nuclear facilities aided by the Agency, with the purpose of preventing a military purpose being served.

(2) Agency access to a system of records showing how the country in question has disposed of materials and facilities received through the Agency.

(3) Agency inspections to account for material which the Agency has supplied. In determining the number of inspections, the possession of irradiated-fuel processing plants and other relevant circumstances are taken into account, and the goal of inspections is taken as limiting the fissile material accounting error to less than .2 Kilograms.

It is noteworthy that Agency safeguards are to apply to all materials supplied, including source materials (natural uranium fuel), installations, and fissile materials.

The majority have consistently held that only safeguards of

this extent can ensure that material is not diverted for weapon purposes. The majority have also held that making safeguards more universally applicable (for instance, to the nuclear powers) is unrealistic and unpractical at present. Let us, they have urged, first get the control of the spread of weapon-capability, then consider existing weapon producers.

The Soviet-bloc countries are found in the minority grouping, as well as a number of Asian and African neutrals, including the United Arab Republic, Afghanistan, Burma, Ceylon, Ghana, India, Indonesia, Iraq, and Morocco. Among the minority, two more or less distinct groupings are evident.

The first is the Soviet-bloc, which is opposed to IAEA safeguards in principle. These countries argue that safeguards should be applied through measures such as the test ban and general disarmament, and not through the IAEA, which after all is devoted to the peaceful applications of atomic energy and not to military applications. The Soviet representative actually made a great point that in the Socialist countries safeguards were unnecessary, and were in fact not applied in bilateral agreements because scientists conducting peaceful research have no interest in weapon production and would in fact be humiliated by unnecessary measures of control. He also argued that most countries to which the safeguards were to apply were poor countries which could not produce weapons for this reason.

A second grouping among the minority are the Asian and African neutrals led by India. This group is not opposed to safeguards in principle, but to the particular format of the IAEA safeguards. Consequently, they have voted with the Soviet bloc almost all the time and have been mistakenly considered part of it. Put simply, the view of this group is that safeguards should be universal, or not at all. The main contention of the Indian delegates can be summarized as follows: (1) It is illogical to apply safeguards only to countries which apply to the Agency for aid, because these are precisely the countries least in a position to make weapons; and at the same time to let countries "go free" which do not apply and which can make weapons because of their more advanced state. (2) It is equally illogical under the Agency system of safeguards to allow aid to countries that have a weapon program; for, since safeguards apply only to facilities to which aid is given, it is possible that the Agency will indirectly aid the weapon programs. (3) Finally, it is illogical, independently of the above conditions, for any safeguard system to include control over source material such as natural uranium, which can be obtained on the world market without safeguards. The only interpretation of such excessively strict safeguards would be that the poor countries, which can produce no weapons in any case, are subject to indirect discrimination and dictation by the larger supplier nations.

India has underlined her sincerity in these criticisms by throwing open all the doors to her atomic laboratories, thus demonstrating to anyone that she is not producing weapons.[64] In addition, she has attempted to offer a compromise solution to the safeguard question, under which safeguards would apply only to fissionable materials, even when the control system is otherwise not different. To date, the only answer to the Indian criticism has been a United States proposal to put four United States research reactors under IAEA safeguards.[60] Needless to say, this has not affected the root of the difficulty.

It is the author's view that the Indian proposals and criticisms attack the most important point in the question of Nth country controls. As noted, this is the recognition that acceptable controls must envisage a degree of restriction of both nuclear and non-nuclear countries, of both rich and poor countries. It is a matter of practical politics, as well as of just principle. In comparison, the United States conception of safeguards may indeed lead to the control of much fissile material, but it leaves the nuclear powers untouched, and perhaps it even aids their weapon programs. The Soviet conception, while recognizing the need for safeguarding weapon-grade material, scuttles any meaningful role for the IAEA by referring the important problem of safeguards to other (equally ineffective) international debating societies.

Despite the significance of the debate on safeguards, the decision reached in favor of the United States safeguards will neither kill the IAEA, as some have claimed, nor will it solve the Nth country problem. As the IAEA continues, capable neither of functioning effectively as a universal distributor of peaceful atomic energy nor as an organ of control, one hopes something will be learned from what looks conspicuously like a "second Baruch Plan."

What Constitutes Sufficient Production Controls?

Before turning to other measures of control, it is useful to look at the IAEA safeguards from a purely technical point of view. In particular, it is of interest to ask of these safeguards a question that should be asked of any arms-control or disarmament measure: are they as simple and as nonrestrictive as they could be, consistent with the goal of preventing independent weapon programs?

As noted in Section 2, the production of weapon-grade plutonium-239 is subject to a simple restriction. If fuel cycles are too long, the product has such a high content of plutonium-240 that its application to weapons becomes impossible. Without actual experience in building bombs, the critical level of plutonium-240 contamination that prevents detonation cannot be determined. Yet it is almost certain that there is such a level, and according to the best information available, it is about 1 percent of the plutonium-240 content.* Even if a contamination with plutonium-240 up to 5 percent were allowable for weapon application, the equivalent fuel cycles would be short and uneconomical. It appears that a sufficient production control for reactors powered by natural uranium is merely the regulation of fuel cycles. This is a simple task.

This measure was recognized by the United States as early as 1946, and its implication for safeguards well understood.** "Denaturing," as the method of plutonium-240 contamination is called, has its limitations. A facility for isotope separation would preclude its usefulness, for example. The limitations are not serious, however. Despite the simplicity of the method, it has not led to the design of simple control measures. If indeed denaturing works in the way described, why has the United States insisted on detailed reports and inspections, and even on the accountability of source materials? One answer is that foolproof safeguards could otherwise not be achieved. While this may indeed be true, it is also unrealistic, for controls must be politically acceptable, as well as effective. It appears quite certain that simpler and yet sufficient systems of safeguards can be designed. With the eventual wide-spread application of reactor controls, such systems will be necessary from an economic point of view as well.

A recent suggestion to involve the IAEA in the business of formulating technical plans for nuclear disarmament is relevant.[61] The sooner the technical questions of disarmament become a matter for international discussion, the more likely is it that the point of view of smaller nations will be taken into account. The double

* See Appendix A.

** A 1946 government press release on denaturing is reproduced in Appendix F (available from the American Academy of Arts and Sciences).

criterion of political acceptibility as well as sufficiency is more likely to be met. At present, with no technical work on controls being performed by the IAEA itself, and with the United States approach dominating the organization, this criterion is not being met.

The Test Ban

It remains to note a third effort at the international control of nuclear weapons: the test ban. It is not my intention to review the voluminous literature on the negotiations or the many technical questions such as the threshold of detectability under various systems. Two points are of interest. Can a universal test-ban agreement solve the Nth country problem from a technical point of view? Can we expect a universal agreement even if the United States and Russia solve their present differences on the test ban and come to terms?

In my view, the answer to the first question is yes. Some writers have doubted that the test ban alone can give 100 percent insurance that some country will not develop untested weapons.[11] Yet judging from the difficult problem of weapon detonation no country could get far without testing, and it would certainly not be able to use its "weapons" as a military threat without first demonstrating that they work. In fact, if the history of United States weapon development is any indication, weapons smaller than a kiloton are probably of an advanced kind; thus for the purpose of Nth country controls, the troublesome question of the threshold of detecting underground-tests may be obviated. Before accepting this (and other points where classified information is crucial), more information must become available.

In regard to the second question, there appears real reason to doubt whether success can be achieved, even if Russia and the United States agree. This is owing to the principle set forth earlier. The test ban, in itself, is *not* disarmament, and has never been considered as such by either side. A universal test ban affects the non-nuclear powers severely, yet it little touches the ability of the nuclear powers to make nuclear war, or even to produce more and better weapons.[65]

From examples at hand, we can see this argument at work in the case of France and China. France has not achieved "full" nuclear status and hence has refused to accede to the trial moratorium. De Gaulle in fact has made quite clear his reasons for a nuclear force: he does not trust anyone, including the United States, to come to his aid with nuclear weapons. China, though she has no weapons, has announced her intention to obtain them, and through her opposition to Khrushchev has shown herself unwilling to negotiate with the West on disarmament, let alone to participate in a test ban.

In fact, even if the negotiations in Geneva had led to success, the resulting treaty would have been of little worth. Without China's signature, the West would not long have trusted the Soviet bloc; without France's signature, the Soviet Union could easily argue the reverse. Mistrust is itself a reason for the failure of arms agreements, and it certainly appears that the failure of the test ban has been owing to the mistrust between Russia and the United States. But it is important to note that the test ban is after all primarily an Nth country directed measure, with only a tension-easing effect on the nuclear powers. As such, it has serious drawbacks if it is separated from more substantial steps on disarmament. The limitations of the test ban in this respect have never been taken seriously by those who have advocated it as a "hopeful first step which will solve the Nth country problem once and for all."

Nth Country Controls and Disarmament

The preceding sections have been an attempt to show that realistic solutions to the Nth country problem will depend on sacrifices by the nuclear powers. It may be said that this is perhaps impossible. In fact, the underlying assumption of many recent proposals for arms control is that nuclear weapons and nuclear powers are here to stay, if for no other reason than that stockpiles are reputedly undetectable, and hence not subject to arms control or to an agreement on disarmament. Yet there are many who believe the Nth country problem can be solved even within the above restriction, and it is interesting for this reason to examine at least one such proposal.

In a recent monograph, Thornton Read [66] has proposed the neutralization of nuclear weapons by what amounts to a negotiated agreement to "close the nuclear club." His proposal includes a reduction of the present membership of the club from four to two (Great Britain and France would rely on the United States). His goal is the achievement of a "stable division" of nations into nuclear and nonnuclear powers, but he rules out the possibility of a "Big-Two Directorate" of the world—an idea "not acceptable to Western ideas of international order." Read in particular proposes the following agreement, which he says satisfies his criteria of meaning the same to everybody and of mobilizing strong feeling, and it does not put the have-not nations at any undue advantage: (1) the possession of nuclear weapons is to be confined to the United States and Russia; (2) all use of nuclear weapons is forbidden, except for reprisal against first use; (3) reprisal is mandatory against first use.

Read makes no mention of any technical measures of inspection and control which would insure compliance with point 1. He believes that the creation of any additional international machinery is too ambitious, since even "as modest a proposal as the Baruch Plan" failed. The treaty is to be implemented by creating a moral revulsion against nuclear weapons, and by emphasizing to the nonnuclear countries the disadvantage of being a member of the nuclear club. In addition, he envisages a second strike deterrent held by Russia and the United States, coupled with a strategy of limited retaliation against prior use, for the enforcement of the treaty conditions. He makes no mention of countries other than those involved in the East-West struggle; for the nonnuclear powers of the West, he assigns a build-up of conventional forces to counter nonnuclear military and political provocations from the Soviet bloc. Read recognizes that China would have to be "coerced" by Russia, that France would be reluctant, and that the United States public would call it appeasement. However, he believes such difficulties can be overcome.

Without denying some ingenious twists of logic in the proposal, my view of such a plan is more skeptical. Countries which either have nuclear weapons now or which have definitely decided to obtain them will not be "coerced" by other than military means to give up their weapons or their intentions so long as other countries continue to hold their position of nuclear power without significant restraint. At least, the history of past attempts indicates this to be the case.

Summary and Conclusions

It has been shown that at least two methods of making nuclear weapons will eventually be available to countries of moderate wealth. At present, the greatest threat of nuclear diffusion through independent acquisition is the increasing availability of large quantities of plutonium. Even though special measures would be needed to utilize the plutonium produced by electrical-power reactors, they are not difficult to achieve in the absence of controls. Despite extensive safeguards through United States bilateral agreements, some countries are not seriously limited by them.

The effect of possible nuclear weapons in many countries will only be felt through appropriate delivery systems. A meaningful delivery capability for small countries in the East-West confrontation is virtually impossible now and will continue to be impossible until (if ever) the delivery race should reach a stable state. Therefore a serious discouragement stands in the way of the prospective members of the nuclear club who are also engaged in the East-West confrontation. On the other hand, poor countries may oppose one another with nuclear weapons outside the East-West struggle and find no serious delivery problems.

Despite the limitation of the small countries to secondary status, the growth of the nuclear club has not been seriously affected. For this reason, realistic proposals for controlling future Nth country developments must be formulated. A look at past efforts leads to the inescapable conclusion that, despite the difficult question of stockpiles, means will have to be found to disarm the nuclear powers along with the nonnuclear powers if control proposals are to be universally acceptable. This is not to deny the difficulty of the task nor to imply that interim measures for arms control aimed at easing tension are not also desirable.

References

1. W. Davidon, M. Kalkstein, and C. Hohenemser, *The Nth Country Problem and Arms Control,* National Planning Association (Washington), 1960.

2. "Report of the NPA Special Project Committee on Security Through Arms Control," *op. cit.*

3. H. Simon, "World-Wide Capabilities for Production and Control of Nuclear Weapons," *Dædalus,* Summer 1959, p. 385.

4. F. Aiken, "Can We Limit the Nuclear Club?" *Bulletin of the Atomic Scientists, 17:* 7, September 1961, p. 263.

5. P. M. S. Blackett, "Thoughts on British Defense Policy," *The New Statesman,* 5 December 1959.

6. E. Teller, "The Feasibility of Arms Control and the Principle of Openness," in D. G. Brennan, ed., *Arms Control, Disarmament, and National Security,* George Braziller (New York), 1961, p. 122.
7. A. Buchan, "The Future of Western Deterrent Power; A View From the United Kingdom," *Bulletin of the Atomic Scientists, 16:* 7, September 1960, p. 277.
8. T. J. Dodd, "Eight Fallacies of the Nuclear Test Ban," speech in the United States Senate, May 12, 1960.
9. A. Wohlstetter, "Nuclear Sharing: NATO and the N + 1 Country," *Foreign Affairs,* April 1961, p. 355.
10. Paul M. Doty, "The Role of the Smaller Powers," in D. G. Brennan, *op. cit.*
11. F. C. Iklé, "Nth Countries and Disarmament," *Bulletin of the Atomic Scientists, 16:* 10 December 1960, p. 391.
12. See for example *The London Times,* 13 October 1960, p. 14.
13. S. Glasstone, *Sourcebook on Atomic Energy,* D. Van Nostrand Co., Inc., (Princeton), 1958, 2nd edition, pp. 385-481.
14. G. I. Pokrovsky, *Science and Technology in Contemporary War,* (translated from the Russian by Raymond L. Garthoff), Frederick Praeger (New York), 1959, p. 61 and p. 139.
15. United States Atomic Energy Commission, *Annual Report to Congress, 1960,* Government Printing Office (Washington), January 1961, pp. 500-504.
16. H. D. Smyth, *Atomic Energy for Military Purposes,* Princeton University Press (Princeton), 1946, Chapter 10.
17. M. Kalkstein and W. Smith, "An Estimate of the Nuclear Stockpile From Unclassified Sources," in D. H. Frisch, ed., *Arms Reduction Program and Issues,* The Twentieth Century Fund (New York), 1961.
18. J. W. Beams, *et al.,* "Tests of the Theory of Isotope Separation by Centrifuging," reference 21, p. 428.
19. K. Cohen, *The Theory of Isotope Separation,* McGraw-Hill Co., Inc. (New York), 1951.
20. *Proceedings, International Symposium on Isotope Separation,* North Holland Publishing Co. (Amsterdam), 1957.
21. *Second United Nations International Conference on Peaceful Uses of Atomic Energy,* United Nations (Geneva), 1958, *4.*
22. W. E. Groth, *et al.,* "Enrichment of Uranium Isotopes by the Gas Centrifuge Method," reference 21, p. 439.
23. J. Kistmaker, *et al.,* "Enrichment of Uranium Isotopes with Ultracentrifuges," reference 21, p. 435.

24. "Santa Fe firm to produce enriched U commercially," *Nucleonics, 17:* 10 October 1959, p. 17.

25. *Ibid.*

26. D. Ciuffa and L. Sani, "Considerations on the Use of Thorium in Power Reactors," *Second United Nations International Conference on the Peaceful Uses of Atomic Energy,* United Nations (Geneva), 1958, *13:* 470.

27. Joint Congressional Committee on Atomic Energy, *Review of the International Atomic Policies of the United States,* Government Printing Office (Washington), 1960, *4,* p. 1397.

28. *Ibid., 5;* pp. 2023-2040.

29. *Proceedings: Second Plowshare Symposium,* Lawrence Radiation Laboratory (Livermore), May 1959.

30. D. Inglis, letter to *The New York Times,* 19 July 1961.

31. D. Inglis, Testimony, Joint Congressional Committee on Atomic Energy, *Hearings on Test Detection,* Government Printing Office (Washington), 1961.

32. Joint Congressional Committee on Atomic Energy, *Review of the International Atomic Energy Policies of the United States,* Government Printing Office (Washington), 1960, *2:* 357 ff.

33. *Ibid.,* p. 466.

34. S. H. Gould, ed., *Science in Communist China,* American Association for the Advancement of Science (Washington), 1961 (26 papers describing the state and progress of various branches of science in China).

35. United States Atomic Energy Commission, *op. cit.,* p. 534 (for cost of nuclear weapons).

36. "Package Plan Calls for 3,900 Missiles," *Aviation Week, 15:* 34, 24 July 1961 (for cost of U. S. "central war force").

37. "46.6 Billion Defense Budget Approved," *Aviation Week, 15:* 37, 14 August 1961, p. 30 (for cost of various segments of the U. S. defense system).

38. "British Score High Missile Costs," *Aviation Week, 14:* 11, 14 March 1960 (gives report on Blue Streak missile).

39. George A. Kelly, "The Political Background of the French A-bomb," *Orbis, 4:* 3, Fall 1960.

40. "French Nuclear Strike Force Debated," *Aviation Week, 14,* 31 October 1960, p. 34 (French military plans and expenditures for next five years).

41. "French Pressing IRBM pace despite U. S." *Aviation Week, 15:* 38, 21 August 1961, p. 32 (discussion of French delivery systems and atomic weapons capabilities and plans).

42. Raymond Aron, "The Future of Western Deterrent Power: A View from France." *Bulletin of the Atomic Scientists, 16:* 7 September 1960, p. 266.

43. P. M. S. Blackett, in Alastair Buchan's *NATO in the 1960's,* reference 44.

44. Alastair Buchan, *NATO in the 1960's,* Frederick Praeger (New York), 1960.

45. Arthur L. Burns, in *NATO and American Security,* Klaus Knorr, ed., Princeton University Press (Princeton), 1959.

46. Klaus Knorr, "The Future of the Western Deterrent: View from the United States," *Bulletin of the Atomic Scientists, 16:* 7 September 1960, p. 271.

47. *Bulletin of the Atomic Scientists, 13:* 6 June 1957, p. 223.

48. Ritchie Calder, "The Non-Nuclear Club," *Bulletin of the Atomic Scientists, 16:* 4, April 1960, p. 123.

49. Stephen King-Hall, *Defence in the Nuclear Age,* Gollancz (London), 1958 (the military argument for nuclear disarmament in Great Britain without American guarantee).

50. Christian Herter, Statement in April 1959.

51. "France Compromises on NATO integration," *Aviation Week,* 3 October 1960.

52. Editorial, *Die Zeit,* 20 October 1961.

53. Ronald Steel, "NATO's Nuclear Crisis," *Commonweal, 74,* 16 June 1961, p. 301.

54. William Green and John Fricker, *The Air Forces of the World,* Hanover House (New York), 1958.

55. *The Acheson-Lilienthal Report,* United States Department of State Publication 2498, Government Printing Office (Washington), 1946 (the Baruch Plan).

56. P. Noel-Baker, *The Arms Race,* Oceana Publications, Inc. (New York) 1958 (for analysis of negotiations).

57. E. Rabinowitch, ed., *Minutes to Midnight,* Bulletin of the Atomic Scientists, Publisher (Chicago), 1950 (for analysis of negotiations).

58. D. D. Eisenhower, speech before the United Nations General Assembly, 8 December 1953.

59. *Statute of the International Atomic Energy Agency,* United Nations (New York), 1956.

60. United States Atomic Energy Commission, *op. cit.,* pp. 204-209.

61. M. Joshi, "Dead or Alive? International Atomic Energy Agency," *Bulletin of the Atomic Scientists, 17:* 3, p. 95.

62. GOV. OR 232 to 238, GC (IV)/COM.2/OR.20, GC (IV)/OR.44, International Atomic Energy Agency (Vienna), 1960 and 1961 (safeguard discussions in the Board of Governors and in the General Conference of the I.A.E.A.).

63. INFCIRC/26, International Atomic Energy Agency (Vienna), 1961 (text of the approved safeguards system of the I.A.E.A.).

64. H. J. Bhaba, Letter to Sterling Cole, Director General of the I.A.E.A., 30 August 1961.

65. G. Seaborg, "Meet the Press" (television program), 29 October 1961.

66. T. Read, "A Proposal to Neutralize Nuclear Weapons," Policy Memorandum #22, Center for International Studies, Princeton University (Princeton), 1961.

N. B.: In preparing this paper, the author assembled many tables and appendices, which include (A) Considerations of Bomb Design, (B) A Primitive Plutonium-Weapons Program, (C) The Manufacture of Thermonuclear Weapons, (D) Tables of Reactors, (E) Delivery Systems, and (F) Denaturing and Controls. Readers interested in this material may obtain copies of these appendices by writing to the American Academy of Arts and Sciences.

DOCUMENTS

OUTLINE OF BASIC PROVISIONS OF A TREATY ON GENERAL AND COMPLETE DISARMAMENT IN A PEACEFUL WORLD

The United States presented this outline to the Eighteen-Nation Committee on Disarmament on 18 April 1962.

SUMMARY

Principles and Process of Disarmament

Disarmament would be implemented progressively and in a balanced manner so that at no stage could any state or group of states obtain military advantage. Compliance with obligations would be effectively verified. As national armaments were reduced, the United Nations would be progressively strengthened.

Disarmament would be accomplished in three stages—the first to be carried out in 3 years; the second, also in 3 years; and the third, as promptly as possible within an agreed period of time. Stage I would be initiated by the United States, the Soviet Union, and other agreed states. All militarily significant states would participate in Stage II; and all states possessing armaments and armed forces, in Stage III.

Transition from one stage of disarmament to the next would take place upon a determination that all undertakings in the preceding stage had been carried out and that all preparations for the next stage had been made.

Disarmament Measures

A. *Armaments.* During Stage I, inventories of major categories of both nuclear delivery vehicles and conventional armaments would be reduced by 30 percent. Fixed launching pads would be reduced with associated missiles. Half of the remaining inventories would be eliminated during Stage II, and final reductions would be made in Stage III. Upon the completion of Stage III, states would have at their disposal only agreed types of nonnuclear armaments for forces required to maintain internal order and protect the personal security of citizens.

Production of armaments during Stage I would be limited to agreed allowances and would be compensated for by the destruction of additional armaments to the end that reductions would not be impaired. In Stage II, production of armaments would be halted except for parts for maintenance of retained armaments. Any further production of national armaments

Reprinted from *Blueprint for the Peace Race,* United States Arms Control and Disarmament Agency Publication 4, General Series 3, May 1962. By permission of the United States Arms Control and Disarmament Agency.

would be ended in Stage III except for production of agreed types of nonnuclear armaments for internal forces.

Military research, development, and testing would be subject to increasing limitations during the disarmament process. During Stage III, appropriate action would be taken to insure that new scientific discoveries and technological inventions of military significance were not used for military purposes.

B. Armed forces. Force levels of the United States and Soviet Union would be reduced to 2.1 million at the end of Stage I. Half of the remaining forces of these two states would be disbanded during Stage II, and final reductions would be made in Stage III. Other states would also progressively reduce their force levels. By the end of Stage III, states would have at their disposal only those agreed forces and related organizational arrangements required to maintain internal order and protect the personal security of citizens.

C. Nuclear weapons. Production of fissionable materials for use in nuclear weapons would be halted in Stage I, and limitations would be imposed on the production of fissionable materials for other purposes. The availability of fissionable materials for use in nuclear weapons would be reduced during Stage I and subsequent stages by safeguarded transfers to nonnuclear weapons purposes.

If nuclear weapons tests had not already been halted under effective international control, arrangements to this end would be undertaken in Stage I. States which had manufactured nuclear weapons would agree in Stage I not to transfer control over nuclear weapons to states which had not manufactured them or to assist such states in their manufacture. States which had not manufactured nuclear weapons would refrain from seeking them. Transfers of fissionable materials between states would be limited to peaceful purposes and would be safeguarded.

Beginning in Stage II, nonnuclear components and assemblies of nuclear weapons would be destroyed and limitations would be imposed on further production or refabrication of nuclear weapons. At the end of Stage II, remaining nuclear weapons would be registered internationally to assist in verifying the fact that by the end of Stage III states would not have such weapons at their disposal.

D. Outer Space. The placing of weapons of mass destruction in orbit would be prohibited in Stage I, and limitations would be imposed on the production, stockpiling, and testing of boosters for space vehicles. States would support increased cooperation in peaceful uses of outer space.

E. Military Bases. Reduction of military bases, wherever they might be located, would be initiated in Stage II, and final reductions would be made in Stage III.

F. Military Expenditures. Military expenditures would be reported throughout the disarmament process.

Verification

The verification of disarmament would be the responsibility of an International Disarmament Organization, which would be established within the framework of the United Nations. Reductions of armaments and armed forces would be verified at agreed locations; and limitations on production, testing, and other specified activities, at declared locations. Assurance that agreed levels of armaments and armed forces were not exceeded and that activities subject to limitation or prohibition were not being conducted clandestinely would be provided through arrangements which would relate the extent of inspection at any time to the amount of disarmament being undertaken and to the risk to the disarming states of possible violations.

Such assurance might, for example, be accomplished through arrangements under which states would divide themselves into a number of zones through which inspection would be progressively extended. By the end of Stage III, when disarmament had been completed, all parts of the territory of states would have been inspected.

Reduction of the Risk of War

To promote confidence and reduce the risk of war during the disarmament process, states would, beginning in Stage I, give advance notification of major military movements and maneuvers, establish observation posts to report on concentrations and movements of military forces, and insure rapid and reliable communications among heads of governments and with the Secretary-General of the United Nations.

An International Commission on Reduction of the Risk of War would examine possible extensions and improvements of such measures as well as additional measures to reduce the risk of war through accident, miscalculation, failure of communications, or surprise attack.

Arrangements for Keeping the Peace

In Stage I, states would undertake obligations to refrain from the threat or use of force of any type contrary to the United Nations Charter. Throughout the three stages of disarmament, states would use all available means for the peaceful settlement of disputes, would seek to improve processes for this purpose, and would support measures to improve the capability of the United Nations to maintain international peace and security.

A United Nations Peace Observation Corps would be established in Stage I, and a United Nations Peace Force, in Stage II. The United Nations Peace Force, which would be equipped with agreed types of armaments and would be supplied agreed manpower by states, would be progressively strengthened until, in Stage III, it would be fully capable of insuring international security in a disarmed world.

OUTLINE OF BASIC PROVISIONS OF A TREATY ON GENERAL AND COMPLETE DISARMAMENT IN A PEACEFUL WORLD

COMPLETE TEXT

In order to assist in the preparation of a treaty on general and complete disarmament in a peaceful world, the United States submits the following outline of basic provisions of such a treaty.

A. Objectives

1. To ensure that (a) disarmament is general and complete and war is no longer an instrument for settling international problems, and (b) general and complete disarmament is accompanied by the establishment of reliable procedures for the settlement of disputes and by effective arrangements for the maintenance of peace in accordance with the principles of the Charter of the United Nations.

2. Taking into account paragraphs 3 and 4 below, to provide, with respect to the military establishment of every nation, for:

(a) Disbanding of armed forces, dismantling of military establishments, including bases, cessation of the production of armaments as well as their liquidation or conversion to peaceful uses;

(b) Elimination of all stockpiles of nuclear, chemical, biological, and other weapons of mass destruction and cessation of the production of such weapons;

(c) Elimination of all means of delivery of weapons of mass destruction;

(d) Abolition of the organizations and institutions designed to organize the military efforts of states, cessation of military training, and closing of all military training institutions;

(e) Discontinuance of military expenditures.

3. To ensure that, at the completion of the program for general and complete disarmament, states would have at their disposal only those non-nuclear armaments, forces, facilities and establishments as are agreed to be necessary to maintain internal order and protect the personal security of citizens.

4. To ensure that during and after implementation of general and complete disarmament, states also would support and provide agreed manpower for a United Nations Peace Force to be equipped with agreed types of armaments necessary to ensure that the United Nations can effectively deter or suppress any threat or use of arms.

5. To establish and provide for the effective operation of an International Disarmament Organization within the framework of the United Nations for the purpose of ensuring that all obligations under the disarmament program would be honored and observed during and after implementation of general and complete disarmament; and to this end to ensure that the International Disarmament Organization and its inspectors would have unrestricted access without veto to all places as necessary for the purpose of effective verification.

B. Principles

The guiding principles during the achievement of these objectives are:

1. Disarmament would be implemented until it is completed by stages to be carried out within specified time limits.

2. Disarmament would be balanced so that at no stage of the imple-

mentation of the treaty could any state or group of states gain military advantage, and so that security would be ensured equally for all.

3. Compliance with all disarmament obligations would be effectively verified during and after their entry into force. Verification arrangements would be instituted progressively as necessary to ensure throughout the disarmament process that agreed levels of armaments and armed forces were not exceeded.

4. As national armaments are reduced, the United Nations would be progressively strengthened in order to improve its capacity to ensure international security and the peaceful settlement of differences as well as to facilitate the development of international cooperation in common tasks for the benefit of mankind.

5. Transition from one stage of disarmament to the next would take place upon decision that all measures in the preceding stage had been implemented and verified and that any additional arrangements required for measures in the next stage were ready to operate.

INTRODUCTION

The Treaty would contain three stages designed to achieve a permanent state of general and complete disarmament in a peaceful world. The Treaty would enter into force upon the signature and ratification of the United States of America, the Union of Soviet Socialist Republics and such other states as might be agreed. Stage II would begin when all militarily significant states had become Parties to the Treaty and other transition requirements had been satisfied. Stage III would begin when all states possessing armed forces and armaments had become Parties to the Treaty and other transition requirements had been satisfied. Disarmament, verification, and measures for keeping the peace would proceed progressively and proportionately beginning with the entry into force of the Treaty.

STAGE I

Stage I would begin upon the entry into force of the Treaty and would be completed within three years from that date.

During Stage I the Parties to the Treaty would undertake:

1. To reduce their armaments and armed forces and to carry out other agreed measures in the manner outlined below;

2. To establish the International Disarmament Organization upon the entry into force of the Treaty in order to ensure the verification in the agreed manner of the obligations undertaken; and

3. To strengthen arrangements for keeping the peace through the measures outlined below.

A. ARMAMENTS

1. Reduction of Armaments

a. Specified Parties to the Treaty, as a first stage toward general and complete disarmament in a peaceful world, would reduce by thirty percent the armaments in each category listed in subparagraph b below. Except as adjustments for production would be permitted in Stage I in accordance with paragraph 3 below, each type of armament in the categories listed in subparagraph b would be reduced by thirty percent of the inventory existing at an agreed date.

b. All types of armaments within agreed categories would be subject to reduction in Stage I (the following list of categories, and of types within categories, is illustrative):

(1) Armed combat aircraft having an empty weight of 40,000 kilograms or greater; missiles having a range of 5,000 kilometers or greater, together with their related fixed launching pads; and submarine-launched missiles and air-to-surface missiles having a range of 300 kilometers or greater.

(Within this category, the United States, for example, would declare as types of armaments: the B–52 aircraft; Atlas missiles together with their related fixed launching pads; Titan missiles together with their related fixed launching pads; Polaris missiles; Hound Dog missiles; and each new type of armament, such as Minuteman missiles, which came within the category description, together with, where applicable, their related fixed launching pads. The declared inventory of types within the category by other Parties to the Treaty would be similarly detailed).

(2) Armed combat aircraft having an empty weight of between 15,000 kilograms and 40,000 kilograms and those missiles not included in category (1) having a range between 300 kilometers and 5,000 kilometers, together with any related fixed launching pads. (The Parties would declare their armaments by types within the category).

(3) Armed combat aircraft having an empty weight of between 2,500 and 15,000 kilograms. (The Parties would declare their armaments by types within the category).

(4) Surface-to-surface (including submarine-launched missiles) and air-to-surface aerodynamic and ballistic missiles and free rockets having a range of between 10 kilometers and 300 kilometers, together with any related fixed launching pads. (The Parties would declare their armaments by types within the category).

(5) Anti-missile missile systems, together with related fixed launching pads. (The Parties would declare their armaments by types within the category).

(6) Surface-to-air missiles other than anti-missile missile systems, together with any related fixed launching pads. (The Parties would declare their armaments by types within the category).

(7) Tanks. (The Parties would declare their armaments by types within the category).

(8) Armored cars and armored personnel carriers. (The Parties would declare their armaments by types within the category).

(9) All artillery, and mortars and rocket launchers having a caliber of 100 mm. or greater. (The Parties would declare their armaments by types within the category.)

(10) Combatant ships with standard displacement of 400 tons or greater of the following classes: Aircraft carriers, battleships, cruisers,

destroyer types and submarines. (The Parties would declare their armaments by types within the category).

2. *Method of Reduction*

a. Those Parties to the Treaty which were subject to the reduction of armaments would submit to the International Disarmament Organization an appropriate declaration respecting inventories of their armaments existing at the agreed date.

b. The reduction would be accomplished in three steps, each consisting of one year. One-third of the reduction to be made during Stage I would be carried out during each step.

c. During the first part of each step, one-third of the armaments to be eliminated during Stage I would be placed in depots under supervision of the International Disarmament Organization. During the second part of each step, the deposited armaments would be destroyed or, where appropriate, converted to peaceful uses. The number and location of such depots and arrangements respecting their establishment and operation would be set forth in an annex to the Treaty.

d. In accordance with arrangements which would be set forth in a Treaty annex on verification, the International Disarmament Organization would verify the foregoing reduction and would provide assurance that retained armaments did not exceed agreed levels.

3. *Limitation on Production of Armaments and on Related Activities*

a. Production of all armaments listed in subparagraph b of paragraph 1 above would be limited to agreed allowances during Stage I and, by the beginning of Stage II, would be halted except for production within agreed limits of parts for maintenance of the agreed retained armaments.

b. The allowances would permit limited production in each of the categories of armaments listed in subparagraph b of paragraph 1 above. In all instances during the process of eliminating production of armaments:

(1) any armament produced within a category would be compensated for by an additional armament destroyed within that category to the end that the ten percent reduction in numbers in each category in each step, and the resulting thirty percent reduction in Stage I, would be achieved; and furthermore

(2) in the case of armed combat aircraft having an empty weight of 15,000 kilograms or greater and of missiles having a range of 300 kilometers or greater, the destructive capability of any such armaments produced within a category would be compensated for by the destruction of sufficient armaments within that category to the end that the ten percent reduction in destructive capability as well as numbers in each of these categories in each step, and the resulting thirty percent reduction in Stage I, would be achieved.

c. Should a Party to the Treaty elect to reduce its production in any category at a more rapid rate than required by the allowances provided in subparagraph b above, that Party would be entitled to retain existing armaments to the extent of the unused portion of its production allowance. In any such instance, any armament so retained would be compensated for in the manner set forth in subparagraph b (1) and, where applicable, b (2) above to the end that the ten percent reduction in numbers and, where applicable, destructive capability in each category in each step, and the resulting thirty percent reduction in Stage I, would be achieved.

d. The flight testing of missiles would be limited to agreed annual quotas.

e. In accordance with arrangements which would be set forth in the annex on verification, the International Disarmament Organization would verify the foregoing measures at declared locations and would provide assurance that activities subject to the foregoing measures were not conducted at undeclared locations.

4. Additional Measures

The Parties to the Treaty would agree to examine unresolved questions relating to means of accomplishing in Stages II and III the reduction and eventual elimination of production and stockpiles of chemical and biological weapons of mass destruction. In light of this examination, the Parties to the Treaty would agree to arrangements concerning chemical and biological weapons of mass destruction.

B. ARMED FORCES

1. Reduction of Armed Forces

Force levels for the United States of America and the Union of Soviet Socialist Republics would be reduced to 2.1 million each and for other specified Parties to the Treaty to agreed levels not exceeding 2.1 million each. All other Parties to the Treaty would, with agreed exceptions, reduce their force levels to 100,000 or one percent of their population, whichever were higher, provided that in no case would the force levels of such other Parties to the Treaty exceed levels in existence upon the entry into force of the Treaty.

2. Armed Forces Subject to Reduction

Agreed force levels would include all full-time, uniformed personnel maintained by national governments in the following categories:

a. Career personnel of active armed forces and other personnel serving in the active armed forces on fixed engagements or contracts.

b. Conscripts performing their required period of full-time active duty as fixed by national law.

c. Personnel of militarily organized security forces and of other forces or organizations equipped and organized to perform a military mission.

3. Method of Reduction of Armed Forces

The reduction of force levels would be carried out in the following manner:

a. Those Parties to the Treaty which were subject to the foregoing reductions would submit to the International Disarmament Organization a declaration stating their force levels at the agreed date.

b. Force level reductions would be accomplished in three steps, each having a duration of one year. During each step force levels would be reduced by one-third of the difference between force levels existing at the agreed date and the levels to be reached at the end of Stage I.

c. In accordance with arrangements that would be set forth in the annex on verification, the International Disarmament Organization would verify the reduction of force levels and provide assurance that retained forces did not exceed agreed levels.

4. *Additional Measures*

The Parties to the Treaty which were subject to the foregoing reductions would agree upon appropriate arrangements, including procedures for consultation, in order to ensure that civilian employment by military establishments would be in accordance with the objectives of the obligations respecting force levels.

C. NUCLEAR WEAPONS

1. *Production of Fissionable Materials for Nuclear Weapons*

a. The Parties to the Treaty would halt the production of fissionable materials for use in nuclear weapons.

b. This measure would be carried out in the following manner:

(1) The Parties to the Treaty would submit to the International Disarmament Organization a declaration listing by name, location and production capacity every facility under their jurisdiction capable of producing and processing fissionable materials at the agreed date.

(2) Production of fissionable materials for purposes other than use in nuclear weapons would be limited to agreed levels. The Parties to the Treaty would submit to the International Disarmament Organization periodic declarations stating the amounts and types of fissionable materials which were still being produced at each facility.

(3) In accordance with arrangements which would be set forth in the annex on verification, the International Disarament Organization would verify the foregoing measures at declared facilities and would provide assurance that activities subject to the foregoing limitations were not conducted at undeclared facilities.

2. *Transfer of Fissionable Material to Purposes Other Than Use in Weapons*

a. Upon the cessation of production of fissionable materials for use in nuclear weapons, the United States of America and the Union of Soviet Socialist Republics would each transfer to purposes other than use in nuclear weapons an agreed quantity of weapons-grade U-235 from past production. The purposes for which such materials would be used would be determined by the state to which the material belonged, provided that such materials were not used in nuclear weapons.

b. To ensure that the transferred materials were not used in nuclear weapons, such materials would be placed under safeguards and inspection by the International Disarmament Organization either in stockpiles or at the facilities in which they would be utilized for purposes other than use in nuclear weapons. Arrangements for such safeguards and inspection would be set forth in the annex on verification.

3. *Transfer of Fissionable Materials Between States for Peaceful Uses of Nuclear Energy*

a. Any transfer of fissionable materials between states would be for purposes other than for use in nuclear weapons and would be subject to a system of safeguards to ensure that such materials were not used in nuclear weapons.

b. The system of safeguards to be applied for this purpose would be developed in agreement with the International Atomic Energy Agency and would be set forth in an annex to the Treaty.

4. *Non-Transfer of Nuclear Weapons*

The Parties to the Treaty would agree to seek to prevent the creation of further national nuclear forces. To this end the Parties would agree that:

a. Any Party to the Treaty which had manufactured, or which at any time manufactures, a nuclear weapon would:

(1) Not transfer control over any nuclear weapons to a state which had not manufactured a nuclear weapon before an agreed date;

(2) Not assist any such state in manufacturing any nuclear weapons.

b. Any Party to the Treaty which had not manufactured a nuclear weapon before the agreed date would:

(1) Not acquire, or attempt to acquire, control over any nuclear weapons;

(2) Not manufacture, or attempt to manufacture, any nuclear weapons.

5. *Nuclear Weapons Test Explosions*

a. If an agreement prohibiting nuclear weapons test explosions and providing for effective international control had come into force prior to the entry into force of the Treaty, such agreement would become an annex to the Treaty, and all the Parties to the Treaty would be bound by the obligations specified in the agreement.

b. If, however, no such agreement had come into force prior to the entry into force of the Treaty, all nuclear weapons test explosions would be prohibited, and the procedures for effective international control would be set forth in an annex to the Treaty.

6. Additional Measures

The Parties to the Treaty would agree to examine remaining unresolved questions relating to the means of accomplishing in Stages II and III the reduction and eventual elimination of nuclear weapons stockpiles. In the light of this examination, the Parties to the Treaty would agree to arrangements concerning nuclear weapons stockpiles.

D. OUTER SPACE

1. Prohibition of Weapons of Mass Destruction in Orbit

The Parties to the Treaty would agree not to place in orbit weapons capable of producing mass destruction.

2. Peaceful Cooperation in Space

The Parties to the Treaty would agree to support increased international cooperation in peaceful uses of outer space in the United Nations or through other appropriate arrangements.

3. Notification and Pre-launch Inspection

With respect to the launching of space vehicles and missiles:

a. Those Parties to the Treaty which conducted launchings of space vehicles or missiles would provide advance notification of such launchings to other Parties to the Treaty and to the International Disarmament Organization together with the track of the space vehicle or missile. Such advance notification would be provided on a timely basis to permit pre-launch inspection of the space vehicle or missile to be launched.

b. In accordance with arrangements which would be set forth in the annex on verification, the International Disaramament Organization would conduct pre-launch inspection of space vehicles and missiles and would establish and operate any arrangements necessary for detecting unreported launchings.

4. Limitations on Production and on Related Activities

The production, stockpiling and testing of boosters for space vehicles would be subject to agreed limitations. Such activities would be monitored by the International Disarmament Organization in accordance with arrangements which would be set forth in the annex on verification.

E. MILITARY EXPENDITURES

1. Report on Expenditures

The Parties to the Treaty would submit to the International Disarmament Organization at the end of each step of each stage a report on their military expenditures. Such reports would include an itemization of military expenditures.

2. *Verifiable Reduction of Expenditures*

The Parties to the Treaty would agree to examine questions related to the verifiable reduction of military expenditures. In the light of this examination, the Parties to the Treaty would consider appropriate arrangements respecting military expenditures.

F. REDUCTION OF THE RISK OF WAR

In order to promote confidence and reduce the risk of war, the Parties to the Treaty would agree to the following measures:

1. *Advance Notification of Military Movements and Maneuvers*

Specified Parties to the Treaty would give advance notification of major military movements and maneuvers to other Parties to the Treaty and to the International Disaramament Organization. Specific arrangements relating to this commitment, including the scale of movements and maneuvers to be reported and the information to be transmitted, would be agreed.

2. *Observation Posts*

Specified Parties to the Treaty would permit observation posts to be established at agreed locations, including major ports, railway centers, motor highways, river crossings, and air bases to report on concentrations and movements of military forces. The number of such posts could be progressively expanded in each successive step of Stage I. Specific arrangements relating to such observation posts, including the location and staffing of posts, the method of receiving and reporting information, and the schedule for installation of posts would be agreed.

3. *Additional Observation Arrangements*

The Parties to the Treaty would establish such additional observation arrangements as might be agreed. Such arrangements could be extended in an agreed manner during each step of Stage I.

4. *Exchange of Military Missions*

Specified Parties to the Treaty would undertake the exchange of military missions between states or groups of states in order to improve communications and understanding between them. Specific arrangements respecting such exchanges would be agreed.

5. *Communications Between Heads of Government*

Specified Parties to the Treaty would agree to the establishment of rapid and reliable communications among their heads of government and with the Secretary General of the United Nations. Specific arrangements in this regard would be subject to agreement among the Parties concerned and between such Parties and the Secretary General.

6. *International Commission on Reduction of the Risk of War*

The Parties to the Treaty would establish an International Commission on Reduction of the Risk of War as a subsidiary body of the International Disarmament Organization to examine and make recommendations regarding further measures that might be undertaken during Stage I or subsequent stages of disarmament to reduce the risk of war by accident, miscalculation, failure of communications, or surprise attack. Specific arrangements for such measures as might be agreed to by all or some of the Parties to the Treaty would be subject to agreement among the Parties concerned.

G. THE INTERNATIONAL DISARMAMENT ORGANIZATION

1. *Establishment of the International Disarmament Organization*

The International Disarmament Organization would be established upon the entry into force of the Treaty and would function within the framework of the United Nations and in accordance with the terms and conditions of the Treaty.

2. *Cooperation of the Parties to the Treaty*

The Parties to the Treaty would agree to cooperate promptly and fully with the International Disarmament Organization and to assist the International Disarmament Organization in the performance of its functions and in the execution of the decisions made by it in accordance with the provisions of the Treaty.

3. *Verification Functions of the International Disarmament Organization*

The International Disarmament Organization would verify disarmament measures in accordance with the following principles which would be implemented through specific arrangements set forth in the annex on verification:

a. Measures providing for reduction of armaments would be verified by the International Disarmament Organization at agreed depots and would include verification of the destruction of armaments and, where appropriate, verification of the conversion of armaments to peaceful uses. Measures providing for reduction of armed forces would be verified by the International Disarmament Organization either at the agreed depots or other agreed locations.

b. Measures halting or limiting production, testing, and other specified activities would be verified by the International Disarmament Organization. Parties to the Treaty would declare the nature and location of all production and testing facilities and other specified activities. The International Disaramament Organization would have access to relevant facilities and activities wherever located in the territory of such Parties.

c. Assurance that agreed levels of armaments and armed forces were not exceeded and that activities limited or prohibited by the Treaty were not being conducted clandestinely would be provided by the International Disarmament Organization through agreed arrangements which would have the effect of providing that the extent of inspection during any step or stage would be related to the amount of disarmament being undertaken and to the degree of risk to the Parties to the Treaty of possible violations. This might be accomplished, for example, by an arrangement embodying such features as the following:

(1) All parts of the territory of those Parties to the Treaty to which this form of verification was applicable would be subject to selection for inspection from the beginning of Stage I as provided below.

(2) Parties to the Treaty would divide their territory into an agreed number of appropriate zones and at the beginning of each step of disarmament would submit to the International Disarmament Organization a declaration stating the total level of armaments, forces, and specified types of activities subject to verification within each zone. The exact location of armaments and forces within a zone would not be revealed prior to its selection for inspection.

(3) An agreed number of these zones would be progressively inspected by the International Disarmament Organization during Stage I according to an agreed time schedule. The zones to be inspected would be selected by procedures which would ensure their selection by Parties to the Treaty other than the Party whose territory was to be inspected or any Party associated with it. Upon selection of each zone, the Party to the Treaty whose territory was to be inspected would declare the exact location of armaments, forces and other agreed activities within the selected zone. During the verification process, arrangements would be made to provide assurance against undeclared movements of the objects of verification to or from the zone or zones being inspected. Both aerial and mobile ground inspection would be employed within the zone being inspected. In so far as agreed measures being verified were concerned, access within the zone would be free and unimpeded, and verification would be carried out with the full cooperation of the state being inspected.

(4) Once a zone had been inspected it would remain open for further inspection while verification was being extended to additional zones.

(5) By the end of Stage III, when all disarmament measures had been completed, inspection would have been extended to all parts of the territory of Parties to the Treaty.

4. Composition of the International Disarmament Organization

a. The International Disarmament Organization would have:

(1) A General Conference of all the Parties to the Treaty;

(2) A Control Council consisting of representatives of all the major signatory powers as permanent members and certain other Parties to the Treaty on a rotating basis; and

(3) An Administrator who would administer the International

Disarmament Organization under the direction of the Control Council and who would have the authority, staff, and finances adequate to ensure effective and impartial implementation of the functions of the International Disarmament Organization.

b. The General Conference and the Control Council would have power to establish such subsidiary bodies, including expert study groups, as either of them might deem necessary.

5. *Functions of the General Conference*

The General Conference would have the following functions, among others which might be agreed:

a. Electing non-permanent members to the Control Council;
b. Approving certain accessions to the Treaty;
c. Appointing the Administrator upon recommendation of the Control Council;
d. Approving agreements between the International Disarmament Organization and the United Nations and other international organizations;
e. Approving the budget of the International Disarmament Organization;
f. Requesting and receiving reports from the Control Council and deciding upon matters referred to it by the Control Council;
g. Approving reports to be submitted to bodies of the United Nations;
h. Proposing matters for consideration by the Control Council;
i. Requesting the International Court of Justice to give advisory opinions on legal questions concerning the interpretation or application of the Treaty, subject to a general authorization of this power by the General Assembly of the United Nations;
j. Approving amendments to the Treaty for possible ratification by the Parties to the Treaty;
k. Considering matters of mutual interest pertaining to the Treaty or disarmament in general.

6. *Functions of the Control Council*

The Control Council would have the following functions, among others which might be agreed:

a. Recommending appointment of the Administrator;
b. Adopting rules for implementing the terms of the Treaty;
c. Establishing procedures and standards for the installation and operation of the verification arrangements, and maintaining supervision over such arrangements and the Administrator;
d. Establishing procedures for making available to the Parties to the Treaty data produced by verification arrangements;
e. Considering reports of the Administrator on the progress of disarmament measures and of their verification, and on the installation and operation of the verification arrangements;

f. Recommending to the Conference approval of the budget of the International Disarmament Organization;

g. Requesting the International Court of Justice to give advisory opinions on legal questions concerning the interpretation or application of the Treaty, subject to a general authorization of this power by the General Assembly of the United Nations;

h. Recommending to the Conference approval of certain accessions to the Treaty;

i. Considering matters of mutual interest pertaining to the Treaty or to disarmament in general.

7. *Functions of the Administrator*

The Administrator would have the following functions, among others which might be agreed:

a. Administering the installation and operation of the verification arrangements, and serving as Chief Executive Officer of the International Disarmament Organization;

b. Making available to the Parties to the Treaty data produced by the verification arrangements;

c. Preparing the budget of the International Disarmament Organization;

d. Making reports to the Control Council on the progress of disarmament measures and of their verification, and on the installation and operation of the verification arrangements.

8. *Privileges and Immunities*

The privileges and immunities which the Parties to the Treaty would grant to the International Disarmament Organization and its staff and to the representatives of the Parties to the International Disarmament Organization, and the legal capacity which the International Disarmament Organization should enjoy in the territory of each of the Parties to the Treaty would be specified in an annex to the Treaty.

9. *Relations with the United Nations and Other International Organizations*

a. The International Disarmament Organization, being established within the framework of the United Nations, would conduct its activities in accordance with the purposes and principles of the United Nations. It would maintain close working arrangements with the United Nations, and the Administrator of the International Disarmament Organization would consult with the Secretary General of the United Nations on matters of mutual interest.

b. The Control Council of the International Disarmament Organization would transmit to the United Nations annual and other reports on the activities of the International Disarmament Organization.

c. Principal organs of the United Nations could make recommendations to the International Disarmament Organization, which would consider them and report to the United Nations on action taken.

NOTE: The above outline does not cover all the possible details or aspects of relationships between the International Disarmament Organization and the United Nations.

H. MEASURES TO STRENGTHEN ARRANGEMENTS FOR KEEPING THE PEACE

1. *Obligations Concerning the Threat or Use of Force*

The Parties to the Treaty would undertake obligations to refrain, in their international relations, from the threat or use of force of any type—including nuclear, conventional, chemical or biological means of warfare—contrary to the purposes and principles of the United Nations Charter.

2. *Rules of International Conduct*

a. The Parties to the Treaty would agree to support a study by a subsidiary body of the International Disarmament Organization of the codification and progressive development of rules of international conduct related to disarmament.

b. The Parties to the Treaty would refrain from indirect aggression and subversion. The subsidiary body provided for in subparagraph a would also study methods of assuring states against indirect aggression or subversion.

3. *Peaceful Settlement of Disputes*

a. The Parties to the Treaty would utilize all appropriate processes for the peaceful settlement of all disputes which might arise between them and any other state, whether or not a Party to the Treaty, including negotiation, inquiry, mediation, conciliation, arbitration, judicial settlement, resort to regional agencies or arrangements, submission to the Security Council or the General Assembly of the United Nations, or other peaceful means of their choice.

b. The Parties to the Treaty would agree that disputes concerning the interpretation or application of the Treaty which were not settled by negotiation or by the International Disarmament Organization would be subject to referral by any party to the dispute to the International Court of Justice, unless the parties concerned agreed on another mode of settlement.

c. The Parties to the Treaty would agree to support a study under the General Assembly of the United Nations of measures which should be undertaken to make existing arrangements for the peaceful settlement of international disputes, whether legal or political in nature, more effective; and to institute new procedures and arrangements where needed.

4. *Maintenance of International Peace and Security*

The Parties to the Treaty would agree to support measures strengthening the structure, authority, and operation of the United Nations so as to improve its capability to maintain international peace and security.

5. United Nations Peace Force

The Parties to the Treaty would undertake to develop arrangements during Stage I for the establishment in Stage II of a United Nations Peace Force. To this end, the Parties to the Treaty would agree on the following measures within the United Nations:

a. Examination of the experience of the United Nations leading to a further strengthening of United Nations forces for keeping the peace;
b. Examination of the feasibility of concluding promptly the agreements envisaged in Article 43 of the United Nations Charter;
c. Conclusion of an agreement for the establishment of a United Nations Peace Force in Stage II, including definitions of its purpose, mission, composition and strength, disposition, command and control, training, logistical support, financing, equipment and armaments.

6. United Nations Peace Observation Corps

The Parties to the Treaty would agree to support the establishment within the United Nations of a Peace Observation Corps, staffed with a standing cadre of observers who could be dispatched promptly to investigate any situation which might constitute a threat to or a breach of the peace. Elements of the Peace Observation Corps could also be stationed as appropriate in selected areas throughout the world.

I. TRANSITION

1. *Transition from Stage I to Stage II would take place at the end of Stage I, upon a determination that the following circumstances existed:*

a. All undertakings to be carried out in Stage I had been carried out.
b. All preparations required for Stage II had been made; and
c. All militarily significant states had become Parties to the Treaty.

2. *During the last three months of Stage I, the Control Council would review the situation respecting these circumstances with a view to determining whether these circumstances existed at the end of Stage I.*
3. *If, at the end of Stage I, one or more permanent members of the Control Council should declare that the foregoing circumstances did not exist, the agreed period of Stage I would, upon the request of such permanent member or members, be extended by a period or periods totalling no more than three months for the purpose of bringing about the foregoing circumstances.*
4. *If, upon the expiration of such period or periods, one or more of the permanent members of the Control Council should declare that the foregoing circumstances still did not exist, the question would be placed before a special session of the Security Council; transition to Stage II would take place upon a determination by the Security Council that the foregoing circumstances did in fact exist.*

STAGE II

Stage II would begin upon the transition from Stage I and would be completed within three years from that date.

During Stage II, the Parties to the Treaty would undertake:

1. To continue all obligations undertaken during Stage I;
2. To reduce further the armaments and armed forces reduced during Stage I and to carry out additional measures of disarmament in the manner outlined below;
3. To ensure that the International Disarmament Organization would have the capacity to verify in the agreed manner the obligations undertaken during Stage II; and
4. To strengthen further the arrangements for keeping the peace through the establishment of a United Nations Peace Force and through the additional measures outlined below.

A. ARMAMENTS

1. Reduction of Armaments

a. Those Parties to the Treaty which had during Stage I reduced their armaments in agreed categories by thirty percent would during Stage II further reduce each type of armaments in the categories listed in Section A, subparagraph 1.b of Stage I by fifty percent of the inventory existing at the end of Stage I.

b. Those Parties to the Treaty which had not been subject to measures for the reduction of armaments during Stage I would submit to the International Disarmament Organization an appropriate declaration respecting the inventories by types, within the categories listed in Stage I, of their armaments existing at the beginning of Stage II. Such Parties to the Treaty would during Stage II reduce the inventory of each type of such armaments by sixty-five percent in order that such Parties would accomplish the same total percentage of reduction by the end of Stage II as would be accomplished by those Parties to the Treaty which had reduced their armaments by thirty percent in Stage I.

2. Additional Armaments Subject to Reduction

a. The Parties to the Treaty would submit to the International Disarmament Organization a declaration respecting their inventories existing at the beginning of Stage II of the additional types of armaments in the categories listed in subparagraph b below, and would during Stage II reduce the inventory of each type of such armaments by fifty percent.

b. All types of armaments within further agreed categories would be subject to reduction in Stage II (the following list of categories is illustrative):

(1) Armed combat aircraft having an empty weight of up to 2,500 kilograms (declarations by types).

(2) Specified types of unarmed military aircraft (declarations by types).

(3) Missiles and free rockets having a range of less than 10 kilometers (declarations by types).

(4) Mortars and rocket launchers having a caliber of less than 100 mm. (declarations by types).

(5) Specified types of unarmored personnel carriers and transport vehicles (declarations by types).

(6) Combatant ships with standard displacement of 400 tons or greater which had not been included among the armaments listed in Stage I, and combatant ships with standard displacement of less than 400 tons (declarations by types).

(7) Specified types of non-combatant naval vessels (declarations by types).

(8) Specified types of small arms (declarations by types).

c. Specified categories of ammunition for armaments listed in Stage I, Section A, subparagraph 1.b and in subparagraph b above would be reduced to levels consistent with the levels of armaments agreed for the end of Stage II.

3. *Method of Reduction*

The foregoing measures would be carried out and would be verified by the International Disarmament Organization in a manner corresponding to that provided for in Stage I, Section A, paragraph 2.

4. *Limitation on Production of Armaments and on Related Activities*

a. The Parties to the Treaty would halt the production of armaments in the specified categories except for production, within agreed limits, of parts required for maintenance of the agreed retained armaments.

b. The production of ammunition in specified categories would be reduced to agreed levels consistent with the levels of armaments agreed for the end of Stage II.

c. The Parties to the Treaty would halt development and testing of new types of armaments. The flight testing of existing types of missiles would be limited to agreed annual quotas.

d. In accordance with arrangements which would be set forth in the annex on verification, the International Disarmament Organization would verify the foregoing measures at declared locations and would provide assurance that activities subject to the foregoing measures were not conducted at undeclared locations.

5. *Additional Measures*

a. In the light of their examination during Stage I of the means of accomplishing the reduction and eventual elimination of production and stockpiles of chemical and biological weapons of mass destruction, the Parties to the Treaty would undertake the following measures respecting such weapons:

(1) The cessation of all production and field testing of chemical and biological weapons of mass destruction.

(2) The reduction, by agreed categories, of stockpiles of chemical and biological weapons of mass destruction to levels fifty percent below those existing at the beginning of Stage II.

(3) The dismantling or conversion to peaceful uses of all facilities engaged in the production or field testing of chemical and biological weapons of mass destruction.

b. The foregoing measures would be carried out in an agreed sequence and through arrangements which would be set forth in an annex to the Treaty.

c. In accordance with arrangements which would be set forth in the annex on verification the International Disarmament Organization would verify the foregoing measures and would provide assurance that retained levels of chemical and biological weapons did not exceed agreed levels and that activities subject to the foregoing limitations were not conducted at undeclared locations.

B. ARMED FORCES

1. Reduction of Armed Forces

a. Those Parties to the Treaty which had been subject to measures providing for reduction of force levels during Stage I would further reduce their force levels on the following basis:

(1) Force levels of the United States of America and the Union of Soviet Socialist Republics would be reduced to levels fifty percent below the levels agreed for the end of Stage I.

(2) Force levels of other Parties to the Treaty which had been subject to measures providing for the reduction of force levels during Stage I would be further reduced, on the basis of an agreed percentage, below the levels agreed for the end of Stage I to levels which would not in any case exceed the agreed level for the United States of America and the Union of Soviet Socialist Republics at the end of Stage II.

b. Those Parties to the Treaty which had not been subject to measures providing for the reduction of armed forces during Stage I would reduce their force levels to agreed levels consistent with those to be reached by other Parties which had reduced their force levels during Stage I as well as Stage II. In no case would such agreed levels exceed the agreed level for the United States of America and the Union of Soviet Socialist Republics at the end of Stage II.

c. Agreed levels of armed forces would include all personnel in the categories set forth in Section B, paragraph 2 of Stage I.

2. Method of Reduction

The further reduction of force levels would be carried out and would be verified by the International Disarmament Organization in a manner corresponding to that provided for in Section B, paragraph 3 of Stage I.

3. Additional Measures

Agreed limitations consistent with retained force levels would be placed on compulsory military training, and on refresher training for reserve forces of the Parties to the Treaty.

C. NUCLEAR WEAPONS

1. Reduction of Nuclear Weapons

In the light of their examination during Stage I of the means of accomplishing the reduction and eventual elimination of nuclear weapons stockpiles, the Parties to the Treaty would undertake to reduce in the following manner remaining nuclear weapons and fissionable materials for use in nuclear weapons:

a. The Parties to the Treaty would submit to the International Disarmament Organization a declaration stating the amounts, types and nature of utilization of all their fissionable materials.

b. The Parties to the Treaty would reduce the amounts and types of fissionable materials declared for use in nuclear weapons to minimum levels on the basis of agreed percentages. The foregoing reduction would be accomplished through the transfer of such materials to purposes other than use in nuclear weapons. The purposes for which such materials would be used would be determined by the state to which the materials belonged, provided that such materials were not used in nuclear weapons.

c. The Parties to the Treaty would destroy the non-nuclear components and assemblies of nuclear weapons from which fissionable materials had been removed to effect the foregoing reduction of fissionable materials for use in nuclear weapons.

d. Production or refabrication of nuclear weapons from any remaining fissionable materials would be subject to agreed limitations.

e. The foregoing measures would be carried out in an agreed sequence and through arrangements which would be set forth in an annex to the Treaty.

f. In accordance with arrangements that would be set forth in the verification annex to the Treaty, the International Disarmament Organization would verify the foregoing measures at declared locations and would provide assurance that activities subject to the foregoing limitations were not conducted at undeclared locations.

2. Registration of Nuclear Weapons for Verification Purposes

To facilitate verification during Stage III that no nuclear weapons remained at the disposal of the Parties to the Treaty, those Parties to the Treaty which possessed nuclear weapons would, during the last six months of Stage II, register and serialize their remaining nuclear weapons and would register remaining fissionable materials for use in such weapons. Such registration and serialization would be carried out with the International Disarmament Organization in accordance with procedures which would be set forth in the annex on verification.

D. MILITARY BASES AND FACILITIES

1. *Reduction of Military Bases and Facilities*

The Parties to the Treaty would dismantle or convert to peaceful uses agreed military bases and facilities, wherever they might be located.

2. *Method of Reduction*

a. The list of military bases and facilities subject to the foregoing measures and the sequence and arrangements for dismantling or converting them to peaceful uses would be set forth in an annex to the Treaty.

b. In accordance with arrangements which would be set forth in the annex on verification, the International Disarmament Organization would verify the foregoing measures.

E. REDUCTION OF THE RISK OF WAR

In the light of the examination by the International Commission on Reduction of the Risk of War during Stage I the Parties to the Treaty would undertake such additional arrangements as appeared desirable to promote confidence and reduce the risk of war. The Parties to the Treaty would also consider extending and improving the measures undertaken in Stage I for this purpose. The Commission would remain in existence to examine extensions, improvements or additional measures which might be undertaken during and after Stage II.

F. THE INTERNATIONAL DISARMAMENT ORGANIZATION

The International Disarmament Organization would be strengthened in the manner necessary to ensure its capacity to verify the measures undertaken in Stage II through an extension of the arrangements based upon the principles set forth in Section G, paragraph 3 of Stage I.

G. MEASURES TO STRENGTHEN ARRANGEMENTS FOR KEEPING THE PEACE

1. *Peaceful Settlement of Disputes*

a. In light of the study of peaceful settlement of disputes conducted during Stage I, the Parties to the Treaty would agree to such additional steps and arrangements as were necessary to assure the just and peaceful settlement of international disputes, whether legal or political in nature.

b. The Parties to the Treaty would undertake to accept without reservation, pursuant to Article 36, paragraph 1 of the Statute of the International Court of Justice, the compulsory jurisdiction of that Court to decide international legal disputes.

2. *Rules of International Conduct*

a. The Parties to the Treaty would continue their support of the study by the subsidiary body of the International Disarmament Organization initiated in Stage I to study the codification and progressive development of rules of international conduct related to disarmament. The Parties to the Treaty would agree to the establishment of procedures whereby rules recommended by the subsidiary body and approved by the Control Council would be circulated to all Parties to the Treaty and would become effective three months thereafter unless a majority of the Parties to the Treaty signified their disapproval, and whereby the Parties to the Treaty would be bound by rules which had become effective in this way unless, within a period of one year from the effective date, they formally notified the International Disarmament Organization that they did not consider themselves so bound. Using such procedures, the Parties to the Treaty would adopt such rules of international conduct related to disarmament as might be necessary to begin Stage III.

b. In the light of the study of indirect aggression and subversion conducted in Stage I, the Parties to the Treaty would agree to arrangements necessary to assure states against indirect aggression and subversion.

3. *United Nations Peace Force*

The United Nations Peace Force to be established as the result of the agreement reached during Stage I would come into being within the first year of Stage II and would be progressively strengthened during Stage II.

4. *United Nations Peace Observation Corps*

The Parties to the Treaty would conclude arrangements for the expansion of the activities of the United Nations Peace Observation Corps.

5. *National Legislation*

Those Parties to the Treaty which had not already done so would, in accordance with their constitutional processes, enact national legislation in support of the Treaty imposing legal obligations on individuals and organizations under their jurisdiction and providing appropriate penalities for noncompliance.

H. TRANSITION

1. *Transition from Stage II to Stage III would take place at the end of Stage II, upon a determination that the following circumstances existed:*

a. All undertakings to be carried out in Stage II had been carried out;
b. All preparations required for Stage III had been made; and
c. All states possessing armed forces and armaments had become Parties to the Treaty.

2. *During the last three months of Stage II, the Control Council would review the situation respecting these circumstances with a view to determining at the end of Stage II whether they existed.*
3. *If, at the end of Stage II, one or more permanent members of the Control Council should declare that the foregoing circumstances did not exist, the agreed period of Stage II would, upon the request*

of such permanent member or members, be extended by a period or periods totalling no more than three months for the purpose of bringing about the foregoing circumstances.

4. *If, upon the expiration of such period or periods, one or more of the permanent members of the Control Council should declare that the foregoing circumstances still did not exist, the question would be placed before a special session of the Security Council; transition to Stage III would take place upon a determination by the Security Council that the foregoing circumstances did in fact exist.*

STAGE III

Stage III would begin upon the transition from Stage II and would be completed within an agreed period of time as promptly as possible.

During Stage III, the Parties to the Treaty would undertake:

1. To continue all obligations undertaken during Stages I and II;
2. To complete the process of general and complete disarmament in the manner outlined below;
3. To ensure that the International Disarmament Organization would have the capacity to verify in the agreed manner the obligations undertaken during Stage III and of continuing verification subsequent to the completion of Stage III; and
4. To strengthen further the arrangements for keeping the peace during and following the achievement of general and complete disarmament through the additional measures outlined below.

A. ARMAMENTS

1. *Reduction of Armaments*

Subject to agreed requirements for non-nuclear armaments of agreed types for national forces required to maintain internal order and protect the personal security of citizens, the Parties to the Treaty would eliminate all armaments remaining at their disposal at the end of Stage II.

2. *Method of Reduction*

a. The foregoing measure would be carried out in an agreed sequence and through arrangements that would be set forth in an annex to the Treaty.

b. In accordance with arrangements that would be set forth in the annex on verification, the International Disarmament Organization would verify the foregoing measures and would provide assurance that retained armaments were of the agreed types and did not exceed agreed levels.

3. *Limitations on Production of Armaments and on Related Activities*

a. Subject to agreed arrangements in support of national forces required to maintain internal order and protect the personal security of citizens and subject to agreed arrangements in support of the United

Nations Peace Force, the Parties to the Treaty would halt all applied research, development, production, and testing of armaments and would cause to be dismantled or converted to peaceful uses all facilities for such purposes.

b. The foregoing measures would be carried out in an agreed sequence and through arrangements which would be set forth in an annex to the Treaty.

c. In accordance with arrangements which would be set forth in the annex on verification, the International Disarmament Organization would verify the foregoing measures at declared locations and would provide assurance that activities subject to the foregoing measures were not conducted at undeclared locations.

B. ARMED FORCES

1. Reduction of Armed Forces

To the end that upon completion of Stage III they would have at their disposal only those forces and organizational arrangements necessary for agreed forces to maintain internal order and protect the personal security of citizens and that they would be capable of providing agreed manpower for the United Nations Peace Force, the Parties to the Treaty would complete the reduction of their force levels, disband systems of reserve forces, cause to be disbanded organizational arrangements comprising and supporting their national military establishment, and terminate the employment of civilian personnel associated with the foregoing.

2. Method of Reduction

a. The foregoing measures would be carried out in an agreed sequence through arrangements which would be set forth in an annex to the Treaty.

b. In accordance with arrangements which would be set forth in the annex on verification, the International Disarmament Organization would verify the foregoing measures and would provide assurance that the only forces and organizational arrangements retained or subsequently established were those necessary for agreed forces required to maintain internal order and to protect the personal security of citizens and those for providing agreed manpower for the United Nations Peace Force.

3. Other Limitations

The Parties to the Treaty would halt all military conscription and would undertake to annul legislation concerning national military establishments or military service inconsistent with the foregoing measures.

C. NUCLEAR WEAPONS

1. Reduction of Nuclear Weapons

In light of the steps taken in Stages I and II to halt the production of fissionable material for use in nuclear weapons and to reduce nuclear weapons stockpiles, the Parties to the Treaty would eliminate all nuclear weapons remaining at their disposal, would cause to be dismantled or converted to peaceful use all facilities for production of such weapons, and would transfer all materials remaining at their disposal for use in such weapons to purposes other than use in such weapons.

2. *Method of Reduction*

a. The foregoing measures would be carried out in an agreed sequence and through arrangements which would be set forth in an annex to the Treaty.

b. In accordance with arrangements which would be set forth in the annex on verification, the International Disarmament Organization would verify the foregoing measures and would provide assurance that no nuclear weapons or materials for use in such weapons remained at the disposal of the Parties to the Treaty and that no such weapons or materials were produced at undeclared facilities.

D. MILITARY BASES AND FACILITIES

1. *Reduction of Military Bases and Facilities*

The Parties to the Treaty would dismantle or convert to peaceful uses the military bases and facilities remaining at their disposal, wherever they might be located, in an agreed sequence except for such agreed bases or facilities within the territory of the Parties to the Treaty for agreed forces required to maintain internal order and protect the personal security of citizens.

2. *Method of Reduction*

a. The list of military bases and facilities subject to the foregoing measure and the sequence and arrangements for dismantling or converting them to peaceful uses during Stage III would be set forth in an annex to the Treaty.

b. In accordance with arrangements which would be set forth in the annex on verification, the International Disarmament Organization would verify the foregoing measure at declared locations and provide assurance that there were no undeclared military bases and facilities.

E. RESEARCH AND DEVELOPMENT OF MILITARY SIGNIFICANCE

1. *Reporting Requirement*

The Parties to the Treaty would undertake the following measures respecting research and development of military significance subsequent to Stage III:

a. The Parties to the Treaty would report to the International Disarmament Organization any basic scientific discovery and any technological invention having potential military significance.

b. The Control Council would establish such expert study groups as might be required to examine the potential military significance of such discoveries and inventions and, if necessary, to recommend appropriate measures for their control. In the light of such expert study, the Parties to the Treaty would, where necessary, establish agreed arrangements providing for verification by the International Disarmament Organization that such discoveries and inventions were not utilized for military purposes. Such arrangements would become an annex to the Treaty.

c. The Parties to the Treaty would agree to appropriate arrangements for protection of the ownership rights of all discoveries and inventions reported to the International Disarmament Organization in accordance with subparagraph a above.

2. International Cooperation

The Parties to the Treaty would agree to support full international cooperation in all fields of scientific research and development, and to engage in free exchange of scientific and technical information and free interchange of views among scientific and technical personnel.

F. REDUCTION OF THE RISK OF WAR

1. Improved Measures

In the light of the Stage II examination by the International Commission on Reduction of the Risk of War, the Parties to the Treaty would undertake such extensions and improvements of existing arrangements and such additional arrangements as appeared desirable to promote confidence and reduce the risk of war. The Commission would remain in existence to examine extensions, improvements or additional measures which might be taken during and after Stage III.

2. Application of Measures to Continuing Forces

The Parties to the Treaty would apply to national forces required to maintain internal order and protect the personal security of citizens those applicable measures concerning the reduction of the risk of war that had been applied to national armed forces in Stages I and II.

G. INTERNATIONAL DISARMAMENT ORGANIZATION

The International Disarmament Organization would be strengthened in the manner necessary to ensure its capacity (1) to verify the measures undertaken in Stage III through an extension of arrangements based upon the principles set forth in Section G, paragraph 3 of Stage I so that by the end of Stage III, when all disarmament measures had been completed, inspection would have been extended to all parts of the territory of Parties to the Treaty; and (2) to provide continuing verification of disarmament after the completion of Stage III.

H. MEASURES TO STRENGTHEN ARRANGEMENTS FOR KEEPING THE PEACE

1. Peaceful Change and Settlement of Disputes

The Parties to the Treaty would undertake such additional steps and arrangements as were necessary to provide a basis for peaceful change in a disarmed world and to continue the just and peaceful settlement of all international disputes, whether legal or political in nature.

2. Rules of International Conduct

The Parties to the Treaty would continue the codification and progressive development of rules of international conduct related to disarmament in the manner provided in Stage II and by any other agreed procedure.

3. United Nations Peace Force

The Parties to the Treaty would progressively strengthen the United Nations Peace Force established in Stage II until it had sufficient armed forces and armaments so that no state could challenge it.

I. COMPLETION OF STAGE III

1. *At the end of the time period agreed for Stage III, the Control Council would review the situation with a view to determining whether all undertakings to be carried out in Stage III had been carried out.*
2. *In the event that one or more of the permanent members of the Control Council should declare that such undertakings had not been carried out, the agreed period of Stage III would, upon the request of such permanent member or members, be extended for a period or periods totalling no more than three months for the purpose of completing any uncompleted undertakings. If, upon the expiration of such period or periods, one or more of the permanent members of the Control Council should declare that such undertakings still had not been carried out, the question would be placed before a special session of the Security Council, which would determine whether Stage III had been completed.*
3. *After the completion of Stage III, the obligations undertaken in Stages I, II and III would continue.*

GENERAL PROVISIONS APPLICABLE TO ALL STAGES

1. Subsequent Modifications or Amendments of the Treaty

The Parties to the Treaty would agree to specific procedures for considering amendments or modifications of the Treaty which were believed desirable by any Party to the Treaty in the light of experience in the early period of implementation of the Treaty. Such procedures would include provision for a conference on revision of the Treaty after a specified period of time.

2. Interim Agreement

The Parties to the Treaty would undertake such specific arrangements, including the establishment of a Preparatory Commission, as were necessary between the signing and entry into force of the Treaty to ensure the initiation of Stage I immediately upon the entry into force of the Treaty, and to provide an interim forum for the exchange of views and information on topics relating to the Treaty and to the achievement of a permanent state of general and complete disarmament in a peaceful world.

3. Parties to the Treaty, Ratification, Accession, and Entry into Force of the Treaty

a. The Treaty would be open to signature and ratification, or accession, by all members of the United Nations or its specialized agencies.

b. Any other state which desired to become a Party to the Treaty could accede to the Treaty with the approval of the Conference on recommendation of the Control Council.

c. The Treaty would come into force when it had been ratified by ____________ states, including the United States of America, the Union of Soviet Socalist Republics, and an agreed number of the following states:

____

d. In order to assure the achievement of the fundamental purpose of a permanent state of general and complete disarmament in a peaceful world, the Treaty would specify that the accession of certain militarily significant states would be essential for the continued effectiveness of the Treaty or for the coming into force of particular measures or stages.

e. The Parties to the Treaty would undertake to exert every effort to induce other states or authorities to accede to the Treaty.

f. The Treaty would be subject to ratification or acceptance in accordance with constitutional processes.

g. A Depository Government would be agreed upon which would have all of the duties normally incumbent upon a Depository. Alternatively, the United Nations would be the Depository.

4. Finance

a. In order to meet the financial obligations of the International Disarmament Organization, the Parties to the Treaty would bear the International Disarmament Organization's expenses as provided in the budget approved by the General Conference and in accordance with a scale of apportionment approved by the General Conference.

b. The General Conference would exercise borrowing powers on behalf of the International Disarmament Organization.

5. Authentic Texts

The text of the Treaty would consist of equally authentic versions in English, French, Russian, Chinese and Spanish.

TREATY ON GENERAL AND COMPLETE DISARMAMENT UNDER STRICT INTERNATIONAL CONTROL. DRAFT BY THE UNION OF SOVIET SOCIALIST REPUBLICS

The Government of the Union of Soviet Socialist Republics presented this draft treaty to the United Nations on 22 September 1962.

Preamble

The States of the world,

Acting in accordance with the aspirations and will of the peoples,

Convinced that war cannot and must not serve as a method for settling international disputes, especially in the present circumstances of the precipitate development of means of mass annihilation such as nuclear weapons and rocket devices for their delivery, but must forever be banished from the life of human society,

Fulfilling the historic mission of saving all the nations from the scourge of war.

Basing themselves on the fact that general and complete disarmament under strict international control is a sure and practical way to fulfil mankind's age-old dream of ensuring perpetual and inviolable peace on earth,

Desirous of putting an end to the senseless waste of human labour on the creation of the means of annihilating human beings and of destroying material values,

Seeking to direct all resources towards ensuring a further increase in prosperity and socio-economic progress in all countries in the world,

Conscious of the need to build relations among States on the basis of the principles of peace, good-neighourliness, equality of States and peoples, non-interference and respect for the independence and sovereignty of all countries,

Reaffirming their dedication to the purposes and principles of the United Nations Charter,

Have resolved to conclude the present Treaty and to implement forthwith general and complete disarmament under strict and effective international control.

Reprinted from *Treaty on General and Complete Disarmament under Strict International Control,* United Nations publication, 24 September 1962. By permission of the United Nations.

PART I. GENERAL

ARTICLE I

Disarmament Obligations

The States parties to the present Treaty solemnly undertake:

1. To carry out, over a period of five years, general and complete disarmament entailing:

The disbanding of all armed forces and the prohibition of their re-establishment in any form whatsoever;

The prohibition and destruction of all stockpiles and the cessation of the production of all kinds of weapons of mass destruction, including atomic, hydrogen, chemical, biological and radiological weapons;

The destruction and cessation of the production of all means of delivering weapons of mass destruction to their targets;

The dismantling of all kinds of foreign military bases and the withdrawal and disbanding of all foreign troops stationed in the territory of any State;

The abolition of any kind of military conscription for citizens;

The cessation of military training of the population and the closing of all military training institutions;

The abolition of war ministries, general staffs and their local agencies, and all other military and paramilitary establishments and organizations;

The elimination of all types of conventional armaments and military equipment and the cessation of their production, except for the production of strictly limited quantities of agreed types of light firearms for the equipment of the police (militia) contingents to be retained by States after the accomplishment of general and complete disarmament;

The discontinuance of the appropriation of funds for military purposes, whether from State budgets or by organizations or private individuals.

2. To retain at their disposal, upon completion of general and complete disarmament, only strictly limited contingents of police (militia) equipped with light firearms and intended for the maintenance of internal order and for the discharge of their obligations with regard to the maintenance of international peace and security under the United Nations Charter and under the provisions of article 37 of the present Treaty.

3. To carry out general and complete disarmament simultaneously in three consecutive stages, as set forth in parts II, III and IV of the present Treaty. Transition to a subsequent stage of disarmament shall take place after adoption by the International Disarmament Organization of a decision confirming that all disarmament measures of the preceding stage have been carried out and verified and that any additional verification measures recognized to be necessary for the next stage have been prepared and can be put into operation when appropriate.

4. To carry out all measures of general and complete disarmament in such a way that at no stage of disarmament any State or group of States gains any military advantage and that the security of all States parties to the Treaty is equally safeguarded.

ARTICLE 2

Control Obligations

1. The States parties to the Treaty solemnly undertake to carry out all disarmament measures, from beginning to end, under strict international control and to ensure the implementation in their territories of all control measures set forth in parts II, III and IV of the present Treaty.

2. Each disarmament measure shall be accompanied by such control measures as are necessary for verification of that measure.

3. To implement control over disarmament, an International Disarmament Organization composed of all States parties to the Treaty shall be established within the framework of the United Nations. It shall begin operating as soon as disarmament measures are initiated. The structure and functions of the International Disarmament Organization and its bodies are laid down in part V of the present Treaty.

4. In all States parties to the Treaty the International Disarmament Organization shall have its own staff, recruited internationally and in such a way as to ensure the adequate representation of all three groups of States existing in the world.

This staff shall exercise control on a temporary or permanent basis, depending on the nature of the measure being carried out, over the compliance by States with their obligations to reduce or eliminate armaments and the production of armaments and to reduce or disband their armed forces.

5. The States parties to the Treaty shall submit to the International Disarmament Organization in good time such information on their armed forces, armaments, military production and military appropriations as is necessary for the purpose of carrying out the measures of the stage concerned.

6. Upon completion of the programme of general and complete disarmament, the International Disarmament Organization shall be kept in being and shall exercise supervision over the fulfilment by States of the obligations they have assumed so as to prevent the re-establishment of the military potential of States in any form whatsoever.

ARTICLE 3

Obligations to Maintain International Peace and Security

1. The States parties to the Treaty solemnly confirm their resolve in the course of and after general and complete disarmament:

(a) to base relations with each other on the principles of peaceful and friendly coexistence and co-operation;

(b) not to resort to the threat or use of force to settle any international disputes that may arise, but to use for this purpose the procedures provided for in the United Nations Charter;

(c) to strengthen the United Nations as the principal institution for the maintenance of peace and for the settlement of international disputes by peaceful means.

2. The States parties to the Treaty undertake to refrain from using the contingents of police (militia) remaining at their disposal upon completion of general and complete disarmament for any purpose other than the safeguarding of their internal security or the discharge of their obligations for the maintenance of international peace and security under the United Nations Charter.

PART II. FIRST STAGE OF GENERAL AND COMPLETE DISARMAMENT

ARTICLE 4

First Stage Tasks

The States Parties to the Treaty undertake, in the course of the first stage of general and complete disarmament, to effect the simultaneous elimination of all means of delivering nuclear weapons and of all foreign military bases in alien territories, to withdraw all foreign troops from these territories and to reduce their armed forces, their conventional armaments and production of such armaments, and their military expenditure.

CHAPTER I

Elimination of the Means of Delivering Nuclear Weapons and Foreign Military Bases in Alien Territories, and Withdrawal of Foreign Troops from those Territories. Control over such Measures

A. *Means of Delivery*

ARTICLE 5

Elimination of Rockets Capable of Delivering Nuclear Weapons

1. All rockets capable of delivering nuclear weapons of any calibre and range, whether strategic, operational or tactical, and pilotless aircraft of all types shall be eliminated from the armed forces and destroyed, except for an agreed and strictly limited number of intercontinental missiles, anti-missile missiles and anti-aircraft missiles in the "ground-to-air" category, to be retained by the Union of Soviet Socialist Republics and the United States of America, exclusively in their own territory, until the end of the second stage. A strictly limited number of rockets to be converted to peaceful uses under the provisions of article 15 of the present Treaty shall also be retained.

All launching pads, silos and platforms for the launching of rockets and pilotless aircraft, other than those required for the missiles to be retained under the provisions of this article, shall be completely demolished. All instruments for the equipment, launching and guidance of rockets and pilotless aircraft shall be destroyed. All underground depots for such rockets, pilotless aircraft and auxiliary facilities shall be demolished.

2. The production of all kinds of rockets and pilotless aircraft and of the materials and instruments for their equipment, launching and guidance referred to in paragraph 1 of this article shall be completely discontinued.

All undertakings or workshops thereof engaged in their production shall be dismantled; machine tools and equipment specially and exclusively designed for the production of such items shall be destroyed; the premises of such undertakings as well as general purpose machine tools and equipment shall be converted to peaceful uses. All proving grounds for tests of such rockets and pilotless aircraft shall be demolished.

3. Inspectors of the International Disarmament Organization shall verify the implementation of the measures referred to in paragraphs 1 and 2 above.

4. The production and testing of appropriate rockets for the peaceful exploration of space shall be allowed, provided that the plants producing such rockets, as well as the rockets themselves, will be subject to supervision by the inspectors of the International Disarmament Organization.

ARTICLE 6

Elimination of Military Aircraft Capable of Delivering Nuclear Weapons

1. All military aircraft capable of delivering nuclear weapons shall be eliminated from the armed forces and destroyed. Military airfields serving as bases for such aircraft and repair and maintenance facilities and storage premises at such airfields shall be rendered inoperative or converted to peaceful uses. Training establishments for crews of such aircraft shall be closed.

2. The production of all military aircraft referred to in paragraph 1 of this article shall be completely discontinued. Undertakings or workshops thereof designed for the production of such military aircraft shall be either dismantled or converted to the production of civil aircraft or other civilian goods.

3. Inspectors of the International Disarmament Organization shall verify the implementation of the measures referred to in paragraphs 1 and 2 above.

ARTICLE 7

Elimination of All Surface Warships Capable of Being Used as Vehicles for Nuclear Weapons, and Submarines

1. All surface warships capable of being used as vehicles for nuclear weapons and submarines of all classes or types shall be eliminated from the armed forces and destroyed. Naval bases and other installations for the maintenance of the above warships and submarines shall be demolished or dismantled and handed over to the merchant marine for peaceful uses.

2. The building of the warships and submarines referred to in paragraph 1 of this article shall be completely discontinued. Shipyards and plants, wholly or partly designed for the building of such warships and submarines, shall be dismantled or converted to peaceful production.

3. Inspectors of the International Disarmament Organization shall verify the implementation of the measures referred to in paragraphs 1 and 2 above.

ARTICLE 8

Elimination of All Artillery Systems Capable of Serving as Means of Delivering Nuclear Weapons

1. All artillery systems capable of serving as means of delivering nuclear weapons shall be eliminated from the armed forces and destroyed. All auxiliary equipment and technical facilities designed for controlling the fire of such artillery systems shall be destroyed. Surface storage premises and transport facilities for such systems shall be destroyed or converted to peaceful uses. The entire stock of non-nuclear munitions for such artillery systems, whether at the gun site or in depots, shall be completely destroyed. Underground depots for such artillery systems and for the non-nuclear munitions thereof shall be destroyed.

2. The production of the artillery systems referred to in paragraph 1 of this article shall be completely discontinued. To this end, all plants or workshops thereof engaged in the production of such systems shall be closed and dismantled. All specialized equipment and machine tools at these plants and workshops shall be destroyed, the remainder being converted to peaceful uses. The production of non-nuclear munitions for these artillery systems shall be discontinued. Plants and workshops engaged in the production of such munitions shall be completely dismantled and their specialized equipment destroyed.

3. Inspectors of the International Disarmament Organization shall verify the implementation of the measures referred to in paragraphs 1 and 2 above.

8. *Foreign Military Bases and Troops in Alien Territories*

ARTICLE 9

Dismantling of Foreign Military Bases

1. Simultaneously with the destruction of the means of delivering nuclear weapons under articles 5-8 of the present Treaty, the States parties to the Treaty which have army, air force or naval bases in foreign territories shall dismantle all such bases, whether principal or reserve bases, as well as all depot bases of any types. All personnel of such bases shall be evacuated to their national territory. All installations and armaments existing at such bases and coming under article 5-8 of the present Treaty shall be destroyed on the spot. Other armaments shall either be destroyed on the spot in accordance with article 11 of the present Treaty or evacuated to the Territory of the State which owned the base. All installations of a military nature at such bases shall be destroyed. The living quarters and auxiliary installations of foreign bases shall be transferred for civilian use to the States in whose territory they are located.

2. The measures referred to in paragraph 1 of this article shall be fully applicable to military bases which are used by foreign troops but which may legally belong to the State in whose territory they are located. The said measures shall also be implemented with respect to army, air force and naval bases that have been set up under military treaties and

agreements for use by other States or groups of States, regardless of whether any foreign troops are present at those bases at the time of the conclusion of the present Treaty.

All previous treaty obligations, decisions of the organs of military blocs and any rights or privileges pertaining to the establishment or use of military bases in foreign territories shall lapse and may not be renewed. It shall henceforth be prohibited to grant military bases for use by foreign troops and to conclude any bilateral or multilateral treaties and agreements to this end.

3. The legislatures and Governments of the States parties to the present Treaty shall enact legislation and issue regulations to ensure that no military bases to be used by foreign troops are established in their territory. Inspectors of the International Disarmament Organization shall verify the implementation of the measures referred to in paragraphs 1 and 2 of this article.

ARTICLE 10

Withdrawal of Foreign Troops from Alien Territories

1. Simultaneously with the elimination of the means of delivering nuclear weapons under articles 5-8 of the present Treaty, the States parties to the Treaty which have troops or military personnel of any nature in foreign territories shall withdraw all such troops and personnel from such territories. All armaments and all installations of a military nature which are located at points where foreign troops are stationed and which come under articles 5-8 of the present Treaty shall be destroyed on the spot. Other armaments shall either be destroyed on the spot in accordance with article 11 of the present Treaty or evacuated to the territory of the State withdrawing its troops. The living quarters and auxiliary installations previously occupied by such troops or personnel shall be transferred for civilian use to the States in whose territory such troops were stationed.

2. The measures set forth in paragraph 1 of this article shall be fully applicable to foreign civilians employed in the armed forces or engaged in the production of armaments or any other activities serving military purposes in foreign territory.

Such persons shall be recalled to the territory of the State of which they are citizens, and all previous treaty obligations, decisions by organs of military blocs, and any rights or privileges pertaining to their activities shall lapse and may not be renewed. It shall henceforth be prohibited to dispatch foreign troops, military personnel or the above-mentioned civilians to foreign territories.

3. Inspectors of the International Disarmament Organization shall verify the withdrawal of troops, the destruction of installations and the transfer of the premises referred to in paragraph 1 of this article. The International Disarmament Organization shall also have the right to exercise control over the recall of the civilians referred to in paragraph 2 of this article. The laws and regulations referred to in paragraph 3 of

article 9 of the present Treaty shall include provisions prohibiting citizens of States parties to the Treaty from serving in the armed forces or from engaging in any other activities serving military purposes in foreign States.

CHAPTER II

Reduction of Armed Forces, Conventional Armaments and Military Expenditure Control over such Measures

ARTICLE 11

Reduction of Armed Forces and Conventional Armaments

1. In the first stage of general and complete disarmament the armed forces of the States parties to the Treaty shall be reduced to the following levels:

The United States of America—1,900,000 enlisted men, officers and civilian employees;

The Union of Soviet Socialist Republics—1,900,000 enlisted men, officers and civilian employees.

. . . .

(Agreed force levels for other States parties to the Treaty shall be included in this article.)

2. The reduction of the armed forces shall be carried out in the first place through the demobilization of personnel released as a result of the elimination of the means of delivering nuclear weapons, the dismantling of foreign bases and the withdrawal of foreign troops from alien territories, as provided for in articles 5-10 of the present Treaty, but chiefly through the complete disbandment of units and ships' crews, their officers and enlisted men being demobilized.

3. Conventional armaments, military equipment, munitions, means of transportation and auxiliary equipment in units and depots shall be reduced by 30 percent for each type of all categories of these armaments. The reduced armaments, military equipment and munitions shall be destroyed, and the means of transportation and auxiliary equipment shall be either destroyed or converted to peaceful uses.

All living quarters, depots and special premises previously occupied by units being disbanded, as well as the territories of all proving grounds, firing ranges and drill grounds belonging to such units, shall be transferred for peaceful uses to the civilian authorities.

4. Inspectors of the International Disarmament Organization shall exercise control at places where troops are being disbanded and released conventional armaments and military equipment are being destroyed, and shall also verify the conversion to peaceful uses of means of transportation and other non-combat equipment, premises, proving grounds, etc.

ARTICLE 12

Reduction of Conventional Armaments Production

1. The production of conventional armaments and munitions not

coming under articles 5-8 of the present Treaty shall be reduced proportionately to the reduction of armed forces provided for in article 11 of the present Treaty. Such reduction shall be carried out primarily through the elimination of undertakings engaged exclusively in the production of such armaments and munitions. These undertakings shall be dismantled, their specialized machine tools and equipment shall be destroyed, and their premises, and general purpose machine tools and equipment shall be converted to peaceful uses.

2. Inspectors of the International Disarmament Organization shall exercise control over the measures referred to in paragraph 1 of this article.

ARTICLE 13

Reduction of Military Expenditure

1. The States parties to the present Treaty shall reduce their military budgets and appropriations for military purposes proportionately to the destruction of the means of delivering nuclear weapons and the discontinuance of their production, to the dismantling of foreign military bases and the withdrawal of foreign troops from alien territories as well as to the reduction of armed forces and conventional armaments and to the reduction of the production of such armaments, as provided for in articles 5-12 of the present Treaty.

The funds released through the implementation of the first-stage measures shall be used for peaceful purposes, including the reduction of taxes on the population and the subsidizing of the national economy. A certain portion of the funds thus released shall also be used for the provision of economic and technical assistance to under-developed countries. The size of this portion shall be subject to agreement between the parties of the Treaty.

2. The International Disarmament Organization shall verify the implementation of the measures referred to in paragraph 1 of this article through its financial inspectors, to whom the States parties to the Treaty undertake to grant unimpeded access to the records of central financial institutions concerning the reduction in their budgetary appropriations resulting from the elimination of the means of delivering nuclear weapons, the dismantling of foreign military bases and the reduction of armed forces and conventional armaments, and to the relevant decisions of their legislative and executive bodies.

CHAPTER III

Measures to Safeguard the Security of States

ARTICLE 14

Restrictions on the Movement of Means of Delivering Nuclear Weapons

1. From the beginning of the first stage until the final destruction of all means of delivering nuclear weapons in accordance with articles 5-8 of the present Treaty, it shall be prohibited for any special devices capa-

ble of delivering weapons of mass destruction beyond the limits of their national territory to be placed in orbit or stationed in outer space, for warships to leave their territorial waters and for military aircraft capable of carrying weapons of mass destruction to fly to.

2. The International Disarmament Organization shall exercise control over compliance by the States parties to the Treaty with the provisions of paragraph 1 of this article. The States parties to the Treaty shall provide the International Disarmament Organization with advance information on all launchings of rockets for peaceful purposes provided for in article 15 of the present Treaty, as well as on all movements of military aircraft within their national frontiers and of warships within their territorial waters.

ARTICLE 15

Control over Launchings of Rockets for Peaceful Purposes

1. The launching of rockets and space devices shall be carried out exclusively for peaceful purposes.

2. The International Disarmament Organization shall exercise control over the implementation of the provisions of paragraph 1 of this article through the establishment, at the sites for peaceful rocket launchings of inspection teams, which shall be present at the launchings and shall thoroughly examine every rocket or satellite before its launching.

ARTICLE 16

Prevention of the Further Spread of Nuclear Weapons

The States parties to the Treaty which possess nuclear weapons undertake to refrain from transferring control over nuclear weapons and from transmitting information necessary for their production to States not possessing such weapons.

The States parties to the Treaty not possessing nuclear weapons undertake to refrain from producing or otherwise obtaining nuclear weapons and shall refuse to admit the nuclear weapons of any other State into their territories.

ARTICLE 17

Prohibition of Nuclear Tests

The conducting of nuclear tests of any kind shall be prohibited (if such a prohibition has not come into effect under other international agreements by the time this Treaty is signed).

ARTICLE 17A

Measures to Reduce the Danger of Outbreak of War

1. From the commencement of the first stage large-scale joint military movements or manoeuvers by armed forces of two or more States shall be prohibited.

The States parties to the Treaty agree to give advance notification of large-scale military movements or manoeuvers by their national armed forces within their national frontiers.

2. The States parties to the Treaty shall exchange military missions between States or groups of States for the purpose of improving relations and mutual understanding between them.

3. The States parties to the Treaty agree to establish swift and reliable communication between their Heads of Government and with the Secretary-General of the United Nations.

4. The measures set forth in this article shall remain in effect after the first stage until the completion of general and complete disarmament.

ARTICLE 18

Measures to Strengthen the Capacity of the United Nations to Maintain International Peace and Security

1. With a view to ensuring that the United Nations is capable of effectively protecting States against threats to or breaches of the peace, all States parties to the Treaty shall, between the signing of the Treaty and its entry into force, conclude agreements with the Security Council by which they undertake to make available to the latter armed forces, assistance and facilities, including rights of passage, as provided in Article 43 of the United Nations Chapter.

2. The armed forces specified in the said agreements shall form part of the national armed forces of the States concerned and shall be stationed within their territories. They shall be kept up to full strength and shall be fully equipped and prepared for combat. When used under Article 42 of the United Nations Charter, these forces, serving under the command of the military authorities of the States concerned, shall be placed at the disposal of the Security Council.

CHAPTER IV

Time-limits for First-Stage Measures Transition from the First to the Second Stage

ARTICLE 19

Time-limits for First-Stage Measures

1. The first stage of general and complete disarmament shall be initiated six months after the Treaty comes into force (in accordance with article 46), within which period the International Disarmament Organization shall be set up.

2. The duration of the first stage of general and complete disarmament shall be 18 months.

ARTICLE 20

Transition from the First to the Second Stage

In the course of the last 3 months of the first stage the International Disarmament Organization shall review the implementation of the first-stage measures of general and complete disarmament with a view to submitting a report on the matter to the States parties to the Treaty as well as to the Security Council and the General Assembly of the United Nations.

PART III. SECOND STAGE OF GENERAL AND COMPLETE DISARMAMENT

ARTICLE 21

Second Stage Tasks

The States parties to the Treaty shall undertake, in the course of the second stage of general and complete disarmament, to effect the complete elimination of nuclear and other weapons of mass destruction, to conclude the destruction of all military rockets capable of delivering nuclear weapons which were retained by the Union of Soviet Socialist Republics and the United States of America after the implementation of the first stage, and to make a further reduction in their armed forces, conventional armaments and production of such armaments, and military expenditure.

CHAPTER V

Elimination of Nuclear, Chemical, Biological and Radiological Weapons. Control over such Measures

ARTICLE 22

Elimination of Nuclear Weapons

1. (a) Nuclear weapons of all kinds, types and capacities shall be eliminated from the armed forces and destroyed. Fissionable materials extracted from such weapons, whether directly attached to units or stored in various depots, shall be appropriately processed to render them unfit for direct reconstitution into weapons and shall form a special stock for peaceful uses, belonging to the State which previously owned the nuclear weapons. Non-nuclear components of such weapons shall be completely destroyed.

All depots and special storage spaces for nuclear weapons shall be demolished.

(b) All stockpiles of nuclear materials intended for the production of nuclear weapons shall be appropriately processed to render them unfit for direct use in nuclear weapons and shall be transferred to the above-mentioned special stocks.

(c) Inspectors of the International Disarmament Organization shall verify the implementation of the measures to eliminate nuclear weapons referred to above in sub-paragraphs (a) and (b) of this paragraph.

2. (a) The production of nuclear weapons and of fissionable materials for weapons purposes shall be completely discontinued. All plants, installations and laboratories specially designed for the production of nuclear weapons or their components shall be eliminated or converted to production for peaceful purposes. All workshops, installations and laboratories for the production of the components of nuclear weapons at

plants that are partially engaged in the production of such weapons shall be destroyed or converted to production for peaceful purposes.

(b) The measures for the discontinuance of the production of nuclear weapons and of fissionable materials for weapons purposes referred to in sub-paragraph (a) above shall be implemented under the control of inspectors of the International Disarmament Organization.

The International Disarmament Organization shall have the right to inspect all undertakings which extract raw materials for atomic production or which produce or use fissionable materials or atomic energy.

The States parties to the Treaty shall make available to the International Disarmament Organization documents pertaining to the extraction and processing of nuclear raw materials and to their utilization for military or peaceful purposes.

3. Each State party to the Treaty shall, in accordance with its constitutional procedures, enact legislation completely prohibiting nuclear weapons and making any attempt by individuals or organizations to reconstitute such weapons a criminal offence.

ARTICLE 23

Elimination of Chemical, Biological and Radiological Weapons

1. All types of chemical, biological and radiological weapons, whether directly attached to units or stored in various depots and storage places, shall be eliminated from the arsenals of States and destroyed (neutralized). All instruments and facilities for the combat use of such weapons, all special facilities for their transportation, and all special devices and facilities for their storage and conservation shall simultaneously be destroyed.

2. The production of all types of chemical, biological and radiological weapons and of all means and devices from their combat use, transportation and storage shall be completely discontinued. All plants, installations and laboratories that are wholly or partly engaged in the production of such weapons shall be destroyed or converted to production for peaceful purposes.

3. The measures referred to in paragraphs 1 and 2 above shall be implemented under the control of inspectors of the International Disarmament Organization.

CHAPTER V A

The Destruction of Rockets Capable of Delivering Nuclear Weapons Which Were Retained after the First Stage

ARTICLE 23A

1. All intercontinental missiles, anti-missile missiles and anti-aircraft missiles in the "ground-to-air" category retained by the Union of Soviet Socialist Republics and the United States of America under paragraph 1 of article 5 shall be destroyed, together with their launching installations and guidance systems.

2. Inspectors of the International Disarmament Organization shall verify the implementation of the measures referred to in paragraph 1 above.

CHAPTER VI

Further Reduction of Armed Forces, Conventional Armaments and Military Expenditures. Control over such Measures

ARTICLE 24

Further Reduction of Armed Forces and Conventional Armaments

1. In the second stage of general and complete disarmament the armed forces of the States parties to the Treaty shall be further reduced to the following levels:

The United States of America — One million enlisted men, officers and civilian employees;

The Union of Soviet Socialist Republics — One million enlisted men, officers and civilian employees.

. . . .

(Agreed force levels for other States parties to the Treaty shall be included in this article).

The reduction of the armed forces shall be carried out in the first place through the demobilization of personnel previously manning the nuclear or other weapons subject to elimination under articles 22 and 23 of the present Treaty, but chiefly through the complete disbandment of units and ships' crews, their officers and enlisted men being demobilized.

2. Conventional armaments, military equipment, munitions, means of transportation and auxiliary equipment in units and depots shall be reduced by 35 from the original levels for each type of all categories of these armaments. The reduced armaments, military equipment and munitions shall be destroyed, and the means of transportation and auxiliary equipment shall be either destroyed or converted to peaceful uses.

All living quarters, depots and special premises previously occupied by units being disbanded, as well as the territories of all proving grounds, firing ranges and drill grounds belonging to such units shall be transferred for peaceful uses to the civilian authorities.

3. As in the implementation of such measures in the first stage of general and complete disarmament, inspectors of the International Disarmament Organization shall exercise control at places where troops are being disbanded and released conventional armaments and military equipment are being destroyed, and shall also verify the conversion to peaceful uses of means of transportation and other non-combat equipment, premises, proving grounds, etc.

ARTICLE 25

Further Reduction of Conventional Armaments Production

1. The production of conventional armaments and munitions shall be

reduced proportionately to the reduction of armed forces provided for in article 24 of the present Treaty. Such reduction shall, as in the first stage of general and complete disarmament, be carried out primarily through the elimination of undertakings engaged exclusively in the production of such armaments and munitions. These undertakings shall be dismantled, their specialized machine tools and equipment shall be destroyed, and their premises and general purpose machine tools and equipment shall be converted to peaceful uses.

2. The measures referred to in paragraph 1 of this article shall be carried out under the control of inspectors of the International Disarmament Organization.

ARTICLE 26

Further Reduction of Military Expenditure

1. The States parties to the Treaty shall further reduce their military budgets and appropriations for military purposes proportionately to the destruction of nuclear, chemical, biological and radiological weapons and the discontinuance of the production of such weapons as well as to the further reduction of armed forces and conventional armaments and the reduction of the production of such armaments, as provided for in articles 22-25 of the present Treaty.

The funds released through the implementation of the second-stage measures shall be used for peaceful purposes, including the reduction of taxes on the population and the subsidizing of the national economy. A certain portion of the funds thus released shall also be used for the provision of economic and technical assistance to under-developed countries. The size of this portion shall be subject to agreement between the parties to the Treaty.

2. Control over the measures referred to in paragraph 1 of this article shall be exercised in accordance with the provisions of paragraph 2 of article 13 of the present Treaty. Financial inspectors of the International Disarmament Organization shall also be granted unimpeded access to records concerning the reduction in the budgetary appropriations of States resulting from the elimination of nuclear, chemical, biological and radiological weapons.

CHAPTER VII

Measures to Safeguard the Security of States

ARTICLE 27

Continued Strengthening of the Capacity of the United Nations to Maintain International Peace and Security

The States parties to the Treaty shall continue to implement the measures referred to in article 18 of the present Treaty regarding the placing of armed forces at the disposal of the Security Council for use under Article 42 of the United Nations Charter.

CHAPTER VIII

Time-limits for Second-Stage Measures
Transition from the Second to the Third Stage

ARTICLE 28

Time-limits for Second-Stage Measures

The duration of the second stage of general and complete disarmament shall be twenty-four months.

ARTICLE 29

Transition from the Second to the Third Stage

In the course of the last three months of the second stage the International Disarmament Organization shall review the implementation of this stage.

Measures for the transition from the second to the third stage of general and complete disarmament shall be similar to the corresponding measures for the first stage, as laid down in article 20 of the present Treaty.

PART IV. THIRD STAGE OF GENERAL AND COMPLETE DISARMAMENT

ARTICLE 30

Third Stage Tasks

The States parties to the Treaty undertake, in the course of the third stage of general and complete disarmament, fully to disband all their armed forces and thereby to complete the elimination of the military machinery of States.

CHAPTER IX

Completion of the Elimination of the Military Machinery of
States Control over such Measures

ARTICLE 31

Completion of the Elimination of Armed Forces and
Conventional Armaments

1. With a view to completing the process of the elimination of armed forces, the States parties to the Treaty shall disband the entire personnel of the armed forces which remained at their disposal after the accomplishment of the first two stages of disarmament. The system of military reserves of each State party to the Treaty shall be completely abolished.

2. The States parties to the Treaty shall destroy all types of armaments, military equipment and munitions, whether held by the troops or in depots, that remained at their disposal after the accomplishment of the

first two stages of the Treaty. All military equipment which cannot be converted to peaceful uses shall be destroyed.

3. Inspectors of the International Disarmament Organization shall exercise control over the disbanding of troops and over the destruction of armaments and military equipment, and shall control the conversion to peaceful uses of transport and other non-combat equipment, premises, proving grounds, etc.

The International Disarmament Organization shall have access to documents pertaining to the disbanding of all personnel of the armed forces of the States parties to the Treaty.

ARTICLE 32

Complete Cessation of Military Production

1. Military production at factories and plants shall be discontinued, with the exception of the production of agreed types and quantities of light firearms for the purposes referred to in article 36, paragraph 2, of the present Treaty. The factories and plants subject to elimination shall be dismantled, their specialized machine tools and equipment shall be destroyed, and the premises, general purpose machine tools and equipment shall be converted to peaceful uses. All scientific research in the military field at all scientific and research institutions and at designing offices shall be discontinued. All blueprints and other documents necessary for the production of the weapons and military equipment subject to elimination shall be destroyed.

All orders placed by military departments with national or foreign government undertakings and private firms for the production of armaments, military equipment, munitions and material shall be cancelled.

2. Inspectors of the International Disarmament Organization shall exercise control over the measures referred to in paragraph 1 of this article.

ARTICLE 33

Abolition of Military Establishments

1. War ministries, general staffs and all other military and para-military organizations and institutions for the purpose of organizing the military effect of States parties to the Treaty shall be abolished. The States parties to the Treaty shall:

(a) demobilize all personnel of these institutions and organizations;

(b) abrogate all laws, rules and regulations governing the organization of the military effort and the status, structure and activities of such institutions and organizations;

(c) destroy all documents pertaining to the planning of the mobilization and operational deployment of the armed forces in time of war.

2. The entire process of the abolition of military and para-military institutions and organizations shall be carried out under the control of inspectors of the International Disarmament Organization.

ARTICLE 34

Abolition of Military Conscription and Military Training

In accordance with their respective constitutional procedures, the States parties to the Treaty shall enact legislation prohibiting all military training, abolishing military conscription and all other forms of recruiting the armed forces, and discontinuing all military courses for reservists. All establishments and organizations dealing with military training shall simultaneously be disbanded in accordance with article 33 of the present Treaty. The disbanding of all military training institutions and organizations shall be carried out under the control of inspectors of the International Disarmament Organization.

ARTICLE 35

Prohibition of the Appropriation of Funds for Military Purposes

1. The appropriation of funds for military purposes in any form, whether by government bodies or private individuals and social organizations, shall be discontinued.

The funds released through the implementation of general and complete disarmament shall be used for peaceful purposes, including the reduction or complete abolition of taxes on the population and the subsidizing of the national economy. A certain portion of the funds thus released shall also be used for the provision of economic and technical assistance to under-developed countries. The size of this portion shall be subject to agreement between the parties to the Treaty.

2. For the purpose of organizing control over the implementation of the provisions of this article, the International Disarmament Organization shall have the right of access to the legislative and budgetary documents of the States parties to the present Treaty.

CHAPTER X

Measures to Safeguard the Security of States and to Maintain International Peace

ARTICLE 36

Contingents of Police (Militia)

1. After the complete abolition of armed forces, the States parties to the Treaty shall be entitled to have strictly limited contingents of police (militia), equipped with light firearms, to maintain internal order, including the safeguarding of frontiers and the personal security of citizens, and to provide for compliance with their obligations in regard to the maintenance of international peace and security under the United Nations Charter.

The strength of these contingents of police (militia) for each State party to the Treaty shall be as follows:*

. . . .

. . . .

* Exact figures to be agreed on.

2. The States parties to the Treaty shall be allowed to manufacture strictly limited quantities of light firearms intended for such contingents of police (militia). The list of plants producing such arms, the quotas and types for each party to the Treaty shall be specified in a special agreement.

3. Inspectors of the International Disarmament Organization shall exercise control over compliance by the States parties to the Treaty with their obligations with regard to the restricted production of the said light firearms.

ARTICLE 37

Police (Militia) Units to be made available to the Security Council

1. The States parties to the Treaty undertake to place at the disposal of the Security Council, on its request, units from the contingents of police (militia) retained by them, as well as to provide assistance and facilities, including rights of passage. The placing of such units at the disposal of the Security Council shall be carried out in accordance with the provisions of Article 43 of the United Nations Charter. In order to ensure that urgent military measures may be undertaken, the States parties to the Treaty shall maintain in a state of immediate readiness those units of their police (militia) contingents which are intended for joint international enforcement action. The size of the units which the States parties to the Treaty undertake to place at the disposal of the Security Council as well as the areas where such units are to be stationed shall be specified in agreements to be concluded by those States with the Security Council.

2. The command of the units referred to in paragraph 1 shall be composed of representatives of the three principal groups of States existing in the world on the basis of equal representation. It shall decide all questions by agreement among its members representing all three groups of States.

ARTICLE 38

Control over the Prevention of the Re-establishment of Armed Forces

1. The police (militia) contingents retained by the States parties to the Treaty after the completion of general and complete disarmament shall be under the control of the International Disarmament Organization, which shall verify the reports by States concerning the areas where such contingents are stationed, concerning the strength and armaments of the contingents in each such area, and concerning all movements of substantial contingents of police (militia).

2. For the purpose of ensuring that armed forces and armaments abolished as a result of general and complete disarmament are not reestablished, the International Disarmament Organization shall have the right of access at any time to any point within the territory of each State party to the Treaty.

3. The International Disarmament Organization shall have the right to institute a system of aerial inspection and aerial photography over the territories of the States parties to the Treaty.

CHAPTER XI

Time-limits for Third-Stage Measures

ARTICLE 39

The third stage of general and complete disarmament shall be completed over a period of one year. During the last three months of this stage the International Disarmament Organization shall review the implementation of the third-stage measures of general and complete disarmament with a view to submitting a report on the matter to the States parties to the Treaty as well as to the Security Council and the General Assembly of the United Nations.

PART V. STRUCTURE AND FUNCTIONS OF THE INTERNATIONAL DISARMAMENT ORGANIZATION

ARTICLE 40

Functions and Main Bodies

The International Disarmament Organization to be set up under article 2, paragraph 3, of the present Treaty, hereinafter referred to as the "Organization," shall consist of a Conference of all States parties to the Treaty, hereinafter referred to as the "Conference," and a Control Council, hereinafter referred to as the "Council."

The Organization shall deal with questions pertaining to the supervision of compliance by States with their obligations under the present Treaty. All questions connected with the safeguarding of international peace and security which may arise in the course of the implementation of the present Treaty, including preventive and enforcement measures, shall be decided by the Security Council in conformity with its powers under the United Nations Charter.

ARTICLE 41

The Conference

1. The Conference shall comprise all States parties to the Treaty. It shall hold regular sessions at least once a year and special sessions, which may be convened by decision of the Council or at the request of a majority of the States parties to the Treaty with a view to considering matters connected with the implementation of effective control over disarmament. The session shall be held at the headquarters of the Organization, unless otherwise decided by the Conference.

2. Each State party to the Treaty shall have one vote. Decisions on questions of procedure shall be taken by a simple majority and on all other matters by a two-thirds majority. In accordance with the provisions of the present Treaty, the Conference shall adopt its own rules of procedure.

3. The Conference may discuss any matters pertaining to measures of control over the implementation of general and complete disarmament

and may make recommendations to the States parties to the Treaty and to the Council on any such matter or measure.

4. The Conference shall:

(a) Elect non-permanent members of the Council;
(b) Consider the annual, and any special, reports of the Council;
(c) Approve the budget recommended by the Council;
(d) Approve reports to be submitted to the Security Council and the General Assembly of the United Nations;
(e) Approve amendments to the present Treaty in accordance with article 47 of the present Treaty;
(f) Take decisions on any matter specifically referred to the Conference for this purpose by the Council;
(g) Propose matters for consideration by the Council and request from the Council reports on any matter relating to the functions of the Council.

ARTICLE 42

The Control Council

1. The Council shall consist of:

(a) The five States which are permanent members of the United Nations Security Council;
(b) . . . (number) other States parties to the Treaty, elected by the Conference for a period of two years.

The composition of the Council must ensure proper representation of the three principal groups of States existing in the world.

2. The Council shall:

(a) Provide practical guidance for the measures of control over the implementation of general and complete disarmament; set up such bodies at the headquarters of the Organization as it deems necessary for the discharge of its functions; establish procedures for their operation, and devise the necessary rules and regulations in accordance with the present Treaty;
(b) Submit to the Conference annual reports and such special reports as it deems necessary to prepare;
(c) Maintain constant contact with the United Nations Security Council as the organ bearing the primary responsibility for the maintenance of international peace and security; periodically inform it of the progress achieved in the implementation of general and complete disarmament, and promptly notify it of any infringements by the States parties to the Treaty of their disarmament obligations under the present Treaty;
(d) Review the implementation of the measures included in each stage of general and complete disarmament with a view to submitting a report on the matter to the States parties to the Treaty and to the Security Council and the General Assembly of the United Nations;

(e) Recruit the staff of the Organization on an international basis so as to ensure that the three principal groups of States existing in the world are adequately represented. The personnel of the Organization shall be recruited from among persons who are recommended by Governments and who may or may not be citizens of the country of the recommending Government;

(f) Prepare and submit to the Conference the annual budget estimates for the expenses of the Organization;

(g) Draw up instructions by which the various control bodies are to be guided in their work;

(h) Make a prompt study of incoming reports;

(i) Request from States such information on their armed forces and armaments as may be necessary for control over the implementation of the disarmament measures provided for by the present Treaty;

(j) Perform such other functions as are envisaged in the present Treaty.

3. Each member of the Council shall have one vote. Decisions of the Council on procedural matters shall be taken by a simple majority, and on other matters by a two-thirds majority.

4. The Council shall be so organized as to be able to function continuously. The Council shall adopt its own rules of procedure and shall be authorized to establish such subsidiary organs as it deems necessary for the performance of its functions.

ARTICLE 43

Privileges and Immunities

The Organization, its personnel and representatives of the States parties to the Treaty shall enjoy in the territory of each State party to the Treaty such privileges and immunities as are necessary for the exercise of independent and unrestricted control over the implementation of the present Treaty.

ARTICLE 44

Finances

1. All the expenses of the Organization shall be financed from the funds allocated by the States parties of the Treaty. The budget of the Organization shall be drawn up by the Council and approved by the Conference in accordance with article 41, paragraph 4 (c), and article 42, paragraph 2 (f), of the present Treaty.

2. The States parties to the Treaty shall contribute funds to cover the expenditure of the Organization according to the following scale: . .

. . . .

(The agreed scale of contributions shall be included in the present article.)

ARTICLE 45

Preparatory Commission

Immediately after the signing of the present Treaty, the States represented in the Eighteen-Nation Disarmament Committee shall set up a Preparatory Commission for the purpose of taking practical steps to establish the International Disarmament Organization.

PART VI. FINAL CLAUSES

ARTICLE 46

Ratification and Entry into Force

The present Treaty shall be subject to ratification by the Signatory States in accordance with their constitutional procedures within a period of six months from the date of its signature, and shall come into force upon the deposit of instruments of ratification with the United Nations Secretariat by all the States which are permanent members of the Security Council, as well as by those States that are their allies in bilateral and multilateral military alliances, and by .... (number) non-aligned States.

ARTICLE 47

Amendments

Any proposal to amend the text of the present Treaty shall come into force after it has been adopted by a two-thirds majority at a conference of all States parties to the Treaty and has been ratified by the States referred to in article 46 of the present Treaty in accordance with their constitutional procedures.

ARTICLE 48

Authentic Texts

The present Treaty, done in the Russian, English, French, Chinese and Spanish languages, all texts being equally authentic, shall be deposited with the United Nations Secretariat, which shall transmit cerified copies thereof to all the Signatory States.

In witness whereof, the undersigned, duly authorized, have signed the present Treaty.

Done at ....

ECONOMIC AND SOCIAL CONSEQUENCES OF DISARMAMENT

REPORT OF THE SECRETARY-GENERAL TRANSMITTING THE STUDY OF HIS CONSULTATIVE GROUP

ACTING SECRETARY-GENERAL'S PREFACE

This report was prepared by a group of experts appointed by the late Secretary-General, Mr. Dag Hammarskjold, under General Assembly resolution 1516 (XV) to assist him in conducting a study of the economic and social consequences of disarmament in countries with different economic systems and at different stages of economic development.

The members of the group acted in their personal capacities and their observations and recommendations were put forward to me on their own responsibility. I am convinced that their report represents a major step forward in the consideration of the economic and social consequences of disarmament and I am pleased to endorse their general findings. It is now my privilege to submit the report to the Economic and Social Council for its consideration and transmittal, along with its comments, to the General Assembly.

The members of the group were: V. Y. Aboltin, Deputy Director, Institute of World Economics and International Relations, Academy of Sciences of the Union of Soviet Socialist Republics; Mamoun Beheiry, Governor, Bank of Sudan; Arthur J. Brown, Head, Department of Economics, University of Leeds, England; B. N. Ganguli, Head, The Delhi School of Economics, India; Aftab Ahmad Khan, Chief Economist, Planning Commission, Government of Pakistan; Oskar Lange, Chairman, Economic Council, Council of Ministers of the Government of the People's Republic of Poland; W. W. Leontief, Professor of Economics, Harvard University, United States; José Antonio Mayobre, Ambassador of Venezuela to the United States; Alfred Sauvy, Director, National Institute of Demographic Studies, Government of France; and Ludek Urban, Economic Institute, Czechoslovakian Academy of Sciences. Mr. Sauvy was represented at the meetings of the second session of the group by Paul Paillat, also of the National Institute of Demographic Studies. Mr. Jacob L. Mosak, Director of the Division of General Economic Research and Policies of the United Nations Secretariat, served as Chairman.

In preparing the report the experts had available replies of Governments to a *note verbale* of the Secretary-General on the economic and

Reprinted from *Economic and Social Consequences of Disarmament,* United Nations publication. By permission of the United Nations.

social consequences of disarmament, which was sent in accordance with the unanimous recommendation of the group. Communications on the subject were also received from a number of the specialized agencies of the United Nations. The replies of Governments, together with the relevant information from the specialized agencies, are reproduced in part II of the report.

The group was assisted in its work by members of the Secretariat from the Department of Economic and Social Affairs at United Nations Headquarters and from the Economic Commission for Europe, collaborating in accordance with that Commission's resolution 1 (XVI).

It is everywhere recognized that the problems of disarmament considered in the present report are among the most vital before the United Nations today. In dealing with its economic and social consequences the experts have adopted the assumption that disarmament, once agreed upon, would proceed rapidly and would be general and complete. They have reviewed the resources devoted to military purposes and the peaceful uses to which these resources might be put when released. They have examined the conversion problems that might arise and the impact of disarmament on international economic relations and on aid for economic development, and they have called attention to some social consequences of disarmament.

It is a source of profound gratification to me, as I am sure it will be to all Governments, that, on a subject that has until recently been so beset by ideological differences, it has now proved possible for a group of experts drawn from countries with different economic systems and at different stages of economic development to reach unanimous agreement. It is particularly encouraging that the Consultative Group should have reached the unanimous conclusion that "all the problems and difficulties of transition connected with disarmament could be met by appropriate national and international measures," and that "there should thus be no doubt that the diversion to peaceful purposes of the resources now in military use could be accomplished to the benefit of all countries and lead to the improvement of world economic and social conditions."

On behalf of the United Nations, I wish to thank the members of the group for their valuable contribution and to express my appreciation to the institutions with which the experts are associated for their willingness to release them from their normal duties so that they might undertake this extremely important task.

U THANT
Acting Secretary-General

Introduction

1. Realization that the disarmament issue is important—as important as the survival of humanity itself—is world-wide. This is exemplified by a resolution adopted in 1959 by the General Assembly in which the question is called "the most important one facing the world today," and in which hope is expressed that "measures leading towards the goal of general and complete disarmament under effective international control

will be worked out in detail and agreed upon in the shortest possible time."[1] This sense of urgency springs mainly from the existence of a threat to mankind that has grown into one of mass destruction. But in part, also, it comes from the consciousness that the resources that make this threat possible, and many more resources devoted to less spectacularly destructive military uses, are being diverted from the tasks of lightening the burdens and enriching the lives of individuals and of society.

2. At the same time, it is seen that disarmament would affect individuals, countries and the entire world economy in many different ways. A substantial part of the world's labour force now earns its living, directly or indirectly, in meeting military demands. To redeploy this force for non-military purposes is an operation large enough to give rise to important problems of economic and social adjustment. Careful advance study is required for full advantage to be taken of the potential benefits disarmament could make possible. The following chapters attempt a survey of the magnitude of both the benefits it would bring and the difficulties that would have to be overcome in the economic and social fields.

3. In many respects the available data fall short of what is needed for a comprehensive and quantitative analysis. Nevertheless, the broad nature and magnitude of the economic and social benefits and the problems of conversion arising from disarmament, and the general lines on which the main problems can be solved, emerge sufficiently clearly from what is already known.

4. This Consultative Group on the economic and social consequences of disarmament has dealt with the subject on the assumption that disarmament, once agreed upon, would be general and complete and also rapid. It has done so in the belief that this was the intention of the General Assembly resolution under which it was appointed,[2] and also because this interpretation gives the clearest form to both the benefits and the difficulties, thereby minimizing the risk that the latter will be under-estimated.

5. The report represents the unanimous findings of the Consultative Group. It deals with the volume of resources devoted to military purposes and the peaceful uses to which these resources might be put when released, and with the transitional or conversion problems that would arise, both at the aggregate level of national production and employment and in particular sectors of the economy. The impact of disarmament on international economic relations is studied as well as the effects of disarmament on the volume and framework of aid for economic development. Finally, some social consequences of disarmament are considered.

CHAPTER 1

Resources Devoted to Military Purposes

6. The most fundamental way in which disarmament affects economic life is through the liberation of the resources devoted to military use and

[1] See *Official Records of the General Assembly, Fourteenth Session, Supplement No. 16,* resolution 1378 (XIV).

[2] The text of General Assembly resolution 1516 (XV), under which the group was appointed, is given in annex 1.

their re-employment for peaceful purposes. This shift in the composition of the aggregate demand for goods and services is simply a large-scale manifestation of a phenomenon that is constantly taking place in all economies as the demand for certain goods and services shrinks while the demand for other goods and services expands; thus disarmament in its economic aspects should not be considered as a unique phenomenon. Short-term shifts in demand on an even larger scale than that which would accompany any agreed disarmament programme have occurred when economies have been converted to war production, or when they have undergone conversion to peacetime patterns of production at the end of the war.

7. It is important, however, that countries, in preparing to disarm, should take stock of the various resources that disarmament would release for peaceful uses. Such a survey would facilitate economic planning and adjustment at all levels, public and private, national and international.

8. To assess the transitional problems that may arise and to determine the peaceful uses to which the resources released may be put, it is necessary to ascertain in some detail the volume and composition of resources so released. An approximation to the volume of resources that would be liberated by disarmament is provided by the published official estimates of military expenditure.[1] On the basis of available data there appears to be general agreement that the world is spending roughly $120 billion annually on military account at the present time. This figure is equivalent to about 8-9 per cent of the world's annual output of all goods and services; it is at least two-thirds of—and according to some estimates may be of the same order of magnitude as—the entire national income of all the under-developed countries. It is close to the value of the world's annual exports of all commodities and it corresponds to about one-half of the total resources set aside each year for gross capital formation throughout the world.

9. The world's armed forces now number about 20 million persons. This figure does not include all those currently employed in supplying military goods or services directly to the armed forces or in producing the raw materials, equipment and other goods that are needed indirectly in the production of military supplies and services. The total of all persons in the armed forces and in all productive activities resulting from military expenditure may amount to well over 50 million.

10. These figures demonstrate that the total volume of manpower and of other productive resources devoted to military use at the present time is very large indeed. The available data do not, however, make it possible to assess with the desired degree of accuracy the volume of resources that disarmament would actually release. For one thing, the existing estimates may not be comprehensive: some categories of military expenditure may be excluded. Further, there may be considerable inconsistency in the pricing of military output compared with the pricing of other production, as also in the relationship between the pay of the armed forces and civilian wages and salaries. For these and other reasons it would be wrong to

[1] Available data on military expenditures in the national budgets of countries are given in annex 2, tables 2-1, 2-2 and 2-3.

interpret the share of military expenditure in total output as a precise measure of the real share of national resources allocated to military purposes, unless appropriate adjustments could be made for coverage, price differentials and other elements of incomparability.

11. Although the data provide an inadequate basis for precise comparisons of the military burdens among countries, it can be safely asserted that within most countries military expenditure accounts for a very significant proportion of total output. In many countries the estimates of military expenditure range between 1 and 5 per cent of gross domestic product, while in others, particularly in some of the larger countries, the corresponding ratio ranges between 5 and 10 per cent.

12. While the burden of armaments is wide-spread, the great bulk of the world's military expenditure is highly concentrated in a handful of countries. Available indications are that about 85 per cent of the world's military outlays is accounted for by seven countries—Canada, the Federal Republic of Germany, France, the People's Republic of China, the Union of the Soviet Socialist Republics, the United Kingdom of Great Britain and Northern Ireland and the United States of America. Total military expenditure in all the under-developed countries amounts to about one-tenth of that of the industrial private enterprise economies. This means that although many under-developed countries devote significant proportions of their resources to military purposes, the great bulk of the resources released by disarmament would be concentrated in a very few countries.[2]

13. It should be noted that an agreed disarmament programme would involve alternate security arrangements. Thus, the recent joint statement of the United States and the Soviet Union on agreed principles for disarmament negotiations provided that "During and after the implementation of the programme of general and complete disarmament there should be taken, in accordance with the principles of the United Nations Charter, the necessary measures to maintain international peace and security, including the obligation of States to place at the disposal of the United Nations agreed manpower necessary for an international peace force to be equipped with agreed types of armaments."[3] While these arrangements would necessitate the continued allocation of funds and resources to military purposes, it may be assumed that these would be small in relation to current expenditure.

14. In order to formulate economic and social policies so as to take full advantage of the opportunities afforded by disarmament, it is necessary for the countries concerned to know in detail the possible alternative uses for the resources released. In general it can be said that the ease and effectiveness with which the various resources liberated by disarmament might be employed for peaceful purposes would depend on the extent to which the composition of the demand for additional civilian uses approximated that of the resources now devoted to armaments. Because of the relative immobility of some resources in the short run, systematic advance

[2] This is less true of manpower than of other resources, since the underdeveloped countries rely much more on numbers of men than on advanced and expensive armaments and equipment.

[3] See General Assembly document A/4879, *Joint Statement on Agreed Principles for Disarmament Negotiations,* submitted by the Soviet Union and the United States.

study is needed so as to minimize wastage in the transitional stage, though in the long run any country's industrial capacity can be adapted to meet the changing pattern of demand.

15. To prepare a list of the resources absorbed by armaments, it is desirable that each country should, at the appropriate time, determine the composition of military expenditure and estimate the productive resources that it absorbs. The latter calculation is straightforward with respect to certain components of military expenditure. The members of the armed forces, for example, constitute a labour supply that would otherwise be available for peaceful purposes. Similiarly, those research facilities employed for military purposes which are adaptable to civilian research are readily identified. Other productive resources, however, are devoted to military use only in an indirect manner which may not be apparent at first glance. While it is clear, for example, that the labour and capacity in ordnance production are employed solely for military purposes, it is impossible to state, without careful analysis, what proportion of the manpower and other resources devoted to, say, coal mining are so employed. If ordnance factories use any coal, some portion of the productive resources of the coal mining industry are engaged, indirectly, in the production of armaments. But to take into account all the inter-industry relationships in a national economy in order to provide a complete picture of the resources absorbed for military purposes requires considerable statistical information and a thorough economic analysis of an economy's productive structure. The degree of elaboration with which statistics should be compiled and economic analysis performed for this purpose varies from country to country according to the complexity and size of the national economy. Analogous considerations apply to the determination of the amount of resources required directly and indirectly to satisfy alternative peacetime needs.

16. Data made available by a number of countries show that military production is highly concentrated in a few industry groups, notably munitions, electrical machinery, instruments and related products, and transportation equipment, including airplanes and missiles. There is a similar concentration in the same industries of the employment resulting from military expenditure.[4] In most other industries military outlays account for a relatively small proportion of total demand. Industries dependent on military expenditure also have a high degree of concentration in certain regions and cities. While this pattern of concentration of output and employment is not necessarily characteristic of all countries, it appears to apply generally to the major military powers.

17. The situation is rather different in those countries that rely upon imports for their supplies of military goods or in which the major part of military expenditure is for the pay and subsistence of the armed forces, rather than for their equipment. In such cases, the resources devoted to military purposes consist essentially of manpower and foreign exchange. This is especially true of the under-developed countries. While disarmament would require all countries to make significant adjustments, the realization of the great potential gains from disarmament in under-de-

[4] See, for example, the reply of the Government of the United States of America.

veloped countries would depend on a major intensification of efforts to promote economic development. Such efforts would be facilitated in so far as military spending were channelled to development expenditure and as scarce foreign exchange resources hitherto directly or indirectly utilized for military objectives were freed for development purposes; and still more to the extent that aid were forthcoming from the industrially advanced countries in the form of both capital equipment and technical assistance.

CHAPTER 2

The Peaceful Use of Released Resources

18. There are so many competing claims for usefully employing the resources released by disarmament that the real problem is to establish a scale of priorities. The most urgent of these claims would undoubtedly already have been largely satisfied were it not for the armaments race.

19. The resources liberated by disarmament within any country could be employed in part to promote economic and social progress at home in part to expand foreign aid. The question of aid to underdeveloped countries is sufficiently important to warrant treatment in a separate chapter (chapter 6). The main civilian purposes for which the freed resources, whether domestic or foreign in origin, could be applied, may be classified as follows:

Raising standards of personal consumption of goods and services;
Expanding or modernizing productive capacity through investment in new plant and equipment;
Promoting housing construction, urban renewal, including slum clearance, and rural development;
Improving and expanding facilities for education, health, welfare, social security, cultural development, scientific research, etc.

Part of the gain from disarmament could also take the form of an increase in leisure as, for example, through a reduction in average working hours without a corresponding reduction in real income, or through an increase in paid vacations.

20. The various claims upon resources listed above are, of course, closely interlinked. A rise in personal consumption may necessitate new investment in industry or agriculture or both. Enlarged aid from the industrial to the under-developed countries may involve expanding capacity for the production of the goods that the latter countries need, notably capital equipment. As regards the under-developed countries themselves, if additional aid is to bring the greatest benefits, a larger volume of investment out of domestic resources is likely to be required; this would be facilitated by the release of internal resources through disarmament.

21. Since it can be assumed that the economy as a whole is highly flexible in the long run, the resources freed by disarmament could ultimately be used for any one or more of the purposes listed above, and in any combination. Labour can be retrained and, where necessary, can move to other areas. As old equipment becomes obsolete it can be replaced

by new equipment oriented to new patterns of demand. In the long run, there should be little difficulty in adapting resources to needs.

22. In the very short run, by contrast, the range of choice may be somewhat more limited. It takes time to turn swords into plough-shares or to make an office clerk or factory worker out of a soldier. Studies in some industrial countries have shown that the productive capacities released from military use would be much more immediately adaptable to the increased output of consumer durables and industrial equipment than to the production of houses, food, clothing or educational facilities. Thus, in the transition period, countries may wish to take into account not merely the unsatisfied needs for higher consumption, investment and foreign aid, but also the extent to which alternative patterns of new expenditure would take full advantage of the particular resources that disarmament would make available. It should, however, be borne in mind that some of the major military powers now have fairly comfortable margins of productive capacity available to them. In these cases it is unlikely that disarmament would generate many new demands that could not fairly readily be satisfied from available resources.[1]

23. In the centrally planned economies, even though they have generally been operating approximately at capacity, the transfer of industrial capacity and labour force to the production of goods for peaceful uses could be achieved in a relatively short time. This transfer could be readily achieved by measures formulated within the framework of the general economic plans which can ensure a desirable balance between demand and resources.

24. In the under-developed countries the principal resource released, apart from the purely financial, would be manpower, both skilled and unskilled. In some cases a significant proportion of industrial and transport capacity would also become available for other uses. In many there would also be considerable savings in foreign exchange. The effective utilization of released resources would depend upon the soundness and vigour of development programmes and the volume and character of aid received.

Personal consumption and productive investment

25. Among the alternative uses of resources released by disarmament, increased personal consumption might well absorb a large share. It is fair to suppose that even in the developed countries there would be strong pressure on Governments to raise the level of living. Disarmament would, in particular, offer an important opportunity to raise incomes of low income sections of the population and to facilitate equalizing the rates of pay for men and women.

[1] See, for example, W. Leontief and M. Hoffenberg, "The Economics of Disarmament," *Scientific American* (New York), vol. 204, No. 4, April 1961, pp. 47-55. An unpublished study made at the Department of Applied Economics, Cambridge, England, suggests that, if military expenditure in the United Kingdom ceased and were replaced in equal parts by increased private consumption, increased domestic fixed capital formation, and increased foreign aid, output would be reduced in only two out of nineteen sectors of the economy (military services, and ship, aircraft and railway vehicle construction) and would be required to expand in most others by between 3 and 6 per cent—the main exceptions being textiles (9 per cent increase) and motor vehicles (14 per cent increase).

26. In most countries, however, not all the resources freed by disarmament would be allocated directly to consumption, no matter what the level of income might be. In the first place, a substantial portion of the released resources would be used for expansion of productive capacities because only such expansion can provide a firm basis for further increases in consumption. Ministers representing the countries of western Europe and North America recently set as a collective target the attainment during the decade from 1960 to 1970 of a growth in real gross national product of 50 per cent for all the countries taken together.[2] In the Soviet Union, according to existing plans for economic development, industrial production should reach, in the course of the present decade, a level two and one half times the present volume. A more rapid rate of growth would also enable countries with a higher degree of industrialization to contribute more effectively—through greater financial and technical assistance and through the widening of markets for exports—to the development of countries that are less advanced industrially.

27. Recent experience in both private enterprise and socialist economies provides a rough guide in judging how much additional investment a specific growth target requires. Among the industrialized private enterprise economies, it appears that during the nineteen fifties a country experiencing a 4 per cent annual rate of growth needed, on the average, to devote about 2 per cent more of gross national product to investment than did a country having a 3 per cent rate of growth.[3] In most of these countries, 2 per cent would constitute a very significant proportion of the resources disarmament would release. In the less developed countries which have low levels of income and saving, the utilization of released resources for capital formation must be considered vitally important.

Social investment

28. Social investment is an important alternative both to private consumption and to industrial and agricultural investment. Its claims rest partly upon the clear urgency of the direct need for improved social amenities, and partly upon the fact that growth of industrial and agricultural productivity is dependent upon developments in education, housing, health, and other fields. Since social investment has had to compete with military claims for state funds, it (like aid to under-developed countries) has probably been particularly affected by the armaments race. Recognition of the necessity to remedy the resulting deficiencies in the stock of social capital is wide-spread among countries at different stages of economic development and with different economic systems. There is no common measure of need according to which it is possible to add up, or to compare, the deficiencies in different fields of social investment or different countries. Nevertheless, the importance of the subject warrants an attempt to set out the main relevant pieces of evidence.

29. In the United States the National Planning Association estimated

[2] Organisation for Economic Co-operation and Development, Press Communiqué, OECD/PRESS/A(61)10 (Paris) 17 November 1961.

[3] For further details, see United Nations, *World Economic Survey, 1959* (Sales No.: 60.II.C.1), chap. 1.

at the end of 1959 the cumulative expenditure requirements for selected government programmes over the next five years.[4] These estimates were not intended to be precise but simply represented a summary of the existing programmes of development and improvement in various fields over the next five years. The significance of these estimates, which imply annual average expenditures of $66 billion, may be judged from the fact that the present spending of the Federal, State and local governments on all these programmes amounts to about $30 billion per year. It is therefore apparent that these programmes could absorb much or most of any resources released by disarmament.

30. In the Soviet Union the task has been set of achieving a sharp improvement in living standards within the next twenty years by raising the income of the population and also by expanding social benefits (education, health protection, social insurance, housing construction, etc.). As stated in an official document, "general and complete disarmament on the basis of an appropriate agreement between States would make it considerably easier to overfulfil the planned improvement in the living standards of the working people."[5]

31. It will be noted that the highest single figure among the programmes for the United States mentioned above is that for urban renewal and development, including slum clearance, low-cost housing and community redevelopment. The problem of urban renewal is worldwide. In 1950 about 80 per cent of the world's population was still living in rural areas. Between 50 and 60 million people are being added to the world's total population every year, mainly to its urban areas. In Asia as many as 500 million persons may be added between 1950 and 1975 to the population of cities with over 20,000 inhabitants. In Latin America, sixty-two cities with over 100,000 people accounted in 1960 for some 40 per cent of the region's total. In Africa a considerably higher rate of growth is taking place in urban areas than in rural areas. Rapid urbanization is characteristic of Europe and North America.

32. The rural and urban environments in many countries are both deteriorating, mainly under the impact of this rapid growth. The social and physical symptoms of this deterioration are bad housing, poor community services and delinquency, the paralysis of city traffic, and in many of the less developed countries an absence of sanitation accompanied by a high incidence of communicable disease. In many metro-

[4] National Planning Association, *Looking Ahead,* March 1960. The estimates covering the next five years were as follows:

		(*$ billion*)
Education		30
Classroom construction	16	
Current operation	14	
Highways and skyways		75
Urban renewal		100
(Slum clearance, low-cost housing and community redevelopment)		
Water supply and conservation		60
Health and hospitals		35
Other programmes		30
(Air pollution, research and development, etc.)		
TOTAL		330

[5] *Programme of the Communist Party,* adopted at the 22nd Party Congress.

politan cities of such less developed countries "squatters' settlements" already contain a considerable part of the population.

33. The magnitude of the resources required for dealing with the problem of urbanization is very large. In India alone, for example, approximately $1 billion a year will be required to house the new inhabitants of cities with over 100,000 people. The provision of city-wide services, utilities and transportation would at least double the needed investment. In Latin America it was estimated by the Organization of American States in 1954 that an annual investment of $1.4 billion was required over a period of thirty years to wipe out the housing backlog, to replace obsolescent dwellings and to provide homes for new households. According to rough estimates by the United Nations Bureau of Social Affairs, as many as 150 million families in the less developed countries are in need of adequate homes. These immense requirements are contributing in many under-developed countries to the maintenance of a level of spending on housing and urban development such that the pressing claims of directly productive sectors have to be curtailed.

34. In the Soviet Union a housing shortage still exists despite the building of dwellings for nearly 50 million people in the last five years. "The housing problem remains acute. The growth of the urban population in the Soviet Union during the past few years is considerably in excess of the estimates."[6] In order to overcome the shortage and house every family in "a separate, comfortable apartment," an increase in twenty years of about 200 per cent would be required in the existing housing facilities. To reach this goal it is required that average annual housing construction be raised from the target of 135 million square metres in 1961-65 to 400 million square metres in 1976-80.[7]

35. Another field in which the supply of social capital is deficient in many countries is road and air transportation.[8] The rapid increase in the stock of automobiles and the lag in road facilities in these countries during the post-war years have been accompanied by extraordinary congestion and numbers of accidents. Airports and other air facilities are also deficient in many under-developed areas as well as in some more advanced economies, and investment in civil aviation will claim a share of the resources freed by disarmament.

36. The development and conservation of natural resources provides another important field for increased outlays in the event of disarmament. In the United States it has been estimated that Federal expenditure requirements up to 1980 in the field of water resource development alone total almost $55 billion, while $173 billion will be needed for non-Federal programmes.[9] The Soviet Union could advance the preparation and implementation of a number of important nature-transforming projects in various parts of the country in order to improve living and

[6] N. Khrushchev, *Report to the 22nd Congress of the Communist Party* (Cross Currents Press, New York, 1961), p. 118.

[7] *Report on the Programme of the Communist Party,* delivered to the 22nd Party Congress; Soviet Booklet, No. 81 (London, 1961), p. 47.

[8] Even countries as industrially advanced as the United States may have such a deficiency. For example, the second largest figure in the National Planning Association estimates cited in the footnote to paragraph 29 is for highways and skyways.

[9] See the reply of the Government of the United States of America.

working conditions for the people. There is, for example, a plan to divert part of the waters of the Pechora, Vychegda and Ob Rivers into the basins of the Volga and the Caspian and Aral Seas. This would bring about a considerable change in the climate and in living conditions in Central Asia and in the southern European part of the Soviet Union. In under-developed countries there are also many important multipurpose schemes for the conservation and the utilization of water resources.

37. The world's demand for water is growing much more rapidly than the supply, and a continuation of present trends implies a growing deterioration in the balance of demand and supply. Increasing supplies of water are needed not merely in order to keep pace with the rapid rise in population, but also in order to meet the still faster growing needs for irrigation and industry. In many countries most of the cheapest sources of supply for water have already been tapped, so that further expansion of supplies necessitates increasingly heavy investment in obtaining access to other sources, including the purification of sea water.

38. Other urgent requirements for natural resource development and conservation exist in the fields of forestry, soil and watershed conservation, rangeland conservation, park and recreational development and fish and wildlife conservation. In the United States the total Federal cost of proposed programmes in these areas over a period of ten years implies an annual rate of almost $4 billion, or almost twice the current rate of expenditure. In addition, scientific research and investigation in the field of natural resources will have to be expanded at considerable cost. In western Pakistan a master plan has been prepared for soil reclamation and conservation in order to combat the twin menaces of water-logging and salinity. The cost during the next ten years is estimated at $1.2 billion.

Investment in Health, Education and Social Services

39. Another major use of the resources released from disarmament is investment to raise standards of health, education and social services. There is an urgent need for improvement in health services throughout the world. In many countries the ratio of doctors, dentists and other medical personnel to the population is inadequate and even falling, and there are also great deficiencies in the supply of hospitals and hospital beds as well as of other basic health facilities. The backlog that many countries have to make up in order to attain the best current levels of hospital facilities is very large. In some of the poorer countries of Europe, for example, the medical facilities available to each doctor have been estimated to be as little as one-fiftieth of those prevailing in the better equipped countries. Yet even in the richest countries there is great need to improve standards of medical services. In Canada and the United States, for instance, the deficit in hospital beds has been estimated at from a quarter to a half of the existing number.[10] In underdeveloped countries the need for improved medical care is obviously greater. This is indicated, for example, by infant mortality rates in excess of 100 per 1,000 in many of these countries as

[10] Royal Commission on Canada's Economic Prospects, *Housing and Social Capital* (Ottawa, 1957), and annual reports of the United States Department of Health, Education and Welfare (Washington, D. C.).

opposed to rates of 20 to 30 per 1,000 in economically advanced countries.

40. An indication of the magnitude of investment requirements for medical care may be gained from projections for the United States. The present rate of construction, plus a limited programme of renovation, modernization and increase in rehabilitation facilities, would require at least $15 billion over the next decade instead of the $9 billion that would be needed if such changes were not carried out.[11] In the Soviet Union it has been officially suggested that hospital accommodation might be increased by 40 per cent (that is, by several hundred thousand beds) at low cost by converting into hospitals part of the buildings now in military use.[12]

41. In most developed countries educational needs are rising and are bound to expand even more rapidly; with the ever wider spread of technical progress there will be a rising premium on a higher educational background, on better scientific and technological skills and on a broader range of knowledge. At the same time greater efforts will be directed towards reducing the drop-out rate of the less talented and towards ensuring that an increasing proportion of the highly talented reach upper levels. The realization of all these purposes would imply the devising of new kinds of education and provision of adequate means so that people keep abreast of the latest developments in knowledge.

42. In the United States, existing standards currently require an expenditure level of $20 billion for school enrollments in kindergarten through twelfth grade, and of $6.7 billion for institutions of higher education. Projections on this basis alone indicate for 1970 a rise of 50 per cent in the first case and of more than 250 per cent in the second case. In a disarmed economy it would also be easier to meet the demands for better standards of education.

43. According to recent estimates, western Europe's expenditure on education may rise from $9 billion in 1958 (including both current and capital outlays) to over $18 billion, on a high estimate, in 1970—an increase of over 100 per cent.[13] As a result, outlays for education may rise from 3.2 per cent of gross national product to 4.0 per cent. Western Europe would also face important problems at the university level if a target were set for raising the European enrolment in the 20-24 year age group from 5 per cent as at present to the United States ratio of over 20 per cent.[14]

44. In the Soviet Union general and polytechnical secondary (eleven-year course) education for all children of school-going age is to be introduced in the next ten years. It is planned that the number of students resident in boarding schools and extended day-care schools should increase from 1.5 million at present to 2.5 million in 1965. The shortage of space in schools has led to using the building facilities in shifts; but teaching

[11] See the reply of the Government of the United States of America.

[12] Embassy of the Union of Soviet Socialist Republics, Washington, D. C., Press Department Release No. 66, 2 February 1960.

[13] Organization for European Economic Co-operation, *Targets for Education in Europe*, by Svennilson, Edding and Elvin, p. 105.

[14] Dewhurst, Coppock, Yates and Associates, *Europe's Needs and Resources*, (New York, 1961) p. 343.

on a shift basis is expected to stop completely in the near future. Besides the extension of secondary school facilities, it is estimated that the present enrolment of 2.6 million students in higher educational establishments will triple by 1980.[15] All these developments will require construction of many more schools and training of a large body of teachers, both of which would be facilitated by disarmament.

45. In the under-developed countries, the magnitude of the educational problem may be seen from the fact that most of them still have illiteracy rates of well over 50 per cent of the population aged fifteen years and over. The cost of educational requirements in under-developed countries for education is exemplified by a recently adopted African programme.[16] On the basis of inventories of educational needs of the countries covered by the African plan[17] the total cost of the programme is expected to increase from $590 millon in the first year to $1,150 million in 1965, $1,880 million in 1970 and $2,600 million in 1980. It is assumed that the share of national income devoted to education will rise from 3 to 4 per cent between 1961 and 1965, and thereafter will increase further, reaching 6 per cent of national income by 1980. This means that the difference, amounting in the same years to $140 million, $450 million, $1,-010 million and $400 million, respectively, would need to be covered by foreign aid.

46. Apart from needs in the fields of health and education, there are urgent requirements for expansion in social services. Even in the most advanced countries, there are pronounced shortcomings in the provision of child welfare services, vocational rehabilitation agencies, community centres and other special services.

47. It is thus clear that, so far as social investment is concerned, there is already a heavy backlog of urgent need, and the recent acceleration of population growth and of technical change make it certain that the need, and the demand, will grow. Social investment therefore is likely to claim an increasing volume of resources, to which disarmament would make a welcome contribution.

Scientific Research for Peaceful Purposes

48. The release of scientific and technical manpower would be one of the important consequences of disarmament. Amongst the major powers a significant part of the national research and development effort currently serves military purposes. The total elimination of military spending would bring about a sizable release of resources for civilian research and development. With disarmament it would thus become possible to encourage programmes of basic scientific research in fields which have hitherto been neglected, and to mobilize great scientific potential for the solution of

[15] Based on information in *Report on the Programme,* op. cit., p. 66, and N. Khrushchev's *Report,* op. cit., p. 122.

[16] United Nations Economic Commission for Africa and United Nations Educational, Scientific and Cultural Organization, *Outline of a Plan for African Educational Development* (UNESCO/ED/180); and *Final Report* (UNESCO/ED/181).

[17] The plan covers only thirty-five States and territories of Africa. It excludes, in particular, the countries bordering on the Mediterranean and the Union of South Africa.

some of the world's greatest problems in such areas as medicine, urban development and reorganization, and the technical problems associated with the economic development of under-developed countries. If human ingenuity, in the space of a very few years, has so vastly increased man's powers for destruction, it should be able to make an equally massive contribution to peaceful and constructive achievement.

49. Not all of the needs described above can be satisfied by single nations acting alone. In some instances their satisfaction will require international co-operation.[18] Serious gaps exist in the permanent world-wide network of meteorological observing stations and in the corresponding telecommunication facilities, and a marked increase is required in the funds available for basic research on improving meteorological services. Furthermore, the funds currently available for assisting meteorological development in the less developed countries are far less than needed to satisfy current demands, not to mention prospective demands. Telecommunications are important to developing economies and there is need to pursue a number of objectives in this field, including the development of networks. There is also considerable scope for international co-operation in developing the world's air transport facilities.

50. Disarmament would also open up possibilities for joint international ventures of an even more ambitious kind, including the utilization of atomic energy for peaceful purposes, space research, the exploration of the Arctic and Antarctic for the benefit of mankind and projects to change the climates of large areas of the world. Joint research into the earth's interior may lead to discoveries that would be of real value to the whole world. In addition, joint projects to assist the development of under-developed countries as well as programmes of co-operation in the social and economic fields could be undertaken. These international projects could have a major impact on world living standards and civilization.

51. It is evident from the foregoing illustrative discussion of the magnitude of current and impending needs that the resources freed by disarmament would not be large enough for the many claims upon them. Though it would take active decisions by Governments in the light of national and international needs to set in motion the necessary programmes for employing the released resources, it seems abundantly clear that no country need fear a lack of useful employment opportunities for the resources that would become available to it through disarmament.

CHAPTER 3

The Impact of Disarmament on National Production and Employment

52. Disarmament would raise both general problems of maintaining the over-all level of economic activity and employment and specific problems in so far as manpower or productive capacity might require adaptation to non-military needs. Structural problems of conversion of the latter type will be discussed in chapter 4. Successful maintenance of the level of

[18] For communications received from specialized agencies of the United Nations on matters discussed in these paragraphs, see volume II of this report (E/3593/Rev.1/Add.1).

aggregate demand, production and employment would facilitate the solution of specific structural or frictional problems. Conversely, economic policies which dealt smoothly and effectively with the structural or frictional problems would help to promote the solution of the general problems. In both cases, careful preparation would be required to ensure that the various stages of the disarmament process were accompanied by as little disturbance of economic life as possible.

53. In the economic life of all countries, shifts in the pattern of demand and in the allocation of productive resources are continually occurring in response to changes in technology, foreign trade, consumer tastes, per capita income, the age distribution of the population, migration, and many other factors. Some industries grow more rapidly than others, while the output of certain industries may even decline in absolute terms. Such shifts involve a transfer of manpower and capital between occupations, industries and regions. The reallocation of productive resources which would accompany disarmament is in many respects merely a special case of the phenomenon of economic growth.

54. There are, however, some aspects of the process of disarmament which would raise problems significantly different from those that have been experienced in the usual process of economic growth. While many of the continuous changes in the composition of demand work themselves out only over a long period of time, it seems reasonable to assume that disarmament, once decided upon, would occur more rapidly—over a period of only a few years. For some components of military demand, the whole of the shift might occur within a very short period of time such as a single year. The reallocation of resources attendant upon disarmament would therefore pose some special problems. The more rapid the rate of growth of an economy, however, the easier it would be to bring about the economic changes disarmament might require.

55. The conversion of resources that would be required as a result of disarmament at the present time would be far smaller, in the aggregate, than that which took place at the end of the Second World War. Thus an examination of the early post-war conversion may help to give perspective to the present problem. The experience of the smaller-scale conversion that followed the end of the hostilities in Korea also deserves consideration.

The Post-War Conversion

56. The post-war conversion was a much larger one and involved a more rapid transfer of resources than total disarmament would require at present. During the last years of the war, the world devoted about one half of its resources to destruction. The real military expenditure and the number of people in uniform were about four times as high as today. The extent of devastation in the areas overrun by armies or bombed from the air was immense. The usual network of trade both within and between countries was thoroughly disrupted. Despite these difficulties, huge armies were quickly demobilized without a significant rise in unemployment in most countries, and the pace of recovery, particularly of industrial output, was impressively rapid.

57. During the post-war conversion, the major concern of economic policy was to restrain, rather than to maintain, over-all demand. This period was characterized by intense pressure of excess demand for both consumption and investment. Most commodities were in short supply. Their distribution was carried out nearly everywhere with the aid of rationing or at least under a system of price controls. The war-time accumulation of liquid savings in the hands of the population guaranteed a high level of continued effective demand. As plant and equipment were released from war production and repaired or replaced, they were immediately turned to producing goods for which demand had remained unsatisfied or deferred in some countries during nearly fifteen years of the Great Depression and the war. Most of the demobilized manpower found employment in civilian occupations, while the total labour force declined, reflecting a voluntary withdrawal of some women, minors and veterans from the labour market. As supply conditions improved, price and distribution controls were progressively eased.

58. There were large arrears not only of consumption but also of investment. The capital stock had in many countries been run down by destruction, obsolescence and lack of maintenance. Technological progress had continued and in fact sharply accelerated in some fields during the war years. But much of it had remained unincorporated in plant and equipment—during the depression because of lack of effective demand, and during the war because of diversion of resources to war-time needs. Residential construction had undergone successive postponement in some countries. These factors led to an upsurge in business and residential investment after the war, financed in part by the accumulated liquid resources of corporations and of consumers and in part by various forms of public assistance.

59. In the United States, by the end of the Second World War, the military budget had accounted for over 40 per cent of the gross national product. Between 1945 and 1946, expenditure on national security was reduced by 80 per cent. The decline in military expenditure was equal to one-third of the gross national product and nearly two-thirds of personal consumption in 1944. By the way of comparison it may be said that the military budget in the United States in recent years has been somewhat less than 10 per cent of the gross national product and about 15 per cent of personal consumption.

60. The decline in total real demand was less than half the drop in military spending because of the advance in all other sectors of demand. The small decline in national output was perhaps no more than could have been expected as a result of voluntary withdrawals from the labour force and from the shortening of working hours.

61. The sharpest increase took place in gross private domestic investment which rose from $21 billion to $51 billion—or from less than 6 per cent of gross national product to about 15 per cent. The rise in consumption also contributed in absolute terms nearly as much as investment, although its relative contribution was not so large. There were also increases in public expenditure for civilian purposes and in net foreign investment. Assistance through UNRRA, other grants and credits to various countries

for relief and rehabilitation helped toward a substantial expansion of United States exports. Thus the economy showed a high degree of flexibility even in the relatively short run.

62. Between August 1945 and June 1946, the size of the United States armed forces was reduced by over 9 million men. There was a small reduction in the labour force as women and minors returned to home and school, and veterans continued their interrupted education. As a result of this, and of the cutting back of overtime, unemployment in 1946 remained below 4 per cent of the labour force, despite the very extensive and rapid demobilization.

63. While the large backlog of demand of private business and consumers was responsible for much of the ease with which the post-war adjustment was made, effective government policies also helped. Taxes were reduced. There was a very great increase in transfer payments, principally veterans' cash benefits and payments related to the veterans' training and education programme. As a result, despite the massive decline in military spending, disposable income fell hardly at all. As regards investment, a large veterans' loan programme helped to finance the purchase of homes and farms, quick settlements were made to business on termination of war contracts, and an easy credit policy was maintained. The Government of the United States of America notes that:

> "Tried measures such as these would be under active consideration again in the event of the acceptance of a disarmament program."[1]

64. In western Europe the conversion process took somewhat longer than in the United States because of the damage or destruction to productive facilities and the fact that the total output had in many cases fallen below pre-war levels. Inflationary pressures were severe. Confidence in currencies was shaken. Many key products, notably coal, steel, certain imported materials, and foodstuffs were in short supply.

65. Despite these difficulties the conversion was relatively rapid. Eighteen months after the cessation of hostilities, industrial output had recovered its pre-war level nearly everywhere except in the Federal Republic of Germany and in Italy. The demobilized armed forces were rather quickly absorbed in employment in civilian occupations. Except in the two countries just mentioned, unemployment declined well below pre-war levels. The recovery of western Europe was assisted by a considerable amount of external aid.

66. In the United Kingdom, it is estimated that at the end of the war, 9 million persons, or 42 per cent of the total working population, were either in the armed forces or engaged in the manufacture of equipment and supplies for them. Sixteen months later, the total number in these two categories had fallen by almost 7 million. Of this total about 1.2 million corresponded to a voluntary decline in the labour force, while involuntary unemployment rose by about 0.7 million. Thus over 5 million people were absorbed into civilian employment in the short space of sixteen months, whereas the corresponding number that would have to be absorbed in the event of disarmament now is just over 1 million. It is note-

[1] See the reply of the Government of the United States of America.

worthy that the number unemployed at any one time never greatly exceeded six or seven weeks' release at the maximum rate reached, and that it stood at this level only so long as releases continued at a substantial rate. Even so, unemployment remained below 4 per cent of the labour force.

67. In some of the under-developed countries, the post-war recovery presented special problems. This was partly because agriculture, which formed a much larger proportion of the output of the underdeveloped than of the developed countries, was generally slower to recover than was industry. The long years of war had led in many cases to heavy exhaustion of farms and livestock and to disturbance of trading patterns. There was a world shortage of fertilizers, and recovery was also delayed in many cases because initially inadequate industrial, transport and mining equipment had been strained beyond its rated capacity during the war. For some time after the war, too, delivery of equipment was delayed by conversion and re-equipment needs in the industrial countries.

68. There is, however, no reason to believe that any future disarmament would be attended, in the under-developed countries, by the same types of problem as prevailed after the Second World War. As indicated previously, the main question in these countries would be whether development programmes could be enlarged and stepped up significantly—and in sufficiently good time—to permit the absorption of the demobilized armed forces and other resources into productive employment.

69. In the Soviet Union, experience of conversion immediately following the Second World War was significantly different from that in other countries, because of the much greater destruction and devastation which had taken place during the war. Much equipment had been damaged or was in a bad state of repair. Plant and equipment constructed during the war had been designed entirely for military purposes, and was therefore somewhat less "convertible" than facilities constructed in peacetime. Superimposed on all this was the problem of transferring workers in the eastern territories—who had been evacuated from areas occupied by the Germans—back to their home districts in the western part of the country. For all these reasons there was a decline in industrial production from 1945 to 1946, concentrated in the producer goods sector. Since some manpower had to be employed in tasks for which it was untrained there was a decline in output per man. These developments, however, were the result of the devastation and dislocation referred to above. The subsequent recovery was very rapid and by 1948 industrial production was already nearly one-fifth above the 1940 level. The circumstances of any future disarmament would be much more favourable to a smooth conversion process than those at the end of the Second World War.

70. In other eastern European countries the conversion process had also to overcome heavy human and material losses caused by the Second World War. In Poland alone, over 6 million people perished during the war and Nazi occupation. The respective Governments had to face the great damage caused to productive capacity, transport and housing, apart from dislocation of populations, monetary disturbances and other difficulties. Recovery was facilitated by the planned direction of the process of

reconstruction and readjustment which was made possible by the gradual nationalization of banking, of most industry and of transportation. The recovery proceeded relatively quickly, so that in 1948 in most countries the pre-war level of production was surpassed.

Conversion After the Korean War

71. In the United States at the end of the Korean hostilities many of the special features associated with demobilization after the Second World War were no longer present. Military spending fell from $62 billion (in 1960 prices) in 1953 to $51 billion in 1954. This was accompanied by a liquidation of inventories that in part was associated directly with the fall in military expenditure itself, and in part reflected some business uncertainty regarding the immediate outlook for demand. The total decline in the national product, however, was less than half the reduction in military spending, largely because of increases in consumption and domestic investment. The latter, in turn, were made possible by a reduction in taxes and a policy of monetary ease which was particularly important in stimulating expenditure on housing. Unemployment, after rising to 5.6 per cent of the labour force in 1954, declined to less than 4.4 per cent in 1955 in the face of further cutbacks in military spending.

72. Characterizing the effectiveness of policies during this period, the Government of the United States of America observes that:

> "Despite the mildness of the 1954 recession it now is clear that fiscal and monetary policies might have been applied with more vigor. The reason they were not is that the decline in defence spending following the Korean War was not treated by the policy makers as a major demobilization requiring strong compensatory action. For this reason the 1953-1954 period does not provide a significant guide to the behavior of the American economy in a disarmament program during the 1960's."[2]

73. In other countries, for which information is available, the degree of involvement in the Korean war was not such that its end provided experience of comparable relevance for the purpose of this study. With the cessation of hostilities in Korea, however, there was a diminution of international tensions which brought about reductions in military expenditure and releases from armed forces in various countries. No significant problems of reabsorption of the demobilized personnel arose in these countries.

Experience in the Centrally Planned Economies

74. The experience of the centrally planned economies in reducing the armed forces is also of interest. In the Soviet Union, the armed forces were reduced from 5.8 million men in 1955 to 3.6 million men in 1958.[3] There were also reductions in military forces in other centrally planned

[2] *Ibid.*

[3] There was a government decision for a further reduction to 2.4 million men in 1960. Statement by Prime Minister Khrushchev reported in *Pravda,* 15 January 1960.

economies during that period. No significant problems were created by the demobilization in these countries since the demand for labour was continually increasing. Discharged officers were absorbed in administrative posts in industry or agriculture and were provided with opportunities for retraining at government expense. In a number of countries in eastern Europe, expansion in output of durable consumer goods was greatly facilitated after 1954 by utilizing the equipment which had earlier been devoted to producing armaments.

Impact on National Production and Employment

75. National experience with general economic policies during previous conversion periods will unquestionably be valuable for policy makers in the future. In adopting a programme of general and complete disarmament, Governments would certainly wish to assess very carefully the probable impact of disarmament on national production and employment, and to examine their economic policies to ensure that these were as well thought out as possible. It would be important to maintain a high general level of domestic demand for goods and services and thereby to support satisfactory levels of output and employment. This is already a well-established objective of national policy, but it would have additional urgency both during the conversion period and also in the long run, after general and complete disarmament had been achieved.

76. The economic measures needed to maintain over-all effective demand are different in the private enterprise economies from those in the centrally planned economies. In the latter, economic decision-making is centralized. Most of the productive capacity is government-owned. The national economic plans are directed toward the achievement of a set rate of growth and higher levels of living. In the private enterprise economies, on the other hand, where the private sectors are much larger than the government sectors, the power to make economic decisions is diffused. Governments must therefore rely heavily, in influencing economic decision-making in the private consumption and investment sectors, on relatively indirect means such as fiscal and monetary policies. In general, the governments of under-developed countries cannot count as readily as those of the more developed countries on an expansion of private investment. Greater attention needs therefore to be given to undertaking whatever volume of expenditure may prove necessary in the government-owned sector in the under-developed countries.

77. Much attention has already been given in the industrialized private enterprise economies to the methods by which total effective demand can be maintained. Member countries are pledged under the United Nations Charter to maintain full employment. A number of Governments have further undertaken in national statements of policy to adopt measures toward that objective. The instruments available for the prevention of any substantial shortfall of demand are well known. Their relative merits, however, vary widely from one country to another and from one time to another because of differences in institutions and attitudes.

78. The nature and magnitude of the task of maintaining total de-

mand at an adequate level to assure the fullest possible employment would depend to some extent upon the purpose to which the resources released from military use were applied. In some cases, it might be decided to use the released resources by reducing taxes on income, particularly of lower income groups. In others, it might be decided to reduce the burden of indirect taxes on mass consumption goods borne mainly by the lower income groups in the community. It might, also, be seen fit to adopt fiscal measures designed to stimulate investment expenditure. In yet other cases importance might be attached to reduction of the public debt. Alternatively, a decision might also be taken to replace military expenditure by other kinds of government expenditure. These different policies would have different impacts upon the level of effective demand. In practice, different combinations of them would be likely to be used in different countries.

79. Disarmament would lead to an immediate reduction of effective demand only in so far as total expenditure of the government-owned sector were reduced. It might seem at first sight that this result would be avoided if tax revenue were reduced by the same amount as government expenditure, but this is not, in general, the case, since some of the increased disposable income would be saved rather than spent. The effect on consumption would depend on which type of tax were reduced, whether direct or indirect, and on which income groups were affected. Generally, reduction in taxes diminishing the burdens on low income groups are the most effective. Even so, however, some fall in income would result under these assumptions. A setback of this kind, unless counteracted by other measures, might also discourage private investment and thus lead to a further fall in income.

80. It should, perhaps, be observed that in so far as it is desired to raise private consumption, the appropriate means cannot lie exclusively in reductions in direct taxation because those benefited by such a measure do not include the poorest sectors of the population whose incomes are too low to be taxed. Supplementary measures of various types would be required to ensure that all parts of the community benefited to some extent from the higher consumption levels made possible by disarmament.

81. The effect of using the money saved by a reduction of military expenditure for repaying public debt would be twofold. On the one hand government expenditure on goods and services would be lower, since debt repayment does not in itself constitute a direct offset to the reduction in military spending. On the other hand, by substituting holdings of money for holdings of public debt some private spending on goods and services would probably be stimulated. The extent of this stimulation is difficult to assess, and would vary with the kind of debt redeemed, but it would be unlikely to offset the deflationary impact of the original reduction in government expenditure.

82. Monetary and fiscal policy could be used to offset the effect of a shortfall in total demand that might result from a decline in government expenditure. Monetary policy, whether operated mainly through interest rates or mainly through a more direct control of credit, gives some scope for the encouragement of both capital formation by business and pur-

chases of durable goods by consumers. Changes in taxation, or transfers, in addition to their immediate effects on purchasing power, to which some reference has already been made, may also be expected to exert some influence on the formation of business capital; tax concessions may be designed to encourage private investment in general or to give special encouragement to investment in particular industries or localities where it will most effectively employ resources formerly in military use. Moreover, although in some countries there are severe limits to the extent to which it is practicable to use unbalanced budgets as a means of adjusting the level of effective demand, such measures, where they are acceptable, are powerful instruments for this purpose. Tax revenue might be deliberately reduced by more than the net reduction in government expenditure brought about by disarmament. In some countries, the changes that have already taken place in the net budget balance of the government sector within small numbers of years appear to have been of the same order of magnitude as those that might be required to offset a shortfall of demand consequent upon disarmament.

83. If a shortfall of effective demand cannot be fully dealt with by the foregoing methods, there always remains the possibility of an increase in civilian government expenditure designed at least in part to help in solving this problem. Expenditure on goods and services is, in general, likely to be more effective for this purpose than transfer expenditure—the increase of grants and subsidies to various sections of the community—but in the not unlikely event of the recipients being disposed to spend nearly all the cash benefits they receive, the difference would be small.

84. The instruments of adjustment referred to above are more highly developed, easier to bring into operation, and may be expected to work more effectively in some countries than in others. Bearing in mind, however, that a substantial part of military expenditure would probably be replaced by other government expenditure in most countries, it may be concluded from the foregoing paragraphs that the maintenance of effective demand in the face of disarmament should not prove difficult. Indeed, it should be practicable not merely to maintain the level of demand during the transition period, but to move forward to the more rapid growth in total real income that a transfer of resources from military use to productive investment would render physically possible.

85. It has been argued that in so far as disarmament might lead to a reduction in the relative size of the government sector, the stabilizing effect that the existence of a substantial public sector exercises upon the general level of activity might be diminished. Military expenditure, however, has itself been notoriously subject to variations which, being unconnected with the requirements of stabilization policy, have disturbed the level of activity in the economies in question and in the world as a whole. Disarmament need not therefore increase the difficulty of economic stabilization, even if it should lead to a fall in the relative size of the government sector.

86. For many under-developed countries, the effect of disarmament upon the industrial countries' demands for primary products, and thus

on the export earnings of the primary producing countries, would be of great importance. So would the methods of dealing with the liquidation of strategic stockpiles. These problems are discussed in chapter 5. It is necessary to add here that the industrial countries' success in maintaining effective demand during the immediate period of disarmament would be of great concern to all primary producing countries. The significance of disarmament for an expansion of aid to under-developed countries is dealt with in chapter 6.

87. The effects of disarmament within the under-developed countries themselves would vary from one to another. In some cases, the ratio of the military budget to the gross domestic product is of the same order of magnitude as in the major military powers (4-10 per cent). In the majority of cases (including most of the larger underdeveloped countries), it is less than 4 per cent. So far as growth rates are concerned, however, the effects of the release for non-military purposes of these proportions of the national resources, whether high or low, might be greater than the figures would by themselves suggest. Both total capital formation and government expenditure are generally smaller in relation to gross domestic product in the under-developed countries than in the richer ones. The ratio of military expenditure to gross domestic capital formation in the majority of under-developed countries for which the data exist lies in the same range (10 per cent and upward) as in the majority of other countries. Thus the contribution of disarmament to their economic growth would be very substantial.

88. Under-developed countries usually obtain their supplies of munitions from abroad either as direct purchases or as grants under military agreements or both. To the extent that these imports are received without payment, their cessation would have little economic impact on under-developed countries. On the other hand, to the extent that these imports have required the expenditure of foreign exchange, disarmament would make it possible to reallocate foreign exchange to imports of capital goods and of other equipment needed for economic growth. There are, however, a few countries which have been receiving considerable foreign exchange from foreign military aid and military expenditure including the outlays of foreign personnel. In consequence, it is important that any disarmament programme should include measures to relieve the strain on the external balances of such countries.

89. Reductions in the military budgets of most under-developed countries would have their main effects through the reduction of manpower in the armed forces and the associated decrease in local expenditure on the products used by the armed forces. The release of unskilled military personnel would to some extent aggravate the already difficult problems of unemployment and under-employment. On the other hand, the members of the armed forces in the under-developed countries are frequently better provided with potentially useful skills than the rest of the population. The more skilled men should be easier to absorb into productive employment and their absorption should contribute substantially to the development of the economy.

90. As was pointed out above with respect to the industrialized pri-

vate enterprise economies, the maintenance of the level of effective demand may require sustaining the level of government expenditure. This consideration appears to apply with greater force to the under-developed countries, where tax reduction may be less effective in stimulating private expenditure than it is in the more developed economies. The need to plan alternative government expenditure would therefore be particularly great.

91. In the centrally planned economies, the maintenance of effective demand while reducing military expenditure would be simply a matter of efficiency of planning techniques. Since decisions concerning the production of military output as well as of investment and consumer goods are co-ordinated through the national economic plan, the substitution of one type of expenditure for another does not raise any basic problems for the maintenance of effective demand. The reply from the Government of the Czechoslovak Socalist Republic indicates that this can be accomplished by certain adjustments in the current economic plans without necessitating the establishment of any special economic institutions. The effect of the decline in armaments expenditure could be largely offset by corresponding increases in investment in plant and equipment and for other purposes such as housing as well as by increases in personal consumption. A rise in personal consumption could be brought about by a reduction in taxation corresponding in magnitude to that part of armament expenditure which was not replaced by investment.

92. In consequence, effective demand could be readily maintained, and the principal problems of conversion would concern the physical adaptation of plants producing armaments to the production of goods for civilian use. The problems of reallocation of resources are discussed in some detail in the reply from the Government of the Polish People's Republic.[4] It is indicated that the period of short-term transition may be divided into three major stages. In the first stage, the main concern would be to utilize the existing military fixed assets and skilled manpower for facilitating an increase in the output of civilian goods and services. The role of new investment and development of additional supplies of raw materials would be relatively minor. It is suggested that the warehouses, transport and communications equipment, repair shops and other capital equipment and raw materials used for military purposes would be converted as far as technically possible to the production of civilian goods. Military personnel with specialized higher education would be transferred to civilian functions in the departments of health, education and social services.

93. The second stage involves an expansion of plant and equipment, in which there is relatively limited or no excess capacity at present, for the absorption of the manpower released from military use. Particular attention would have to be paid to overcoming the shortages of raw materials that might develop. For this purpose, an increase in the domestic output of these commodities as well as in exports to pay for imports would be called for. With an adequate expansion of productive capacities and of the raw materials base, it would then be possible in the third stage to

[4] See the reply of the Government of the Polish People's Republic.

reap the full benefits of conversion—in the form of a higher rate of growth of the economy and of levels of living than is currently envisaged.

CHAPTER 4

Structural Problems of Conversion

94. Even with the successful maintenance of total effective demand during a period of disarmament, significant problems of adjustment would remain in specific sectors and areas of the economy. Part of the personnel released by the armed forces and the armaments industry would have to be trained or retrained so as to permit absorption into peacetime occupations. Some plant and equipment would have to be converted. Productive capacity might contract in some industries, and might have to be expanded in others. Where the manufacture of armaments has been concentrated in particular regions, it would be necessary either to shift resources out of those regions to other areas of growing demand, or alternatively to undertake schemes of redevelopment. The necessary steps would have to be taken to modify the direction of research and of technological development.

95. It has already been suggested that the broad problem of readaptation of industry and manpower resulting from disarmament is not basically dissimilar from that experienced in the normal process of economic growth. For example, a decline in demand for coal in western Europe and North America has created special problems in the coal mining communities. The position in some of the textile towns is similar. In the centrally planned economies, problems of this type can be handled by planning. In private enterprise economies, where adjustments may be delayed because of such circumstances as immobility of some labour or capital and rigidity of prices, they can be dealt with by special government measures.

96. The higher the rate of growth of the economy, the easier the process of adaptation. In the longer run, disarmament would allow each country to raise the rate of investment and to adapt productive capacity more adequately to the needs of the population and to the requirements of economic growth, both in the private enterprise and the centrally planned economics.

97. In the shorter run, the smoothness of the transition would largely depend on the ability of Governments to anticipate the types of problem that might arise, and on the adequacy of preparations. This calls for an adequate assessment of the direct and indirect demands of military expenditure on each industrial sector and region, and of the extent to which a replacement of military by other expenditure would involve a modification of the structure of demand. Such a confrontation of military demands and of civilian alternatives can be carried out in detail only by national Governments. The present discussion sets out only some of the more important considerations involved.

98. The resources now supplying military requirements could be adapted to peacetime needs partly by shifts within industries and plants, and partly by shifts between industries.

(a) Shifts within industries and plants. In a large number of cases, it may be possible for a given plant to shift the nature of the end-product from military equipment to durable consumer goods and investment goods while using the same productive equipment and manpower. For instance, there might be a shift from tanks to tractors, from military to civilian aircraft, from naval vessels to merchant ships, or from electronic equipment for military purposes to television sets. This might be a relatively easy procedure, in many cases involving little more than changes in designs, retooling, and minor adaptations of skills, particularly in plants and enterprises which already produce both military and civilian goods.

(b) Shifts between industries. Other cases, however, might call for a more complex form of conversion requiring the output of some industries to be completely stopped or sharply curtailed and that of others to be correspondingly expanded. Many ordnance factories might cease to produce altogether. In some countries, the total output of aircraft, ships and boats would have to be reduced since civilian demand for such products would not fully offset the fall in military demand. On the other hand, a considerable expansion of output in the cement, brick, glass and building industries might be required should there be a shift in expenditure in favour of civilian construction. Shifts of this type cannot be accommodated within the same plant but require instead a movement of resources from one industry to another.

99. Shifts between industries would necessitate acquisition of different types of skill by the working force as well as new investment in plant and equipment. They would take a somewhat longer time to accomplish than shifts within industries, the length of time depending on how major or far-removed were the shifts. If the two industries were to have a similar resource content—as do the aircraft industry and the general engineering industry, for instance—the adaptation would be easier and would take a shorter time than if the two industries were to differ significantly in resource content—as do the aircraft industry and the building materials industry, for example. The extent to which the conversion would involve shifts within industries and plants as opposed to shifts between industries can be judged from studies made in a number of countries.

The Problem of Inter-Industry Shifts

100. In the United States, owing to the concentration of military expenditure in a limited number of industries, only a few industries would be affected sharply by reductions in military demand. Professor Leontief has prepared a hypothetical study of the inter-industrial ramifications of conversion in the United States on the assumption that military expenditure is replaced wholly by increases in expenditure on other kinds of goods and services in proportion to their shares in total demand in 1958.[1] Such a reallocation of military expenditure would release 1,320,000 employees from the contracting industries for employment elsewhere. Over four-fifths of the decline in employment would be in four industries—aircraft

[1] W. Leontief and M. Hoffenberg, "The Economic Effects of Disarmament", *Scientific American* (New York), vol. 204, No. 4, April 1961, pp. 47-55.

and parts (which includes missiles), radio, ordnance, and ships and boats (see annex 3, table 3-1). Employment would be totally eliminated in the ordnance industry and would fall by more than 90 per cent in the aircraft and parts industry; expansion of demand for civilian aircraft would have only a minor influence on output in the latter industry.

101. In addition to the 1,320,000 employees released from contracting industries, the 2,530,000 members of the armed forces and about 790,000 civilian employees of military agencies would become available for alternative employment. Thus, about 4.5 million persons—some 6 or 7 per cent of the total labour force in employment in 1958—would, on these assumptions, have to change their employment from one industry group to another or find civilian instead of military employment.

102. Professor Leontief estimates the number absorbed into expanding sectors to be some 600,000 less than that released from the military establishment and the contracting industries. This difference, taken literally, would imply that an increase of about 1 per cent in total government and private expenditure, spread over the duration of the disarmament process, would be required to preserve the general level of employment. It is, however, a residual figure which should be treated with reserve, since it is less than the margin of error of this hypothetical calculation.

103. A similar calculation, though with less narrowly defined industry groups, has been made for the United Kingdom by Professor J. R. N. Stone and his colleagues of the University of Cambridge, Department of Applied Economics. The assumption in this case is that military expenditure is replaced as to one-third by increased private consumption expenditure, one-third by fixed capital formation at home, and one-third by increased foreign aid. The only industrial group in which output (and hence employment) is estimated to decline is that including the manufacture of ships and aircraft, in which the fall is about 20 per cent (see annex 3, table 3-2). Including the members of the armed forces themselves, and civilian employees of the military establishment, the number of persons required to change their "industry group" would be about 900,000, or between 3½ and 4 per cent of the labour force.

104. In both cases, these calculations indicate the numbers who would have to move from one industry to another (or out of direct military employment) in the event of very rapid disarmament. If the operation were to extend over a number of years, the change per annum would be only a fraction of the total. Moreover, a substantial proportion of the shrinkage in the armed forces and in the contracting industries might take place through the normal process of turnover, thereby diminishing the number of persons actually required to move from one kind of employment to another.

105. The replies received from a number of other countries of western Europe indicate that the problem of shifts from one industry to another would be a relatively small one.[2] According to these replies, the rate of economic growth is now limited by labour shortages and it could be accelerated if manpower were released from military uses.

[2] See volume II of this report (E/3593/Rev.1/Add.1).

106. Under-developed countries generally have been meeting their requirements for military goods and services by imports, so that their disarmament would release foreign exchange rather than industrial workers. As indicated in chapter 3, it would also free members of the forces with many useful skills and training. Some of these would be absorbed by the growing labour market; others could be usefully employed in the development of social capital by construction of minor irrigation works, feeder-roads and other community development projects, which would help to mitigate the already acute problem of under-development.

107. In some of the semi-industrialized countries, however, the newly started basic industries which manufacture, for example, chemical fertilizers, heavy machine tools, heavy vehicles, aircraft and electronic equipment, have been serving both military and civilian needs. In the event of disarmament these industries could concentrate, without any transitional difficulty, on the manufacture of capital goods so urgently needed for both consumer goods industries and capital goods industries. Transport capacity, particularly vehicles, released from military uses, would supplement the inadequate transport facilities available in the present stage of their development.

108. In the centrally planned economies, as indicated previously, productive capacity is usually fully utilized. Thus it would be necessary to convert plants producing military equipment to production of durable consumer goods and of such investment goods as can be produced in them with only minor retooling. Such conversion could be achieved rapidly. Many plants producing military equipment produce also certain goods for civilian purposes. In Poland, for instance, plants which manufacture military equipment also account for about 50 per cent of the national output of motor cycles and scooters, 80 per cent of the sewing machines, 70 per cent of the washing machines and 30 per cent of the refrigerators produced in the country.[3] The reply of the Government of the Czechoslovak Socalist Republic mentions experience with conversion of a number of plants from military production to production of medium-sized trucks, tractors and television sets, in all of which no more than 3 to 4 per cent of the productive equipment was found to be unutilizable after conversion.[4]

109. In the longer run, disarmament would make possible substantial increases of investment, so that the more adequate adaptation of productive capacity to the needs of the population and to the requirements of economic growth could proceed fairly rapidly. In Poland, for instance, it is estimated that total disarmament would allow the total amount of capital investment to rise by over 9 per cent as compared with the level of 1962.[5] In Bulgaria an increase of investment by 10 to 12 per cent would be possible in consequence of disarmament.[6] A considerable increase in investment would also take place in Hungary.[7]

[3] See the reply of the Government of the Polish People's Republic.
[4] See the reply of the Government of the Czechoslovak Socialist Republic.
[5] See the reply of the Government of the Polish People's Republic, Addendum.
[6] See the reply of the People's Republic of Bulgaria.
[7] According to the reply of the Government of the Hungarian People's Republic, military expenditure in 1959 was 2.5 thousand million forints while total investment

110. The replies of the Governments of the centrally planned economies state that there will be no difficulty in absorbing released manpower. In countries such as Czechoslovakia, the German Democratic Republic and Hungary, the supply of labour in recent years has not kept pace with growing labour requirements. In Poland it is estimated that in the next few years the increase of the industrial labour force will be drawn mainly from the natural increase of the urban population with relatively little influx of workers from agriculture to industry. In these circumstances it would appear that demobilization of manpower might slow down the transfer of labour from agriculture to industry. But the increase of investment following disarmament would raise considerably the requirement of labour for industry and construction. The final effect, therefore, would be to stimulate rather than to slow down the transfer of labour from agriculture to industry. In the Soviet Union the absorption of demobilized personnel would be greatly facilitated by the growing demand for manpower in the rapidly expanding eastern territories. The construction of new industrial centres and the expansion of cultivation of land in the less populated Asian parts of the Soviet Union, particularly in Siberia, has generated a demand for labour which cannot be fully met by local resources. Migration to these territories is being encouraged and disarmament would provide a welcome source for addition to the manpower required.

Special Problems

111. The preceding analysis of the changes resulting from the process of reallocation of military expenditure to other purposes suggests that the net shifts in employment and output would be relatively small. As already indicated, however, special problems would arise from a concentration of the military effort in certain industries or areas. These problems may be broadly classified as follows:

(i) Adaptation of skills to peace-time requirements.

(ii) Problems of assistance to particular enterprises, industries and localities, heavily oriented to military use.

(iii) Reorientation of research and technological development.

(i) *Adaptation of skills*

112. In some instances, the skills that are essential for service in the armed forces or in some of the major industries producing military goods may not be readily adaptable to the requirements of civilian employment. Consequently, there would arise a necessity to retain part of the skilled manpower and to train some of the unskilled.

113. (a) Armed personnel and employees in the Ministry of Defence. Most of the officers in modern armed forces have received training that would fit them easily for technical, engineering, medical and similar posts in civilian life. As the reply of the Government of the United States of

---

was 19.5 thousand million forints. If only half of the military expenditure were turned to investment, the latter would increase by about 6.5 per cent.

America indicates, 85 per cent of the commissioned officers in that country have completed some form of college training. However, some of the senior officers in the armed forces have been trained for purposes significantly different from those that are needed in civilian life. A special effort would have to be made to find suitable employment for them. Some of them might be called on to serve in various capacities in the international organs to be set up for control of disarmament. Some would find useful occupations in civilian activities where their organizational abilities may be a special requirement. Since the number of officers is usually not very large, it should not be hard to absorb them into civilian life.

114. The demobilization of the non-professional members of the armed forces would involve a much larger number of persons. But most of these men have been drawn from civilian life where they were previously engaged in non-military occupations. They are usually young and relatively mobile. Military service has often interrupted their education. In many cases, however, they have acquired new technical skills while in military service. In most of the under-developed countries, the regular armed forces possess a much higher level of industrial and technical skills than the civilian population; this would tend to give them a relatively greater chance of being absorbed into civilian employment, particularly in an expanding economy.

115. The release of the armed forces, over some years, would imply only that the number of new entrants for that period would be augmented by this special factor. In some countries, particularly in Europe, which are faced with shortages of manpower, the availability of a larger labour force could indeed contribute to an acceleration of the rate of economic growth. Moreover, the financial resources released by disarmament should make it possible to arrange for termination pay and special allowances for various types of training. For instance, the Government of the United States carried out, after the Second World War, a large programme for education, training and job placement for demobilized army personnel. Nearly 8 million veterans took advantage of the training programme. Similarly, 2 million, or one-third of the eligible veterans of the Korean war have benefited from such training facilities.[8]

116. The reply of the Government of the Polish People's Republic indicates the magnitudes involved in re-employing the non-professional members of the armed forces. It is anticipated that a majority of the draftees from rural areas would return to the countryside to help in the projected intensification of agriculture. Some 20 to 30 per cent are expected to be employed in plants which now produce military equipment but could immediately be converted to produce investment goods, export commodities and raw materials. This would further facilitate the productive employment of the remainder.

177. (b) Industries producing military goods. As pointed out above, the problem of conversion in the industrial countries[9] is likely to be a short-term one for most industries. In industries depending heavily on

[8] See the reply of the Government of the United States of America.

[9] Owing to virtual absence of major military goods industries in the under-developed countries, this question has relatively limited relevance to them.

military orders, many of the employees possess a level of skill that should find gainful employment in other branches of production,[10] so long as over-all effective demand is rising. Moreover, where some form of retraining or additional training would be needed for employment, it could be acquired through the facilities for apprenticeship and on-the-job training often provided by individual firms or plants for their new labour force. Even so, there might be some special cases which would require special assistance to encourage the adaptation of skills to new jobs. Such help could be provided through opportunities for vocational training financed by such means as termination pay or other special measures.

118. In this age of automation the demand for highly skilled labour is rising faster than the demand for semi-skilled and unskilled. Therefore a significant number of those who would be released in the latter categories might be faced with difficult problems, particularly if they were of an advanced age. While the experience of a much more extensive demobilization and conversion at the end of the Second World War suggests that the problems thus arising are by no means insuperable, governments should stand ready to assist the reabsorption of such workers into productive employment.

(ii) *Particular enterprises and localities*

119. Owing to the concentration of military output in a few industries, termination of military contracts would bear specially upon the activities of particular enterprises. These would have a choice of three courses of action: complete shut-down, the adaptation of existing plant and equipment to the production of other goods through major retooling, and investment in entirely new plants. Similar problems on a much larger scale were faced at the end of the last war and tackled with a considerable degree of success.

120. The geographical distribution of the activity based on military expenditure is very uneven in many countries. The readjustments necessitated by disarmament would therefore impinge particularly heavily on certain areas and localities. Various forms of public and other assistance would thus prove necessary to facilitate readjustment. Measures of three types would be required. First, attempts should be made to diversify the structure of employment by developing new industries where possible. Secondly, adequate relocation allowances should be provided to facilitate the movement of those who are mobile to areas where the labor market is expanding. Thirdly, adequate relief should be granted to those whose attachment to the locality is too deep or whose age is too advanced to contemplate moving to other areas. The costs of the necessary measures would be very small in relation to the resources that disarmament would release.

[10] Of the 2.5 million persons employed directly or indirectly in producing military goods and services in the private sector in the United States in 1960, nearly 1.5 million, or 60 per cent of the total, possessed various types of skills such as professional, technical, managerial, clerical or skilled craftsmanship. See the reply of the Government of the United States of America.

(iii) *Reorientation of research and technological development*

121. In the centrally planned economies Governments have always played a major role in promoting research and development. In the private enterprise economies also, this role has expanded everywhere in recent years, particularly through the growth of research for military purposes. In the United Kingdom, direct military expenditure is responsible for nearly two-fifths of the total spent on research and development. Approximately half of the research and development effort in the United States is financed out of the military budget; this part of research is highly concentrated in a few industries.

122. The magnitude of the task of shifting scientific and technical personnel to non-military fields of research would differ from country to country, but the estimates that have been made for the United States may have some relevance elsewhere. In that country, expenditure on research and development is six to seven times higher per dollar of military demand than per dollar of final civilian demand.[11] Therefore, on the hypothetical assumption of an unchanged proportional allocation of funds to science by the civilian sector, the reply of the Government of the United States of America estimates that a reallocation of total military expenditure to civilian purposes would lead to a reduction of about 40 per cent in spending for research and development. The corresponding decline in the employment of scientific personnel would amount to only half the decline in research and development spending, or about 20 per cent.[12]

123. No reduction in the actual employment of scientific and technical personnel need be feared, however, because the demand for civilian research would increase rapidly. Indeed, one of the main reasons why scientific research is still far from adequately applied in many civilian fields is the fact that highly qualified personnel have been scarce, and have been pre-empted by military demands. A more adequate supply of specialists would make it possible to open up new fields of inquiry, hitherto virtually neglected, as well as to devote larger resources to existing lines of scientific investigation in both the developed and under-developed countries. The scope for peaceful research in the physical, chemical, biological and human sciences is unlimited, and the potential benefits to the whole of humanity incalculable.

CHAPTER 5

The Impact of Disarmament on International Economic Relations

124. Disarmament would be bound to have favourable effects on the development of international economic relations. The political *détente* that would accompany an international disarmament programme would in itself imply that nations were willing to reconsider their economic relations

[11] See the reply of the Government of the United States of America.

[12] The smaller decline in employment is due in part to the fact that the materials and equipment content of research expenditures is much higher for military than for civilian research and in part to the fact that more scientists and engineers are required in posts not directly connected with research and development in the non-military industries than in the military.

with one another. The consequent relaxation of international tensions would provide a sound basis for reduction of trade barriers and for modification of existing trade agreements and trading practices. In the long run this would encourage an expansion of international trade, a more rational international division of labour and a more effective use of the world's resources. In the short term it might help conversion by generating new demand for exports from existing sources of supply that could be satisfied fairly easily from existing capacities.

125. The relaxation of international tension would benefit trade through the elimination of the concern with national defence as a factor affecting national trade policies. The needs of national defence have long been accepted as a legitimate reason for the pursuit of discriminatory and protectionist policies.[1] Among the justifications advanced for the protection of agriculture and mining in many industrial countries has been the need to guarantee an adequate national supply of food and raw materials. In many instances, the domestic production of manufactured goods, as well, has been promoted on security grounds, to the detriment of international trade. Security is not the only consideration in such cases, and may not even be the decisive one; nevertheless, it carries considerable weight with Governments at the present time. After disarmament, however, its force would be lost, and an opportunity would be afforded to re-examine and improve the framework of world trade.

126. An important aspect of this matter is trade between the centrally planned economies and the rest of the world. Although this trade has been rising in relation to world trade in recent years, its share is still low in comparison with the levels prevailing before the Second World War and, especially, in comparison with the share of these economies in world output and with the levels that could be achieved under favourable conditions in the future. The centrally planned economies are expanding rapidly and form a growing market, particularly for durable producers' goods and raw materials. At the same time, they are capable of serving as a source of supply to the rest of the world for certain primary products and manufactures. The obstacles that stand in the way of closer economic relations between state trading and private enterprise economies are not basically of a technical character. To a considerable extent they reflect mutual lack of confidence. A lessening of international tensions and a rebuilding of confidence would help to remove them.

127. Disarmament would bring about a change in the composition and rate of growth of output and thus affect the structure and rate of expansion of world trade. While the composition of the non-military production that would replace military output cannot be precisely foreseen, it appears to be a safe assumption that all the main categories of civilian output would increase their share in national product. In so far as increased investment and greater economic aid would accelerate the rate of economic growth in developed and under-developed countries, a more rapid

[1] It is true that at certain times national security considerations have led to higher trade flows in particular directions than might otherwise have taken place; strategic stockpiling, for example, has stimulated purchases of some commodities. However, this stimulus has not been an unmixed blessing, and in any case stockpiling is no longer significant in world trade.

expansion of world trade could be anticipated. However, there are more immediate effects that might follow the shift in demand; these hinge on the difference between the import content of military expenditure and the import content of the increments to consumption, investment and foreign aid that disarmament would facilitate.

128. It is possible in principle to estimate the import content of any country's military expenditure, as well as of the civilian expenditure that would replace it, by means of an analysis of an economy's inter-industry structure. Such an analysis would indicate whether a shift from military expenditure to, say, housing construction would result in a net increase or a net decrease in the demand for imports both in the aggregate and for specific commodities.

129. Some exports of primary products, such as petroleum, rubber and most metallic ores depend significantly at present on direct and indirect demand generated by military purchases. An estimate of this dependence with respect to the United States economy is summarized in annex 3, table 3-3. These figures show, for instance, that the direct and indirect demand for copper generated by United States military expenditure in 1958 amounted to 7.8 per cent of that year's total world supply and to 7.4 per cent of the supply in 1959. On the assumption that the demand generated by the combined military outlays of all industrialized countries may be about twice as large as that computed for the United States alone, the table indicates that some 15-16 per cent of world copper output has served, directly and indirectly, military purposes (see columns 3 and 4). For tin, nickle, lead and zinc the corresponding figure is over 9 per cent; for petroleum, between 8 and 9 per cent. In view of the well-known sensitivity of the prices of these products to changes in demand, the elimination of all armament expenditure, if there were no offsetting rise in civilian demand, could have a seriously adverse effect on the income of those under-developed countries whose exports consist largely of such raw materials.

130. Table 3-4 (in annex 3) shows, however, that the demand of the United States and of the world for these raw materials would be reduced only fractionally—by less than 2 per cent—if the elimination of military expenditure were accompanied by a corresponding increase in private and public non-military expenditure. These hypothetical estimates, it should be noted, are based on the assumption that private consumption, investment, non-military government purchases and other categories of non-military demand would all increase in the same proportion. However, since the content of these raw materials in military production does not differ significantly from that of the most important categories of non-military production, the impact on over-all demand for the items listed in the table would appear to be only marginal for any likely change in the composition of civilian demand.

131. Since the importance of military expenditure for most other primary commodities is smaller than for those discussed above, its cessation, even if not offset by an equal increase in non-military expenditure, would produce a smaller percentage of reduction in demand for them. The reallocation of military expenditure to non-military purposes would prob-

ably bring about a net increase in this demand. The hypothetical calculations made for the United States and the United Kingdom, for instance, suggest that this reallocation would increase the demand for both food and clothing and thus for foodstuffs and textile materials in general.

132. Since disarmament may be expected to result in an acceleration of economic growth, it should stimulate the growth of demand for primary production in general. Coupled with the fact that disarmament should be associated with a tendency for the advanced countries to open their markets more widely to foodstuffs, for instance, this would make for a substantial growth of primary commodity trade. Accelerated economic growth would be still more powerful in increasing total demand for manufactures. In the past, an increased world demand for manufactures has normally been associated with increased international trade in them. The tendency to reduce trade barriers should be particularly important in enabling developing countries to increase their exports of manufactures to the more highly developed.

133. The over-all impact of disarmament on the trade of under-developed countries is likely to be favourable, not only because of the acceleration of economic growth but also because of the greatly expanded aid to be expected from the more advanced countries. Both private enterprise and centrally planned economies should also be prepared to open their markets more widely to under-developed countries once the trade restrictions imposed for security reasons are lifted. There might, however, be instances in which declines in demand for particular commodities would cause appreciable difficulties. In these cases consideration should be given to special aid for the countries concerned, in the same way as for particular industries or areas within the principal disarming countries.

134. The immediate impact of disarmament on international economic relations during the conversion period is a matter that needs to be given careful study along with the other conversion problems already discussed in chapters 3 and 4. Changes in the level of aggregate economic activity associated with disarmament in the major industrial countries would be a major determinant of the level of international trade during the conversion period. In the international field, as in the domestic, nations need to be prepared to take whatever measures may prove appropriate to facilitate the reallocation of resources and to ensure that any temporary dislocations of economic life that might occur are minimized. The degree to which special policies might be called for would depend partly on the speed of the disarmament process.

135. If appropriate steps are taken it should be possible even in the short run to avoid any significant reductions in the general level of primary product prices, but it needs nevertheless to be realized that any failure to achieve this goal could have serious consequences. For many of the countries mainly dependent on the export of primary commodities, a percentage decline in their export earnings which might appear small arithmetically could cause grave damage. For example, a 6 per cent drop in their average export prices, were it to take place, would imply for the under-developed countries a decline in their foreign exchange earnings equivalent to something like one-half of all official economic grants and

loans currently received from abroad in a year.[2] Recessions in activity in the industrial countries have caused declines of this order of magnitude in the recent past. Concerted international action would, therefore, be required to prevent any such decline in the prices and incomes of primary producing countries as a result of disarmament.

136. Even with favourable prospects for total trade, however, special problems might arise during the conversion period for particular countries or for trade in particular commodities. One such problem stems from the fact that new countries have been receiving considerable foreign exchange from military aid and military expenditure, including the outlays of foreign personnel. In these cases, special attention should be given to the possibility of arranging future programmes of developmental assistance, and especially their timing, so as to avoid adverse effects on their balances of payments.

137. A more wide-spread problem relates to particular countries that are largely dependent on the export of those commodities for which world demand might suffer a temporary decline. In conjunction with the formulation of any disarmament programme, therefore, it is highly desirable that a detailed study be undertaken on the changes in demand for the various primary commodities which would result from disarmament. The reduction of strategic stockpiles of primary commodities should be planned in such a way as to cause a minimum of disturbance to international markets, and consideration should be given to the adequacy of already existing compensatory measures and the possibility that additional measures might be required during the conversion period. Regardless of the technique employed, no country should be allowed to suffer a disruption to its economic life, even temporarily, as a result of disarmament.

CHAPTER 6

The Effects of Disarmament on the Volume and Framework of Aid for Economic Development

138. The promotion of economic and social development in under-developed countries is one of the most important ways in which the resources released by disarmament could be put to use. Two-thirds of the world's population lives in countries that obtain only a modest part of the benefits which modern technology and science are capable of providing. The peoples of the under-developed areas are determined to raise their levels of living, and the peoples of the more industrialized countries have undertaken to help them do so. Progress has been made since the Second World War in raising real incomes per capita in many under-developed countries. The planning of economic and social development has been intensified in some and initiated in others, and the mobilization of domestic resources

[2] In 1956-1959 the sum of net official donations and official net long-term lending to under-developed countries averaged $3.2 billion annually, or about 12.6 per cent of the $25.2 billion annual average value of these countries' exports during the same period. (See, respectively, United Nations, *International Flow of Long-term Capital and Official Donations, 1951-1959* (Sales No.: 62.II.D.1), table 3 and United Nations, *Monthly Bulletin of Statistics,* February 1962, table 43. The two sets of statistics differ somewhat in country coverage.)

for national development has become a major policy objective. In many instances, domestic resources have been supplemented by foreign loans, grants, private capital flows and technical assistance.

139. National efforts and international co-operation in the development of the under-developed countries have so far not brought about the desired acceleration of economic growth. The average rate of growth in per capita income over the past decade was still less than 2 per cent per annum, and possibly as little as 1 per cent.[1] The absolute gap between per capita incomes of rich and poor countries has been progressively widening.[2] Even if future growth in the developed areas is left out of account and the present levels of income in the developed areas are taken as a target, the recent experience of under-developed areas still appears disappointing. In under-developed areas the average level of real income per capita is now less than one-sixth—and in many of them less than one-tenth—of that enjoyed in such countries as Belgium, Denmark, Norway and the United Kingdom. Consequently, a future growth rate no higher than 2 per cent per annum could be expected to raise the level of living in poor countries to that now prevailing in the countries just mentioned only after a very long time.

140. An acceleration of the rate of growth of under-developed countries depends upon many factors, including the adoption of appropriate national development programmes and, in many cases, social and institutional reforms. Among these programmes an important role must be assigned to encouragement of productive investment both from domestic and foreign resources. To this end world disarmament could make a major contribution. Despite the inadequacies of the available statistics, it appears that the world's military expenditures far exceed the combined gross investment expenditures of the less developed areas; they are probably at least five times as large and may be much greater. A much larger volume of resources could thus be allocated to investment for productive development in these countries even if only a fraction of the resources currently devoted to military purposes were used in this way.

141. Assuming that the necessary national development programmes and social and institutional reforms were effectively realized, under-developed countries would be able to absorb a considerably larger flow of productive investment. The consequent effect upon the rate of growth may be illustrated by a hypothetical example in which it is assumed that these countries devoted half of the resources liberated by disarmament to investment in productive capacity and that at the same time the rate of total capital flow from more advanced countires (both private enterprise and centrally planned) rose to around $15 billion annually, or somewhat more than 1 per cent of their aggregate national product. This is a modest increase in view of the 8 or 9 per cent they now devote to military pur-

[1] Owing to the margin of error in the population estimates of many underdeveloped countries (especially the inter-censal estimates), estimates of real income in these areas, which are rather crude in any case, are subject to an even wider margin of error when expressed in per capita terms.

[2] To narrow the gap, under-developed areas must experience a substantially higher growth rate than the more advanced areas, since in the higher-income areas a given rate of growth implies much larger absolute increments to income.

poses. Under these conditions, the less advanced countries might be expected to increase their annual rate of growth of national product from, say, 3 per cent to 5 per cent. Assuming an annual rate of population growth of around 2 per cent, this could mean a trebling of the rate of increase in per capita income from 1 per cent to 3 per cent.

142. The hypothetical example just given is based on certain assumptions concerning income and investment and their interrelationship in under-developed areas. Although different sets of assumptions would inevitably lead to somewhat different estimates of acceleration in the rate of growth in under-developed areas, there clearly emerges the general conclusion that disarmament could bring about a marked increase in the rate of growth of real income in the poorer parts of the world.

143. These conclusions are reinforced by a comparison of the volume of resources now being devoted to military use with the various estimates made in recent years of the external financial needs of the under-developed countries. Four relatively comprehensive estimates of global aid requirements are available,[3] apart from a number of estimates of aid needed for specific purposes. In these calculations, the total amount of foreign capital required by the under-developed areas, over and above their domestic resources devoted to investment, is estimated to range from $6 billion to $10 billion annually. These figures are based on conservative assumptions: the target rates of growth of per capita real income are about 2 per cent, and the computations are based on assumed ratios between increments to real income and, on the one hand, increments to employment, or, on the other hand, increments to the stock of capital, which past experience suggests are reasonable but which could conceivably turn out to have underestimated the capital needs should conditions prove to be less favourable than anticipated. After allowing for the present flow of foreign capital through existing institutions and arrangements, the authors cited believe that there is a deficiency of about $3 billion a year that needs to be made good in order to achieve the modest annual rate of growth in income of 2 per cent per capita.[4]

144. Two further questions arise. First, would disarmament release in sufficient quantity the particular resources required for economic development? Secondly, is the present institutional framework of aid to under-developed countries likely to be affected by disarmament?

145. In the longer run, productive capacities can be adapted to any

[3] These estimates of financial needs are based on fragmentary data. They have been compared in a United Nations document prepared for the Committee on a United Nations Capital Development Fund: *The Capital Development Needs of the Less Developed Countries* (A/AC.102/5). The earliest estimate is contained in a report prepared for the United Nations: *Measures for the Economic Development of Under-Developed Countries* (Sales No.: 51.II.B.2). Its estimates concerned the nineteen-fifties, and were based on data for 1949 and earlier years. The second estimate is contained in Max F. Millikan and W. W. Rostow, *A Proposal: Key to an Effective Foreign Policy* (New York, 1956). It is based on data for 1953 and earlier years. The third estimate, contained in Paul G. Hoffman, *One Hundred Countries, One and One Quarter Billion People* (Washington, 1960), is based on information available in 1959, and concerns the decade of the nineteen-sixties. The fourth is contained in P. N. Rosenstein-Rodan, "International Aid for Under-developed Countries," *Review of Economics and Statistics* (Cambridge, Mass.) XLIII (May, 1961) and covers the years 1962-1976.

[4] *Ibid.*

changed patterns of demand, and provided that the needs of under-developed countries are known in sufficient detail, no serious problems should arise in matching resources to uses. Even in the short run, however, it seems probable that a significantly large proportion of the resources absorbed for military use would indeed prove to be of a type useful for investment in under-developed countries. An important proportion of military expenditure absorbs the output of heavy industry and of the engineering and construction industries. The output of these industrial sectors could undoubtedly make a valuable contribution to the industrialization of the less developed areas and to their accumulation of social capital. Transporation and communication equipment, for example, is an important component of military expenditure and is urgently required by under-developed countries. When a disarmament programme is adopted it would be desirable for Governments to estimate what resources would become available for peaceful purposes in the various stages of the programme. In the light of these data and detailed information concerning the resources which under-developed countries could usefully employ in their developmental programmes, it would be possible for Governments to assess the share of the released resources to be allocated to the investment needs of the less industrialized parts of the world.

146. Disarmament would also release personnel, such as scientific research workers and engineers, who could be utilized for other purposes. In the event of disarmament, it should prove possible for the industrialized countries to provide greater technical assistance and thereby help remove one of the serious limitations to development efforts in these countries. Furthermore, disarmament would free from military service in both the more advanced and the less developed countries large groups of young people. Past experience in utilizing their good will and enthusiasm in a number of countries indicates that when completely freed from military preoccupations, many of them could make an important contribution to economic and social development in under-developed areas.

147. With respect to the impact of disarmament on the framework and structure of aid to under-developed countries several points need to be made. If we leave out of account—as seems proper in the present context—short-term finance of all kinds, private grants, and military and defence-support aid, the principal international flows of capital to under-developed countries consist of (1) official grants, (2) official loans and credits on non-commercial terms, (3) long-term loans and credits on commercial terms made by national governments and by international authorities, and (4) private long-term loans or direct investment. Unlike capital flows of the last three types, official grants do not, of course, burden the recipient country's balance of payments. Official loans and credits on non-commercial terms are less burdensome than public or private lending on commercial terms: hence the distinction between the second and third categories.

148. Comprehensive statistics of loans and grants to under-developed countries are not available according to the fourfold classification just mentioned. However, an impression of the over-all magnitude and composition of loans and grants to under-developed countries can be obtained

from various sources.[5] During the past few years the total net flow of capital, as just defined, from private enterprise developed countries to under-developed countries averaged between $3.5 billion and $4 billion annually. About half represented official grants. The remainder consisted mostly of private lending.

149. In the fifteen years from 1945 to 1960 the sum total of credits granted by the centrally planned countries to under-developed countries and of mutual assistance among the centrally planned countries themselves amounted to about 52 billion old roubles. In the earlier years the greater part of the credits was granted to other centrally planned economies; in more recent years the emphasis has shifted to credits to under-developed countries.

150. The increased international flow of capital to under-developed countries that is certain to result from disarmament could take any one or more of the forms referred to above. Their relative importance would be likely to change, however, since each of them would be affected somewhat differently by the implementation of a disarmament programme.

151. As regards the flow of private capital, it may be assumed that this would continue to respond to commercial considerations. Diminished world tension resulting from disarmament, coupled with additional means of encouraging private foreign investment in under-developed countries, might be expected to lead to a greater movement of private capital into these countries.

152. At the present time, nine-tenths or more of official grants and loans are given under bilateral programmes. Bilateral and multilateral programmes of aid each have their own particular advantages and disadvantages, and many of the considerations which now prompt Governments to favour bilateral rather than multilateral aid might continue to hold good even in a disarmed world. On the other hand, in so far as political circumstances have had any weight in determining the direction and form of aid, effective disarmament and the related lessening of international tensions should improve the prospects for more cooperative international action.

153. The discussions that have been held in the Economic and Social Council and the General Assembly during the past eight years concerning the need for an increased flow of aid through an international fund within the framework of the United Nations have frequently emphasized the importance of the savings to be derived from general disarmament. The basic position of the General Assembly on this matter remains resolution 724 (VIII), adopted unanimously in 1953. Under this resolution the General Assembly made the following declaration:

"We, the Governments of the States Members of the United Nations, in order to promote higher standards of living and conditions of economic and social progress and development, stand ready to ask our peoples, when sufficient progress has been made in internationally supervised world-wide disarmament, to devote a portion of the savings achieved through such disarmament to an

[5] See *International Flow of Long-term Capital and Official Donations, 1951-1959* (Sales No.: 62.II.D.1) chap. 1, and *World Economic Survey, 1960* (Sales No.: 61.II.C.1), pp. 119-121.

international fund, within the framework of the United Nations, to assist development and reconstruction in under-developed countries."

154. It should be realized that the repayment of loans granted on commercial terms may impose heavy burdens on the balances of payments of these countries. Concern has already been expressed in recent years regarding the heavy accumulated indebtedness of a number of countries and the growing difficulties they have been experiencing in servicing outstanding loans. It seems urgent that as large a proportion of economic aid as possible should take the form of grants or "soft" loans. Disarmament would likely facilitate the increased flow of such aid. This is so because the savings afforded by disarmament would provide the aid-giving countries with a favourable opportunity to increase their assistance without imposing an additional burden on civilian expenditure. This should also lead to a desirable broadening of the existing basis of aid to include types of projects not adequately covered under existing policies, and should therefore facilitate a balanced execution of development plans. Increased aid in the fields of social investment should also become possible, as it is now generally recognized that substantial investment in health facilities and particularly in education is a prerequisite for obtaining the maximum benefits from other development efforts.

155. Because the competing claims in developed countries are also urgent, there is a serious possibility that the financial resources released by disarmament might be rapidly absorbed by purely national aims. It is therefore desirable that an appropriate proportion of these resources should be allocated to international aid in its various forms simultaneously with their use for domestic purposes.

156. It must be emphasized that foreign aid can play only a supplementary role in the development of these countries and that the responsibility for initiation and intensification of development efforts would continue to lie entirely with the governments and peoples concerned. There are many countries in which foreign exchange resources are by no means the only nor even the main limitation on the rate of economic growth. Such countries are not likely to be in a position to utilize larger amounts of aid effectively unless they take the domestic measures necessary to encourage such growth. There is reason to look to the major powers to be generous in allocating resources freed by disarmament to the development of under-developed countries. But there is also every reason to look to the under-developed countries themselves to create the conditions favourable to their economic growth. In this as in other fields discussed in this report, advance planning and preparation are likely to enhance greatly the favourable impact of general disarmament.

CHAPTER 7

Some Social Consequences of Disarmament

157. The economic and social consequences of disarmament are inextricably intertwined. As already discussed, it would be possible to bring about a significant improvement in many aspects of social life, provided

that some of the resources released by disarmament were earmarked for fields such as education and scientific research, health, housing and urban development. An idea of the magnitude of the needs in these fields has been given in chapter 2. There are, however, some aspects of social life which elude measurement, but which none the less greatly affect individual and family life and on which smoother human relations within and between nations largely depend.

158. In a disarmed world, a general improvement could be expected in the level of living and in the conditions of under-privileged and low-income groups such as the old and retired people whose share in the social well-being is often meagre, even in the more developed countries. With the end of the armaments race, Governments would accord these social objectives a higher priority than in the past. The implementation of measures discussed in chapter 2 would lead to a cumulative diffusion of social benefits.

159. The more rapid rate of economic growth and the increase in productivity that may be expected to result from disarmament might well permit a reduction in working hours, an improvement in the conditions of work and a lengthening of paid vacations. To take full advantage of the resultant longer leisure and the higher level of living, wider cultural facilities would be required. In this context, education acquires special significance as a means of disseminating culture.

160. In the domain of personal and family life, disarmament and recession of the threat of war would decrease tensions which often bring about psychosomatic illnesses. Human life would acquire a new meaning, once war and preparations for war were eliminated. The whole prospect of life would be brightened, especially for young people about to enter a profession or found a family. There would no longer be any separation from the family for compulsory military service, so that the psychological, moral and material evils which this creates would be avoided. A greater stability in the family nucleus would be likely to exert a favourable influence on morality.

161. The very fact of disarmament would lead to a diminution of tensions between nations and races. The tendency to divert individual and national frustrations into national and racial hatreds would be lessened significantly.

162. In a disarmed world, the danger that security considerations and armed forces might play an excessive role in forming the values of the community would be eliminated. It is important to note, however, that attention would need to be paid to constructive outlets for individual and collective aspirations.

163. If confidence is one of the necessary conditions for concluding a disarmament agreement, an increase of confidence would also be one of its happiest consequences. A decrease in tensions and in the influence of groups interested in armaments would bring about a profound change in the form and content of international relations. Political and economic conflict between nations, with its attendant risk of war, would more rapidly be replaced by constructive emulation. Scientific co-operation between nations would advance more rapidly, and the peaceful utilization of sci-

ence and technology would be accelerated. The arts, too, would greatly benefit from an extension of international exchanges. All the great civilizations in the past have gained from such cultural contacts and have exerted their influence beyond their own frontiers. Disarmament would remove the main barriers to the far greater exchanges that are now technically possible. Humanity would thus be able to carry out co-operatively the projects which lie beyond the resources of a single country or a group of countries.

164. In short, disarmament would release resources from uses in which they are not only wasted but also in many ways make the remainder of mankind's wealth less effective in promoting welfare than it would otherwise be. In reckoning the gains from it, one must take into account a general easing of tension and frustration and an enhanced possibility of co-operation that would reinforce the direct economic contribution of the resources released.

165. In view of this, as well as the conclusions reached in previous chapters, there should be no doubt that the diversion to peaceful purposes of the resources now devoted to military expenditure could and should be of benefit to all countries and would lead to improvement of world social conditions.

CHAPTER 8

Summary and Conclusions

166. The present level of military expenditure not only represents a grave political danger but also imposes a heavy economic and social burden on most countries. It absorbs a large volume of human and material resources of all kinds, which could be used to increase economic and social welfare throughout the world—both in the highly industrialized countries, which at the present time incur the bulk of the world's military expenditures, and in the less developed areas.

Resources devoted to military purposes

167. There appears to be general agreement that the world is spending roughly $120 billion annually on military account at the present time. This corresponds to about one-half of the total gross capital formation throughout the world. It is at least two-thirds of—and according to some estimates, of the same order of magnitude as—the entire national income of all the under-developed countries.

168. It is important that countries, in preparing to disarm, should take stock of the various resources that disarmament would release for peaceful uses. In the major military powers, military production is highly concentrated in a few industry groups. In those countries that rely upon imports for their supplies of military goods or in which the major part of military expenditure is for the pay and subsistence of the armed forces, rather than for their equipment, the resources devoted to military purposes consist essentially of manpower and foreign exchange.

The peaceful use of released resources

169. There are so many competing claims for usefully employing the resources released by disarmament that the real problem is to establish a scale of priorities. The most urgent of these claims would undoubtedly already have been largely satisfied were it not for the armaments race.

170. Increased personal consumption might well absorb a large share of the released resources. A substantial portion of them, however, would be used for expansion of productive capacities because only such expansion can provide a firm basis for further increases in consumption. In the less developed countries, the utilization of released resources for capital formation must be considered vitally important.

171. Social investment is an important alternative both to private consumption and to industrial and agricultural investment. Its claims rest partly upon the clear urgency of the direct need for improved social amenities, and partly upon the fact that growth of industrial and agricultural productivity is dependent upon developments in education, housing, health, and other fields.

172. The release of scientific and technical manpower would make it possible to encourage programmes of basic scientific research in fields which have hitherto been neglected. Disarmament would also open up possibilities for joint international ventures of an ambitious kind, such as the utilization of atomic energy for peaceful purposes, space research, the exploration of the Arctic and Antarctic for the benefit of mankind and projects to change the climates of large areas of the world.

173. Thus, though it would take active decisions by Governments in the light of national and international needs to set in motion the necessary programmes for employing the released resources, it seems abundantly clear that no country need fear a lack of useful employment opportunities for the resources that would become available to it through disarmament.

Impact on national production and employment

174. Disarmament would raise both general problems of maintaining the over-all level of economic activity and employment and specific problems in so far as manpower or productive capacity might require adaptation to non-military needs. In the economic life of all countries, shifts in the pattern of demand and in the allocation of productive resources are continually occurring. The reallocation of productive resources which would accompany disarmament is in many respects merely a special case of the phenomenon of economic growth.

175. The post-war conversion was a much larger one and involved a more rapid transfer of resources than total disarmament would require at present. Nevertheless, huge armies were quickly demobilized without a significant rise in unemployment in most countries. The pace of recovery, particularly of industrial output, was impressively rapid. During the post-war conversion, however, the major concern of economic policy was to restrain, rather than to maintain, over-all demand.

176. Much attention has already been given in the industrialized

private enterprise economies to the methods by which total effective demand can be maintained. Monetary and fiscal policy could be used to offset the effect of a short fall in total demand that might result from a decline in military expenditure to the extent that it were not offset by a rise in civil government expenditure. Bearing in mind that a substantial part of military expenditure would probably be replaced by other government expenditure in most countries, it may be concluded that the maintenance of effective demand in the face of disarmament should not prove difficult.

177. For many under-developed countries, the effect of disarmament upon the industrial countries' demands for primary products, and thus on the export earnings of the primary producing countries, would be of great importance. So would the methods of dealing with the liquidation of strategic stockpiles.

178. In the centrally planned economies, the maintenance of effective demand while reducing military expenditure would be simply a matter of the efficiency of planning techniques. In consequence, effective demand could be readily maintained, and the principal problems of conversion would concern the physical adaptation of plants producing armaments to the production of goods for civilian use.

Structural problems of conversion

179. Even with the successful maintenance of total effective demand during a period of disarmament, significant problems of adjustment would remain in specific sectors and areas of the economy. The resources now supplying military requirements could be adapted to peace-time needs partly by shifts within industries and plants. This might be a relatively easy procedure, in many cases involving little more than changes in designs, retooling, and minor adaptations of skills, particularly in plants and enterprises which already produce both military and civilian goods. Shifts between industries would necessitate new investment and acquisition of different types of skill by the working force. In the longer run disarmament would allow each country to raise the rate of investment and to adapt productive capacity more adequately to the needs of the population and to the requirements of economic growth, both in the private enterprise and the centrally planned economies.

180. Hypothetical studies on the assumption that military expenditure is replaced wholly by increases in expenditure on other kinds of goods and services suggest that in the event of very rapid disarmament some 6 or 7 per cent (including the armed forces) of the total labour force in the United States and 3½ to 4 per cent in the United Kingdom would have to find civilian instead of military employment or change their employment from one industry group to another. These shifts would be small if spread out over a number of years and would be greatly facilitated by the normal process of turnover. The higher the rate of growth of the economy, the easier the process of adaptation.

181. Under-developed countries generally have been meeting their requirements for military goods and services by imports, so that their

disarmament would release foreign exchange rather than industrial workers. It would also free members of the forces, many with useful skills and training. Some of these could be usefully employed in the development of social capital. In some of the semi-industrialized countries, newly started basic industries could concentrate, without any transitional difficulty, on the manufacture of capital goods.

182. In the centrally planned economies, where productive capacity is usually fully utilized, it would be necessary to convert plants producing military equipment to production of durable consumer goods and of such investment goods as can be produced in them with only minor retooling. This could be done rapidly.

183. Some special problems would arise with regard to re-employment and training of manpower and reorientation of scientific research. While most members of the armed forces have received training that would fit them easily for civilian life, a special effort would have to be made to find suitable employment for the rest. The domobilization of the non-professional members of the armed forces would imply only that the number of new entrants for that period would be augmented by this special factor.

184. In industries depending heavily on military orders, many of the employees possess a level of skill that should find gainful employment in other branches of production, so long as over-all effective demand is rising. Even so, there might be some special cases which would require special assistance to encourage the adaptation of skills to new jobs. The uneven geographical distribution of the activity based on military expenditure would give rise to a need for various forms of public and other assistance to facilitate readjustment.

185. The task of shifting scientific and technical personnel to non-military fields of research in some countries would be considerable. No reduction in the actual employment of scientific and technical personnel need be feared, however, because the demand for civilian research would increase rapidly.

Impact on international economic relations

186. Disarmament would be bound to have favourable effects on the development of international relations. The political *détente* that would accompany an international disarmament programme would in itself imply that nations were willing to reconsider their economic relations with one another. The relaxation of international tensions would provide a sound basis for reduction of trade barriers and for modification of existing trade agreements and trading practices. An important consequence of this would be a substantial increase in trade between the centrally planned economies and the rest of the world.

187. Since disarmament may be expected to result in an acceleration of economic growth, it should stimulate the growth of demand for primary production in general. Accelerated economic growth would be still more powerful in increasing total demand for manufactures. The over-all impact of disarmament on the trade of under-developed countries is likely

to be favourable, not only because of the acceleration of economic growth but also because of the greatly expanded aid to be expected from the more advanced countries.

188. Some exports of primary products, such as petroleum, rubber and most metallic ores, depend significantly at present on direct and indirect demand generated by military purchases. Provided, however, that military expenditure were fully replaced by public and private non-military spending, the impact on over-all demand for these commodities would be only minor. There might, however, be instances in which declines in demand for particular commodities would cause appreciable difficulties. In these cases consideration should be given to special aid for the countries concerned, in the same way as for particular industries or areas within the principal disarming countries. For most other primary commodities, the reallocation of military expenditure to civilian use would probably bring about a net increase in demand.

189. During the conversion period changes in the level of aggregate economic activity associated with disarmament in the major industrial countries would be a major determinant of the level of international trade. It is believed that significant fluctuations in the general level of international trade could be avoided, but it should nevertheless be realized that any failure to achieve this goal could have serious consequences. Regardless of the technique employed, no country should be allowed to suffer a disruption to its economic life, even temporarily, as a result of disarmament.

Effects on the volume and framework of aid for economic development

190. National efforts and international co-operation in the development of the under-developed countries have so far not brought about the desired acceleration of economic growth. A much larger volume of resources could be allocated to investment for productive development in these countries even if only a fraction of the resources currently devoted to military purposes were used in this way. Disarmament could thus bring about a marked increase in the rate of growth of real income in the poorer parts of the world.

191. Bilateral and multilateral programmes of aid each have their own particular advantages and disadvantages, but in so far as political circumstances have had any weight in determining the direction and form of aid, effective disarmament and the related lessening of international tensions should improve the prospects for more co-operative international action. Since repayment of loans granted on commercial terms may impose heavy burdens on the balances of payments of the under-developed countries, as large a proportion of economic aid as possible should take the form of grants or "soft" loans.

192. Because the competing claims in developed countries are also urgent there is a serious possibility that the financial resources released by disarmament might be rapidly absorbed by purely national aims. It is therefore desirable that an appropriate proportion of these resources should be allocated to international aid in its various forms simultaneously with their use for domestic purposes.

193. Foreign aid, however, can play only a supplementary role in the development of these countries and the responsibility for initiation and intensification of development efforts would continue to lie entirely with the Governments and peoples concerned.

Some social consequences

194. In a disarmed world, a general improvement could be expected in the level of living, including an increase in leisure. With the end of the armaments race, Governments would accord social objectives a higher priority. The psychological, moral and material evils of compulsory military service and of stationing troops away from their homes would be avoided; so would the danger that security considerations and the armed forces might play an extensive role in forming the values of the community. Scientific co-operation and the arts would benefit from an extension of international exchanges.

Conclusion

195. The Consultative Group is unanimously of the opinion that all the problems and difficulties of transition connected with disarmament could be met by appropriate national and international measures. There should thus be no doubt that the diversion to peaceful purposes of the resources now in military use could be accomplished to the benefit of all countries and lead to the improvement of world economic and social conditions. The achievement of general and complete disarmament would be an unqualified blessing to all mankind.

ANNEXES

ANNEX 1

Terms of Reference

Resolution 1516 (XV), adopted by the General Assembly

Economic and social consequences of disarmament

The General Assembly,

Recalling its resolution 1378 (XIV) of 20 November 1959,

Conscious that the impact of disarmament is likely to set in motion great changes in the domestic economies of States and in international economic relations, as a result of the progressive diversion of human and material resources from military to peaceful purposes,

Recognizing that effective action at the national and international levels will need to be taken to make use of material and human resources becoming available as a consequence of disarmament, in order to promote social progress and better standards of living in the world,

Bearing in mind the importance of comprehensive and systematic studies in this field to enable Member States, especially those which are under-developed, to make the necessary economic and social adjustments in the event of disarmament,

Convinced that it is both timely and desirable to undertake such studies,

1. *Requests* the Secretary-General to examine:

(*a*) The national economic and social consequences of disarmament in countries with different economic systems and at different stages of economic development, including, in particular, the problems of replacing military expenditures with alternative private and public civil expenditures so as to maintain effective demand and to absorb the human and material resources released from military uses;

(*b*) The possible development of structural imbalances in national economies as a result of the cessation of capital investment in armaments industries, and the adoption of possible corrective measures to prevent such imbalances, including expanded capital assistance to the under-developed countries;

(*c*) The impact of disarmament on international economic relations, including its effect on world trade and especially on the trade of under-developed countries;

(*d*) The utilization of resources released by disarmament for the purpose of economic and social development, in particular of the under-developed countries;

2. *Recommends* that the Secretary-General should conduct the proposed examination with the assistance of expert consultants to be appointed by him with due regard to their qualifications and to the need of geographical representation and intimate knowledge of countries with different economic systems and at different stages of economic development;

3. *Appeals* to Governments of Member States to give full co-operation to the Secretary-General in the fulfilment of the task entrusted to him;

4. *Requests* the Secretary-General to submit a preliminary report on the results of the examination to the Economic and Social Council at its thirty-third session;[a]

5. *Requests* the Economic and Social Council to transmit the report with its views to the General Assembly at its seventeenth session.

948th plenary meeting,
15 December 1960.

ANNEX 2

Official military expenditure statistics

1. Information concerning military expenditure is contained in the official public accounts of central Governments and the national accounts

[a] In response to a suggestion by the Group of Experts, made at their first session, the Economic and Social Council agreed to defer consideration of this item to its thirty-fourth session.

dealing with gross national or material product and related data. Countries differ, however, in their definitions of military expenditure, and information concerning their methods of classification is commonly not available. It is therefore impossible in many instances to determine the content of the official statistics from an economic and social point of view. Some expenditures that would be considered as military from this viewpoint may be excluded from the official data, while others that would be considered as non-military may be included. In addition, there are commonly differences within countries in the basis of pricing of military output as compared with that of the output of the rest of the economy. These differences alone, even if the coverage of the expenditure statistics were appropriate, would make it impossible to indicate with any precision the proportion of resources devoted to military purposes. Furthermore, different countries have different economic structures and patterns of prices, so that in comparing countries one would obtain different ratios of military expenditure to national product and its components merely from using the different price patterns. For all these reasons, official statistics of military expenditure have only limited value as a basis for measuring the economic burden imposed by the armaments race.

2. The following tables include the most readily available official statistics on military expenditure and compare these with domestic product and fixed capital formation. These three tables cover industrial private enterprise, under-developed and centrally planned countries respectively. In accordance with usual statistical practice, the concept of domestic product in the first two tables is different from that in the third table. In tables 2-1 and 2-2, domestic product includes output originating in both "material production" and services. In table 2-3, domestic product includes output originating in material production only. A further difference is that domestic product in tables 2-1 and 2-2 is gross, depreciation not having been deducted from gross investment or income, while domestic product in table 2-3 is net of depreciation. Accordingly, military expenditure is compared with a more broadly defined measure of product in tables 2-1 and 2-2 than in table 2-3.

Table 2-1

INDUSTRIAL PRIVATE ENTERPRISE COUNTRIES: MILITARY EXPENDITURE AS STATED IN BUDGET ACCOUNTS, COMPARED WITH OTHER STATISTICS, 1957-1959[a]

Country, period and currency unit	Military budget expenditure	Gross domestic product[a]	Gross domestic fixed capital formation	Military budget expenditure as percentage of	
				Gross domestic product	Gross domestic fixed capital formation
AMERICA, NORTH					
Canada (million dollars):					
1957	1,668.5[b]	32,347.0	8,590.0		
1958	1,424.7[b]	33,186.0	8,292.0		
1959	1,506.1[b]	35,110.0	8,456.0		
Average 1957-1959	1,533.1[b]	33,548.0	8,446.0	4.6	18.4
United States (million dollars):					
1957	43,270.0[d]	441,764.0	76,981.0[e]		
1958	44,142.0[d]	443,869.0	72,270.0[e]		
1959	46,426.0[d]	481,253.0	80,374.0[e]		
Average 1957-1959	44,613.0[d]	455,628.0	76,542.0[e]	9.8	58.3[e]
ASIA					
Japan[b] (billion yen):					
1957	176.0	10,135.8	2,727.0[e]		
1958	178.0	10,414.8	2,772.8[e]		
1959	189.0	12,561.4	3,509.6[e]		
Average 1957-1959	181.0	11,037.3	3,003.1[e]	1.6	6.0[e]
EUROPE					
Austria (million schillings):					
1957	1,714.0	121,800.0[f]	27,000.0		
1958	1,986.0	126,700.0[f]	28,400.0		
1959	1,989.0	134,600.0[f]	30,700.0		
Average 1957-1959	1,896.0	127,700.0[f]	28,700.0	1.5[f]	6.6
Belgium (million francs):					
1957	16,638.0	550,100.0	95,900.0		
1958	16,433.0	547,600.0	91,600.0		
1959	18,047.0	565,700.0	95,400.0		
Average 1957-1959	17,039.0	554,467.0	94,300.0	3.1	18.1

Table 2-1 (continued)

Country, period and currency unit	Military budget expenditure	Gross domestic product[a]	Gross domestic fixed capital formation	Military budget expenditure as percentage of	
				Gross domestic product	Gross domestic fixed capital formation
EUROPE (*continued*)					
Denmark (million kroner):					
1957	941.0[b]	32,939.0	5,705.0		
1958	973.0[b]	34,374.0	6,020.0		
1959	1,015.0[b]	38,100.0	7,025.0		
Average 1957-1959	976.0[b]	35,138.0	6,250.0	2.8	15.6
Finland (billion markkaa):					
1957	18.4	1,112.0	294.5		
1958	20.6	1,186.3	303.0		
1959	22.4	1,259.6	331.2		
Average 1957-1959	20.5	1,186.0	309.6	1.7	6.6
France (million new francs):					
1957	14,120.0	211,200.0	39,100.0		
1958	14,190.0	239,100.0	43,100.0		
1959	15,830.0	258,400.0	45,100.0		
Average 1957-1959	14,713.0	236,200.0	42,433.0	6.2	34.7
Germany (*Federal Republic*) (million Deutche mark):					
1957	7,547.0[b]	214,200.0	46,650.0		
1958	8,824.0[b]	228,510.0	50,350.0		
1959	9,403.0[b]	247,520.0	57,200.0		
Average 1957-1959	8,591.0[b]	230,077.0	51,400.0	3.7	16.7
Ireland (million pounds):					
1957	8.1[b]	545.0	77.2	1.5	10.5
Italy (billion lire):					
1957	496.1[d]	15,638.0	3,434.0		
1958	543.6[d]	16,656.0	3,481.0		
1959	548.9[d]	17,656.0	3,730.0		
Average 1957-1959	529.5[d]	16,650.0	3,548.0	3.2	14.9
Netherlands (million guilders):					
1957	1,725.0	35,120.0	9,044.0		
1958	1,546.0	35,830.0	8,210.0		
1959	1,438.0	38,170.0	9,120.0		
Average 1957-1959	1,570.0	36,373.0	8,791.0	4.3	17.9

Table 2-1 (continued)

Country, period and currency unit	Military budget expenditure	Gross domestic product[a]	Gross domestic fixed capital formation	Military budget expenditure as percentage of: Gross domestic product	Military budget expenditure as percentage of: Gross domestic fixed captial formation
EUROPE (*continued*)					
Norway (million kroner):					
1957	986.6[d]	28,826.0	8,187.0		
1958	967.8[d]	28,645.0	9,067.0		
1959	1,058.7[d]	30,294.0	8,799.0		
Average 1957-1959	1,004.4[d]	29,255.0	8,684.0	3.4	11.6
Sweden (million kronor):					
1957	2,450.0[d]	52,558.0	10,605.0		
1958	2,663.0[d]	54,825.0	11,615.0		
1959	2,748.0[d]	58,386.0	12,926.0		
Average 1957-1959	2,620.0[d]	55,256.0	11,715.0	4.7	22.4
Switzerland (million francs):					
1957	930.1	30,800.0	7,700.0[g]		
1958	1,019.1	32,000.0	7,300.0[g]		
1959	972.4	33,400.0	8,000.0[g]		
Average 1957-1959	973.9	32,067.0	7,667.0[g]	3.0	17.7[g]
United Kingdom (million pounds):					
1957	1,429.7[b]	21,719.0	3,340.0		
1958	1,467.7[b]	22,623.0	3,476.0		
1959	1,504.0[b]	23,741.0	3,631.0		
Average 1957-1959	1,467.1[b]	22,694.0	3,482.0	6.5	42.1
OCEANIA					
Australia[d] (million pounds):					
1957	183.4	5,751.0	1,408.0[h]		
1958	172.0	5,829.0	1,522.0[h]		
1959	181.9	6,250.0	1,613.0[h]		
Average 1957-1959	179.1	5,943.0	1,514.0[h]	3.0	11.8[h]
New Zealand[b] (million pounds):					
1957	24.2	1,096.0	245.0		
1958	25.5	1,154.0	242.0		
1959	27.3	1,247.0	251.0		
Average 1957-1959	25.7	1,166.0	246.0	2.2	10.4

(*Continued on p. 386*)

Table 2-1 (footnotes, continued)

SOURCE: United Nations, *Statistical Yearbook* and *Yearbook of National Accounts Statistics*, various issues.

[a] For differences between the concept of domestic product used in table 2-1 and 2-2, as compared with table 2-3, see para. 2 of this annex.

[b] Fiscal years beginning 1 April.

[c] Including increase in stocks of local government enterprises.

[d] Fiscal year ending 30 June.

[e] Excluding government expenditure on equipment.

[f] Gross national product.

[g] Including increase in stocks.

[h] Including expenditure on maintenance of roads and expenditure on motor vehicles for personal use.

Table 2-2

UNDER-DEVELOPED PRIVATE ENTERPRISE COUNTRIES: MILITARY EXPENDITURE, AS STATED IN BUDGET ACCOUNTS, COMPARED WITH OTHER STATISTICS, 1957-1959[a]

				Military budget expenditure as percentage of	
Country, period and currency unit	*Military budget expenditure*	*Gross domestic product*[a]	*Gross domestic fixed capital formation*	*Gross domestic product*	*Gross domestic fixed capital formation*
AFRICA					
Sudan[b] (million pounds):					
1957.............	3.4	...	26.2		
1958.............	4.9	...	42.8		
1959.............	5.0	...	38.2		
Average 1957-1959	4.4	...	35.7	...	12.3
Union of South Africa (million pounds):					
1957.............	18.1[c]	2,345.0	485.0		
1958.............	19.6[c]	2,411.0	544.0		
1959.............	21.8[c]	2,518.0	525.0		
Average 1957-1959	19.8[c]	2,425.0	518.0	0.8	3.8
AMERICA, LATIN					
Argentina (million pesos):					
1958.............	6,924.8[d]	318,400.0	65,610.0		
1959.............	15,589.4[d]	604,547.0	107,985.0		
Average 1958-1959	11,257.1[d]	461,474.0	86,798.0	2.4	13.0

Table 2-2 (continued)

Country, period and currency unit	*Military budget expenditure*	*Gross domestic product*[a]	*Gross domestic fixed capital formation*	*Military budget expenditure as percentage of*	
				Gross domestic product	*Gross domestic fixed capital formation*
AMERICA, LATIN (*continued*)					
Brazil (billion cruzeiros):					
1957.............	34.6	1,063.1	124.5		
1958.............	40.8	1,299.3	165.6		
1959.............	41.1	1,837.4	228.5		
Average 1957-1959	38.8	1,399.9	172.9	2.8	22.4
Chile (million escudos):					
1957.............	73.1	2,252.7[e]	247.0		
1958.............	82.2	2,971.8[e]	309.9		
1959.............	91.1	4,163.0[e]	405.0		
Average 1957-1959	82.1	3,129.2[e]	320.6	2.6[e]	25.6
Colombia (million pesos):					
1957.............	288.6	17,651.0	2,630.0		
1958.............	306.4	20,477.0	3,350.0		
1959.............	274.7	22,995.0	3,919.0		
Average 1957-1959	289.9	20,374.0	3,300.0	1.4	8.8
Costa Rica (million colones):					
1957.............	13.4	2,302.7[f]	434.8		
1958.............	12.8	2,465.0[f]	404.0		
1959.............	13.1	2,529.8[f]	451.4		
Average 1957-1959	13.1	2,432.5[f]	430.1	0.5[f]	3.0
Ecuador (million sucres):					
1957.............	289.0	12,007.0	1,561.0		
1958.............	282.0	12,355.0	1,586.0		
1959.............	273.0	12,424.0	1,553.0	2.2	17.6
El Salvador (million colones):					
1957.............	19.2	1,218.2[g]	...		
1958.............	19.0	1,249.9[g]	...		
1959.............	17.0	1,226.7[g]	...		
Average 1957-1959	18.4	1,231.6[g]	...	1.5[g]	...

Table 2-2 (continued)

Country, period and currency unit	Military budget expenditure	Gross domestic product[a]	Gross domestic fixed capital formation	Military budget expenditure as percentage of: Gross domestic product	Military budget expenditure as percentage of: Gross domestic fixed capital formation
AMERICAN, LATIN (*continued*)					
Guatemala (million quetzales):					
1957	8.9[b]	652.5	97.5[h]		
1958	9.7[b]	647.0	97.4[h]		
1959	9.9[b]	659.1	84.1[h]		
Average 1957-1959	9.5[b]	652.9	93.0[h]	1.5	10.2[h]
Honduras (million lempiras):					
1957	8.9	688.3	94.1	1.3	9.5
Mexico (million pesos):					
1957	791.7	103,000.0[i]	15,544.0		
1958	861.5	114,000.0[i]	16,282.0		
1959	971.0	122,000.0[i]	18,066.0		
Average 1957-1959	874.7	113,000.0[i]	16,631.0	0.8[i]	5.3
Peru (million soles):					
1957	1,083.8	34,342.0[e]	9,149.0		
1958	1,265.4	37,691.0[e]	8,643.0		
Average 1957-1958	1,174.6	36,016.0[e]	8,896.0	3.3[e]	13.2
Venezuela (million bolivares):					
1957	419.3[b]	23,847.0	5,950.0[j]		
1958	572.0[b]	24,585.0	5,964.0[j]		
1959	630.2[b]	24,904.0	6,721.0[j]		
Average 1957-1959	540.5[b]	24,445.0	6,212.0[j]	2.2	8.7[j]
ASIA					
Burma[k] (million kyats):					
1957	368.5	5,429.0	1,018.0		
1958	407.6	5,299.0	1,135.0		
1959	403.3	5,493.0	1,015.0		
Average 1957-1959	393.1	5,407.0	1,056.0	7.3	37.2
Cambodia:					
1957	...	...	...	4.0	...

Table 2-2 (continued)

Country, period and currency unit	*Military budget expenditure*	*Gross domestic product*[a]	*Gross domestic fixed capital formation*	*Military budget expenditure as percentage of*	
				Gross domestic product	*Gross domestic fixed capital formation*
ASIA (*continued*)					
Ceylon (million rupees):					
1957.............	39.9[k]	5,382.0	660.6		
1958.............	64.1[k]	5,662.6	682.6		
1959.............	72.4[k]	6,032.9	805.5		
Average 1957-1959	58.8[k]	5,692.5	716.2	1.0	8.2
China (Taiwan):					
Average 1957-1959	...	...	...	10.8[l]	...
Federation of Malaya (million dollars):					
1957.............	160.6	5,310.0	610.0	3.0	26.3
India[c] (million rupees):					
1957.............	2,828.0	114,100.0[m]	...		
1958.............	2,787.0	124,800.0[m]	...		
Average 1957-1958	2,808.0	119,450.0[m]	...	2.4[m]	...
Indonesia (million rupiah):					
1957.............	6,052.0	171,000.0[n]	7,600.0		
1958.............	11,085.0	180,200.0[n]	8,299.0		
1959.............	8,788.0	210,000.0[n]	8,895.0		
Average 1957-1959	8,642.0	187,100.0[n]	8,265.0	4.6[n]	104.6
Israel (million pounds):					
1957.............	197.1[c]	3,054.0[o]	829.0[j]		
1958.............	217.1[c]	3,501.0[o]	897.0[j]		
1959.............	251.1[c]	4,022.0[o]	961.0[j]		
Average 1957-1959	221.8[c]	3,526.0[o]	896.0[j]	6.3[o]	24.8[j]
Korea (Republic of) (billion hwan):					
1957.............	112.9	1,615.7	200.9		
1958.............	127.8	1,706.8	219.4		
1959.............	141.1	1,840.0	265.0		
Average 1957-1959	127.3	1,720.8	228.4	7.4	57.8
Lebanon (million pounds):					
1957.............	39.1	1,503.0[m]	...		
1958.............	45.6	1,325.0[m]	...		
Average 1957-1958	42.4	1,414.0[m]	...	3.0[m]	...

Table 2-2 (continued)

Country, period and currency unit	Military budget expenditure	Gross domestic product[a]	Gross domestic fixed capital formation	Military budget expenditure as percentage of: Gross domestic product	Military budget expenditure as percentage of: Gross domestic fixed capital formation
ASIA (*continued*)					
Pakistan:					
Average 1957-1958	...	...	...	3.0[l]	...
Philippines (million pesos):					
1957.............	157.0[b]	10,119.0	890.0		
1958.............	181.1[b]	10,666.0	851.0		
1959.............	183.6[b]	11,161.0	901.1		
Average 1957-1959	173.9[b]	10,649.0	881.0	1.6	19.7
Syrian Arab Republic (million pounds):					
1957.............	140.0	2,514.0[p]	266.0	5.6	52.6
Thailand (million baht):					
1957.............	1,566.7	44,670.0	6,434.0	3.8	24.4
1958.............	1,389.7	45,458.0	6,669.0		
1959.............	1,439.0	49,010.0	7,334.0		
Average 1957-1959	1,465.1	46,379.0	6,812.0	3.2	21.5
Turkey (million lires):					
1957.............	959.1[q]	30,668.0	4,033.0		
1958.............	956.2[q]	38,652.0	5,278.0		
1959.............	1,146.1[q]	46,640.0	7,463.0		
Average 1957-1959	1,020.5[q]	38,653.0	5,591.0	2.6	18.3
EUROPE					
Greece (million drachmas):					
1957.............	4,500.0	80,772.0	12,531.0		
1958.............	4,560.0	85,750.0	15,320.0		
1959.............	4,590.0	88,515.0	18,470.0		
Average 1957-1959	4,550.0	85,012.0	15,440.0	5.4	29.5
Portugal (million escudos):					
1957.............	1,754.0	57,396.0	8,808.0		
1958.............	1,845.6	59,017.0	9,625.0		
Average 1957-1958	1,799.8	58,206.0	9,216.0	3.1	19.5
Spain (million pesetas):					
1957.............	10,881.0	437,200.0[l]	...	2.5[l]	...

SOURCE: United Nations, *Statistical Yearbook* and *Yearbook of National*

Accounts Statistics, various issues, except for Cambodia, China (Taiwan) and Pakistan, the source for which is United Nations, *Economic Survey of Asia and the Far East*, 1960 (Sales No.: 61.II.F.1), table 32, p. 83.

[a] For differences between the concept of domestic product used in tables 2-1 and 2-2, as compared with table 2-3, see para. 2 of this annex.

[b] Fiscal year ending 30 June.

[c] Fiscal year beginning 1 April.

[d] Fiscal year ending 31 October.

[e] Including a statistical discrepancy.

[f] Including current international transfers.

[g] At market prices of 1950.

[h] Including increase in stocks.

[i] Gross national product.

[j] Including change in stock of livestock held on farms.

[k] Fiscal year ending 30 September.

[l] Ratio to net national product.

[m] Net domestic product at factor cost.

[n] Gross domestic product at factor cost.

[o] Including interest on public debt.

[p] Net domestic product at factor cost of 1956.

[q] Year beginning 1 March.

Table 2-3

CENTRALLY PLANNED COUNTRIES: MILITARY EXPENDITURE AS STATED IN BUDGET ACCOUNTS, COMPARED WITH OTHER STATISTICS, 1957-1959[a]

				Military budget expenditure as percentage of	
Country, period and currency unit	*Military budget expenditure*	*Net domestic product*[a]	*Gross fixed investment*[b]	*Net domestic product*	*Gross fixed investment*
Bulgaria (million leva):					
1957	1,540	32,089	5,172		
1958	1,729	34,863	6,321		
1959	1,628	42,198	10,103		
Average 1957-1959	1,632	36,383	7,199	4.5	22.7
China (mainland) (million yuan):					
1957	5,510	93,500[c]	12,400[c]		
1958	5,000	125,400[c]	21,400[c]		
1959	5,800	152,500[c]	24,800[c]		
Average 1957-1959	5,437	123,800[c]	19,533[c]	4.4[c]	27.8[c]
Czechoslovakia (million korun):					
1957	9,319	...	29,090		
1958	8,933	...	31,470		
1959	8,789	...	36,094		
Average 1957-1959	9,014	...	32,218	...	28.0

Table 2-3 (continued)

Country, period and currency unit	Military budget expenditure	Net domestic product[a]	Gross fixed investment[b]	Military budget expenditure as percentage of	
				Net domestic product	Gross fixed investment
Eastern Germany (million marks):					
1958	1,650	64,899	9,798	2.5	16.8
Hungary (million forints):					
1957	1,912	107,310	11,100		
1959	2,500	126,500	30,500		
Average 1957 and 1959	2,206	116,905	20,800	1.9	10.6
Poland (million zloty):					
1957	10,136	301,400	47,356		
1958	11,220	321,300	52,106		
1959	14,259	345,800	61,653		
Average 1957-1959	11,872	322,833	53,705	3.7	22.1
Romania (million lei):					
1957	3,817	...	13,966[d]		
1958	3,597	...	15,234[d]		
1959	3,446	...	17,803[d]		
Average 1957-1959	3,620	...	15,668[d]	...	23.1[d]
Soviet Union (million roubles):[e]					
1957	95,000	1,258,000[f]	237,800		
1958	93,600	1,357,000[f]	273,580		
1959	93,700	1,466,000[f]	309,330		
Average 1957-1959	94,100	1,360,333[f]	273,570	6.9[f]	34.4
Yugoslavia (million dinars):					
1957	158,300	1,829,400	550,000		
1958	178,500	1,833,600	587,000		
1959	195,600	2,269,000	750,000		
Average 1957-1959	177,500	1,977,300	639,000	9.0	27.8

SOURCE: Division of General Economic Research and Policies of the United Nations Secretariat, based on official sources.

[a] For differences between the concept of domestic product used in tables 2-1 and 2-2, as compared with table 2-3, see para. 2 of this annex.

[b] In state and co-operative sector, excluding capital repairs. Figures for China (mainland) pertain only to budgetary fixed investment; figures for Eastern Germany exclude co-operative investment from own resources.

[c] Product and investment in 1952 prices.

[d] Investment in 1959 prices.

[e] Before exchange of 1961.

[f] Product in 1960 prices.

ANNEX 3

Analytical tables illustrating certain hypothetical economic changes during disarmament

TABLES FOR CHAPTERS 4 AND 5

Table 3-1

CHANGES IN EMPLOYMENT IN THE UNITED STATES FOLLOWING A REALLOCATION[a] OF MILITARY EXPENDITURE, 1958

Production sectors	*Change in employment in man years (thousands)*	*As percentage of employment in the production sector*
(a) *Showing decline*		
Armed forces	−2,532	100.0
Civilian employment of military agencies	−791	100.0
Aircraft and parts	−705	93.1
Radio	−172	31.6
Ordnance	−142	100.0
Ships and boats	−137	57.1
Instruments	−31	12.6
All others	−133	...
TOTAL DECLINE	*−4,642*	...
(b) *Showing increase*		
Non-military government service and domestic service	1,196	
Trade	752	7.9
Professional and service	565	7.6
Restaurants, hotels, amusements	244	9.4
Banking, finance	204	8.6
Business services	136	5.2
Railroads, trucking	64	3.5
Automobile and other repairs	28	7.9
Other transportation	16	3.1

Table 3-1 (continued)

Production sectors	*Change in employment in man years (thousands)*	*As percentage of employment in the production sector*
(b) *Showing increase (continued)*		
Construction	188	7.1
Food products	77	8.0
Textile mill	58	6.4
Lumber, wood products	50	5.1
Motor vehicles	34	5.3
Livestock, poultry	31	7.3
Non-metallic minerals	27	4.2
All others	344	...
TOTAL INCREASE	*4,014*	...

SOURCE: Based on data in W. Leontief and M. Hoffenberg, "The Economic Effects of Disarmament," *Scientific American*, April 1961.

[a] The estimates relate to reallocation of total military purchases to each demand category proportionally to its 1958 share.

Table 3-2

INFLUENCE OF DISARMAMENT[a] ON VARIOUS INDUSTRIAL SECTORS IN THE UNITED KINGDOM, 1959

Industrial sector	*Changes in net output*		
		As percentage of	
	£ million 1959	*Gross national product*	*Net output of sector*
I. *Showing declines*			
Military services	−547	−2.7	−100.0
Ships, aircraft, etc	−124	−0.6	−19.8
TOTAL	−671		
II. *Showing expansion*			
Distribution	126	0.3	4.9
Transport	42	0.2	2.6
Other services	24	0.3	0.5
Engineering	96	0.5	4.6
Building	84	0.4	7.1
Motors	59	0.3	13.9
Textiles	47	0.3	8.7
Metals	43	0.2	6.4
Coal, etc	38	0.2	4.1
Chemicals	33	0.1	5.2
Food	33	0.2	4.0

Table 3-2 (continued)

Industrial sector	Changes in net output: £ million 1959	As percentage of: Gross national product	As percentage of: Net output of sector
II. *Showing expansion* (*continued*)			
Agriculture	30	0.2	3.5
Other manufactures	27	0.2	3.5
Clothing	20	0.1	6.0
Gas, water, electricity	19	0.1	3.5
Wood	11	0.1	5.6
TOTAL	732		

SOURCE: Unpublished study by the University of Cambridge, Department of Applied Economics.

[a] Assuming that armament expenditure is distributed equally among personal consumption, capital formation and foreign aid.

Table 3-3

DIRECT AND INDIRECT MILITARY DEMAND FOR SELECTED RAW MATERIALS
(*As percentage of their total world supply 1958 and 1959*)

	1958 U.S. military demand[a]		Estimated aggregate military demand of industrial countries[b]	
	1958	1959	1958	1959
	Column 1	Column 2	Column 3	Column 4
Crude Petroleum	4.5	4.1	8.9	8.3
Natural rubber (crude)	1.5	1.4	3.0	2.9
Metallic ores:				
Copper	7.8	7.4	15.7	14.7
Nickel	6.0	4.8	12.0	9.5
Tin	4.9	4.7	9.8	9.3
Lead and zinc	4.7	4.7	9.4	9.4
Molybdenum	4.2	3.4	8.3	6.8
Bauxite	3.5	3.3	7.1	6.6
Iron ore	2.6	2.5	5.3	4.9
Manganese	1.3	1.3	2.7	2.6
Chromite	1.1	1.1	2.3	2.2

SOURCES AND METHODS: Direct and indirect military demand for raw material was computed from the worksheets for "The Economic Effects of Disarmament" (by W. W. Leontief and Marvin Hoffenberg, *Scientific American*, April, 1961) obtained from the Harvard Economics Research Project. World supplies of natural rubber are from *Rubber Statistical Bulletin*,

(*Continued on page 396*)

Table 3-3 (footnotes, continued)

16:2 (November 1961), p. 2. World supplies of mineral are from U.S. Department of the Interior, *Minerals Yearbook*, 1959, vol. I, pp. 124, 125.

[a] Generated by $41,585 million of goods and services purchased under the U.S. military budget of 1958.

[b] As a rough approximation, assumed to be equal to twice the U.S. military expenditure.

Table 3-4

CHANGE IN WORLD DEMAND FOR SELECTED RAW MATERIALS AFTER PROPORTIONAL REALLOCATION OF MILITARY PURCHASES TO OTHER DEMAND CATEGORIES

(*As percentage of world supply, 1958 and 1959*)

	After reallocating 1958 United States military purchases[a]		*After reallocating 1958 military purchases of industrial countries*[b]	
Item	*1958*	*1959*	*1958*	*1959*
Crude petroleum	−0.09	−0.08	−0.18	−0.16
Natural rubber (crude)	0.05	0.05	0.10	0.09
Metallic ores:				
Copper	−0.96	−0.90	−1.92	−1.81
Nickel	−0.76	−0.60	−1.51	−1.21
Tin	−0.33	−0.32	−0.67	−0.63
Lead and zinc	−0.32	−0.32	−0.64	−0.64
Molybdenum	−0.06	−0.05	−0.11	−0.09
Bauxite	−0.52	−0.48	−1.04	−0.96
Iron ore	−0.04	−0.03	−0.07	−0.07
Manganese	−0.02	−0.02	−0.04	−0.04
Chromite	−0.02	−0.02	−0.03	−0.03

SOURCE: See table 3-3. The figures in this table were derived by multiplying the appropriate entries in table 3-3 by those in column 2 of W. Leontief and M. Hoffenberg, op. cit., table 8.

[a] Equal to $41,585,000,000.

[b] Assumed equal to twice the United States military expenditure.

Notes on Contributors

EMILE BENOIT, born 1909, is chairman of the panel on the economic impacts of disarmament of the United States Arms Control and Disarmament Agency, a consultant to the United States State Department and to the United Nations Secretariat, as well as professor at the Graduate School of Business, Columbia University.

LEWIS C. BOHN, born 1924, served for some years as a specalist in arms limitation at the RAND Corporation, and then with the Systems Research Center. Presently a consultant in the field of disarmament, he is preparing a book on nonnuclear strategies for keeping the peace and promoting freedom.

DAVID F. CAVERS, born in 1902, is Fessenden Professor of Law at Harvard University. Since 1947 he has contributed numerous articles to general and legal periodicals on the regulation of the peaceful uses of atomic energy and on the control of atomic armaments.

BERNARD T. FELD, born in 1919, is professor of physics at the Massachusetts Institute of Technology, chairman of the Subcommittee on International Meetings of the Committee on Public Responsibilities of Scientists of the American Academy of Arts and Sciences, vice-chairman of the Federation of American Scientists, and president of the Council for Abolishing War.

LAWRENCE S. FINKELSTEIN, born 1925, is vice-president of the Carnegie Endowment for International Peace. His articles on trusteeship, colonial problems, Southeast Asia, arms control, and the United Nations have appeared in numerous publications. The present essay was written while he was research associate at the Harvard University Center for International Affairs, during a leave of absence from his present post.

ROGER FISHER, born in 1922, is professor of law at Harvard University and member of the Harvard-MIT joint seminar on arms control, as well as consultant on disarmament to the United States Department of Defense.

CHRISTOPH HOHENEMSER, born in 1937, is a specialist in low-energy nuclear physics who has devoted intensive research to the problems of disarmament, and is co-author of *The Nth Country Problem and Arms Control.*

ROBERT W. KASTENMEIER, born in 1924, is Member of Congress for the 2nd Congressional District of Wisconsin, and has been particularly active in the domain of disarmament policy and arms control.

RICHARD C. RAYMOND, born in 1917, is manager of the Technical Military Planning Operation, Defense Systems Department, of the General Electric Company, Santa Barbara, California.

HERBERT RITVO, born in 1915, was editor of *Ost Probleme* (Frankfurt, Bonn) for several years, then Soviet affairs analyst for Radio Free Europe (Munich), and is now research associate at the Center for International Studies, the Massachusetts Institute of Technology.

LEONARD S. RODBERG, born in 1932, is project officer, United States Arms Control and Disarmament Agency, on leave of absence from the Physics Department of the University of Maryland.

THE EARL RUSSELL, O.M., F.R.S., born 1872, mathematician, philosopher, essayist, and Nobel Laureate, is widely known for his life-long efforts in the cause of world peace.

LOUIS B. SOHN, born in 1914, is Bemis Professor of International Law at Harvard University and consultant to the United States Arms Control and Disarmament Agency.

ARTHUR I. WASKOW, born in 1933, is member of the Senior Staff of the Peace Research Institute in Washington, and author of *The Limits of Defense*.